A

B O O K

The Philip E. Lilienthal imprint
honors special books
in commemoration of a man whose work
at University of California Press from 1954 to 1979
was marked by dedication to young authors
and to high standards in the field of Asian Studies.
Friends, family, authors, and foundations have together
endowed the Lilienthal Fund, which enables UC Press
to publish under this imprint selected books
in a way that reflects the taste and judgment
of a great and beloved editor.

The publisher gratefully acknowledges the generous contribution to this book provided by the Philip E. Lilienthal Asian Studies Endowment Fund of the University of California Press Foundation, which is supported by a major gift from Sally Lilienthal.

THE THREE FACES OF CHINESE POWER

David M. Lampton · # THE THREE FACES OF CHINESE POWER

Might, Money, and Minds

University of California Press

Berkeley   Los Angeles   London

University of California Press, one of the most
distinguished university presses in the United States,
enriches lives around the world by advancing scholarship in the humanities, social sciences, and natural
sciences. Its activities are supported by the UC Press
Foundation and by philanthropic contributions from
individuals and institutions. For more information,
visit www.ucpress.edu.

University of California Press
Berkeley and Los Angeles, California

University of California Press, Ltd.
London, England

Library of Congress Cataloging-in-Publication Data
Lampton, David M.

The three faces of Chinese power : might, money,
and minds / David M. Lampton.
    p.   cm.
Includes bibliographical references and index.
ISBN 978-0-520-24951-6 (cloth : alk. paper)
ISBN 978-0-520-25442-8 (pbk. : alk. paper)
    1. China—Foreign relations.   2. China—Military
policy.   3. China—Economic policy.   4. China—
Cultural policy.   I. Title.
JZ1734.L35   2008
327.51—dc22   2007033319

Manufactured in the United States of America

17   16   15   14   13   12   11   10   09
10   9   8   7   6   5   4   3

This book is printed on New Leaf EcoBook 50, a 100%
recycled fiber of which 50% is de-inked post-consumer
waste, processed chlorine-free. EcoBook 50 is acid-free
and meets the minimum requirements of ANSI/ASTM
D5634–01 (*Permanence of Paper*).

To my grandchildren,
Zoe Vittoria and William Hawking

CONTENTS

ILLUSTRATIONS

PREFACE

This book is about what will prove to be one of the transformative developments of the twenty-first century—China's resumption of a position of power and influence in the world. This volume addresses the character and use of Chinese power, not only because it is important how Beijing employs its growing strength, but also because it is essential that Americans consider how they understand and employ their own power. Chinese power provides a mirror in which Americans can contemplate their own conception of power, its uses, and its limitations. In the early twenty-first century the United States must rediscover the multifaceted character of power, particularly the utility of its noncoercive faces.

To address the admittedly broad subject of Chinese power I have had to cover a broad sweep of history, a broad range of topics and fields, and a vast expanse of real estate. I have thus needed, and received, the assistance of a great many persons in the United States, in China, throughout Asia, and elsewhere whom I wish to acknowledge and thank. I trust that the individuals who assisted me will find their contributions reflected in the following pages, but I alone am responsible for any inadvertent errors of fact, interpretation, omission, or commission that may remain.

The University of California Press has been my publisher of choice over the past years, and I wish to express my particular gratitude to Sheila Levine for her constant encouragement and constructive criticism. At every stage of this book's conceptualization, development, and production I have benefited greatly from working with Reed Malcolm, my acquisitions editor at the press. I want to thank him and the press for the care that went into the review of this manuscript, the suggestions for revision, the editing, and not least the production of this volume under the Philip E. Lilienthal imprint. The two anonymous academic reviewers of this volume have my profound appreciation for their many constructive and important suggestions, which substantially improved the initial manuscript.

As I moved through the writing and editing process, I benefited enormously from the editing assistance of Ms. Krista Forsgren, who not only improved the volume's organization and writing but also provided great intellectual stimulation. She asked probing questions throughout, such as "What do you mean?" "Is this true?" "Is this relevant?" "Is this the best example?" I will always be in Krista's debt for her help on this and earlier books. To the splendid copy editor Elisabeth Magnus I express my great appreciation, as I do to Chalon Emmons, who skillfully guided this volume through production at UC Press.

I have been very fortunate to have had superb research assistance both at the School of Advanced International Studies (SAIS) of Johns Hopkins University and at the Nixon Center over the substantial period necessary to research, write, and produce this volume. Each of the individuals acknowledged below gave not only of their research skills but also of their intellectual insight, contributions for which I am grateful: Liza Davis (SAIS and Nixon Center), Amanda Egan (Nixon Center), Janie Hsieh (SAIS), Kong Bo (SAIS), Yang (Bonny) Lin (University of Michigan), Tabitha Grace Mallory (SAIS), Matthew Jacob Platkin (Stanford), and Laura Tanner (Nixon Center).

My academic colleagues at SAIS also have been enormously helpful in providing intellectual advice and support along the way. I particularly want to thank Frederick Z. Brown (a fellow at the SAIS Foreign Policy Institute) who traveled with me to Vietnam in March 2006 and used his vast network of contacts and enormous personal knowledge of the country to advance this project and my education about the region. I will always be grateful for his help during that journey and for his intellectual input thereafter. Dzung Pham, vice president of trade and investment at Sandler, Travis & Rosenberg, also deserves special thanks for his help in making arrangements for my productive trip to Hanoi and Ho Chi Minh City. Four other SAIS colleagues deserve an expression of gratitude for their ongoing intellectual interaction with me during various phases of research and writing: Ji Zhaojin, Pieter P. Bottelier, David Brown, and Charles F. Doran. Zhaojin has been particularly supportive throughout the entire process, including providing me with research materials and her sharp analysis. Finally, I wish to thank my Australian friend and colleague Richard Rigby for helping arrange my trip to his beautiful country in June 2005 and the Kettering Foundation for including me in its sustained dialogue with China over many years.

Projects such as this also require institutional support, and I am particularly grateful to the dean of SAIS, Jessica P. Einhorn, for her multidimensional support of me and this project. Likewise, Edward B. (Ted) Baker Jr., the former senior associate dean for finance and administration at SAIS, provided me with a supportive environment of unparalleled quality and depth, a contribution for which I shall always be appreciative. Also, for a portion of the period it took to research and write this book I was affiliated with the Nixon Center, whose president, Dimitri K. Simes, and executive director, Paul J. Saunders, were supportive, including providing for research assistance.

While conducting interviews in China and in neighboring countries, I received intellectual and/or logistical support from a great many persons beyond those mentioned above. I can mention only a few here: Chan Heng Chee (Singapore's ambassador to the United States); Sylvia Bay and Selina Ho (Singapore); Douglas Ramage (Asia Foundation, Indonesia); and Nancy Yuan (Asia Foundation, Washington, DC). Most of all, I wish to thank the many interviewees in China, Indonesia, Australia, Vietnam, Taiwan, Singapore, Korea, and Japan for the opportunity to learn from them. In the text I have identified these sources to the degree I thought prudent and appropriate given their positions in and out of government.

I express my appreciation to my family last because I want them and the reader to have this as the concluding thought. An entire family writes a book, not the nominal author. In a million ways they react to the author's running commentary of thoughts and problems throughout the protracted process of research and writing and provide almost imperceptible guidance as well as emotional support. Family members also give of themselves by forgoing time together and suffer through the author's preoccupations of mind even when they are together. For all this and more I thank my wife of nearly forty years, Susan, and my entire family.

Finally, I dedicate this volume to my two grandchildren, Zoe and William, not just because I love them, but because this book deals with an important determinant of their futures. How we relate to China now and how China relates to the rest of the world will greatly shape their lives.

David M. Lampton
Washington, DC
August 2007

Introduction

And the peaceful rising of China is probably going to be the most momentous happening, probably, in the first half of this century for sure.

DEPUTY SECRETARY OF STATE RICHARD L. ARMITAGE, December 10, 2004

Although the U.S. motive for developing economic and trade ties with China is private profit, this has objectively spurred China's economic prosperity and technical advance. China's economic prosperity and technical advance will naturally promote the strengthening of its military power. This, however, is precisely what makes the United States worried and wary. This is a contradiction and paradox in U.S. long-term strategy toward China. A similar paradox on the Chinese side is: Only a U.S. economic decline can lead to a decline in its national strength, thus easing its strategic pressure on China. However, a U.S. economic slide will certainly have quite a big negative impact on China's economy, and in addition the various changes in world politics in the process of U.S. decline will not necessarily be favorable to China.

WANG JISI, then at the Chinese Academy of Social Sciences, January 2005

THE DOUBLE GAMBLE

China's elite and public opinion leaders have a national grand strategy. For them, the next twenty years provide a strategic opportunity. In a February 23, 2004, Politburo study session, General Secretary and President Hu Jintao could not have been clearer when he said, "Take a broad view of the world while analyzing the situation; see clear-headedly the serious challenges posed by the intensifying international competition; see clear-headedly the difficulties and risks in the road ahead; [and] grasp firmly and conscientiously use well this period of important strategic opportunity."[1] The next twenty years are expected to be an era of continuing American dominance in which Beijing's principal tasks are to get along with Washington while relentlessly building the nation's military, economic, and ideational power. At the end of this period China will be better able to defend and advance its interests. And while most Chinese hope to build a cooperative relationship with America in the coming decades, they are also aware of other possibilities, just as they are mindful of the many uncertainties that stand between the present day and twenty years of continued, uninterrupted, high-speed growth.

For America, Beijing's strategy presents a dilemma. Out of apprehension of how China's growing power may be used, some Americans think that seeking to constrain that growth now would be prudent, anticipating that it will become ever more difficult to do so as time passes. Other Americans ask themselves whether it is within their capabilities to succeed in constraining Chinese growth, given the unwillingness of other nations to cooperate and the strength of China's own internal growth dynamic. Further, they suspect that such an effort would foster the conflict it was designed to avoid. And, there are issues of justice—would not such an effort amount to trying to keep 20 percent of the world's people poorer than they otherwise would be? Many other questions arise as well, not the least of which is whether an incompetently governed and weak People's Republic of China (PRC) spilling its problems into the international arena is a greater problem for global security and welfare than a strong and stable China. Moreover, in pursuing an adversarial course, Americans would forego the positive opportunities of cooperation, ceding those benefits to competitors in Europe, Japan, and elsewhere and making the world as a whole poorer for the inability to jointly address transnational issues.

The present circumstance, therefore, requires both nations to take a historic gamble with respect to China's current and prospective future ascent. For Chinese, the gamble is that the Americans will countenance, indeed cooperate with, their rise, even as they have misgivings and as some in the U.S. government and elsewhere in society periodically contemplate taking a more confrontational path. And for America, the bet is that a powerful China two or more decades hence, woven into the fabric of international society and a beneficiary of the globalization that energized its growth in the first place, will become, in the words of one Chinese scholar in Shanghai, "a responsible, decent role model for others." In the phraseology of the U.S. government in September 2005, the hope was (and remains) that China will progressively become more of "a responsible stakeholder" in the international system.

BACKGROUND

When Richard Nixon journeyed to China in the winter of 1972, and during the two succeeding decades, there was a comfortable illusion that its problems were so massive, and the accumulated societal, economic, organizational, ideological, and demographic considerations so burdensome, that China's rise would be gradual at best. In 1978, while the average population enrolled in higher education in low-income countries was 2 percent, in China the rate was half that.[2] These modest expectations for progress were born of China's post-1949 decades of wrenching domestic turmoil, counterproductive economic policies, intellectual isolation, destruction of domestic social capital, and a bullying foreign policy. Indeed, this turmoil was reflected in Mao Zedong's very definition of his era as one of "war and revolution." Economically, Mao created a Chinese workforce without material incentives or the promise of individual or family fulfillment.

Nixon did not premise his move toward China in the early 1970s so much on the Middle Kingdom's economic future or its innovative people as he did on its utility in compounding the strategic challenges confronting the Soviet Union. China was useful because it was there and it was big. Any thoughts of what China could become were secondary when the new diplomatic relationship was begun in 1972; China was in the darker years of the decade-long Great Proletarian Cultural Revolution. Nixon, however, did dimly perceive that China's rise would not be forever deferred and that when it occurred it would transform the world; keeping China angry and isolated was unwise.

Along with Deng Xiaoping's succession to Mao in 1977–78 came a gradual redefinition of the current era as one of "peace and development." Deng's redefinition of the era and his innovative policies in the late 1970s and 1980s generated optimism abroad concerning the prospects for sustained growth in China, though the tragic events surrounding June 4, 1989, fed a still underlying skepticism about the country's future. Most projections of growth and China's mounting strength in the first half of the 1990s were hedged by equally cogent analyses about how the PRC's future would be shaped by uncertainties, not the least political.

By the latter half of the 1990s, however, China's sustained, rapid growth and the accumulated changes of the preceding two decades had so exceeded all modest and hedged expectations that the rest of the world began to ask itself what a rapid increase in Chinese comprehensive power meant for its own economic competitiveness and military security and what opportunities and dangers might be embedded within this success. Moreover, sustained, rapid Chinese growth contrasted with economic malaise in Japan and Europe; the rest of Asia was working its way through the Asian Financial Crisis and its aftermath in the late 1990s and into the new millennium. Slipping below the radar, therefore, China had become an engine of global economic growth, alongside America, as other economies sputtered. For the rest of the world, it was as if 20 percent of world's people, who had for decades been in the bleachers episodically watching a sporting event below, were now emptying onto the field to play—the game would never be the same.

For its part, China began to act differently. It moved from being a prickly state most comfortable dredging up past humiliations, a nation that eschewed any hint of a desire to play a leadership role, to a more self-assured state. This new, more confident China desired to be perceived as a globally responsible power, even a nation that upon occasion could promote ideas designed to exert influence, the first being the "New Security Concept" of the latter half of the 1990s.[3] It moved from being a state that resisted the internal implications of globalization to one that embraced them as a driver of its own economic and social reform, even suggesting that other states make similar changes if they wanted Chinese investment. For instance, when Cheng Dawei, a Chinese expert on the World Trade Organization (WTO), was in Quito, Ecuador, in July 2004, she was reported to have said that "China has the capacity to invest in Ecuador and all of Latin America if conditions are stable and the rules of the game are clear."[4] Cheng was making the same business-related demands for discipline, transparency, stability, and predictability of potential recipients of Chinese direct foreign investment that others had made of the PRC since the dawn of the reform era—indeed, demands that foreigners had been making of China since the early nineteenth century. These demands, however, do not extend to human rights and environmental conditions, as seen in chapter 4. By the new millennium, Beijing had become a leading promoter of free-trade areas throughout the world and had made it clear that if an invitation to join the G-7/8 were extended, it would accept. China had gone from trying to build a Third World United Nations (to compete with the UN) in the 1960s to wanting the UN to be the principal legitimator of the use of force and economic sanctions in the international system. The PRC had gone from being an extremely poor nation eschewing any hint of capitalism to a nation moving rapidly forward by embracing it.

Simultaneously, China began to wrap the iron fist of its armed forces in a velvet glove, approaching NATO to initiate a strategic dialogue in late 2002. Also in late 2002 (first with Kyrgyzstan), the People's Liberation Army (PLA) began to engage in confidence-building measures and joint exercises with other nations—the British,

French, Indian, Pakistani, Russian, and Central Asian militaries, and even the United States by 2006–7. In the aftermath of the tsunami that hit large swaths of South and Southeast Asia in December 2004, Beijing sent a small number of its military personnel on humanitarian missions to some affected areas. With respect to nonproliferation initiatives, Beijing became more constructive and more active, notably on the Korean Peninsula, both by fostering multilateral talks that sought to denuclearize the Korean peninsula and by encouraging Pyongyang to move forward with economic reforms and trade (as China had done). Kim Jong Il was a repeat visitor to areas of rapid economic development in the PRC. In May 2004, Beijing entered the Nuclear Suppliers Group and formally sought to join the Missile Technology Control Regime (MTCR), something it had declined to do for years because of the organization's nonuniversal character. It was Washington, ironically, that balked at China's entry into MTCR, apprehensive about possible technology transfer and not wishing to "reward" Beijing for what the United States viewed as problematic proliferation behavior.[5]

Nonetheless, the iron fist of Beijing's coercive potential also was visible, and it was becoming more lethal. On the coercive side, China justified its growing missile force aimed at Taiwan with the language of "deterring" the island's de jure independence. In space, in 2003 China launched its first manned flight, with more ambitious missions to the moon and beyond charted for the next few decades. Military purposes were embedded within this effort, just as such objectives had been central to the American space program at its inception decades earlier. On the high seas, the PRC Navy ranged ever farther from Chinese shores (circumnavigating the globe for the first time in July 2002), in part fearful that China's growing energy imports could be disrupted by potential adversaries, including the U.S. Navy. And in the Himalayas Beijing began cooperating with Kathmandu in Nepal's struggle against its own Maoist insurgency: post-Mao China was opposing the Maoist residue on its borders.[6]

In sum, at the turn of the millennium, China began to use a different vocabulary in its interactions with the world, its behavior and interests began to change, and it sought to shape events, particularly in its region but also beyond, rather than assume its more traditional reactive posture. By 2007, Beijing was quite far along the road of this historic change, but the pace and precise direction of future evolution remained uncertain.

This book is about China's growing power, the diversity of this power, the uneven growth among its various forms of power, and what this means for the rest of the world, not least America. In the following pages I ask: How might outsiders think about the power of the PRC? How have the Chinese thought about their own power in the past, and in what ways do they think about it now? What dimensions of Chinese power are changing, how is the "mix" of power types evolving, and what are the vulnerabilities and uncertainties to which China's continued development is subject? And what do the answers to these questions mean for the rest of the world?

As to implications for a United States that often refers to itself as "the sole remaining superpower" and "the indispensable nation," it is appropriate to recall Hans Morgenthau's wisdom expressed not long after the conclusion of World War II, advice that should resonate with America as it is embroiled in a global war against terror and bogged down in the Middle East and Central Asia.

> A nation that at a particular moment in history finds itself at the peak of its power is particularly exposed to the temptation to forget that all power is relative. It is likely to believe that the superiority it has achieved is an absolute quality to be lost only through stupidity or neglect of duty. A foreign policy based on such assumptions runs grave risks, for it overlooks the fact that the superior power of that nation is only in part the outgrowth of its own qualities, while it is in part the result of other nations compared with its own.[7]

Yet while acknowledging China's mounting coercive, economic, and ideational power, we must avoid exaggeration. In the 1980s, Japan's economic achievements were projected forward in time and across all dimensions of national capability, but many of these projections did not come to pass. China's power is growing, a fact with a number of consequences for itself and the rest of the world. Nonetheless, there will be bumps, perhaps major bumps, in the road of economic performance over time, and China has yet to bring its political system into greater alignment with social and economic changes in the country. Effective governance in China cannot be assumed; this is the biggest challenge of all. Catastrophic political convulsion is possible, though I judge it to be improbable in the near and middle future. Consequently, Beijing's leaders, probably for decades, will be preoccupied at home, though economic, physical, and political interdependencies increasingly will pull their attentions abroad as well. Then there is Taiwan, a continuing policy challenge to Beijing that could derail its policies and performance by distracting and deflecting the elite's attention from the domestic agenda and by conceivably bringing the PRC into conflict with America and Japan.

It is likely that the biggest challenges China will present the rest of the world will be in the domains of economics and ideas, not military power. Negative Chinese impacts on the world are likely to result less from malign intentions than from the headlong drive for economic growth, which will have enormous, and largely unintended, spillover effects globally. According to the International Energy Agency, for instance, it is likely that the PRC will surpass the United States as "the world's biggest emitter of CO_2 before 2010." Indeed, in 2007 the Netherlands Environmental Assessment Agency said the threshold had been crossed in 2006.

China's growing multidimensional participation in the world is a staggering opportunity as well as a challenge. In the twentieth century, for the most part, other countries did not have to compete intellectually and economically with 20 percent of the earth's population, but that competition will be a defining feature of the twenty-first century. If America is to compete effectively, it will require huge investment in domestic educational systems to maintain our nation's innovative edge, provide more cost-effective health care, move away from dependence on foreign liquid energy, place greater emphasis on restoring America's depleted soft-power resources, and resist the impulse to overrely on military power. Above all, what China's rise requires is reform in America and elsewhere in the "developed world." China's rise underscores the fact that "development" is not a permanent condition; rather, it is a process of continual adaptation to new circumstances.

As I write this introduction in Hong Kong in January 2007, the U.S. and Hong Kong dollars continue to drop in value as the Chinese RMB or *yuan* gradually gains strength. The *South China Morning Post* reported on January 12 that "Starbucks in Shenzhen has declined to accept Hong Kong or U.S. dollars [which used to freely circulate there] since last month." This reminds one that while currency values reflect many fluid forces, fundamentally they constitute a collective assessment about relative futures and the expected consequences of national choices. World markets currently are expressing greater confidence in the choices being made in Beijing than in Washington.

With respect to foreign affairs and security, the words of K. S. Nathan are worth remembering when Americans wonder if their natural advantages in Asia are declining in the face of China's rise: "Asians won't accept the leadership of each other, but will accept the involvement of the United States."[8] The key word is *involvement*, not domination.

ONE · Thinking about Power

China is applying the strategy of the long
wait to get the big catch [of fish].

VIETNAMESE OFFICIAL,
Hanoi, March 2006

A POLICY PROCESS PERSPECTIVE ON POWER

This book is about China's power and its implications for the rest of the world.

During the last three millennia, countless theorists, politicians, and statesmen have spent their lives thinking about power. They have asked how power is distributed within and among societies; how power ought to be distributed; what the practical consequences of various power distributions are; how shifts in relative power positions fuel conflict; what the nature and varied uses of different forms of power are; and how one acquires and uses power. Confucius, Plato, and Aristotle contemplated how power "ought" to be distributed and institutionalized. In Sun Tzu's *The Art of War* (a manual on strategy written in China hundreds of years before the beginning of the Common Era) and in the work of Machiavelli we find sophisticated expositions on how to use power both within and among states. Wielders of power and analysts as varied as Chairman Mao Zedong, sociologist Amitai Etzioni, and political scientist Joseph Nye have been concerned with various kinds of power and their respective uses. In the work of Robert Dahl, we learn about the consequences of power dispersion for policy outcomes, while in the writings of Edward Banfield the politician is portrayed as a venture capitalist whose currency is political influence accumulated and expended in the course of decision making.

Though power has been a ubiquitous theoretical concept and practical concern, its definition has been elusive. For Max Weber, "Power is the probability that one actor within a social relationship will be in a position to carry out his own will despite resistance, regardless of the basis on which this probability rests."[1] For Hans Morgenthau, "When we speak of power, we mean man's control over the minds and actions of other men. . . . In international politics in particular, armed strength as a threat or a potentiality is the most important material factor making for the political power of a nation."[2] Notably, while Morgenthau emphasized hard military power, he did not ignore that power also was manifest in the ability to sway the minds of others. In contrast to Morgenthau, John Mearsheimer comes close to equating power with force—"Power is based on the particular material capabilities that a state possesses. The balance of power, therefore, is a function of tangible assets—such as armored divisions and nuclear weapons—that each great power controls."[3]

Joseph Nye advances a parsimonious, broader, and more productive definition, one most compatible with the usage in the remainder of this volume: "Power is the ability to achieve one's purposes or goals."[4] This is a definition to which I would add only two (italicized) words—Power is the ability to *define and* achieve one's purposes or goals. In complex, mass societies and in the international system, simply *deciding* what to do is often extremely difficult. And once the decision is made, great effort is required to maintain consensus (both domestically and internationally) and to achieve congruence between policy intent and policy outcomes. The congruence between intention and outcome is continually degraded as policy moves through national bureaucracies and civic organizations, across national boundaries, and through international organizations. These difficulties give rise to the concept of efficiency, or what Nye calls "smart power." *Smart power,* as I use the term, is the capacity to define goals and implement policy with the most efficient use of resources, which means the optimal mix of power types.[5]

Exercising power is to be distinguished from merely having an impact. A mindless brute has impact, but the exercise of power involves the purposeful use of resources to achieve goals efficiently. Power is demonstrated when a leader or national leadership efficiently achieves goals throughout the entire cycle of policy making, from agenda setting to formulation, implementation, and subsequent adaptation. A powerful nation is one that authoritatively sets its own agenda as well as the international agenda over a broad range of issues, wins support for (or compliance with) its policies both internally and externally, influences the implementation process so that there is a high degree of correspondence between initial intentions and actual outcomes, and desists from pursuing policies that prove ineffective or counterproductive.

This policy-process perspective on power emphasizes the myriad points at which potential power resources can be deflected from achieving intended outcomes. The smart-power approach also points to the need for an effective nation to use all forms of power available in an optimal mix to address a problem. This brings us to the three forms of power that are the focus of this book.

THE THREE FACES OF POWER

In his classic *A Comparative Analysis of Complex Organizations,* Amitai Etzioni notes that "power differs according to the *means* employed to make the subject comply. These means may be physical, material, or symbolic,"[6] or what Etzioni respectively calls coercive, remunerative, and normative power. Coercive power relies on inflicting physical or psychological pain or deprivation. Remunerative power is the realm of material inducement; if one talks of economic sanctions, however, coercion and remunerative power bleed into one another. Normative power relies on the capacity to motivate through the force of ideas and win compliance through creating group norms with which individuals wish to identify. If group norms are used to ostracize, this too bleeds into coercion. Only in the area of normative power will I broaden Etzioni's concept into "ideational power," power deriving from human intellect, power expressed in the creation and dissemination of knowledge and compelling ideas. Considerably broader than normative power, "ideational power" explicitly includes leadership, human intellectual resources, innovation, and culture. While close in definition to Joseph Nye's "soft" or "attractive" power,[7] "ideational power" is broader than "soft power" inasmuch as it explicitly embraces innovation; it is narrower inasmuch as it excludes the attractive aspects of material inducements.

With this typology of power, "organizations [as well as regimes and nations] can be ordered according to their power structure, taking into account which power is predominant, how strongly it is stressed compared with other organizations in which the same power is predominant, and which power constitutes the secondary source of control."[8] Comparing the national strategies and foreign policies of Mao Zedong and his successors Deng Xiaoping, Jiang Zemin, and Hu Jintao, for instance, one sees a dramatic shift away from strategies relying heavily on coercion and normative ("revolutionary") appeals both at home and abroad and toward remunerative incentives and strategies relying on specific dimensions of ideational power, notably reassurance. More emphasis is placed on attracting support for China than seeking to compel it, taking advantage of the fact that "seduction is always more effective than coercion."[9] As one Chinese scholar put it, "For Chinese this is an evolving process. The first generation [Mao Zedong] paid more attention to military power; the second generation [Deng Xiaoping] placed more emphasis on comprehensive national strength. The third generation [Jiang Zemin], in the late 1990s, began to pay more attention to soft power."[10]

The power wielder is like a conductor, seeking to employ the most efficient combination of power types to achieve objectives. This is difficult. Organizations relying on coercive power may alienate the objects of the exercise of power, thereby rendering normative appeals less effective. Similarly, organizations liberally employing remunerative incentives may find normative suasion less potent. Nonetheless, organizations, regimes, and nations usually employ all three power types, even when using one degrades the utility of others. Organizations, regimes, and nations can be compared and differentiated by the power they possess in various forms, their preferred "mix," and the scope and scale of the goals they pursue and actually achieve.

This volume is organized around the uses, effectiveness, and limitations of these three types of Chinese power. The first four chapters deal with defining and then discussing the three types of power. Chapter 5 surveys the reaction of China's neighbors to its growing power and the various mixes employed by Beijing. Chapter 6 analyzes the challenges that could retard China's continued acquisition of power or change the mix of power types that Beijing employs. The volume concludes with an exploration of what the three faces of Chinese power mean for America and the world.

THE INTERNATIONAL POWER CYCLE AND ITS IMPLICATIONS

The growth of a nation's power is significant in that new achievements become possible, yet mounting power also produces reactions elsewhere in the international system, responses that occasionally lead to cooperation but often lead to conflict. These reactions arise from several phenomena described and analyzed by scholars, including Charles Doran, Hans Morgenthau, Ronald Tammen, and John Mearsheimer. In this volume I draw heavily on the thinking of Charles Doran.

> A state's foreign policy expectations are tied to change on its power cycle, but power and role get out of sync because actors and system do not adjust readily to changes in relative power. On the upside of the power curve, the increase in power tends to exceed acquisition of role. The system is reluctant to yield role

to the ascendant actor, or the rising state may prefer to postpone role gratification and responsibility until it could do so more easily (with greater confidence) and on its own terms (with less competition). On the downside of the curve, there is a tendency for role to exceed power, leading to overextension. Allies and dependent client states do not want the once-ascendant state to step aside, and elites accustomed to the benefits power bestowed do not want to yield role and face a different, more constricted, foreign policy setting. Long latent in statecraft, these power-role gaps are shoved to the fore of diplomatic awareness and priority in critical intervals of suddenly altered security circumstance, greatly escalating the tension. They then abruptly demand adjustment.[11]

To start, an increase of one nation's *relative share* of international power implies a *relative decline in the share* of power held by other actors, a decline that nations try to resist. Second, nations develop *roles* or patterns of behavior that reflect their capabilities and govern their use of power and create preferences for particular power mixes. When a nation's relative power declines (especially when it does so precipitously), its capacity to play its preexistent role diminishes, but its expectations about its own role often change more slowly. This causes dissatisfaction and stresses within and among both the previously dominant power(s) and the "upstart" rising power. The nation in relative decline resents its diminished influence (often equated with reduced security), and the rising power resents the lag between its new capabilities and the respect or role it is accorded in the international system. The Chinese see this problem, both generally and with respect to Sino-American relations. As the scholar Wang Zaibang put it in late 2005, "The United States' continued desire to lead the world based on its own values will inevitably run into bigger problems as its own power falls short."[12]

Contemporary Russia, the United States, China, Japan, Germany, and India all demonstrate various aspects of this phenomenon. It has been painful for a dramatically weaker post–Cold War Russia to adjust to its more modest power position. Long after the Soviet Union vanished, Russia acted as though it were entitled to have disproportionate influence over nearby states that were formally part of that union. Turning to the United States, the resistance to a potentially reduced role in international affairs is nowhere so apparent as in *The National Security Strategy of the United States of America* (September 2002),[13] where the administration of George W. Bush declared, "Our forces will be strong enough to dissuade potential adversaries from pursuing a military build-up in hopes of surpassing, or equaling, the power of the United States." A senior foreign policy analyst in Beijing expressed

Chinese anxieties about whether Washington would ever be reconciled to a strong PRC: "The Bush administration promotes the idea of U.S. primacy, and [China] is so worried that the U.S. will never accept China as an equal or competitor. . . . Some in the U.S. say that the U.S. will not allow another country to challenge it; . . . so it is making a negative impact on China's grand strategy."[14] As another Chinese analyst put it, "The major problem is that the U.S. has not solved what is China's legitimate role under the sun."[15] At the extreme end of the continuum of Chinese worries is the possibility that the United States would use war to maintain its dominance in the face of a possible relative decline of power.[16]

Speaking more broadly, in this early part of the twenty-first century, economically powerful Japan and Germany and a rising India all want their influence acknowledged by the UN with permanent seats on the Security Council. Yet current Permanent Members generally resist such an expansion of seats (particularly with veto rights) as a move that would dilute their power. Doran's key point is that it is the function of diplomacy to cushion the disconnect between expectations and roles as international systems change; war is not inevitable in moments of great change, but it is more likely.

John Mearsheimer's work presents a darker understanding of the origins and implications of changing power relationships among nations: in his view, there is virtually no role for diplomacy or intelligent leadership. For Mearsheimer, military (coercive) capability is the most useful form of power in the junglelike international arena. Growing economic actors have increasing capacity to acquire additional military strength, which Mearsheimer presumes they will do because hegemony is the surest way to survive in the anarchic, predatory international environment. In his view, expanding economies beget growing militaries; the growing interdependence that liberal internationalists hope will moderate conflict is largely a snare and a delusion; and economic interdependence as often as not ignites conflict.[17]

Mearsheimer's view ignores the potentialities for cooperative security strategies and slights security dilemmas—circumstances in which one nation's quest for absolute security creates insecurity among others, thereby generating an upward competitive spiral. Despite these considerations, his zero-sum perspective is deeply entrenched among practitioners and analysts of international affairs in China, in the United States, and around the world. Mearsheimer's theory of "offensive realism" puts his Hobbesian view in stark relief.

> In sum, my argument is that the structure of the international system, not the particular characteristics of individual great powers, causes them to think and

act offensively and seek hegemony. . . . I assume that the principal motive behind great-power behavior is survival. In anarchy, however, the desire to survive encourages states to behave aggressively. . . . In international politics, however, a state's effective power is ultimately a function of its military forces and how they compare with the military of rival states. . . . This privileging of military power notwithstanding, states care greatly about latent power, because abundant wealth and a large population are prerequisites for building formidable military forces.[18]

Thus for Mearsheimer the times turn profoundly dangerous when a new, large power begins a rapid ascent in the international system, thereby setting off a relative diminution in the power of previously more dominant actors and whetting its leaders' appetite for global military clout. Such moments are dangerous for the rising power because the dominant nation, along with other less powerful states, may seek to bandwagon against the aspirant. This possibility accounts for Beijing's anxiety about an American-led "new containment strategy" and its fear of a Japan-U.S. alliance aimed at the PRC. Such moments are perilous for other actors as well because the rising power may overestimate what its new capacities enable (or entitle) it to achieve. The latter peril is apparent with respect to Beijing's expectations regarding Taiwan. A rising China no longer feeling supine before others may calculate (or miscalculate) that it can resolve the Taiwan issue unilaterally on terms favorable to itself. Conversely, the United States may seek to maintain security commitments even if its capacities are no longer able to sustain them. Changing power relationships change a nation's interests and capacities, but commitments and sense of role and obligation may change more slowly.

When Mearsheimer visited the PRC in 2003, he found considerable sympathy for his vision of international politics and the causes of war.[19] As one senior Chinese scholar put it, "So [also] in China there are people who think the peaceful rise [of China] is a self-delusion."[20] Nonetheless, the question is being actively debated in China, with others arguing that "we should also not neglect the restraining and regulating effects of international regimes, as well as the directing role played by economic integration and interdependence."[21] In late 2005 one university vice president at an international relations institution in China described the debate as being conducted between the "mainstream" of "cooperative internationalists" and a more insurgent but significant group that believes that war is likely or inevitable as China rises—"the new nationalists." The avenues of expression for the nationalists are more numerous on the Internet and in less establishment publications. The cooperative internationalists believe that interdependence, balance-of-power politics in a multipolar world, "win-win solutions," and wise statesmanship can reduce the chances of conflicts between the major powers. The outcome of the debate, which has its analogue in America, will have considerable bearing on China's posture in the emerging world order.

I now consider Chinese perspectives on power: the development of this thinking over the centuries and current attitudes and debates about power among leaders, intellectual elites, and the citizenry. I conclude with a discussion of whether, or to what degree, the PRC has a national grand strategy. I believe that there is a widely shared national strategy, with dissenters to be sure. This strategy places primacy on economic and ideational power. China has made considerable progress in increasing important dimensions of "comprehensive national strength" in the estimation of regime leaders and intellectuals. At the same time, there is deep and abiding anxiety about weaknesses, particularly internal deficiencies; these are discussed in chapter 6.

CONTINUITIES AND CHANGES IN CHINESE UNDERSTANDINGS OF POWER

TRADITIONAL THINKING AND MODERN MANIFESTATIONS

When one speaks with Chinese officials, military officers, and academics, they almost universally talk about the use of power from what Alastair Iain Johnston calls the Confucian-Mencian paradigm. This model emphasizes strategy, places importance on deception and manipulation of the opponent, leaves a significant role for accommodation, and employs diversified instruments of power. Brute force is not the most highly esteemed instrument of power in this genre of thinking.[22] However, when one examines actual historical and contemporary Chinese behavior, there is abundant discussion and employment of force. Indeed, contemporary PRC strategic analysts point out that historically China has used force often: "There had been more than 6,000 battles in 4,000 plus years from the twenty-sixth century B.C. when Shen Nong Shi (the Holy Farmer) attacked the Fu Sui Tribes (Tribes of Axe and Flint) to the end of [the] Qing Dynasty (1644–1911). This figure was more than one-third of the total numbers of the battles that had happened around the world during the same period."[23] The key question is: As China's power increases, will the use of force and physical intimidation increasingly characterize its international behavior?

Deng Xiaoping's statement made shortly after June 4, 1989, contributes to foreign anxiety about China's true intentions. "Adopt a sober perspective; maintain a stable posture; be composed; conserve your strength and conceal your resources; don't aspire to be the head; do something eventually."[24] Though some Chinese assert that this comment referred to not assuming the mantle of ideological leader as the Soviet Union collapsed, and others assert that it simply was a call to maintain a "low profile," it has reinforced the idea abroad that China will be patient in its assertiveness but eventually will employ newly acquired power to settle old scores, realize new aspirations, and secure new interests. It is reassuring, however, that although China's power has grown significantly since the 1980s its frequency of using force has not increased. As Johnston notes, almost all instances of China's external use of force in the communist era have had something to do with its borders and sovereignty.[25] In the final analysis, however, as Andrew Scobell argues, "Two strands of strategic culture, both shaped by an ancient and enduring civilization, exist: a distinctly Chinese pacifist and defensive-minded strand, and a Realpolitik strand favoring military solutions and offensive action."[26]

Chinese thinking about power has been embodied in discussions of "war" for about two and a half millennia—wars with enemies from within and without.[27] Systematic thinking on the subject goes back to around China's Warring States Period (453–221 BCE), the era when Sun Tzu, the fount of Chinese thinking on war, wrote. Sun Tzu referred to war as "a matter of vital importance to the State; the province of life or death; the road to survival or ruin. It is mandatory that it be thoroughly studied."[28] His core idea is that war is about producing submission, not simply using armed force. Brute force is one means of producing submission but not the most prized. In this tradition, discussion of war focuses on the combined utilization of force, material inducements, and ideas, and the distinction between domestic and foreign conflict is blurred.

Means to produce submission include the integrated use of diplomacy, superior knowledge of the antagonist and his weaknesses (temperamental, social, governmental, and economic), psychological pressure and isolation, undermining of the opponent's bases of domestic support, and hiding of one's own material, psychological, and societal weaknesses (and strengths). War and politics involve the calculated use of strategy to produce submission using normative, economic, and coercive resources, with the greatest skill demonstrated when the employment of raw force is minimized.

Sun Tzu's thinking has been central to discussions of the uses of power throughout the centuries, with his influence most visible in the eleventh century's *Seven*

Military Classics (used to prepare military officers and imperial examination takers in the Ming Dynasty), the contemporaneous classic *Unorthodox Strategies*, and Mao Zedong's core military writings of the mid- and late 1930s.[29] Mao's essays reflect his familiarity with Sun Tzu's work both directly and through his reading of Chinese classic stories such as *Water Margin* and *Romance of the Three Kingdoms*.

Dating to the fourteenth century, *Three Kingdoms* is replete with stratagems to produce submission or destruction of opponents. The stronger or weaker party in any given circumstance depends upon context and the use of appropriate strategy as well as tactics, not simply upon a comparison of material balances. One stratagem, "The Chain Plan," is emblematic of the calculating, context-dependent, comprehensive style of Chinese thinking, in which one's assets must be assessed in relationship to the other's weaknesses, whether material, organizational, intellectual, or spiritual. The materially weak can overcome those with greater abundance by being intelligent and inducing the opponent to act in ways contrary to his own interests.

Chapters 8 and 9 of *Three Kingdoms* recount the story of Governor Wang Yun's successful attempt to bring down the self-styled "imperial rector," Minister Tung Cho [Dong Zhuo], a man who sought to overthrow the emperor and who was so brutal that he brought the head of a guest to the dinner table to gratuitously intimidate his remaining retainers. Governor Wang Yun, a keen observer of human frailty, persuaded the "flowering" maiden Sable Cicada to participate in a conspiracy to become romantically involved with Tung Cho's adopted son, Lu Pu [Lu Bu]. Once the son was betrothed to the maiden she would "take every opportunity to turn away their [Tung Cho's and Lu Pu's] countenances from each other, cause the son to kill his adopted father and so put an end to the great evil."[30] Wang and Sable Cicada craftily ignited the conflicting lusts of father and son, manipulating the jealous adopted son to assassinate his father and thereby eliminate the threat to the throne. In the process, Wang Yun expended few of his own resources while accomplishing tasks enormously important to the state.

> Just introduce a woman,
> Conspiracies succeed;
> Of soldiers, or their weapons,
> There really is no need.
> They fought their bloody battles,
> And doughty deeds were done;
> But in a garden summer house
> The victory was won.[31]

This may seem an interesting detour through somewhat tangential intellectual terrain, but I often have been struck in the course of my interviews and documentary research with the complexity and indirection of Chinese thought. A Chinese policy analyst recounted, for instance, how Beijing addressed a dilemma it had faced in early 2003 following Beijing's November 8, 2002, vote in support of UN Security Council Resolution 1441 promising Saddam Hussein's Iraq that "serious consequences" would be visited upon it if it did not fully cooperate with UN weapons inspectors. In the wake of 1441's passage, Baghdad was not sufficiently cooperative in Washington's view, and in January 2003 the Bush administration began to press Beijing and others on the UN Security Council to support a second, explicit resolution authorizing the use of force.

Beijing did not wish to explicitly endorse the use of force for a host of reasons, including fear that fundamentalist Islamic groups and states might seek to retaliate by energizing some of China's own nineteen million Muslims. In addition, Chinese leaders simply had an aversion to big-power intervention in sovereign states, reflecting, in part, a sensitivity acquired from China's own past humiliations. However, Beijing had a countervailing consideration: it did not wish to become estranged from Washington. Moreover, PRC leaders calculated that after the presumed victory in Iraq the United States would be sitting on the world's second- to fourth-largest oil reserves, precisely as the PRC was becoming more dependent upon imported energy. Chinese leaders expected America to win the anticipated conflict with Iraq and wanted to be in a position to benefit by being perceived as more cooperative with Washington than Paris, Berlin, and Moscow were.

Beijing therefore undertook a diplomatic stratagem to get Pakistan, a PRC ally and crucial vote (at the time Pakistan was temporarily on the UN Security Council), not to support the American proposal for a second resolution (while downplaying its own opposition to Washington). The hope was that the Bush administration would see that its support on the Security Council was insufficient and decide not to proceed with a vote. This would obviate the necessity for Beijing to vote directly against Washington, permit the Bush administration to argue that the UN already had approved a use of force in 1441 with the phrase "serious consequences," and allow China to say that it had not explicitly authorized the use of force against Iraq. The Chinese policy analyst explained:

China avoided war on its watch as chair of the UN Security Council [November 2002] with UN Resolution 1441—the wording was not based on principle—it didn't reject war, it just postponed it [until China was not chair of the Security

Council]. All this shows China's weakness. We tried to convince Pakistan not to vote for the second resolution; Pakistan was caught between the United States and China and in fact went with China. This was the most successful Chinese policy in a decade. China did not directly hurt the United States and escaped the retaliation faced by France and Germany. China's hard power is not great, but its diplomatic wisdom and implementation were very successful. Because China understands that its hard power will not be adequate for twenty years, we use China's ever-increasing soft power to offset insufficient hard power.[32]

Despite their preference for diplomacy, force is one tool that Chinese throughout their long history have often been willing to use. One need only recall Korea and the Taiwan Strait in the 1950s; Vietnam, the Sino-Indian border, and the Sino-Soviet border in the 1960s; Vietnam again in the 1970s; the South China Sea in the 1970s, 1980s, and 1990s; and the Taiwan Strait in the mid-1990s. Each of these instances in which force was employed had its own rationale and was limited, facts that are in themselves instructive. But one cannot conclude that Chinese foreign policy is averse to the use of force if Chinese leaders believe it is the most effective instrument of state power. As Michael Swaine and Ashley Tellis explain, "The historical record suggests that the Chinese state has frequently employed force against foreign powers but generally followed a pragmatic and limited approach to the use of such force. Specifically, it has employed force against foreigners primarily to influence, control, or pacify its strategic periphery and generally has done so when it possessed relative superiority."[33] In short, when Chinese conclude that force is the most effective way to secure vital objectives, and that the collateral costs of using force are manageable, their inhibitions to its use are not great.

SIZE AND NUMBERS MATTER

Because China is such a large country in terms of geography and population, its leaders have long known that power must be considered in both its per capita and its aggregate forms. Size *and* numbers matter.

One of China's most forward-looking contemporary thinkers, Zheng Bijian, often talks of China's "division" and "multiplication" problems. In referring to his country's 1.3 billion population he explains, "The multiplication problem is that no matter how small a problem [is], when multiplied by 1.3 billion [it becomes huge]. The division problem is that no matter how much capital [you have], when divided by 1.3 billion it is a very small amount of capital."[34] Of course, the reverse also is true. Even though financial or other resources and capabilities may be small on a per capita basis, a government able to extract and concentrate those dispersed resources has at its disposal an enormous aggregate. And here the Chinese have some potential advantages. China's political system is capable of extracting and aggregating resources (with limitations noted in chapter 6), even as its small per capita resource base is a huge impediment to progress.

Mao Zedong always viewed China's geographic expanse and massive population as defensive assets in the face of possible invasion—"Lure the enemy deep." China's masses were seen as an offset to America's technological lead, as demonstrated clearly during the Korean War, when Chinese infantry formations could take an enormous pounding from far superior U.S. artillery but keep coming. This is not to say that Chinese do not value human life or understand the implications of the "revolution in military affairs"—they do. But they also recognize that size and numbers can be assets, particularly if your adversary has a low threshold for pain, as Chinese are prone to think is true for Americans. Numbers and *will* can be a powerful combination.

Enormous aggregates are seen as important not simply in terms of coercive power but also in terms of economic and ideational power. One of the PRC's principal assets in attracting foreign capital is the sheer scale of the potential domestic market to which the investor would have access. Deng Xiaoping once referred to China as a "big piece of good meat" that foreigners might savor,[35] and one senior Chinese official described the Chinese market as "a big cake" over which various foreigners were competing.[36]

Diplomatically, Chinese often sanctify their national demands and policy objectives by invoking the alleged shared sentiments of 1.3 billion people, in effect arguing that China's titanic population size lends moral standing to Beijing's arguments. The implied assertion that what 20 percent of the world's population wants ought to count for something would seem to be based on an ethos of a democratic world order, such as that called for by Jiang Zemin in his statement that the PRC is "in favor of promoting democracy in international relations."[37]

COMPREHENSIVE NATIONAL POWER

In subsequent chapters I examine each category of power (coercive, remunerative, and ideational) in depth. The focus here, however, is on how Chinese analysts think about their current national circumstances in quantitative terms. Whether methodologically well grounded or not, the idea of "comprehensive national power" (CNP, *zonghe guoli*) shapes the way Chinese understand their national circumstance and strategy. Though the broad conclusions of various Chinese studies of CNP overlap considerably, there are also important divergences and debates between those analysts who stress, more than the others, the rapidity with which the PRC's relative share of global power is growing and those who stress, more than the others, the challenges confronting China's growth trajectory. The idea of CNP resonates with the thinking of traditional strategists such as Sun Tzu, whose first chapter in *The Art of War* is entitled "Estimates."

In his work on Chinese conceptions of CNP, Michael Pillsbury emphasizes the degree to which many PRC analyses employ methodologies "unique to China" in addition to more standard internationally employed quantitative approaches.[38] Somewhat in contrast, I have been struck by the degree to which PRC research in the last half of the 1990s and the first part of the new millennium draws on international concepts and categories of data.

For Huang Shuofeng CNP is "the combination of all the powers possessed by a country for the survival and development of a sovereign state, including material and ideational ethos, and international influence as well."[39] CNP, in short, is the sum total of coercive, economic, and ideational power of a nation. The concept, however, is difficult to unassailably operationalize. How is one to measure resources, assess their relative importance, combine economic, coercive, and intellectual indicators into one unified measure, and distinguish between *potential* strength and that which can actually be mobilized for state purposes?

In 2002, two of China's most creative economic and social thinkers, Professors Hu Angang and Men Honghua in Beijing, published a study of China's CNP (updated in 2007). Arguing that "the status (or position) of a country in the international community is in essence associated with the rise and fall of its national power, the increase and decrease of strategic resources," they posed the following questions:

> What is comprehensive national power (CNP)? What are strategic resources that make up CNP? What kinds of strategic resources are most important in the twenty-first century? What advantages and disadvantages [does] China enjoy in strategic resources vis-à-vis other great powers? Where [does] China stand in the world with regard to CNP? Has it grown or lost in /sic/ strength over the past 20 years? How is China's CNP changing as compared with the United States, Japan, India and Russia, which are closely associated with China's national interests and geopolitical strategy? How should China raise its CNP and how should it make full use of its advantage[ous] strategic resources and constantly improve its disadvantaged strategic resources? What are the objectives of China's grand strategy? How to put it into execution?[40]

Hu and Men focus on hard power in their quantitative assessments, even though they note that less tangible, soft power cannot be ignored and even though a few of their indicators touch on soft power. Taking their cue from Michael Porter's work, they measure as principal components of CNP physical resources, human resources, infrastructure, knowledge resources, and capital.[41] They further divide these resources into eight categories with twenty-three indicators. To create each indicator, they employ data from the World Bank's *World Development Indicators* and other comparable sources (such as Barro and Lee's global education data bank).[42] Each indicator is developed by calculating China's resource as a percentage of the global resource total.[43] China's ranking is then compared to the rankings of India, Japan, Russia, and the United States along each of the twenty-three dimensions. These separate indicators are then combined according to a weighting index to produce a total CNP measure for various points in time for each nation.

Each indicator is compromised by issues of data accuracy and comparability across nations and time, not to mention questions about what each indicator actually measures or how one should rank their relative importance and then aggregate these weighted indicators into one meaningful measure of CNP. As Hu and Men acknowledge, most of the indicators ignore the problem of "resource quality." Some indicators, like central government spending and military spending, ignore the fact that significant expenditures in China occur outside the budget entirely, in nontransparent corners of the budget, or by organizations not categorized as "military." Data reliability has changed over time; there is also the problem of whether to emphasize per capita or aggregate indicators. Parenthetically, when Chinese wish to emphasize their weaknesses, they speak in per capita terms; when they seek to impress, they speak in aggregate terms.

It is telling that Hu and Men chose to compare China to the United States, Japan, Russia, and India—these are the nations that PRC elites and opinion makers measure themselves against. As one Chinese put it to me, "I always have in mind the United States. Confucius said, 'See the best and do the best.' Aim high and you'll get the middle. If you aim at the middle, you get low. So we have to set high goals."[44]

Hu and Men come to a number of conclusions about China's relative power position that are derived from their data covering the years 1980 through 2003.[45] First, the United States remains far and away number one in CNP, though its global share has declined somewhat. America's share of global power is about 2.2 times China's, though the PRC is narrowing the gap: "[The] CNP of China was only 1/5 (21%) that of the United States in 1980, 1/4 (25.5%) in 1990. But by 2000, it was more than 1/3 (39%) that of the United States."[46] By 2003, it had reached 44 percent. Second, China

TABLE I Comprehensive National Power Index for Five Major Countries
(% of World Total)

Country	1980	1985	1990	1995	2000	2003	Change in 1980–2003
China	4.736	5.306	5.646	7.163	8.770	9.991	5.255
India	3.376	3.615	3.735	4.008	4.543	4.868	1.492
Japan	6.037	6.337	7.317	8.535	7.729	6.998	0.961
Russia	—	—	3.271	2.808	2.925	2.934	—
USA	22.485	22.022	22.138	21.903	22.518	22.274	−0.211
Five-country total	—	—	42.107	44.417	46.485	47.065	—

SOURCE: Hu Angang and Men Honghua, "The Rise of Modern China (1980–2000): Comprehensive National Power and Grand Strategy," *Strategy and Management*, no. 3 (2002).

NOTE: This table was updated by Professor Hu in 2007 from the original published version. Correspondence with author, March 3, 2007. [Non-data edits by author.]

increased its lead over both India and USSR/Russia considerably during 1980–2003. Third, China has surpassed Japan; Hu and Men assert that "China has risen to the second world power."[47] These broad assessments are shared by other Chinese agencies and scholars: one respected analyst at the China Institute of Contemporary International Relations commented in 1998, "Few people would disagree that China's overall national strength will still be far behind the United States, but may catch up with Japan and will be sure to exceed Russia."[48] Another Chinese scholar put it this way: "In the twenty-first century, like it or not, the United States will continue to play a leading role in the world."[49] By 2006, a multinational survey of public opinion concerning how nations view their own influence in relationship to other nations revealed that Chinese saw their influence as second only to that of the United States, though they felt China "should have more influence than the United States and that they would achieve equal influence with the United States within ten years."[50]

These conclusions can be assailed from several directions. In the information age, industrial-age measures of strength are somewhat less salient; comparing the head count of various militaries, for example, is less germane given the revolution in military affairs. Moreover, there is the issue of whether to use Purchasing Power Parity (PPP) as a measure of economic performance as opposed to exchange rate calculations. PPP calculations yield per capita GDP figures for the PRC that are about four times those obtained by exchange rate methods.[51] Further, Chinese analysts may be making a mistake by projecting Japan's sub-par economic performance of the 1990s into the new millennium in straight-line fashion,[52] and it is similarly unlikely that China will sustain its recent blistering growth rates indefinitely: as an economy grows and matures, growth rates tend to slow. Finally, as underscored in chapter 6, there are enormous economic, demographic, and sociopolitical disruptions that could deflect China from its current path of sustained, high growth. Indeed, an extensive *People's Daily* article in August 2004 reported that ninety-eight foreign and domestic experts had warned of ten major vulnerabilities to stable continued progress and counseled that "one must think of danger in time of peace as the eleventh Five-Year Plan (2006–10) is being drawn up."[53] One astute Chinese interviewee put it this way: "People in China are less optimistic about its [China's] future than people outside China. The whole posture is very defensive. They [Chinese] are very worried about food, energy, environment, disease."[54]

Hu and Men's policy conclusions and recommendations correspond with widely shared assumptions undergirding policy in China today. They say that China should:

1. "Intensify investment in human capital" to maintain economic growth and continue to climb in international power rankings. China must boost workforce quality, improve general citizen education and health, reduce absolute poverty, and so forth.

2. Develop "new energy sources and renewable energy . . . and fully utilize internationally available strategic resources based on [the] market mechanism and environmental-friendly sustainable development model."

3. Increase the efficiency of capital utilization.

4. Improve the efficiency of the taxation system and increase net government extraction from the economy.

5. "Raise sharply the percentage of defense spending in GDP to enhance the defense capabilities."

6. Increase China's ideational power, stressing "international institutions, international prestige, cultural influence, and other soft factors."[55]

Of course, such objectives and recommendations have embedded within them painful choices and powerful constituencies in favor of divergent paths. Regarding Hu and Men's first and fifth recommendations, for instance, how can Chinese leaders balance human and defense investment—guns versus *doufu* (tofu)? With a rapidly aging citizenry, not to mention a nation with a far-flung and still massive rural population, how can health care be provided when technology, pharmaceuticals, and the growth in chronic disease are all rapidly driving up costs? How should health and education expenditures be prioritized, and what level(s) and types of education are most important to emphasize? How can the central government increase revenues without dampening economic incentives at local levels and in the growing private sector? How can leaders balance economic growth with environmental considerations? Similarly, it is easier to call for improving the efficiency with which capital is allocated than to actually produce systemic change in this respect: local officials resist relinquishing power over the allocation of capital, crony capitalism is deeply embedded, and local officials' promotions are based on their localities' growth rates (which creates incentives for making loans locally and misreporting up and down the administrative hierarchy). The very politics of producing change makes it hard to devise and implement a strategy.

GRAND STRATEGY AND DEBATE

There is disagreement in China about whether the country's leaders have a "grand strategy" to boost CNP and guide its subsequent use. Many Chinese observers speak of their nation's foreign policy from the perspective that the relatively centralized political system creates opportunity for strategic consensus and that the PRC's size entitles Beijing to think globally. As one Chinese scholar put it not so delicately, "It is the privilege of great countries to have grand strategies—not Papua New Guinea."[56] On the other hand, many also recognize that as Chinese society (and its bureaucracy) become increasingly pluralized, consensus is becoming progressively more difficult to achieve and maintain. One respondent heatedly argued: "We have no grand strategy. The basic approach of our government is an instantly reactive approach, though many [Chinese analysts] suggest China should have a long-term objective."[57] Other analysts claim that China has a "camouflaged" or implicit strategy. Still others claim that China has a self-evident and clearly stated goal and a strategy to attain it: "In the coming twenty years the relative gap between China's overall national strength and that of the United States will be reduced to two-fold from three-fold, making the country [China] a world power with dominant ability."[58] In my own opinion, there is an implicit consensus on broad goals *and* the means to achieve them, but debates and conflicts will continually arise along the way over priorities and thresholds of risk. One almost universally shared goal in the PRC—indeed in China for the last 150 years or more, since the Qing Dynasty went into decline—is to make China rich and powerful and to regain the nation's former status as a great power that controls its own fate.

FIGURE 1

In 2006 guards watch the construction site of the National Stadium, "The Bird's Nest," the main venue for the 2008 Beijing Olympic Games. China's leaders and people hope that their hosting the Games will strengthen the country's infrastructure, spur economic modernization and China's role in globalization, and mark the nation's formal reemergence as a great power. Cancan Chu/Getty Images.

There is a broad consensus strategy for achieving this goal. However, it leaves two decisive questions unanswered. First, will the international system (the United States in particular) resist and seek to retard China's movement along its chosen path? Second, what domestic and foreign policies will best ensure the levels of economic growth *and* domestic stability that will enable the strategy to proceed and to succeed? These two questions must be addressed as Chinese society and government pluralize, with various elite, opinion-shaping, and popular groups adopting divergent policy preferences. With increasing pluralization, political groups can form to promote their own concerns, thereby creating the risk that political conflict could rip asunder the more general strategic consensus. For instance, as domestic inequality has grown with economic development, more domestic voices are raised about the wisdom of China's bet on globalization. A final obstacle concerns the general drift toward leaders with less strength in an increasingly bureaucratized system. One Chinese scholar put it this way: "With Mao Zedong and Deng Xiaoping you had leaders with strategic vision; now we have weak leaders and a strong, fragmented society [and] policy structure."[59]

Swaine and Tellis provide a parsimonious description of what they call the PRC's "calculative security strategy." The security component upon which Swaine and Tellis primarily focus is designed to foster the international conditions under which domestic development can proceed with minimum external interference and maximum external support. "The notion of 'calculative' strategy is . . . a pragmatic approach that emphasizes the primacy of internal economic growth and stability, the nurturing of amicable international relations, the relative restraint in the use of force combined with increasing efforts to create a more modern military, and the continued search for asymmetric gains internationally."[60] Swaine and Tellis anticipate that this strategy will endure until at least 2015–20.

In his political report to the Sixteenth Party Congress on November 8, 2002, President Jiang Zemin put the strategy crisply, saying, "The first two decades of the 21st century are a period of important strategic opportunities, which we must seize tightly and which offers bright prospects. . . . We need to concentrate on building a well-off society . . . in this period. . . . The two decades of development will serve as an inevitable connecting link for attaining the third-step strategic objectives for our modernization drive. . . . A new world war is unlikely in the foreseeable future. It is realistic to bring about a fairly long period of peace in the world and a favorable climate in areas around China."[61] A key component of this strategy has been developing cooperative relations abroad, most importantly with Washington, even as Beijing has tried to find other friends. In making friends elsewhere, Beijing has realized that the frustrations of others with U.S. policy can be an asset. As one senior Chinese scholar put it,

> As China's power has grown [it has] wanted to make itself more charming, more effective, to limit counter-reactions. And, as China grew into the international system, it talked more responsibly, played by common rules, got into international organizations—soft power. It started with realism [and changed to neoliberalism]. . . . I have two conclusions: (1) It is important to have economic power, and it should also be converted into military power. In the 1980s and into the 1990s we needed to convert more into military [power]. It is not enough to be rich; be strong too. . . . (2) We need to get soft power and we have seen the failure of George W. Bush as an indication of how important it [soft power] is to being a big power. Regarding soft power, [China's leaders] want China to be seen as a responsible power. How to achieve this? Emphasize the UN's role, and at the regional level promote regional economic integration

FIGURE 2

Chinese President Jiang Zemin and U.S. President George W. Bush in Shanghai at the October 2001 APEC summit, their first meeting after the September 11 terrorist attacks on the United States. In the attacks' immediate aftermath, President Jiang articulated a PRC policy that opposed terrorism and supported initial American moves. This was a turning point in U.S.-China relations. Reuters/Corbis.

and build regional economic and security institutions. . . . [I]t is not enough to work at these levels; we must also build domestic political civilization—more balanced development and more attention to the needy. . . . There is a general consensus about the direction in which China should move, [a consensus] developed in the mid- and late 1990s. How to be a constructive middle power? [There is] a mind-set of elite/opinion leaders, and with this mind-set [we have] developed policies on different issues.[62]

A clear logic is at work, a logic linking the need to maintain cooperative relations with the external world (particularly the United States), with the requirement to constrain Washington through multilateral bodies and world opinion and to become an increasingly influential nation with substantial ideational power. The basic concept is that by following a nonconfrontational path in the short and medium term China will become a major force in the world.[63] As one Chinese scholar explains,

> Regarding hard power, China is betting that in twenty years things will change. Now we have a $1.4 trillion GNP, but after twenty years of 7.8 percent annual growth we will requadruple our GNP and reach the level of $4–5 trillion. The United States is at the level of $11–12 trillion now, and given 3 percent per annum growth, by 2020 the United States will have a GNP of $17 trillion—China will be about one-third [the U.S. level]. . . . Today China spends US$30 billion [official budget] on its military. By 2020, it will be four times higher, and at least for the last decade-plus China's military budget has increased at the rate of GNP increase, about 12 percent. By 2020 our military budget would be $180 billion at this rate of growth—almost 50 percent of the U.S. military budget of last year [2003]. I don't know where the U.S. budget will go. . . . And these figures don't include [China's] off-budget procurement. . . . Our grand strategy is that by 2020 China matters and China's hard power will appear. If we are premature to meet the challenge of the United States we will lose our chance.[64]

Importantly, however, this scholar did not fall prey to the gravest danger in such thinking—the tendency to project today's performance indefinitely into the future. During the same interview, this respondent argued that many things could deflect China from the path described above and that its leaders recognized the dangers. These considerations argue that China should keep the window of opportunity open and should avoid strategic challenge for as long as possible—well beyond the next twenty years. "Growth will weaken the Chinese Communist Party. . . . Also, the oil supply cannot sustain China's quadrupling GNP again. The world supply cannot do it. And China's ecological and financial system cannot stand a quadrupling of GNP either. No water supply; no electricity. We can't absorb the waste [effluents]. So the grand strategy is very questionable. The competition for energy alone will cause external problems. Energy-scarce countries will hate China."[65]

Returning to the subject of grand strategy, all of these considerations have led to the development of a widely shared, implicit sense concerning China's goals, the broad steps needed for their achievement, and the obstacles that will be confronted along the way. In the words of another senior Chinese scholar,

We have a camouflaged strategy. There is one world, it is dominated by the capitalist democracies, and we want to join that world. We should be part of this world, join the G-8 and make it the G-9. We already are part of the WTO and most existing regimes. We have no problem. If we want to be rich, adopt norms, and these norms are favorable [to China], so we don't have to be hasty in changing regimes because we are part of the advanced world. So our strategy is this, but we can't say it. Our goal is to become a capitalist country.[66]

The "calculative security strategy" is the cocoon protecting domestic economic and social development, and the principal features of the domestic strategy are increased use of markets and material incentives; modernization of science, technology, education, and management; use of the international economic system to provide skills, capital, information, competition for domestic firms, and export markets; and a growing domestic consumption class that provides stability and can drive internal growth, investment, and innovation so that China is not as export dependent as the earlier modernizing Asian tiger economies and Japan. This strategy acknowledges that there will need to be fundamental changes in the role of the government and Chinese Communist Party (CCP) in the economic system (from economic player to regulatory referee), along with the creation of more predictable legal and judicial institutions. The vision currently does not include extensive political liberalization (see chapter 6). A key aspect of this strategy is to use the resulting urban and industrial growth to absorb the hundreds of millions of surplus rural citizens, and to do all this while avoiding regime-threatening internal instability.

One Chinese scholar described the evolution of China's national strategy as follows:

Mao Zedong and Deng Xiaoping had the same goals—to make China rich and strong. Mao used alliances to do it; Deng pursued interdependence as a way to develop, integration into the world, outsourcing technology and capital. Mao emphasized idea ["normative"] power to mobilize people, and Deng attached more importance to material aspects, incentives. In terms of military strategy, Mao was very defensive—guerrilla or people's war and development of nuclear weapons were for political reasons. Deng placed a lot of importance on economics; after the economy was strong he would spend more on the military. After the fall of the USSR, Deng switched to more emphasis on the military, in part as a reward for June 4. This was a change in strategy, not just an adjustment. The world was more threatening; China was the only socialist country left, Vietnam and North Korea aside. . . . Also, by then the government felt more able to spend.[67]

Though there is a consensus about Deng's broad national strategy in both its security and its domestic development dimensions, and though this consensus has lasted for a quarter-century and probably will endure for a considerable time into the future, the forces of entropy (the tendency toward disorganization over time) continually put pressure on the strategy. In the course of policy specification and implementation, winners and losers are created. Over time, the losers seek to challenge the strategy or its implementation, at least around the edges. Debate over the strategy becomes more intense as social and governmental pluralization proceeds and greater resources foster divisive debates over how the new strength should be used and distributed. Finally, in the two decades following the chaos of the Great Proletarian Cultural Revolution most Chinese were willing to attach primacy to social stability and postpone fundamental political reform, but as memories of Mao Zedong's depredations as well as the more recent June 4, 1989, violence recede the population increasingly resents the government's authoritarian constraints and grows progressively bolder in confronting them. While Deng Xiaoping, with all his revolutionary and postrevolutionary credentials, had enough clout to make a strategy stick, each subsequent generation of leaders may well have diminished capacities in this respect.

The tendency toward entropy is well described by Chinese citizens themselves:

Modernization has led to a lack of consensus. This is the future—more lack of consensus. In noncrisis circumstances, there is a lack of consensus. . . . In the Politburo Standing Committee, nine votes are important, not just one. You see it in the regional governments like Shanghai, Zhejiang, Fujian, [and] Guangdong having major voices. There is a lack of consensus.[68]

So the positive side is that leaders are keeping a clear mind and they have the capability to keep control, but the negative side is that more people are involved [in the policy process]. We have an independent public opinion, to some extent. With . . . freer media and independent society this is good for the long run, but not so in the short run—it is too emotional.[69]

Consequently, over time three significant modifications have revealed the internal and external pressures to which the strategy has been subject. The first change was in 1989, when the relative priority of the military rose in the modernization strategy. In every year between 1980 and 1988, the official Chinese military budget had either declined in current Chinese dollars or gone up by a low single-digit percentage. In 1980, official Chinese military spending was 16 percent of total central government expenditure, and by 1988 it had dropped to 8.1 percent. From 1989 through 2005, however, the official military budget on average grew by 15.4 percent annually; this larger expenditure constituted 12.7 percent of total central government budgetary expenditure in 2004.[70] The second change was in 1997, when China moved toward a more active role in global affairs, in part as a result of the Asian Financial Crisis and Washington's relative passivity in that period. The most recent change has been evident under Jiang Zemin's successor, Hu Jintao, who has emphasized promoting economic growth and social welfare among regions and groups left behind by the previous trickle-down domestic development. Looking ahead, a principal question is when and how China's leaders will put accelerated political change on the agenda, a topic addressed in chapter 6.

The first change reflects a military unhappy with its budget as it faced a more capable and assertive United States, a Taiwan seemingly drifting farther from the mainland, and the demise of previous communist brethren regimes. The second reflects the anxieties that a growing Chinese military generates in Asia, the PRC's need to reassure its neighbors, and the opportunity for Beijing to use multilateral organizations and its growing economic clout to restrain a powerful Washington and hem in an independence-minded Taiwan. And the third change reflects the need to maintain tolerable domestic stability in the face of widening economic and social gaps at home and gaping holes in the social safety net. These pressures have resulted in a modified consensus strategy that provides great room for debate, if not conflict. Each of these changes is addressed in greater detail in subsequent chapters.

TWO GREAT CHALLENGES

Two sets of considerations most worry China's leaders as they seek to implement their strategy. First, how can rising material and political expectations be managed as change proceeds, and can social stability be maintained given these undeniable changes? Second, as China becomes stronger, how can Beijing reduce the likelihood that the dominant power (or powers) will seek to retard, or reverse, China's ongoing acquisition of strength? Will the international system remain comparatively benign, thereby permitting China to remain focused on internal growth and stability? In this vein, a 2003–5 debate in China, over whether to describe China's strategy as that of a "peaceful rise" *(heping jueqi)*, is particularly instructive.

The phrase *peaceful rise* was first coined in November 2003 by the chairman of the China Reform Forum Zheng Bijian[71] as a way to reassure the outside world (particularly the PRC's neighbors and Washington) that China's ascendance would not follow the destructive paths of Germany and Japan in the first half of the twentieth century or the Soviet Union throughout much of that same century. The phrase was used by General Secretary and President Hu Jintao, along with Premier Wen Jiabao, the following month and into 2004 and was a rhetorical attempt to reassure skeptics in the United States and elsewhere who had started speaking regularly of a "China threat." After intense debate that may have included discussion in the Standing Committee of the Politburo,[72] President Hu Jintao, in his April 24, 2004, remarks to the Boao Forum on Asia, dropped the term *peaceful rise*, using *peaceful development path* instead.[73] This substitution reflected leadership jockeying between Hu and his predecessor Jiang Zemin and the debate outlined below. The argument leading up to Hu's speech illustrates the forces that both shape China's strategy and continually subject it to pressure. One of several PRC analysts who described the debate summed it up as follows:

Zheng Bijian suggested *peaceful rise*. [But] former ambassador to Russia Li Funing [and many other ambassadors] raised criticisms. It is not a good idea to stress a rising China. *Jueqi,* this is stronger in Chinese than *rise* is in English [the Chinese word conveys the idea of "thrusting up" or "rising abruptly"]. So they [the ambassadors] say [the phrase] is no good for China. Another group of opponents is in academic circles, and they say [the phrase] demonstrates a lack of knowledge. There is no historical base for this [peaceful rise]. No country ever rose peacefully. Consider Japan and Germany. Others in the academic circles say, How can you say China is rising when Chinese per capita GDP is $1,000? [Another scholar mentioned by name] considers that the idea of a peacefully rising China further reduces China's ability to deal with Taiwan independence because if your strategy focuses too much on "peaceful" then there is a restraint on your power. The third group is from the PLA [People's Liberation Army]—if "peaceful rise" is the stated strategy, they are concerned with the possibility that the PLA will be disadvantaged in the budget. [By way of contrast, the term substituted by Hu Jintao,] *peaceful development*, is a very ordinary term and gradually will become meaningless.[74]

Despite this debate, however, both *peaceful development* and *peaceful rise* remained in usage, showing that Beijing remained dedicated to the task of reassuring the outside world about its intentions, even if it could not reach internal unanimity about the vocabulary for doing so. Indeed, in the fall of 2005 Zheng Bijian wrote an article for *Foreign Affairs* magazine entitled "China's 'Peaceful Rise' to Great-Power Status"; Deputy Secretary of State Robert Zoellick referred to Zheng's thinking in a major September 21, 2005, policy address on China; and Zheng responded to Zoellick's remarks about a month later, saying, "What I want to stress is that it is economic globalization that has created conditions for the peaceful rise of China. Therefore, the Chinese Communist Party doesn't intend to challenge the existing international order, nor will it advocate undermining or overthrowing it by violent means."[75] He went on to talk about the need for pragmatism in policy and the conflict-reducing effects of global interdependence. In the conference at which Zheng's November 2005 address was delivered, a Chinese scholar summarized China's effort to reassure the world of its nondisruptive intentions and called upon others to accept China's peaceful rise, saying: "China has spent a lot of time learning from past rising powers like Russia, Japan, and Germany so as to avoid the mistakes of past rising powers. The United States should spend time learning how previous dominant powers dealt with rising powers [peacefully]."[76]

From ancient times Chinese leaders have appreciated the varied forms of power and have understood that its varied forms should be employed in an optimal mix that changes according to internal and external conditions. There is, on the one hand, a role for the decisive use of force, or what Mao called "battles of quick decision" and "annihilation." Theorists and practitioners from Sun Tzu to Mao Zedong, Deng Xiaoping, and Jiang Zemin have not hesitated to use force when they deemed it necessary. On the other hand, almost all instances of Chinese use of force in the post-1949 era have reflected anxiety about periphery defense—though one must acknowledge that China had little capacity for power projection farther afield, so that the PRC's future actions as it acquires enhanced capabilities are still uncertain. What constitutes the periphery to be defended could change as PRC capabilities and interests expand. For instance, one Chinese scholar noted to a group of U.S. congresspersons that the Middle East had become a part of China's salient periphery in a way that it had not been when China had been self-reliant in oil prior to 1993.[77]

Leaders and citizens of the PRC generally see themselves as getting stronger along all three dimensions of power (coercive, remunerative, and ideational), although they also recognize that:

- China today is considerably weaker than the United States in terms of comprehensive power and will remain so for the foreseeable future.

- China's clout in the Asian-Pacific region is greater than it is in the broader international system.

- China has an approximate twenty-year window of opportunity to stay focused domestically.

- Continued national progress remains hostage to both internal and external developments.

China's leaders from Deng Xiaoping through Jiang Zemin to Hu Jintao have adopted and adapted a consensus grand strategy that emphasizes securing the external conditions conducive to internal economic growth and social change. To these ends, the preponderant part of China's elite has moved toward a concept of cooperative, multilateral security. *At the same time,* there is seriousness of purpose in modernizing China's military and using it, if need be, in the Taiwan Strait and in the more distant future to protect the nation's resource lifelines. Moreover, there is a perceptible rift between those intellectuals and leaders in the PRC who subscribe to a more cooperative view of international relations and those who espouse a Chinese form of "offensive realism" in which it is seen as a delusion to believe that the current world hegemon (the United States) will acquiesce to its own loss of power.

The current circumstances require China and the United States to each make a bet—a double gamble. For China, the bet is that America and the outside world will maintain an external environment in which China's growth can proceed according to the evolving development strategy that has worked relatively well since 1978. Washington is expected to maintain such an environment for many reasons, one of which is that it is preoccupied with more imminent global threats to its national security and needs China's assistance (great or small) in addressing them. Another reason is that China's potential market is an economic prize for which the advanced nations of the world are already competing, thereby giving China leverage.

For America, the bet since the 1970s has been that as China grows and becomes enmeshed in global interdependence, the liberal internationalist impulse in the PRC will exert progressively more influence over Chinese policy. The argument is that as China benefits from globalization it will become an increasingly staunch maintainer of the system from which it derives huge gains (a "responsible stakeholder," in the 2005 words of then U.S. Deputy Secretary of State Robert Zoellick). Each nation has made its respective bet because progress to date fosters the hope for progress in the future and because there really is no realistic alternative.

Nonetheless, each nation has embedded within its social, economic, and political systems individuals and social groups that are uncertain, or openly skeptical, of their own country's bet. Each national leadership hedges its bet by having (and creating more) military capability in reserve and developing allies and friends elsewhere in the international system—what I call "hedged integration." The hedging strategy of each country understandably creates anxiety (and military counter-reactions) in the polity of the other. China and the United States, therefore, are wedded to strategies that foster continued debate and anxiety at home but to which there currently is no feasible alternative. Politicians in both nations will continue to struggle to maintain internal support for a strategy that has many domestic skeptics.

History and power cycle theory suggest that the moments when relative power begins to change among great states are moments of uncertainty, if not danger. These moments necessitate that there be statesmen in both the ascendant state and the dominant state. In the ascendant state (China), leaders must be careful not to misjudge what their new capacities can accomplish and should not fail to reassure the dominant state and others that they are mindful of others' core interests. In the currently dominant state (the United States), the task is to adapt policies and international structures to incorporate the arrival of the new power in such a way as to preserve for itself as much leverage as possible and to build the ascendant nation into what Ronald Tammen calls the "coalition of the satisfied."[78] The United States, in this case, cannot cling to peripheral interests that its power is no longer adequate to secure at reasonable cost.

TWO · Might

People think of armies as instruments of war, but they
are much more.

WILLIAM PERRY,
former U.S. Secretary of Defense,
January 2005

As the PLA [People's Liberation Army] has opened
to the world, it has realized it needed to modernize—
it is backward compared to the other instruments of
state power. The PLA faces competition from the private
sector for recruitment, and patriotism is not enough to
get them the personnel they need.

SENIOR SINGAPORE FLAG OFFICER,
June 2005

This chapter deals with changes in China's coercive power during the reform era, future trends, and the place of coercion in China's overall power repertoire. Two central themes emerge. First, although China is becoming stronger in terms of coercive power, it is also becoming smarter in terms of its ability to use coercive, economic, and ideational power in combination to reassure others and thereby reduce the anxieties and reactions that this growing coercive capability might otherwise create. This said, anxiety among China's neighbors and more distant states persists. Second, although China's coercive power is growing, it has distinct limitations.

Might, as metaphorically used here, represents coercive power, that form of power resting "on the application, or the threat of application, of physical sanctions . . . ; generation of frustration through restriction of movement; or controlling through force the satisfaction of needs such as those for food, sex, comfort, and the like."[1] The principal tools of coercion in the realm of international politics are militaries or other instruments of brute force, economic embargoes and sanctions aimed at dramatically affecting welfare in the target society, and international isolation—the diplomatic version of prison. The three broad forms of power around which this book is organized (coercive, remunerative, and ideational) are not entirely discrete. The use of material goods as rewards is clearly remunerative power. However, when the promise of gain morphs into the threat of pain (through withholding essential material resources), remunerative power becomes coercion. Similarly, one expression of ideational power is the use of "acceptance" and "positive response" to promote desired behavior.[2] However, when isolation and the creation of pariah status are employed, these methods slip into coercion; and in "shame" or "face" cultures, outcast status is a particularly potent means of control. Thus the three faces of power have multiple expressions.

China has mounting capabilities to intimidate, punish, and isolate. While not all of these capabilities need cause alarm, some do. Uncertainty arises because coercive power can be used defensively or offensively, with a key determinant being the intentions of the power holder. Intentions are difficult to determine and may change—increased capabilities, in the context of new and far-flung interests to protect, for example, may stimulate the adoption of more ambitious objectives. A further complication is that coercive power can be self-limiting—economic sanctions may boomerang, for example. And instruments that normally are thought of as coercive can be used in certain circumstances to reassure.

Like other sophisticated power wielders, the Chinese use force as one note in a chord of three. As Beijing increases its coercive capacities, it simultaneously employs growing economic and ideational strength to, for example, weaken the support that Washington may seek to mobilize to respond to possible PRC coercion against Taiwan. As a Chinese intelligence agency journal put it in 2004, "China hopes to improve relations with Japan so that the latter would no longer support American military policy toward Taiwan."[3] Similarly, Beijing seeks to deter Taipei with missiles, constrain and lure it with ever tighter economic integration, and attract it by appealing to a shared Chinese culture.

China's growing coercive capabilities are the first of the three power types to be examined, not because this is the dominant face of Beijing's power currently, but rather because this is the aspect upon which so many outside observers focus. We also start with coercive power because to a considerable extent the use of different faces of power has evolved from coercion under Mao Zedong, to economic power under Deng Xiaoping, to ideational power in the post-Deng era. The PRC's overall strategy emphasizes economic and intellectual power. Thus if other nations concentrate their responses to the PRC in the coercive realm they will miss the central challenges posed and weaken their own national capacities to compete on Beijing's chosen fields—economics and ideas.

Within the category of coercive power, I first examine military components, then discuss economic instruments of coercion and isolation.

MILITARY MODERNIZATION: THREATS AND RESPONSES

At the outset of the post-Mao era of reform in the late 1970s and throughout the 1980s, military modernization was the fourth priority of the "four modernizations" (industry, agriculture, science and technology, and the military). The resources devoted to military modernization rose in the 1990s as China's economy gained strength, as communist regimes in Eastern Europe and the Soviet Union collapsed, and as mutual strategic suspicion between Beijing and Washington increased following the June 4, 1989, violence in the PRC. The PLA increasingly chafed at its modest allocation of resources as it witnessed the revolution in military affairs that was first dramatically displayed in 1991 by the United States in the First Gulf War. In 1994 China's most senior uniformed military officer, Liu Huaqing, put it this way to a group led by former Defense Secretary Robert McNamara: "When China modernizes we will have more resources. . . . But if we don't have economic growth now we will not modernize [the military] later."[4] As Liu anticipated, more resources have become available to the PLA since then, and military modernization is picking up steam, with China's 2004 *White Paper on National Defense* stating, "The role played by military power in safeguarding national security is assuming greater prominence."[5] Some historical context is useful for understanding the current state of military power in the PRC.

In July 1975, when Deng Xiaoping surveyed the PRC military, he summarized the problems of the PLA in five words: "bloating, laxity, conceit, extravagance and inertia."[6] The PLA did not perform well against the Vietnamese in 1979. Thereafter, first Deng and then his successors Jiang Zemin and Hu Jintao continually sought to shrink the total number of PLA personnel; reestablish and then upgrade the military education system; build a noncommissioned officer corps; gradually create a more secure nuclear deterrent; reduce the dominance of ground units in the force structure and decision-making system; elevate the positions and capabilities of the strategic and missile forces (second artillery), navy, and air force; revolutionize the technological level of all services and functions such as logistics, intelligence, command, control, and communications; and increase mobility and joint operational capabilities.

From the late 1970s until 1989, military budgets generally represented a declining share of both total government expenditure and GDP; during a few of those years officially announced military budgets actually declined in current Chinese dollars. Lack of funds encouraged PLA units to go into an assortment of sideline businesses that, in turn, fostered corruption, weakened the chain of command, created foreign policy problems (e.g., proliferation), and diminished professionalism.[7] These are some of the reasons that from mid-1998 onward an earnest effort has been made to get the military out of many ancillary businesses. As these sources of revenue have shrunk, compensating monies have been appropriated within the budget, thereby driving up apparent expenditures more than "real total" expenditures, though by an unknown margin. Officially announced military budgets from 1990 to 2005 largely rose by double digits,[8] reflecting not only the "budgetization" of military expenditure but also China's economic growth and the perceived need to increase military spending in the wake of the Tiananmen violence of 1989, in which the PLA had played a decisive role. Moreover, the 1991 display of U.S. military superiority in the Gulf War, the 1996 dispatch of two U.S. carrier groups to the waters off Taiwan, a move that Beijing found it difficult to respond to, and the 1999 Kosovo War also created a rationale for increased military spending. Finally, a major contributor to rising military spending has been the need to keep military pay somewhat competitive with compensation in the civilian sector.

The discussion of China's improving military capabilities must be understood against the backdrop of more than a quarter-century of significant, wrenching, and incomplete transformation. As elaborated below, and as the work of David Shambaugh and many others describes in great detail, significant progress has been made in reducing the size of costly ground forces, increasing air and naval capabilities, developing reconnaissance and communications infrastructures, augmenting service educational and training levels, and developing doctrine more appropriate to the most probable military contingencies, particularly increasing the capacity to bring coercive power to bear in the Taiwan Strait.

Despite the progress, however, there is considerable distance yet to be covered, and as China moves forward so do the armed forces of others, notably the United States. Areas of weakness include security of strategic retaliatory forces, ability of the different branches of the military to act as one integrated force, sensing and communications systems, and conventional power projection and force sustainability at great distances. Beijing's 2006 defense white paper acknowledged the protracted nature of the military modernization task by saying that the goal was "building informationized armed forces and being capable of winning informationized wars by the mid-21st century."[9]

THREATS

Beijing has four main security concerns. To start with, Beijing fears (and currently assumes) that the United States would intervene to protect Taiwan if the PRC used force against the island. A declaration of de jure independence by Taipei would compel Beijing to respond coercively, but U.S. intervention would be militarily, economically, and diplomatically catastrophic for everyone, not least the PRC. However, a lack of response by the PRC would undermine the regime's legitimacy with its own people. Given this dilemma, Beijing's chosen course has been to increase its military strength in hopes of deterring a Taiwan declaration and, failing that, deterring a U.S intervention. U.S. intervention could conceivably produce an escalatory sequence culminating in a nuclear exchange.[10] This nexus of Taiwan-related concerns is Beijing's most pressing external security worry.

A second anxiety is that the PRC's strategic nuclear deterrent is at least theoretically vulnerable to the combination of a first strike (possibly conventional), the U.S. development of national missile defense, and the transfer of antiballistic missile (ABM) capabilities to China's neighbors (most notably Taiwan and Japan).[11] What has Beijing concerned is the combination of still very numerous U.S. strategic warheads, very accurate U.S. conventional weapons that could theoretically strike nuclear facilities first, the desire of George W. Bush's administration to develop more usable (smaller) nuclear weapons and its somewhat greater emphasis on pre-emption in addressing threats, and an ABM system that could theoretically neutralize what was left of China's small retaliatory force.

Third, the presence of a large and growing percentage of China's GDP in coastal areas vulnerable to air and sea threats is a concern Beijing is addressing.[12] From 1978 to 1980, 32.7 percent of China's total GDP was located in coastal areas; by 1995–97, that percentage had risen to 41.7. Doctrinally, therefore, Beijing wants to push the space for potential conflict offshore. This requires enhanced naval and air capabilities, as well as the means to command, control, and coordinate fast-moving and far-flung forces.

Finally, the nation's increasing dependence on imported strategic resources, notably oil, that are concentrated in volatile areas, especially the Middle East, is an increasing concern in Beijing. China was a net oil exporter through 1992, but the U.S. Department of Energy estimates that by 2025 the PRC will be 73 percent dependent on oil imports, and the U.S. Department of Defense estimates that this figure could reach 80 percent. China's own figures indicate that 48 percent of China's oil imports came from the Middle East in 2001, and this figure is estimated to jump to 80 percent by 2010.[13] John Calabrese reports that in 2005, 58 percent of China's oil imports came from the Middle East.[14] Chinese leaders are obsessed with the risk that sea-borne fuel imports, carried overwhelmingly on the flagships of other nations, could be interrupted in a number of ways, including by the U.S. Navy.

Beijing is desperately seeking to diversify both sources and means of conveyance of energy and other resources and to acquire energy reserves (equity oil) around the world, sometimes paying above world market prices.

DIMENSIONS OF MILITARY MODERNIZATION

To counter these vulnerabilities and assuage these concerns, the PRC has been strengthening military capabilities, most notably in the air, on the sea, and in space, as well as giving increased attention to cyberspace. To increase capabilities along each dimension, the PLA emphasizes "informationization,"[15] or the capacity to bring real-time command, guidance, sensing, and intelligence information to forces when and where it is needed and to degrade the adversary's corresponding capabilities. This reorientation began in 1985 and has been reflected in larger budgets, procurements of foreign weapons systems, force restructuring, promotions/ organizational changes, and doctrine. The most dangerous aspect of U.S.-China relations is the extent to which each military has taken the other as its hypothetical opponent for many planning and exercise purposes.[16]

A principal objective of Chinese military modernization is to create more balance among the branches of the military. "Once the unchallenged heart and soul of the People's Liberation Army (PLA), Chinese ground forces remain the dominant service in the military in terms of manpower, resources, doctrine and prestige. The other services, however, are clearly in the ascendance, while the ground forces have been in a long, slow decline."[17] Modernization is taking place along the dimensions of budgeting, procurement, force restructuring and education, organizational change, doctrine, joint operations, and command and control.

> *Budgeting.* The official (publicly released) defense budget as a whole has increased (in the double-digit range) every year from 1990 through 2007.[18] There is debate over the actual size of the PLA budget because items that reasonably could be counted in the "defense" category are not included, such as procurement of foreign-manufactured weapons, research and development, and subsidies from local governments. Consequently, many non-Chinese analysts would agree that the PRC's defense budget is about twice as large as the published number, putting China at a level of military expenditure roughly comparable to that of Russia, Japan, or the United Kingdom. Beijing may well be moving previously off-budget items into the reported budget, so that "in three to four years [2006–7] the official budget should reflect reality rather better."[19] Also noteworthy is that many

defense-related expenditures in the U.S. budget are not in the Defense Department's appropriation (e.g., military retirement, nuclear weapons in the Department of Energy).[20] Between 2002 and 2006, China's military budget grew at about the same rate as the budget as a whole but not as rapidly as some components of the total budget, such as those for rural support, health, education, and welfare. Given the decision of the Party Central Committee in October 2006 "putting people first," the tension between military and domestic spending promises to become a bigger issue.[21]

Procurement. The lion's share of the PLA's procurement expenditures for foreign weapons and weapons-related technology has gone for air, naval, and strategic deterrence systems. According to Beijing's *White Paper on National Defense, 2004,* "The PLA will promote coordinated development of firepower, mobility and information capability, enhance the development of its operational strength with priority given to the Navy, Air Force and Second Artillery Force, and strengthen its comprehensive deterrence and war fighting capabilities."[22] As one senior Chinese military officer explained to me, "In terms of procurement monies, modernization of the air force and the navy is taking more money and moving ahead more rapidly because these services require the purchase of major, new, and very expensive systems. So they, along with the second artillery [missiles], take more procurement resources. However, the land army is so large and personnel costs are such a big item that the amount of money going into the land army from the overall budget is still very large."[23]

Force Restructuring and Education. The entire Chinese military has shrunk from about 4 million people in 1978 to 2.35 million in 2002, though some of these personnel have been moved into the People's Armed Police (which has domestic missions and as of 2006 a total force of 660,000). The PLA aimed to reach a total force size of 2.3 million by the end of 2005, a goal that was achieved. The idea has been to dramatically reduce the number of land troops, increase the capabilities of remaining land forces, and utilize the saved resources for overall modernization of the air force, the navy, and strategic forces. After personnel reductions, the ground forces constituted 73 percent of total forces, the navy 10 percent, and the air force 17 percent.[24] As the PLA has shifted its balance toward more high-tech services while shrinking and upgrading its ground forces, military education and the development of a noncommissioned officer corps have become central aspects of the overall modernization program. High-quality human resources are the key to a modern military.

Organizational Change. In 2004 the Central Military Commission (CMC) expanded its number of members from four to seven by adding the commanders of the navy, the air force, and the second artillery.[25] This signaled an increased role for these services in decision making long dominated by the land army and was an attempt to increase joint operations capabilities.[26] Organizational changes, however, have gone far beyond this since the 1980s to include slimming down the military's national command authority, the CMC; reducing the number of officers and boosting the noncommissioned officer ranks; creating a General Armaments Department (in April 1998) to try to improve the defense industry structure and improve weapons research; reducing the number of military regions from eleven to seven (in 1985) to increase efficiency and coordination; reforming the logistical and service support systems by using more outsourcing and closer integration with the civilian economy; developing and improving expeditionary and special operations units and capabilities; expanding the People's Armed Police (responsible for border control, internal security, some key construction projects, and gold prospecting); and greatly enlarging and improving the military education system, particularly since the late 1990s but beginning in the 1980s.

Doctrine. Whereas traditionally China has emphasized in-depth territorial defense by land forces, it now embraces the concepts of "active defense" and "fighting local wars under modern, high-tech conditions" offshore in short-duration conflicts. *Informationization* has become the buzzword for the process necessary to accomplish this. The Chinese Navy is placing particular emphasis on submarines and is moving ahead briskly in this direction. Most fundamentally, as the United States has moved forward with its "transformation" agenda, Chinese doctrine has also been evolving, placing emphasis on conventional force modernization, information and cyberwar operations, missile-centered strikes, and seizing of the initiative.[27]

Joint Operations. Since the late 1980s, the PRC has been making progress in joint operations capability at the campaign level, though less progress has been achieved with respect to interservice cooperation or tactical-level joint operations.[28] A fundamental problem is that a "[land] army-dominated General Staff perpetuates combined arms operations, at best augmented by parallel air, navy, and missile forces operations, rather than facilitating joint integration."[29] Progress is being made in developing a joint logistics system and rapid reaction forces. Further, Shambaugh reports that since 1993 there has been an "increase in joint and combined-arms exercises."[30] As the PRC improves its capacity to have its various service branches act on the battle-field as one force, its mobility, flexibility, and ability to effectively strike at greater distances will increase.

Command and Control. Progress is being made in the integration of intelligence, surveillance, and reconnaissance capabilities, but in 2004 the U.S. Department of Defense judged that China's capability in this respect would "not be achieved for many years."[31] One reason is an organizational problem—reporting upward through vertical stovepipes rather than having effective and timely horizontal communication across branches and units at more decentralized levels.

As a result of all these developments, discussed more fully below, the PLA of the early twenty-first century is far different from the force Deng Xiaoping criticized in 1975. A foundation has been created that, when considered against the backdrop of anticipated sustained economic (and budgetary) growth, should contribute to even more rapid progress in the future. Nonetheless, China has a long way to go to achieve the capabilities it now envisions. By the time Beijing achieves its current objectives, it is hard to say where the new frontier of U.S. and Western technology and organization will be.

THE USES OF MILITARY POWER

Military power has four broad uses—homeland defense, deterrence, power projection, and reassurance. These categories conceptually overlap to some extent. Nuclear deterrence relates to power projection, homeland defense, and in some cases reassurance. When one country places another under its nuclear umbrella, the move can be one of reassurance as well as deterrence, as in the case of the United States and Japan in the post–World War II era, most recently in the wake of the October 2006 detonation of a nuclear device by North Korea. Placing Japan under the U.S. nuclear umbrella was part deterrence (of the Soviet Union before 1991) and part reassurance for both Tokyo (which was protected) and Beijing (which was reassured that the incentives for Japan to go nuclear had been reduced).

Chinese leaders and analysts are confident that their homeland is secure from occupation or any system-threatening conventional ground attack. Further, although terrorism poses a danger to China, the Chinese tend to be much less concerned about this threat than Americans, and less concerned about proliferation and the dangers it presents: 69 percent of Americans surveyed in 2006 saw the possibility of unfriendly countries becoming nuclear powers as a "critical" threat, while only 28 percent of Chinese did.[32] Nonetheless, Chinese businessmen and diplomats have been killed (and in Iraq taken hostage) in diverse places throughout Central and South Asia (particularly Pakistan), the Middle East, and beyond. In 2003 the then deputy chief of staff of the PLA, General Xiong Guangkai, announced that "the so-called East Turkestan terrorists have launched over 260 terrorist attacks in China since 1990, claiming 170 lives and leaving 440 wounded."[33] During the first nine months of 2004, seventy Chinese were attacked or killed overseas, with incidents (not all terrorist) occurring in Kyrgyzstan, Pakistan, and Afghanistan. This rising danger led the PRC Foreign Ministry to establish a new department for "external security affairs."[34] In April 2007, nine Chinese workers were killed by Ethiopian rebels.[35]

Nonetheless, the threats that most concern Beijing are internal—system legitimacy, social stability amid profound domestic transformation, and "separatist tendencies" in China's western areas such as Xinjiang and Tibet (see chapter 6). From Beijing's perspective, the 2001 formation of the Shanghai Cooperation Organization, or SCO (now consisting of four Central Asian states plus Russia and China), was designed to stabilize China's western border by ensuring that external ethnic and religious groups residing in neighboring states would not link up with "domestic separatists."[36] Over time the SCO's purposes have broadened, particularly in the economic realm: an underlying objective now is to offset growing U.S. power in the region, which Beijing sees as "a new potential military threat."[37] The SCO has broadened not only functionally but also in terms of participating countries, with Uzbekistan joining the antecedent organization's original five full members in 2001, followed by Mongolia (2004), Iran, India, and Pakistan (2005) as "observers." Membership of all four observer countries was under discussion as of 2006. Any thought of possible Iranian membership is particularly distressing to Washington; Tehran is widely viewed as having embarked on a nuclear weapons development effort and as being a principal state supporter of terrorism. The SCO also is enhancing its military coordination, as demonstrated by joint SCO exercises.[38]

The Chinese leadership believes that an external land attack of a system-threatening scale is not on the horizon, a view reflected in the strategic assessment of the November 2002 Sixteenth Party Congress that the PRC had an approximately two-decade-long window of opportunity to focus on internal development. This perspective has been operative since the mid-1980s and is seen in Beijing's continuing reduction of the size of its land army and the measured pace at which it is upgrading army equipment. The most obvious reason for this strategic assessment has been productive relations with the United States and the former Soviet Union. Even with the fragmentation and demise of the Soviet Union and the more ambivalent strategic posture of the United States since 1989, conflict with any other major power remains highly unlikely (outside the Taiwan Strait) for the foreseeable future. China is improving its diplomatic relations with almost every country on its periphery, with ties to Japan being the most precarious (see chapter 5).

This assessment is reinforced by an underlying confidence about China's defensive capabilities stemming from the country's geographic size, population mass, and ethnic homogeneity—all of which are sizable deterrents to any conventional attack (beyond border encroachments). As one PRC international relations expert put it, "We are focused on land, hence we calculate power that way and think that [for others] to attack us they need a lot more [power]. So we are strong enough to defend ourselves."[39] Mao's guerrilla warfare strategy relied on luring invaders deep, exhausting them, and counting on attrition to erode the invader's domestic support. Technology took a back seat to mass and scale in homeland defense, and it still does in the non-nuclear domain. As one Chinese general put it to me, "No leader of any country will be so stupid as to launch a big invasion, so the likely scenario is border conflict or a long-distance strike, and in that case how can people's war come into play?"[40]

Another factor facilitating homeland defense is the massive construction of communications and transport infrastructure, which is knitting China together as never before. New economic and communication lines act as "reinforcing bars" for territorial cohesion. The world has not seen a national road-building effort such as China's since President Dwight Eisenhower backed the creation of the National System of Interstate and Defense Highways in the 1950s—an effort that had both economic and military rationales. In late 2004, China's Ministry of Communications reported that the PRC had become second in the world in total expressway mileage and third in total road mileage. In 2001 Beijing adopted a National Expressway Network Plan guiding road construction for the following thirty years. The plan calls for a network consisting of five vertical and seven national trunk lines and eight additional highways in the west.[41] Even before this initiative, from 1990 to 2003, China spent US$241.5 billion on road construction,[42] and it plans to spend a very large amount over the three decades starting from 2006.

Further, through a series of negotiations and border adjustments since 1978, the PRC has stabilized relations with neighboring states considerably, using diplomacy to fortify homeland defense.[43] China and Russia signed border agreements in 1991, 1994, and 2004, when the last, small contested portions of the 4,300-kilometer-long Sino-Russian border were basically delimited (see chapter 5). Vietnam and China signed a land border treaty in December 1999, and China and Nepal signed an agreement stabilizing trade with Tibet in 2000. In the 1990s, various agreements were signed with Laos, Mongolia, and Bhutan. With respect to the Central Asian states in the wake of the Soviet implosion of 1991, China "kept only 20 percent of the land disputed with Kazakhstan, 30 percent of the land it disputed with Kyrgyzstan, and with Tajikistan conceded the majority of its claim to the Pamir Mountains."[44] The 4,677-kilometer-long border with Mongolia was "finalized" in late 2005, with Beijing conceding substantial portions of its claims.[45] Discussions between New Delhi and Beijing about their troubled border (over which a brief armed conflict had been waged in 1962) started in July 1989 with meetings of the China-India Joint Working Group. The Working Group's activities were further accelerated as a result of the September 1993 Sino-Indian Agreement on the Maintenance of Peace and Tranquillity. Though the discussions have progressed slowly and were interrupted by India's and Pakistan's 1998 nuclear tests, they have continued, in part representing Beijing's desire to offset improved U.S.-India relations. Indeed, in July 2004, cross-border trade (halted in 1962) resumed between China and the state of Sikkim, and in October 2004 on a visit to India, State Councilor Tang Jiaxuan said that Beijing supported "a bigger role for India in the international community, including in the United Nations Security Council."[46]

Taken together, improved security along China's land periphery, along with other factors such as infrastructure development and the coastal concentration of economic assets, has turned Beijing's defense focus toward the seas, skies, heavens, and cyberspace. A senior Chinese military officer summed up the overall situation as follows: "The gap between the air force, the navy, the second artillery, and the U.S. or Western forces is much bigger than the gap of the land army in terms of defensive ability. Basically, in terms of land defense we have improved relations with neighbors and we have very big forces. But in the air [force] and navy we are much less strong. So in terms of modernization, yes, we are changing more in the navy and air force, but the gap is bigger there."[47]

Deterrence is the use of threat to dissuade an opponent from initiating an attack or taking some other unwanted step. Coercive diplomacy, in contrast, uses threat "to persuade an opponent to do something, or to stop doing something."[48] In general, it is easier to succeed at deterrence than coercive diplomacy because dissuading others from a contemplated action is easier than forcing them to reverse course or to make a move that they resist.

A deterrent threat can be nuclear or conventional and can use any power type (coercive, remunerative, or ideational) singly or in combination. Whatever the face of power employed, the threat must be credible to be successful. Credibility can be achieved only when the adversary believes that the promised damage will be unacceptable and that the deterring party has the will and ability to deliver. The instrument of threat must be able to survive a disarming first strike. In their respective work on Chinese deterrence doctrine, Shen Dingli, Sun Xiangli, and Evan Medeiros make clear that Beijing views deterrence, and what is necessary to achieve it, largely in these terms.[49] Major General Peng Guangqian and his colleagues at the Academy of Military Science put it in more traditional Chinese terms:

> Without a real deterrent force as the mainstay, strategic deterrence is unlikely to attain the expected effect. . . . In a description of classical literature *The Romance of the Three Kingdoms*, the essential reason why Zhuge Liang can fool Sima Yi by the "Stratagem of the Empty City" [a ruse by which a lightly defended city opens its gates in the face of attack, presenting a face of absolute confidence, suggesting to the attacking commander that within the city is a huge defending force, with the result that the attacker unilaterally retreats] lies in the fact that there is really a powerful army under Zhuge's command. If Zhuge's total military strength were utterly incomparable with the rival, however suspicious Sima Yi might be he could not certainly be confused by the fabricated false appearance.[50]

The seemingly precise definition of deterrence masks great uncertainties: How does one assess the deterring party's will? What are the deterrent target's capacities to initiate a disarming first strike? Can the acquisition of a deterrent itself become provocative and precipitate conflict? What is "unacceptable" damage to various actors? And once escalation begins, how can it be controlled? In addition, we need to know more about how Chinese leaders might think about the conduct and escalation of a nuclear conflict once it had begun, or how China might respond to a conventional attack on its nuclear deterrent.

Beijing has been most interested in preventing two sets of contingencies. The first set concerns Taiwan. Keeping Taiwan from becoming independent is not only a question of nationalism and sovereignty (and therefore of regime security as described above) but also a security issue narrowly understood—Beijing wishes to deny other powers the use of the nearby island group to threaten the mainland and strategic sea lanes of communication. Beijing also wishes to deter Taipei from acquiring nuclear weapons (efforts twice stopped by Washington), but it is unclear whether mainland threats reduce or enhance that prospect.

The PRC's predominantly conventional "deterrent" forces against Taiwan date to the mid-1990s with then Taiwan President Lee Teng-hui's push for more international breathing space, the 1995–96 missile "crisis" in the Strait, and Beijing's subsequent buildup of ballistic missiles in the vicinity of the island. For Beijing, Taipei's actions since the mid-1990s have been practically a linear move away from the "one China principle." By 2004, Taipei was pushing to have Washington join it in openly rejecting the "one China policy." Beijing's missiles and other forces, therefore, have been aimed at deterring the island from declaring de jure independence and Washington from supporting or defending such a move if it occurs. Of course, PRC missiles could become the leading edge of a strategy to coerce Taiwan into submission (reunification). With their terminally guided maneuverable warheads, they represent a potential threat to U.S. forces stationed in Japan or elsewhere in the region, notably U.S. aircraft carriers, as John Negroponte, then U.S. Director of National Intelligence, told the Senate in early 2007.[51] While Beijing may view its forces as a deterrent, others may see them as provocative and offensive.

As to what Beijing considers enough conventional power to aim in Taiwan's direction to deter "secession," no one outside China knows. According to the U.S. Defense Department's report to Congress in 2005, the PRC was annually adding between 75 and 120 short-range ballistic missiles (300–600 kilometers in range) to its existing inventory.[52] The Pentagon believed that these missiles numbered between 710 and 790 in 2006.[53] This is in addition to its overall military modernization and gradual acquisition of an amphibious assault capability. It also is worth noting that while "China's nuclear weapons serve only two goals: nuclear deterrence and nuclear counter-strike/retaliation," China's conventional missile force aimed at Taiwan is central to a war-fighting strategy in which there is a role for a preemptive missile strike.[54]

With its strategic deterrent, the PRC hopes to dissuade the United States (or other countries) from employing or threatening to use nuclear weapons (or other WMDs) against China's population or small nuclear force or attacking its strategic forces with conventional (or other exotic) weapons. China's nuclear deterrent dates back to Beijing's detonation of a device on October 16, 1964, a development that was the culmination of an enormous decade-long effort to protect itself from Washington's implicit and explicit nuclear threats during the 1950s and 1960s and to subsequently protect itself from the Soviet Union. As Mao put it in 1956, "If we are not to be bullied in the present-day world, we cannot do without the bomb."[55] By about the mid-1980s, China had a nuclear stockpile bigger (by some reckonings) than the combined forces of the French and British.[56] As of 2003 the PRC had about 250 strategic nuclear weapons and 120 nonstrategic nuclear weapons according to the generally accepted view, though there remains a range of estimates.[57] Norris and Kristensen have asserted that in 2006 the number was about 200.[58]

Chinese deterrence theorists, like their counterparts in the United States, have sought to maintain their nation's assured capacity to retaliate after withstanding a first strike (nuclear or conventional) on its nuclear force.[59] From the PRC's earliest days, its leaders, most notably Mao Zedong, believed they did not need a massive nuclear arsenal to deter the United States from attacking either conventionally or with nuclear weapons. Lewis and Xue report that "in defining the nuclear weapons program, Mao had limited its scale—China's nuclear weapons 'won't be numerous even if we succeed'—and he argued that the program's success would 'boost our courage and scare others.'"[60] Since then Beijing's belief in not needing a massive arsenal has been strengthened by subsequent developments. These developments include Presidents Kennedy's and Johnson's decisions not to risk attempts to preemptively destroy China's nuclear development program and small arsenal thereafter,[61] the Vietnam War (during which Washington eschewed bombing near the Chinese border and invasion of North Vietnam for fear of sliding into war with Beijing), and the evidence provided in Vietnam, Somalia, and Iraq that the U.S. tolerance for casualties is low. The U.S. willingness to attack a non-nuclear Iraq in March 2003 but not to attack a possibly nuclear North Korea further confirms Beijing in this belief.

Nonetheless, there is uncertainty in Washington about what Beijing considers to be adequate retaliatory and assured destruction capability beyond having the capacity to launch nuclear "key point counter strikes"—key points being places whose destruction would either dramatically affect the opponent's war-making ability or deliver "a strong psychological blow."[62] One U.S. estimate is that the PRC seeks (or seeks to maintain) the capability to hold one or two American cities hostage after absorbing a first strike and would want the assurance of having about twenty warheads capable of penetrating U.S. defenses.[63] The Office of the Secretary of Defense's Mark Stokes said in 2002 that "China's nuclear forces generally are believed to follow a countervalue strategy that targets population centers [in part reflecting the inability of the Chinese ICBM force to hit smaller, military targets, though this deficiency is being corrected]. China has sufficient nuclear weapons to hold approximately 15–20 million U.S. citizens at risk, or about 5–10 percent of the total U.S. population."[64] This contrasts with the Cold War "overkill" capabilities of the United States and former Soviet Union, which could have annihilated multiples of the adversary's entire population.

Two developments have caused Beijing to be concerned about the security of the substantial portion of its nuclear deterrent that still resides in fixed sites (though this will change with a nuclear-armed, submarine-launched, multiple-warhead missile force and land-mobile missiles): (1) increasingly accurate and still numerous U.S. nuclear and conventional warheads and (2) the American development and gradual deployment of a layered antiballistic missile system.[65] Taken together, these developments create the *theoretical* possibility that Washington could launch a preemptive nuclear or conventional strike on China's slow-to-launch missiles in silos. After this hypothetical first strike, whatever PRC retaliatory capability remained could hypothetically be neutralized by missile defenses under U.S. control.[66] In the world of actual warfare and faulty intelligence, military planners would have to be reckless to assume that China would have no residual force capable of reaching the United States. Beijing, however, cannot fully discount this possibility and therefore hedges by moderately enlarging and modernizing its nuclear forces.

A U.S. missile defense that was perceived to "work" would to some extent weaken the PRC's deterrent and thereby stimulate some degree of expansion of Chinese strategic forces beyond what they otherwise would be. As of 2006, the U.S. National Missile Defense (NMD) plan envisioned "a layered" system capable of destroying missiles in their boost, midcourse, and terminal phases. The distinction between theater missile systems provided to Taiwan and Japan, those based on U.S. platforms and bases outside U.S. territory, and NMD systems located on American soil is becoming increasingly blurred.[67] All this calls into question Beijing's capacity to inflict unacceptable damage on the United States (and possibly Taiwan) in the event the PRC is attacked or Taiwan declares de jure independence. With the George W. Bush administration's elevation of "preemption," or more accurately preventive war, as a doctrinal concept in the wake of 9/11, Chinese confidence in

American intentions has eroded. Further shaking Beijing's confidence in U.S. intentions has been the Bush administration's publicly announced, and congressionally resisted, desire to develop "smaller," more usable nuclear weapons. It could have been only partially reassuring for Beijing to read a 2006 report from the Office of the U.S. Secretary of Defense saying that the PRC's planned upgrades to its land-based strategic forces "will make China's ICBM force more survivable."[68] All these developments have given rise to debate of unknown depth in China as to the desirability of continuing its "no first use" policy.[69]

These worries were articulated in the following closely paraphrased comment by a PLA general grade officer with whom I spoke in 2005:

> If I list the order of emphasis of modernization [among services], the second artillery [missiles], our strategic deterrent force, should come first—both nuclear and conventional weapons, the latter to deter splittism. Modernization is needed to increase the safety and security of the nuclear arsenal. No one wants problems. [We want] to increase the survivability of some of our arsenal from a first strike and increase the ability of our penetration. The United States is deploying its ballistic missile defense; this is a challenge to the second artillery, since it can intercept [our missiles] in the boost phase. Another purpose [of modernization] is to increase [the number] of nukes—they are political, we don't need many. [But] we need to keep the deterrent credible to some extent.[70]

Efforts to keep the PRC nuclear and conventional missile arsenal credible include making its retaliatory force more mobile to avoid targeting; developing missile systems capable of being launched rapidly (e.g., solid rather than liquid fuel); diversifying delivery platforms to include a new generation of submarine ballistic missiles that may be coming on line faster than outsiders expected; developing decoys and multiple warhead systems to confuse and overwhelm defenses; improving the accuracy and guidance of each warhead; developing systems that can put at risk U.S. space-borne guidance and sensing systems; and multiplying the number of conventional missiles aimed at Taiwan. With respect to its naval deterrent, for instance, in 2004 the PLA said that "the capability of nuclear counterattacks is also enhanced."[71] In 2004 the U.S. Department of Defense described China's broader missile program, reporting that "a ballistic missile modernization program is under way to upgrade all classes of missiles, both qualitatively and quantitatively. Beijing intends to improve its nuclear deterrence by increasing the number of warheads that can target the United States and augmenting the nuclear force's operational contingencies in East Asia. . . . China currently has about 20 ICBMs capable of targeting the United States. This number could increase to about 30 by 2005 and may reach up to 60 by 2010."[72] To put this in perspective, in April 2006 the U.S. Department of State announced that the United States had deployed 5,966 strategic warheads on ICBMs, submarine-launched ballistic missiles (SLBMs), and heavy bombers.

In summary, China has a relatively small but growing and gradually more capable nuclear inventory. There is, however, no apparent intention to quickly build up to anything approximating Cold War scale. The organizing principle of China's nuclear force modernization is that of guaranteeing a sufficient deterrent. A key uncertainty for outsiders is the Chinese definition of *sufficient;* to a large extent, it will depend on U.S. actions.

Worrisome to China's neighbors is the possibility that as its nuclear and conventional missile forces modernize, Beijing may find new uses for them beyond deterrence—for example, fighting wars. Chinese leaders may search for categories of nuclear forces that avoid the Hobson's choice of a single, massive, suicidal launch against the United States and doing nothing—as the United States did in the 1960s when it developed the concept of "flexible response."

POWER PROJECTION

Power projection is the capacity to deliver coercive power in an effective manner beyond one's borders. The farther from one's borders, and the greater the coercive power that can be delivered, the greater one's ability to project coercive power. Although in July 2002 components of the PLA Navy made their first around-the-world voyage, and although the following year China launched and recovered its first manned space mission—the third nation to do so—the PRC "continues to lack the capability to project significant power beyond its borders."[73] Beyond the projection capacity represented by Beijing's strategic nuclear deterrent, the capacity to strike another society most conspicuously exists across the Taiwan Strait, where, as of 2006, Beijing had deployed between 710 and 790 increasingly accurate short-range missiles.

The rather modest pace of the PRC's ground-force modernization has been consistent with both the underlying confidence of Chinese in their homeland defense and the need to conserve resources. In contrast, the PLA's conventional missile, naval, and air forces have a mission of "active offshore defense." This requires "more modern warships and submarines capable of operating at greater distances from China's coast for longer periods."[74] In turn, a larger navy operating ever farther from China's shores with greater troop-lift capacity requires air power that can protect those vessels and aircraft flight management systems to control battle space. This requires aircraft with longer ranges and greater capacity to loiter over distant locations and eventually platforms such as aircraft carriers. Consequently, Beijing has active construction programs to create these systems, and "its force projection capabilities play a central role in procurement decision-making."[75] By the U.S. Defense Department's reckoning, Beijing's capabilities are far behind those of U.S and allied forces in the region, and the PRC still lacks a capability to move large numbers of troops simultaneously and securely in amphibious and/or airborne operations.[76] Nonetheless, China is increasing its capabilities to inflict damage on U.S. forces that might seek to engage in conflict near the mainland's shores, more particularly in the Taiwan theater.

Five factors almost guarantee enhanced future projection capacities, though the rate of progress is uncertain. First, projection has a central role in China's evolving military doctrine. Each of the services is acquiring capacities that, over a decade or two, will significantly enhance their abilities. These doctrinal changes reflect the fact that China is seeking to move the site of future conflict out of its own territory. For instance, current military training assumes cross-water and long-distance troop movements. Moreover, China increasingly has both civilian and military personnel under the UN umbrella all over the world and wants the capacity to extract them in emergencies with its own resources, something it has been unable to do in crises in the Solomon Islands, Tonga, and southern Lebanon. Second, China's space program is moving ahead, a program with both civilian and military rationales. Third, deterring Taiwan from declaring de jure independence, Beijing believes, requires the capacity to quickly inflict unacceptable damage on the island and raise the costs of intervention for America, if not deterring it altogether. Fourth, the PRC's growing economy and improved human resources mean that Beijing will increasingly possess the material, technological, and human wherewithal to enhance power projection. China's defense industries are improving.[77] Fifth, China increasingly depends on strategic resources imported over extended supply lines. Beijing feels obliged to secure these supply routes, a task that has become part of the Chinese Navy's evolving mission. In interviews Chinese military officers repeatedly refer to protecting "China's maritime interests." All this requires effective power projection. A conversation with a senior Chinese military officer, paraphrased below, signals this direction.

DML: It seems to me that people [I met recently in China] were
                  obsessed with protecting energy supply lines and securing
                  access to resources. Is this increased dependence going to lead
                  China to modernize and extend its military power projection
                  to protect those strategic resources?

CHINESE OFFICER: The major reason we are increasing power projection is to
                  keep Taiwan from going independent, not to guard resources.
                  That is secondary.

DML: But as you get more dependent on resources from abroad, just
                  like the United States, won't you want to secure those lines [of
                  supply], and doesn't this mean power projection?

CHINESE OFFICER: Yes, development and interdependence are processes
                  [guocheng], and "processes have their logic."[78]

One important aspect of China's emerging power-projection capacity is its underappreciated space program. This program is relevant in terms of China's projection of military power as well as its projection of ideational power, a subject addressed in chapter 4. Moreover, the space program has contributed to China's economic development inasmuch as its rocket lift capacity has generated revenue from other countries desiring to place objects in space, among which have been U.S. payloads. In the longer run, the space program should strengthen, reflecting China's growing research and development capacities (see chapter 4). All these efforts will have other economic spin-offs, and a central purpose of the space program is to drive societal and economy-wide innovation in both the state and nonstate sectors; in turn, societal innovation will energize the space program. As the white paper *China's Space Activities in 2006* put it, "Increasing the capability for independent innovation is a strategic basis for developing the space industry."[79]

In 2003, China became the poorest (in per capita terms) nation to put a man in space (with the Taikonaut Yang Liwei eating fried rice and freeze-dried pork shreds with garlic sauce). This feat is part of a space program that by 2010 aims to establish an earth observation system, an independently operated global broadcasting and telecommunications system, and an independent satellite navigation and positioning system. Longer-term goals include "carrying out pre-study for outer space exploration centering on the exploration of the moon."[80] Having put a man in space in 2003 and two more men in October 2005 (who then conducted scientific experiments there), China plans a lunar orbiting in Chang-e-1 by the end of 2007,[81] a space walk in 2007, docking and rendezvous in 2009–12,[82] and an unmanned lunar

FIGURE 3
Beijing Space Control Center during China's first manned space flight, Shenzhou-5, October 15, 2003. This mission was part of China's long-term space effort, which includes missions to the moon and thereafter Mars. Xinhua/Xinhua Photo/Corbis.

landing, the construction of a lunar base, the launch of a space station, and the establishment of a Mars base at some point.[83] The program is ambitious, and we will have to see how it progresses.

The lunar orbiter was initially budgeted at $175 million (1.4 billion RMB).[84] Potential payoffs for such missions include prestige in the context of the Olympic Games and advances in meteorology, manufacturing, agriculture, computing, materials science, navigation, electronics, satellite (distance) education, and earth resources and other sensing technologies.[85]

As the ultimate high ground, space also has military importance, though it is not always possible to disentangle civilian and military purposes—for example, in the use of geographic positioning systems (GPS). Chinese military figures and the government assert their support for "the non-weaponization of space," but how Beijing will react to possible future U.S. moves remains to be seen, and space has many military uses that need not involve "weapons" per se. Chinese analysts are quite straightforward, saying that space capabilities "possess a strong deterrent value."[86] In January 2007 China destroyed one of its own aging satellites in orbit in an apparently successful test, thereby demonstrating the ability to interfere with the satellite systems of others, systems that, while not weapons per se, are central to modern war fighting and much else. This test alarmed other space powers.

The PLA plays a major, but somewhat nontransparent, role in the PRC's space activities. The Chinese space expert He Sibing announced that China's Shenzhou spacecraft program had by the end of 2003 "carried equipment for military surveillance, Shenzhou-4 had devices for intercepting radar and telecommunications signals, and Shenzhou-5 carried a camera that can resolve features on the ground as small as 1.6 metres across."[87] The white paper *China's Space Activities in 2000* stated, "Remote-sensing and telecommunications satellites account for 71% of the total number of satellites developed and launched by China. These satellites have been widely utilized in all aspects of economy, science and technology, culture, and national defense." Beijing has an active and growing program for electronic intelligence gathering.[88]

One U.S. Naval War College analyst has stated that in the "potential coming space race" "it is likely the United States and China will be the primary—though not the only—competitors."[89] This race, whatever its dimensions, will have military characteristics as well as important implications for both economic and ideational power. One indication of the scope of Chinese space activity, plans, and aspirations is that during President Hu Jintao's November 2004 trip to South America he signed a $260 million agreement with Argentina on a satellite communication system. On that same trip, President Hu signed two agreements with Brazil on space technology, building upon prior cooperation in the launch of satellites in 1999 and 2003. China also has space arrangements with Sweden, Russia, Algeria, Chile, Japan, Peru, Malaysia, France, Venezuela, Nigeria, Bangladesh, Iran, South Korea, Mongolia, Thailand, India, Pakistan, Ukraine, Canada, Britain, and Germany, launching a PRC-made satellite for Nigeria in May 2007.[90] In October 2005, China signed the Asia-Pacific Space Cooperation Organization Convention (APSCO); the organization's headquarters is in Beijing. Turkey joined in mid-2006. Finally, Beijing initially cooperated with the EU's Galileo GPS (geographic positioning system) program[91] but curtailed its participation because the EU took steps (under U.S. pressure) to limit technology transfer to China and set access conditions that do not ensure an uninterrupted signal.[92] In parallel, China's own indigenous GPS, Beidou, appears to be moving forward faster than Galileo.[93]

It is indicative of U.S. security-related concerns with China's space efforts that after visiting with NASA's Michael Griffin in early 2006, the vice administrator of China's National Space Administration Luo Ge said he found reticence about Sino-American cooperation in this area. He expressed interest in bilateral cooperation but said, "We don't have the ticket yet."[94] Misgivings in the U.S. Congress were on display in March 2006 House Hearings of the Appropriations Subcommittee on State, Justice, and Commerce, and Related Agencies. And later that year, when Griffin, on a trip to China, was asked about space cooperation with the PRC, he said, "We have to have a great degree of trust. If not, there is a real danger in the mix."[95]

Notwithstanding the great potential of China's space program, there also are important questions about the relative payoffs of investment in this area. Beijing's financial resources to invest in the program remain limited though uncertain: Western estimates of yearly space expenditures vary, with the high-end estimates being in the $2 billion per year range as compared to NASA's FY 2004 Operating Plan Budget of $15.378 billion[96] (which does not include either private or other public sector space expenditures). For its part, Beijing asserts that it has spent approximately 20 billion RMB (about US$2.46 billion at the mid-2006 exchange rate) over thirteen years on its manned space program.[97] In early 2006 Luo Ge was reported to have said China spent about $500 million annually, with the caveat that Chinese budgets are "very complicated."[98] Because the PRC's modernization needs (in both the military and civilian sectors) are enormous, space programs are in tight competition for resources. It is unclear whether the manned space program that started in 1992 is the most efficient way to produce gains in either military capabilities or economic modernization. The former commander-in-chief of Pacific forces, Admiral Dennis Blair, provided a balanced assessment of the Chinese program in December 2004: "I think that Chinese military space activities are part of a decision to leapfrog to a new technological level, to bypass the development process that the U.S. military went through since the 1957 Sputnik. The key question is whether they can do it. The United States has a pretty good insight into their [China's] program. Their record is pretty mixed."[99]

Beyond enhanced power projection (including space-based assets and counter-space capabilities) and technological spin-offs, PRC achievements in space tell the rest of the world that China is on a trajectory for greatness. The fact that by 2000 Beijing had created a global satellite TV broadcasting capacity (and by 2010 plans to be able to independently operate its own worldwide satellite broadcasting system) means that the reach of Chinese ideas is global. Similarly, while the space program may be seen as a contributor to, and expression of, military and economic power, cooperating with other societies presumably enhances China's attractiveness (ideational power). An offer to include Taiwan residents in space activities would hold out potential for influence on the island, for example.

Returning to the broader subject of power projection, sizable constraints still impede Beijing's drive. First, acquiring effective power-projection capacity is very expensive and brings military desires into conflict with urgent domestic needs. Ultimately, an important component of the regime's legitimacy resides in putting goods on the shelves and meeting basic human needs, a cornerstone of President Hu Jintao's policies. Chinese civilian leaders widely share the belief that Moscow's overspending on its military was a major reason for the collapse of the USSR, and they do not want to make the same strategic error.

Second, China's efforts to project power significantly will depend on the progress it makes in modernizing its defense industries. These industries vary widely in quality, with missiles, shipbuilding, and information technologies on the strong side and the aviation industry considerably weaker. While acknowledging the important progress that has been made since the late 1990s, the most recent and exhaustive available study of China's defense industries still concludes: "China's defense industry now has the *potential* to become more competitive with the defense industries of the world's advanced military powers in key sectors within a moderate (10–20 years) amount of time" (emphasis in original).[100] The current weaknesses of China's domestic defense industry are evidenced in the role of Russia (and to a lesser extent Israel)[101] as principal suppliers of advanced technology to the PLA. That Beijing relies to a considerable extent on Russian technology, which in many areas is considerably behind U.S. technology, reveals the weaknesses of the PRC's defense industries, recent gains aside. One Russian official referred to Moscow's extensive cooperation with China's military aviation effort as a "Russian mini-industry of aviation."[102] Indeed, in 2004–5 Beijing was doing its best to persuade the European Union to end its arms embargo against the PRC, a move that, by creating competitive pressures among all international arms sellers, would give Beijing additional leverage.

Third, China's modest, though growing, power-projection capabilities have perverse diplomatic consequences, as demonstrated in chapters 5 and 6. Overall, PRC foreign policy is designed to reassure others that China presents no threat, a line embodied in the New Security Concept first articulated by then foreign minister Qian Qichen. However, by expanding the capacity to project power on the sea and in the air the PRC inevitably becomes potentially more of a consideration in a world in which national defense forces think in worst-case terms—particularly in Asia, where distrust of neighbors runs deep. Vietnam keeps a wary eye on China; Russians still worry about their sparsely inhabited (and defended) far east; and Japan worries about the impact of Beijing's progress on its own regional role and security. China's neighbors consequently look for reassurance from more distant, bigger powers, notably the United States. Consequently, as the PLA expands its reach, Beijing's diplomacy has become more reassuring.

During his participation in the November 2004 ASEAN + 3 summit in Vientiane, Laos, Chinese Premier Wen Jiabao went out of his way to reassure neighbors to the south that his country "will not budge an inch as China grows stronger. The development of China constitutes no threat to other countries. Even a stronger China will by no means seek hegemony in whatever form in the region."[103] At the same time, China and the Philippines (which in 1995 had military tensions over Mischief Reef in the Spratly Islands) agreed to hold security discussions and exchange military delegations, as well as increase cooperation in the areas of security, rescue, and counterterrorism.[104]

A Chinese scholar recounted the dilemma China has faced as its power has grown. "We used to hide our power—deny our power. But then this became increasingly impossible as our strength increased. . . . We had to find ways to reassure people, use power constructively, because our power became increasingly undeniable."[105] And reassurance, particularly in its own neighborhood, is necessary, given the endemic distrust in the region. A late 2006 Pew poll found that while 95 percent of Chinese who were surveyed thought that the PRC's growing military power was a "good thing," 93 percent of Japanese, 76 percent of Russians, and 63 percent of Indians thought it was a "bad thing."[106]

Militaries and other coercive state appendages such as law enforcement agencies are used to reassure as well as to punish, repel, compel, and deter. Reassurance can be part of an ideational power strategy in which values and ideas are shared in the process of interaction between militaries and law enforcers. Part of reassurance is encompassed in what one Chinese analyst calls "negative [military] cooperation," which "refers to two parties hav[ing] cooperation to prevent themselves from [having] military clashes."[107] In the 1980s and 1990s, the PLA gradually increased its interactions with foreign armed forces through delegation trips, functional exchanges, arms control negotiations, arms purchases, growing participation (initially as "observers" and now in a variety of roles) in UN peacekeeping operations, and postings of military attachés abroad,[108] not to mention "Track Two" interactions with a broad range of nongovernmental organizations around the world. By 2004, Beijing had established military relations with more than 150 countries. That the PLA is becoming relatively more transparent is a good indicator that Beijing has more confidence in its strength—the weak are reluctant to be open.

In late 2002, a qualitative change in the scale and breadth of such interactions occurred. Starting in October of that year, the PRC began a sprint of military exercises that foreigners were invited to observe and in some cases participate in. This started with Kyrgyzstan and proceeded first to other members of the SCO, then to Pakistan and India (both maritime search-and-rescue exercises) the following year; and then to France, Britain, Pakistan, India, Germany, Australia, and Mexico in 2004. In 2004, sixty foreign military officers from sixteen countries were invited to "Iron Fist—2004." In late 2004 Moscow and Beijing announced that the first Sino-Russian joint military exercises would be held in Chinese territory in 2005, to the consternation of some in the U.S. diplomatic and security communities. Also in late 2004, in connection with the visit of a Chinese military delegation to Kazakhstan, Beijing announced that it had given the Kazakhs thirty-seven million RMB in material and technical assistance, that many Kazakh military personnel were enrolled in PLA schools, and that a dozen others had graduated from Chinese universities.[109] All such interactions served the twin purposes of reassurance and deterrence. In 2006 Beijing and Washington agreed to joint search-and-rescue exercises, and in March 2007 two Chinese naval vessels visited Indonesia, a nation that has long been wary of Chinese military power, as we shall see in chapter 5.

Though China's National Defense University (NDU) began interacting with foreign militaries and enrolling foreign officers in brief, rather segregated classes in the 1990s, the scale of activity and the number of institutions involved broadened thereafter. In 2004 the Ministry of National Defense began two-week training courses for young African military officers, and the Submarine Academy of the Chinese Navy began a forty-five-day training course for Asians and Africans in charge of offshore salvage operations. Some of these programs have included U.S. allies such as Germany. In explaining these programs, NDU President Pei Huailiang emphasized reassurance: "The courses have not only deepened officers' understanding to [sic] China's history and culture, reform and opening-up, and policy of national defense, but also enhanced the mutual understanding and trust between Chinese and world armies."[110]

In another first, in June 2004 the PLA's Academy of Politics in Xi'an cooperated with the International Committee of the Red Cross to conduct a seminar on armed conflict and international humanitarian law. The academy in Xi'an is where the military's political commissars and legal advisors are trained. Twenty Asian nations were invited to participate.[111] Since 2002 China has been running a large UN police training center in the vicinity of Beijing.[112]

The participation of Chinese forces in UN peacekeeping operations, initially as "observers" in small numbers and later as full participants in larger numbers, is an important development that generally reassures the international community.[113]

FIGURE 4

In August 2005, Chinese and Russian forces held their first joint military maneuvers, called "Peace Mission 2005." This eight-day exercise involved ten thousand troops from several services in the two nations' militaries. The undertaking partly reflected improved relations between Beijing and Moscow and their common desire to balance U.S. power in Asia. Li Gang/China Features/Corbis.

Allen and McVadon report that only in 1990 did China start having "observers" participate in PKOs, the first instance being the UN Truce Supervision Organization in April 1990. From December 1991 to September 1993, Beijing put eight hundred troops in Cambodia under the auspices of the Transitional Authority of the UN, and from 1991 to 2004 China had hundreds of observers in Kuwait, Western Sahara, Mozambique, Liberia, Afghanistan, Sierra Leone, East Timor, Ethiopia and Eritrea, Bosnia and Herzegovina, Cote d'Ivoire, and Burundi, as well as troops in the Congo, troops and police in Liberia, and police in Kosovo and Haiti.[114] In May 1997 Beijing "decided that, in principle, the PRC would take part in the UN's stand-by arrangements and would provide military observers and civilian policemen to UN peacekeeping operations."[115]

Like other forms of reassurance behavior, Chinese participation in the realm of international peacekeeping increased dramatically (from a low base) in the new millennium. This expanded level of activity is evident in the number of missions, their increasing intrusiveness, the move from just sending observers to dispatching police and troops, the relative cost burdens Beijing is willing to bear, and the number of Chinese personnel sent to such operations. The PRC (accurately) says that "it provides more military observers, civilian policemen, and troops to peacekeeping operations under the roof of the United Nations than any of the other four permanent members of the UNSC [United Nations Security Council], which increasingly prefer to operate outside the U.N. framework."[116] As of July 2006, China had 168 police, 63 military observers, and 1,417 troops for a total of 1,648 participants in UN peacekeeping operations, compared to 587 for France, 370 for the United Kingdom, 340 for the United States, and 305 for Russia.[117] And in the wake of the summer 2006 war between Hezbollah and Israel Beijing pledged to deploy 1,000 personnel in southern Lebanon (where they subsequently removed land mines, among other things). That same year Beijing sent substantial contingents to Liberia and Sudan. All this reflects the increasing global reach of Chinese foreign policy, as well as the desire to compete for recognition with Taiwan and the rise of new leaders in Beijing who are less encumbered by past taboos.

In September–October 2004, for instance, about 125 Chinese riot police (with three months' prior training) went to Haiti for a half-year mission as the first Chinese forces deployed in the Western Hemisphere. Vice-Minister of Public Security Meng Hongwei noted, "They are contributing to world peace. They shoulder the heavy responsibility of maintaining stability in the country." In its summary report, the Chinese Embassy in Washington concluded, "Nearly 300 Chinese peacekeepers have been sent around the world—in East Timor, Bosnia-Herzegovina, Liberia, Afghanistan, Kosovo, and Haiti."[118] Since 1990, "six Chinese servicemen lost their lives and dozens [were] wounded in UN peacekeeping operations."[119]

In the wake of the December 2004 tsunami that struck vast reaches of Southeast and South Asia, Beijing employed its military forces in a reassurance role, in this case bringing limited humanitarian assistance. Previous Chinese humanitarian missions had taken place in Afghanistan and North Korea, but on a very limited scale. The January 5, 2005, front page of *China Daily* proclaimed, "PLA Troops Active in Tsunami Relief Work," noting that "aircraft carrying more than $7.6 million worth of Chinese mainland relief materials as well as items from Hong Kong have been sent to the afflicted region in the past week."[120] In interviews that I held with the Chinese military and other government organizations, it became clear that Beijing wanted to make two things clear to me regarding its assistance: its capabilities to undertake these kinds of missions were modest, and China's ability to project even limited power into the region for humanitarian purposes could spark anxiety among neighbors. As one ministerial-level official put it to me at the time, "Excessive troops may trigger reactions."[121]

Reassurance strategies also utilize nonmilitary instruments of coercive power, notably law enforcement agencies. One example involving the United States is the Container Security Initiative (CSI), initiated by the U.S. Customs Service, now within the U.S. Department of Homeland Security. This initiative stems from the fact that "50 percent of the world's trade, 21 of the world's 30 top container seaports, and 23 of the world's 30 busiest airports" are in the Asia-Pacific region.[122] The world's top twenty ports (which account for roughly two-thirds of U.S. cargo imports) were the initial focus of CSI. The plan was to station personnel in these ports and work with local law enforcement to inspect high-risk cargo before it was sent to the United States. China has several very big ports on the CSI list—Hong Kong, Shanghai, and Shenzhen (Shekou)—and these three harbors account for two-thirds of China's total port trade.[123] Initially, it was not clear (especially given China's unhappy experience with "treaty ports" and extraterritoriality in the nineteenth century and the first half of the twentieth) whether the PRC would consider cooperating; there was some domestic opposition to the idea. Even so, in May 2003 Hong Kong joined the program—a critical decision, since it alone ships more than six thousand containers a day to the United States. Two months later, the Chinese government signed a "cooperation declaration" regarding Shanghai and Shenzhen that was implemented by early 2005.[124]

This kind of PRC activity has not been limited to Sino-American efforts. In his address to ASEAN, Japanese, and Korean summit partners in November 2004, Premier Wen Jiabao recommended that "given the increasingly pronounced problem in maritime safety and security," "positive consideration be given to stronger cooperation within the 10 + 3 [ASEAN plus China, Japan, and South Korea] in this respect."[125]

Through its diplomacy, China is starting to discuss and develop new forums and structures to provide regional security outside the framework of America's bilateral alliances—structures such as the Six-Party Talks in Northeast Asia. In October 2004, for instance, Beijing and Moscow jointly announced that they would "facilitate the formation in the Asia-Pacific region of an entire cooperation system of security and cooperation with equal rights for all participating states."[126] The following month, Beijing held the first-ever ASEAN Regional Forum (ARF) Security Policy Conference, "with the objective of intensifying the participation of national defense officials in the ARF."[127] Beijing, in short, has some new ideas regarding regional cooperation and reassurance and is advancing them to interested audiences.[128]

Another instance of reassurance concerns China's space program. By making its space efforts more collaborative (as enumerated in the above-mentioned space agreements) and hence transparent, Beijing promotes reassurance at the same time that it presumably gains technologically. The United States has been reluctant to cooperate much in this area, but such cooperation would be mutually reassuring.

One of the oldest dimensions of China's reassurance strategy concerns its nuclear weapons capabilities, since this was the area in which the PRC's capacity to project power was demonstrated earliest—in October 1964. Because China's non-nuclear neighbors have had anxieties about Beijing's nuclear forces, China has promoted two concepts designed to reassure these nations over the last five decades— a "no first use" nuclear policy and nuclear-free zones. Chinese Premier Wen Jiabao reiterated Beijing's support for ASEAN's nuclear-free zone policy during the already mentioned summit in Vientiane, Laos, in November 2004. In its 2004 *White Paper on National Defense,* Beijing again mentioned that it "pursues a policy of no first use of nuclear weapons, and undertakes unconditionally not to use or threaten to use nuclear weapons against non-nuclear-weapons states or nuclear-weapon-free zones."[129] Of course, were war to break out, Chinese leaders might reevaluate prior declarations about restraint—fighting wars is different from deterrence or reassurance. In its 2006 annual report to Congress, the Office of the U.S. Secretary of Defense asserted that the no-first-use policy "may be under discussion" in Beijing. It is hard to see why the PRC would explicitly reverse itself on this policy given the "peaceful rise" theme of its overall diplomacy.[130] Nonetheless, the possibility that conventional weapons could be used to attack China's nuclear deterrent, combined with the possibility of preemption, has, according to Professor Shen Dingli, "stirred up debate [in Beijing] on the validity of NFU [no first use]."[131]

ECONOMIC COERCION

Economic power, remuneration, is a form of positive inducement, a fungible means by which to bend others to one's will. That expression of the Chinese face of economic power is the topic of chapter 3. Here we focus on the coercive utility of economic power.

Economic coercion can be evidenced in procurement decisions, the leverage that derives from being the home to substantial foreign investment, and the ability to impose economic sanctions. To start, Beijing has substantial clout stemming from its ability to dictate major domestic procurement decisions in the context of fierce international business competition. The Washington director of government affairs for Caterpillar Corporation put the PRC's importance to the company this way when speaking to U.S. congressional staff: "Forty percent of the world's construction is in China—if we are not number one in China, we are not number one in the world."[132] Another well-known example is the competition between Boeing and Airbus for sales in China, a competition that has at times influenced decision makers in Washington or Brussels as they have considered whether to initiate, continue, or curtail policies Beijing finds objectionable. Yet another clear example of China using its procurement leverage to change a foreign interlocutor's policies occurred in 1992 when Beijing did not permit French firms to bid on Guangzhou subway contracts in retaliation for Paris's decision to sell Mirage jet fighters to Taiwan. It did not take Paris long to change its policies and decide against future sales.

Some Chinese economic leverage is also evident in the facts that Taiwan entrepreneurs have invested around $100 billion on the mainland, 38 percent of the island's total exports went to the PRC (including Hong Kong) in 2005, and 71 percent of Taiwan's foreign direct investment (FDI) is in the PRC.[133] From time to time, Beijing has threatened specific Taiwan entrepreneurs and companies with economic reprisals if they express unacceptable views. For the most part these threats have been ineffective and counterproductive, and they have been dropped, though it is hard to precisely measure their self-censoring impact on the island.

Finally, China can place direct economic pressure on wayward states, particularly those along its borders. One example of this is the PRC's reported temporary interruption of oil flows to North Korea in February 2003, a move intended to induce Pyongyang to sit down at a multilateral negotiating table to discuss its nuclear weapons program(s).[134] In 2006 Beijing applied economic pressure on the Democratic People's Republic of Korea (DPRK) by freezing its assets in the Macau Special Administrative Region (SAR) Branch of the Bank of China[135] and later that year reportedly again interrupted oil flows to the Hermit Kingdom.[136] In the wake of Pyongyang's October 2006 nuclear detonation and PRC-backed UN sanctions in reaction, in late 2006 to early 2007, the Hong Kong SAR more strictly enforced ship safety standards on North Korean vessels than it had before, in one case keeping a DPRK commercial vessel out of circulation for more than two months.[137] Similarly, "In November 2002, when the Dalai Lama visited Mongolia, China suspended rail services between the two countries for two days, a none-too-subtle reminder of Beijing's ability to control Mongolia's chief trade route."[138] This is an interesting case of coercive economic power doing battle with attractive spiritual (ideational) power.

It is true that many of the coercive economic tools available to Beijing may be difficult to use and have limited utility. First of all, China reaps huge domestic employment gains by virtue of Taiwan and other FDI; in December 2004 the PRC Ministry of Commerce announced that "the jobs of 80 million Chinese are directly related to foreign trade."[139] To punish foreign investors who generate domestic employment is to threaten China's own interests and perhaps its stability. Second, Beijing must preserve its reputation for having a stable investment environment if it wishes to keep FDI flowing in. Third, some of the industries that have invested in China, such as shoes, could be moved elsewhere with manageable transition costs. Fourth, due to interdependent global production chains, often if Beijing seeks to punish one part of the chain through sanctions, it inadvertently will affect a great number of others it may not wish to offend. Economic sanctions against Taiwan's electronics industry, for example, would affect global supply and China's own capacity to export. Fifth, in the case of North Korea, applying economic sanctions to get compliance on nuclear proliferation may rank lower than avoiding a sanctions-induced collapse in Pyongyang, which might, in turn, spew refugees into China's already economically distressed northeast. Finally, many of China's undertakings in joining the WTO and other multilateral organizations require that political and foreign policy decisions not interfere with market-driven international economic competition.

Considering these factors and many others, Taiwan Professor Chen-yuan Tung concluded, "Overall, in terms of both the initiation and outcome of economic sanctions, China has no economic leverage over Taiwan and the island's vulnerability with respect to cross-Strait economic relations is almost non-existent."[140] This may be overstated, but it does point to the difficulty of using economic leverage coercively. The difficulties stem from interdependence and Beijing's overriding strategy of maximizing growth to maintain political stability at home and influence abroad.

The remaining coercive instrument in China's national tool kit is the power of diplomatic isolation—the international relations equivalent of jail.

ISOLATION AS AN INSTRUMENT OF COERCION: THE TAIWAN CASE

Isolation is only one method in China's four-part strategy to prevent Taipei from moving toward de jure independence in the short and medium terms and to achieve some form of political integration in an indeterminate long run. The other three are increased economic integration across the Strait, increased cultural contact, and military deterrence. The four methods can work against one another and compromise other Chinese foreign policy goals. What may be designed to prevent independence (coercive threat) may alienate Taiwan's citizens and thereby reduce the chances of peaceful reunification and raise anxieties among China's other neighbors.

The degree to which both the Republic of China (ROC) and the PRC have used isolation as a principal instrument to subdue each other since 1949 is extraordinary. From 1949 until 1971 (when the ROC occupied the "China seat" at the United Nations), Taipei fought on every diplomatic battlefield to deny Beijing representation in international organizations or other forms of international participation and legitimacy. Washington was an indispensable ally in this endeavor. Then, when Richard Nixon acquiesced to Beijing's assumption of China's UN seat in 1971 and Jimmy Carter normalized relations with the PRC in the late 1970s, Taiwan became the more isolated society. Since then, Beijing has forced it into greater and greater "official" isolation. By the late 1990s, this struggle had become a diplomatic trench war in which the two nations competed to buy the recognition of small, often corrupt regimes (e.g., Vanuatu), with only twenty-four countries recognizing the ROC as of mid-2007.

Why have attempts at mutual isolation been so prominent in the nearly six-decade struggle between Taipei and Beijing? And why is Beijing increasingly able to tighten this noose of isolation?

To start, both sides of the Taiwan Strait find lack of dignified treatment, the absence of a respectable name and place for their society, intolerable—a reaction with origins deep in Chinese history and culture, human psychology, and modern nationalism. Early manifestations of these sensibilities can be found in Confucius's *Analects* (book 13, verse 3). "Tzu-lu said, If the prince of Wei were waiting for you to come and administer his country for him, what would be your first measure? The Master said, It would certainly be to correct language. Tzu-lu said . . . Why should language be corrected. The Master said, . . . If language is incorrect, then what is said does not concord with what was meant, what is to be done cannot be effected."[141] Put in plain English—If you say the wrong thing, your intention is unclear; if your intention is unclear, the right action cannot be taken; and, if the correct action cannot be taken, the intended aim cannot be realized.

Buried in this formulation is a compulsion, shared equally by Taipei and Beijing, to make reality conform to names, or to use names to create new realities. To be sure, other peoples and cultures are concerned about words, titles, and names, but the Chinese pay particular attention in this regard. This helps explain the impenetrable word and symbol games played over Taiwan's status and name. Regarding status, is Taiwan a country? A province? A customs area? An international health entity? In terms of name, is the island the Republic of China (ROC)? The ROC on Taiwan? The ROC (Taiwan)? The Republic of Taiwan (ROT)? Chinese Taipei? China, Taipei? Taipei, China? Or Taiwan? Since 1972, Beijing has been successful in persuading an ever-growing number of countries to recognize the PRC as "the sole legitimate government" of all of China; having each new partner at least "acknowledge," if not "recognize," Beijing's claim that Taiwan is a part of China; and dissuading other countries, multilateral organizations, and even private companies from using names for the island that would suggest otherwise. For instance, in the Olympic Games and APEC, Taiwan's name is "Chinese Taipei"; in the Asian Development Bank it is "Taipei, China." In the World Trade Organization, Taiwan was admitted under the name of the "Separate Customs Territory of Taiwan, Penghu, Kinmen and Matsu" or "Chinese Taipei."

This fixation over names is also evident in Taiwan, where in 2001 President Chen Shui-bian announced his intention to place the word Taiwan on the island's passport, which had previously borne only the name Republic of China. The actual change occurred in September 2003. This in turn, sensitized Beijing further to even the word Taiwan, and private companies, in turn, often sought refuge in referring to the island as Taipei, fearing to use any word that might be construed to indicate nation-state status for the island. Similarly, in the run-up to Taiwan's Legislative Yuan elections of December 2004, President Chen tried to win votes for his "Pan Green" coalition by calling for changing the name of the island's offices in the United States from "The Taipei Economic and Cultural Representative Office in the United States" (TECRO) to "The Taiwan Economic and Cultural Representative Office in the United States" (TECRO)—the sole difference being "Taipei" and "Taiwan," with the latter suggesting statehood in a way that the former (the name of a city) did not. In mid-2007, President Chen was backing a referendum to occur along with the March 2008 presidential election, this time asking voters to express their views on whether Taiwan should be admitted to UN membership under the name of Taiwan. In the delicate cross-Strait context, this was a dangerous move.

A second reason that international isolation has been such an important tool in the struggle over Taiwan's status concerns regime legitimacy in both societies. For the PRC, post-1949 legitimacy rested on China's resumption of the dignified role in the world that had been stripped away from it in the nineteenth century and the first half of the twentieth century. The Chinese Communist Party's revolutionary objective could not be fulfilled until Beijing represented China on the world stage and China was unified. Taiwan was, and remains, the principal item of unfinished territorial business. For its part, from 1949 to 1971 the ROC waged its war against

Mao Zedong in part by isolating the PRC internationally and thereby weakening the communists' legitimacy both internationally and domestically.

On Taiwan, a significant fraction of the island's population has a distinct sense of identity. This sense of separateness has its origins in the psychology of a people occupied by Japan from 1895 to 1945 and subsequently "occupied" by Kuomintang "outsiders" *(waishengren)* after World War II. This identity was strengthened in the years since 1949 by a combination of initial KMT ("mainlander") repression and martial law (ended in 1987), followed by dramatic successes in democratization and economic development. All this has convinced many of the island's people that they are distinct and entitled to their own autonomous status in the international community. Even some of those mainlanders who came over around 1949 have come to feel this way, resenting past KMT corruption and repression, and reflecting their own socialization (often through intermarriage) and the emerging democratic ethos on the island.

The third reason isolation is an important instrument derives from regional economic integration and China's central role in it. The PRC has a mounting ability to deny Taiwan the full economic benefits of participating in some of the PRC-inspired and nascent free-trade areas forming, such as the "ASEAN + 3" arrangement under discussion. Taiwan will be excluded unless it submits to the "one China principle." Nicholas Lardy and Daniel Rosen argue that Taiwan would gain much more from inclusion in regional free-trade integration in East and Southeast Asia than from a similar arrangement with the United States.[142] Or as Rosen puts it more bluntly, "Taiwan's status quo economic condition is eroding with [Beijing-driven] regional trade integration from which Taiwan is excluded. . . . Taiwan is being deliberately frozen out of regional economic arrangements [by Beijing]."[143] We return to this topic in chapter 3.

Beijing's capacity to isolate Taiwan diplomatically and economically gains strength from the global attraction of the PRC's domestic market (and the leverage China thereby enjoys), its importance in key international organizations, its mounting military strength, its increasing investments abroad, and the mainland's strategic role in global production chains. China's leverage induces others to implicitly or explicitly choose between Beijing and Taipei. For example, Pretoria switched diplomatic recognition from Taipei to Beijing in 1998, and by 2004 South Africa had become China's largest trade partner in Africa.

While there are many reasons for the weak investment climate in Taiwan, this cumulative isolation diminishes Taiwan's attractiveness as a destination for FDI (which on an annualized basis fell by more than half between 2001 and 2004).[144]

Domestic investment on Taiwan also declined significantly between 2000 and 2003. Unsurprisingly, Taipei feels trapped as the noose of isolation tightens and Washington demands that Taipei do nothing to upset the "status quo," a dynamic status quo that generally evolves in a direction adverse to the island. A senior official in one important Pacific nation candidly explained: "The Chinese are now talking about our representation in Taipei and want us to use it to put pressure on Taiwan as America is doing. We do it. We have been quite concerned for a year and a half about Taiwan upsetting the status quo—to move toward sovereign, legal status."[145]

Taiwan's frustration and outrage with big-power pressure to minimize "provocations" as Beijing tightens the noose were expressed in a *Taipei Times* editorial of December 2004: "The terminology of contemporary politics is being defined by China alone. In applying these rules, China seems to have brought the rest of the world under its wing, with the US following China's lead in the use of this terminology, seemingly unaware of [the] danger. China is trying to bury Taiwan alive with the term 'status quo,' and unfortunately, the US might be serving as Beijing's unwitting accomplice."[146] In June 2007 in Taipei, Foreign Minister James Huang told me, "Regarding the status quo, we need to maintain a dynamic status quo. You [the United States] define it . . . according to your interests. Please, support Taiwan democracy. Please, support adequate international space."[147]

Beijing's growing ability to isolate Taiwan is demonstrated by the Gilbert-and-Sullivan-like contest between Taipei and Beijing in late 2004 over securing the diplomatic recognition of Vanuatu, a small nation consisting of eighty-three coral and volcanic islands in the Western Pacific, with a population of about two hundred thousand and an economy where pigs are one medium of exchange. The saga became public shortly after the prime minister of Vanuatu, Serge Vohor, paid a secret visit to Taipei in November 2004 and signed a recognition agreement with Taipei, even though his government had recognized Beijing since 1982 and had received millions of dollars in aid over the years.[148] A Vanuatu government spokesman explained, "As we often say here, the 'one China' policy will not take you to heaven."[149] Prime Minister Vohor explained his thinking (that the PRC's financial assistance was inadequate) by saying, "It was no use asking for a carton of Coca Cola and getting a [single] can."[150] It was reported that Taipei had offered somewhere between $20 million per year and $6 billion overall for the recognition shift.[151]

Over the five weeks that followed the prime minister's move, the situation deteriorated, with intense infighting in the Vanuatu government between the prime minister and the foreign minister, who disagreed with him about the shift. Taiwan Vice Foreign Minister Y. M. Kau paid a low-profile visit to Vanuatu to try to salvage things for Taipei in the face of increasing pressure on the tiny nation from Beijing. There were even reports of physical contact between Prime Minister Vohor and the PRC's Ambassador Bao Shusheng. To add to the confusion, on November 24 Australia stated that it would end aid to Vanuatu "unless it cracked down on corruption and improved the island's governance."[152] Taiwan Foreign Minister Chen Tang-sun proceeded to tell Australia not to "meddle" in Taiwan-Vanuatu affairs.

The denouement came when Prime Minister Vohor was deposed after receiving a no-confidence vote from his parliament. The vote occurred on the eve of Taiwan's hotly contested December 12, 2004, Legislative Yuan elections, the results of which dashed President Chen Shui-bian's hopes of gaining a working "Pan Green" majority in the island's legislature. The Vanuatu affair probably had little to do with the election results, but the fiasco's timing enraged Taiwan Foreign Minister Chen Tang-sun, who said, "The parliament [in Vanuatu] chose to call the vote on the eve of Taiwan's elections. Obviously China is behind all this. It's all too apparent that Beijing intends to influence the elections here."[153] Chen probably ascribed more foresight and influence to Beijing than was warranted, though it remains unknown (publicly) what inducements Beijing offered Vanuatu's government to spurn Taipei. In the immediate aftermath of Vohor's ouster, Taiwan diplomats were ordered to leave Vanuatu, with the PRC ambassador saying: "This is good news," "They should have left long ago," "I really don't know what they [the Taiwan diplomats] are going to say to the media," and "This has been a farce."[154]

Adding an exclamation point to this episode, about five weeks later, Chinese Foreign Minister Li Zhaoxing and the foreign minister of Grenada, Elvin Nimrod, announced that Grenada had switched recognition to Beijing, bringing the number of countries recognizing Taipei down to twenty-five. In short, Beijing and Taipei are each expending diplomatic and financial resources struggling over recognition, each feeling that every victory, no matter how paltry, reinforces its own legitimacy. In June 2007 the game continued with Beijing wooing Costa Rica into its fold, setting off fear in Taipei that others in Latin America would follow suit.

If Vanuatu was farce, SARS (severe acute respiratory syndrome) and Taipei's quest to participate in the work of the World Health Organization (WHO) were closer to tragedy. In November 2002 an outbreak of what initially was called atypical pneumonia began in southern China. This development was concealed from the central authorities in Beijing early on and then, once known in the capital, was kept from the general public until well into the New Year. The epidemic spread to Hong Kong, Singapore, Canada, Vietnam, and Taiwan, and by the time it had run out of steam in mid-2003 it had killed 774 persons around the world and sickened over

8,098, with the most cases in the PRC, the second greatest number in Hong Kong, and Taiwan ranking third at 346 cases, of which 37 were fatal.

This public health crisis became an instance of Beijing's isolation strategy at work when Taipei asked for direct interaction with (and participation in) the WHO. Beijing demanded that all Taipei contacts with the WHO and WHO's World Health Assembly (WHA) be mediated through the PRC, thereby conferring no independent status on the Taiwan government and legitimating Beijing's claim to represent all of China, including Taiwan. Vice Premier and Minister of Public Health Wu Yi made Beijing's position crystal clear at the height of the epidemic when she told the WHA on May 19, 2003, "Inviting Taiwan to participate in the WHO is unlawful, illogical and unreasonable. . . . First, there is no legal ground for a region or a province of a sovereign state to join an inter-governmental international organization. . . . The Central Government of China is willing to consider favorably Taiwan's request for more outside assistance in epidemic control."[155] In a demonstration of Beijing's ability to control the issue, Taiwan was not listed on the WHO general meeting agenda in Geneva.

For much of the world, it seemed that Beijing was more interested in isolating Taiwan than in isolating the SARS virus. The U.S. Congress passed resolutions calling on the Bush administration to support Taiwan's efforts to participate in the work of the WHO, and public health authorities around the world criticized Beijing—without tangible results. On the other hand, Taipei, even as its people were dying from SARS, saw in the tragedy an opportunity to advance the cause of Taiwan's autonomous identity: its stock position was, "Taiwan is one of the few countries in the world excluded from the WHO and its related agencies for what few deny is for purely political reasons."[156] Taipei couldn't resist referring to itself as a "country," despite knowing that this vocabulary would strengthen Beijing's resolve. Meanwhile, the U.S. State Department had an unwavering position that tried to find a middle route between the two sides—"We have urged the World Health Organization and its members to find appropriate ways for Taiwan to participate, including observer status. We will continue to do so. The United States does not support Taiwan's membership in organizations that require statehood for membership."[157]

The Vanuatu and SARS incidents are only two of many examples that demonstrate the capacity of Beijing to isolate Taiwan. This power derives from the growing strategic and economic interests that other countries have in not alienating the PRC. As a senior Australian official put it to me: "There is a moral dilemma for Australia. Taiwan has done all we could have wanted—markets and democracy—but China is rising so fast. And our interests with the PRC are great."[158] In the final analysis, however, the PRC's isolation efforts to some extent work against the reassurance efforts that its diplomacy otherwise pursues. Moreover, the competition between Taipei and Beijing for influence in impoverished countries contributes to corruption and poor governance in the battleground areas, which in turn can explode into antiethnic Chinese feeling, as it did in the Solomon Islands in the spring of 2006, when three hundred PRC businesspersons and family members had to be evacuated.[159]

Beijing's capacity to diplomatically and economically isolate Taiwan is mounting. In late 2006 Beijing made it clear that if the pro-Taiwan, economic nationalist opposition candidate Michael Sata were elected president in Zambia, Chinese "investors" could end their involvement there.[160] Though this strategy has the unfortunate side effect, from Beijing's perspective, of alienating Taiwan's people and (sometimes) the citizens of battleground nations (such as Zambia, where there was subsequent anti-Chinese violence), using this form of power is less risky than force and has fewer adverse side effects than blatant economic sanctions.

In Beijing's overall strategy toward Taiwan, the coordinated use of coercive power is apparent—deterrence through military instruments, regional economic marginalization (while pursuing cross-Strait economic integration), and diplomatic isolation. Along with these coercive measures, in 2006 Beijing began to vigorously use the power of economic attraction when Premier Wen Jiabao visited Pacific island countries and promised those "that have diplomatic ties with China" reduced tariff barriers, augmented development assistance, and augmented investment.

Two conclusions on China's might are important above all others. First, China's military and coercive strength is growing, but, as a senior U.S. military officer in China put it to me in 2005, we should not "build [the PRC into] an eight-foot giant" militarily. China's armed forces have improved markedly over the last quarter-century, and they will continue to do so, but the road ahead is long and the horizon of catching up tends to retreat. During the period ahead, America's military will not be standing still. Second, the face of power upon which Beijing is concentrating is not coercive but economic and intellectual power. If America diverts its primary attention to the military realm instead of strengthening its own economic and intellectual capabilities, it will be playing the wrong game, on the wrong field, with the wrong team.

A subtext throughout this chapter is that using coercion often hurts the power wielder as much as the target. Employing brute force can cause others to take up arms or seek powerful allies such as Washington. Economic sanctions can boomerang. And isolation further alienates the population one is seeking to woo.

The PRC has considerable homeland defense and deterrent capabilities and modest but growing force-projection power. Because China is nearer to its many land and sea neighbors than it is to the United States and Europe, its neighbors are most sensitive to Beijing's behavior and capabilities. For the most part, China's neighbors want America to be an active participant in the region (see chapter 5). Beijing is aware of all this, as it is aware of the danger of investing too much in military modernization too early in its own development process. Sensibly, Beijing is simultaneously reassuring neighbors and more distant powers about its pacific intentions as it increases its deterrent and power-projection capacities.

The crucial strategic point is that Beijing is becoming more powerful while at the same time seeking to minimize the incentives for others to ally against it. If successful, Beijing will achieve its principal aim of becoming stronger without eliciting external responses that would force it to prematurely divert resources from internal development to war-fighting capacity. In his *The Origins of Alliances,* Stephen Walt argues that, in judging how to respond to powerful neighbors and states in the international system, leaders are most driven by their assessments of "balance of threat" (rather than "balance of power"). That is why, for instance, Washington has had relatively conciliatory relations with Canada and Mexico despite obvious U.S. predominance and why the stronger United States had more allies during the Cold War than a weaker Soviet Union, when balance-of-power theory would suggest the inverse. Because of their judgments about the probable uses of U.S. power, neither Canada nor Mexico has sought to ally with others to offset or deter Washington.

Overall, if power is the ability to define and achieve broad purposes efficiently, China has been demonstrating "smart power." The observer must be impressed with the strategic coherence of Beijing's acquisition and use of coercive power. It has put coercion in the background, maintained a reassuring focus on domestic development, and become somewhat more transparent and reassuring to neighbors. Beijing has largely reserved its bare fists—coercive strategies of deterrence and isolation—for dealing with Taipei, whose threatened independence is the one issue on which the bulk of the international community is either indifferent or rhetorically lined up with the PRC, and even here it has used the lure of economic integration as well.

Finally, Beijing has sought to weaken the commitment of U.S. allies to side with Washington should cross-Strait tensions escalate or conflict break out. It has done so by concentrating on giving incentives for cooperation with Beijing to as many key actors in the international system as possible. Growing economic power has provided the principal means to accomplish this. By developing economic ties with America's traditional allies in the EU, the Republic of Korea, Japan, Australia, and Israel, China has fostered a context in which U.S. allies now balance their interests between Beijing and Washington. In East Asia, China's status as a major purchaser of what everyone in the region has to sell, and its lead role in regional economic integration, provide ample reasons to cooperate with the PRC. Walt's observation about the crucial role of a nation's domestic economic power in generating international support applies to both the United States and China in the post-9/11 world: "The domestic situation of the United States [*or China*] may be more important than anything else. External events impinge on U.S. [*or Chinese*] power; internal conditions generate it. . . . It is far more important to maintain a robust and productive economic system than it is to correct minor weaknesses in defense capability or to control the outcome of some insignificant clash in the developing world."[161]

In this light it is important not to take actions that unnecessarily stimulate Beijing to divert more resources to a faster acquisition of coercive power and that simultaneously divert America's attentions from its own more fundamental challenges in the realms of economics and ideas. We turn now to the economic realm.

THREE · Money

Money and material resources are a convertible form of power—they purchase coercive capabilities, confer normative power, are attractive, and provide the means to disseminate ideas. This chapter addresses the utilities, limitations, and effects of China's multiple expressions of economic power.

Since 1978, China's approximately 20 percent of the world's population has been regaining its "normal" relative weight in the global economy. Over most of the past two thousand years China has accounted for between 22 and 33 percent of world GDP. Only in the second half of the nineteenth century and the twentieth century did China's share of global GDP fall dramatically, reaching 4.5 percent in 1950, where it stayed until after 1973.[1] Since about 1978, China has been recapturing its share of global GDP, according to the International Monetary Fund (IMF)—in 1990 China's share was at 5.61 percent, increasing to 11.02 percent in 2000, 14.39 percent in 2005, and an estimated 15.83 percent in 2007.[2]

Putting it differently, in 1990 China's per capita GDP (expressed in PPP terms) was about 6.82 percent of the United States' per capita GDP; by 2000 it was 10.79

percent.[3] These figures reveal two aspects of China's reality—it has come a long way in a short period of time, and it has an enormous distance yet to travel. The challenge the PRC presents other societies is to reform their economic and social structures, find their comparative advantage as the PRC's economic progress presumably continues, and move further up the value-added chain.

The confidence that this economic progress gives China's leadership was revealed to me on December 7, 2003. Premier Wen Jiabao listened patiently as one of his American guests at the Waldorf Astoria Hotel in New York City argued that China should revalue its currency, the RMB or *yuan*. The American was seeking Beijing's help in stemming the tide of the PRC's mounting trade surplus with Washington and producing currency realignment. The guest's argument was that China's trade surplus was politically unsustainable in Washington, that other Asian economies would not revalue their currencies until Beijing did, that the Euro was bearing too much of the burden of global exchange rate adjustment, that the PRC's current account surplus and mounting foreign exchange holdings were indicators of the Chinese dollar's undervaluation, and that therefore the PRC should revalue by 20 to 25 percent. After listening carefully, the premier simply answered: "I'll give you some facts. The U.S. deficit [with China] is a result of the double deficits [the U.S. trade and budget deficits]." His point was that America's national savings rate was inadequate and that Washington needed to put its own fiscal and savings house in order before making demands of others.[4] Li Ruogu, deputy governor of the People's Bank of China, subsequently made a related point: "China's custom is that we never blame others for our own problem[s]. . . . The U.S. has the reverse attitude, whenever they have a problem, they blame others."[5]

The premier's confidence was grounded in about twenty-five years of nearly double-digit economic growth, the tsunami of FDI flooding into the PRC, and the growing sophistication of China's technocratic leaders. China's elite believes that the nation's sustained, high-speed economic growth translates into international influence. As one Chinese analyst put it, "China contributed more than 1 percent to Japan's, South Korea's, and Southeast Asia's GDP growth last year [2004], so we have room for maneuver with these countries to secure a friendly environment [for] China's development."[6]

This bravado coexists, however, alongside deep apprehensions. China's high-speed growth also creates and empowers forces that threaten stability at home. China's post-Jiang Zemin elite know that raw GDP growth alone is insufficient to maintain domestic stability indefinitely and that increasing attention must be devoted to the more equitable distribution and the quality of that growth. The leaders also know that fundamental political change cannot be deferred in perpetuity, though they apparently hope to leave this task largely to their successors.

There are other apprehensions as well, including the anxiety about whether rapid economic expansion can be sustained given deep-seated institutional rigidities, increasing dependence on overseas strategic resources, environmental limitations at home, protectionist impulses abroad, and the ever-present volatility of economic activity itself. The confidence born of growth contends with fears that growth will spark domestic and external conflict, slow precipitously, or push China's physical, institutional, and social systems to the breaking point. While these vulnerabilities will be examined in detail in chapter 6, here we focus on the considerable power that China's remarkable post-1978 economic performance confers. Economic power gives others incentives to cooperate and contributes to China's ideational power, its attractiveness, since there is a tendency to see virtue in economic success.

SOURCES OF CHINA'S ECONOMIC STRENGTH

Almost every country is in search of growth opportunities—jobs, particularly export-oriented jobs. Because of China's past performance, great size, modest but rapidly climbing consumption levels, and governmental progrowth policies, there is a widespread perception that the PRC has promising growth prospects for years to come, particularly with the rollout in 2004 of the policy promoting consumption-driven growth. In 2005, a breathless Lester Brown wrote an article entitled "China Replacing the United States as World's Leading Consumer."[7] The expectation for continuing high-speed growth in China rests on five attributes: (1) the PRC's national investment and savings rates; (2) a relatively educated and healthy citizenry; (3) a rapidly growing middle class and private sector; (4) the intimate connections between Chinese on the mainland and ethnic Chinese living abroad; and (5) the continuity and content of Beijing's economic policies. While there are problems in each domain, overall these attributes have greatly enhanced productivity and fueled PRC growth, and there is no compelling reason to forecast major changes any time soon. Indeed, in its 2007 study *Dancing with Giants*, the World Bank estimates that China's average contribution to world growth in the 2005–20 period will be 15.8 percent, second only to the United States and far ahead of India.[8]

NATIONAL INVESTMENT AND SAVINGS RATES

Plentiful savings and productive investment are keys to sustained, high-speed growth. China has very high national savings and gross capital formation (and fixed asset investment) rates, though the utilization of these resources is inefficient. Indeed, since 2004, Beijing has been trying with only limited success to boost consumption and reduce investment as a source of growth.[9] The investment-to-GDP ratio in 2003 was somewhere between 31.7 percent and 42.3 percent (the size and measurement of China's GDP and scale of gross capital formation are debatable).[10] By 2005, Chinese were investing somewhere around forty-five cents out of each dollar produced. Even with the inefficient use of these resources, high-speed growth is almost inevitable. If China increases the efficiency with which investment resources are employed, this should permit high-speed growth to continue for a considerable period, even if savings and investment rates decline somewhat. Looking at domestic savings alone, the IMF reports that China's "gross national savings" rate was 47.6 percent in 2003 and reached a rate of around 50 percent in 2005.[11]

These numbers are most striking when contrasted to the rates in the United States. Former Secretary of the Treasury Larry Summers put it most succinctly:

> In the last year [2003], the net national savings rate of the United States has been between 1 and 2 percent. That is to say, if one adds personal savings, corporate savings, and government savings—in this case government dissavings—and calculates them as a ratio of NNP [net national product], one is left with a figure between 1 and 2 percent. . . . It represents the lowest net national savings rate in American history. . . . At 1.5 percent, the national savings rate is about half what it was in the late 1980s and early 1990s, when national saving was last a major item on the U.S. policy agenda. In fact, net investment has declined over the last four to five years in the United States, suggesting that all of the deterioration of the current account deficit can be attributed to reduced savings and increased consumption rather than to increased investment.[12]

In short, Americans are buying and consuming and Chinese are saving, investing, and selling—as China's premier so bluntly pointed out in late 2003.

A RELATIVELY EDUCATED AND HEALTHY CITIZENRY

China is a nation of contradictions, one of which is that while it is poor and faces enormous health and educational challenges, it also has a relatively healthy and educated workforce that makes it a formidable international competitor. Educational and health deprivations, particularly in the central and western belts of the country and in mountainous regions, remain acute problems—60 percent of China's poor are in the western reaches of the country, where 30 percent of the country's total population lives. China's government reported that in 2003 about one billion persons had no health insurance.[13] At the start of the millennium, the PRC accounted for about 17 percent of global tuberculosis cases (about 270,000 deaths annually), with a 70 percent higher prevalence rate in the poorer central and western provinces.[14]

On the other hand, China has a comparatively educated, healthy, and still young workforce. World Bank figures report that adult literacy (age fifteen and older) in 2002 was about 95 percent for males and 87 percent for females, with a rate of 99 percent among young (age fifteen to twenty-four) males and females in that same year. These literacy figures (using a modest definition of literacy) nearly equal those of Thailand and Russia. While the net enrollment ratio of primary school–age children in China dropped slightly in 1990–2003 to 95 percent (financing for rural schools is particularly problematic), the percentage of secondary school–age children enrolled in China rose from 49 to 67 percent in the same period, and the percentage of the population in tertiary education more than quadrupled, although there are quality problems given this rapid expansion. Consequently, China is not simply a nation with cheap labor; it also possesses a relatively inexpensive and *capable* workforce.

Turning to the high end of labor force skills, in 2002 China and the United States granted approximately equal numbers of graduate-level engineering degrees, though China granted almost 3.5 times as many undergraduate engineering degrees.[15] Moreover, entering class sizes in engineering schools in China are growing rapidly. The Chinese figures, however, include many degree holders that are not included in comparable U.S. figures. A study by McKinsey & Company, for example, says that of China's about 1.6 million "engineers" only about 10 percent are "suitable for work in multinationals."[16] Even discounting for quality and definitional differences, however, the PRC will have an enormous and deepening pool of technically proficient human resources. South Korean and Japanese firms were investing heavily in the lower Yangzi region in 2005 because "they are increasingly interested in more technology and capital-intensive projects—a reflection of the high level of education and skills in the local workforce."[17]

In terms of health, China has a profile much superior to other countries (at its level of per capita income), though there are vulnerabilities. The most worrisome weaknesses include the high rate of smoking among adult males (53 percent in 1998–2002), the problem of HIV/AIDS infection, air and water pollution, tuberculosis (China ranks number two globally, with perhaps 45 percent of the population "infected with a latent form" of the disease),[18] syphilis, hepatitis B, and the ever-present danger of a pandemic of mutant avian or animal flu, all topics addressed in more detail in chapter 6.

Nonetheless, life expectancy in China has climbed four years since 1980, reaching age seventy-one in 2003—a figure close to that found in the world's "high-income countries" (seventy-eight), and eight years longer than in India.[19] Infant mortality, an indicator of public health, dropped substantially in China during the reform era, from forty-nine in 1980 to thirty per thousand live births in 2003—a rate slightly better than in Brazil and less than half that of India.[20] In short, China has a comparatively healthy workforce with high rates of basic education and a rapidly growing higher education sector. However, the combination of longer life spans and an aging workforce, in part due to the one-child policy, creates the future twin problems of a rapidly aging population with mounting chronic disease and a low worker-to-retiree ratio. These facts warn against straight-line projections, as discussed in chapter 6.

A GROWING MIDDLE CLASS

Because the definition of *middle class* is debatable, its size is difficult to determine. For example, should the definition be subjective or objective? A survey in Guangdong Province reported that "most of those surveyed thought themselves to be middle class," something that *subjectively* could be true for respondents but *demonstrably* would not be true if any reasonably rigorous criteria of income, occupation, and lifestyle were applied.[21]

Though Chinese analysts generally prefer the terms *middle stratum* or *middle income*, the size of the middle class depends on the income, lifestyle, occupation, ownership, and other criteria that are applied. In October 2004 researchers at the Chinese Academy of Social Sciences (CASS) concluded that China's middle class accounted for 19 percent of the PRC population (247 million persons) and was projected to reach 40 to 45 percent by 2020.[22] The analysts' definition was based on a level of family assets ranging from US$18,137 to US$36,275. By contrast, China's National Bureau of Statistics estimated that 75 million persons would be in the middle class in 2005 and 170 million in 2010, using a definition of annual household income for a family of three of US$7,230 to US$60,240, a huge range.[23] Thus in 2004 one could find size estimates of China's middle class that ranged from 2.8 percent of the population to 19 percent. In 2005 the CASS Institute of Sociology estimated the size of the middle class as a percentage of the working population—12 percent.[24] And in mid-2007 the Research Office of the State Council, using an income definition, said 6.15 percent of the population (80 million persons) were considered middle class.[25] If one looks to Western estimates of China's middle class, Goldman Sachs defines the middle class as beginning at the threshold of $3,000 per capita annual income and estimates that by 2011 China's middle class thus defined will constitute 28 percent of the population. They project that by around 2025 this number will be over 1.1 billion persons.[26]

Whatever the current presumed size of the Chinese "middle class," there is consensus about a second point—it is growing rapidly. This is a crucial fact for foreign investors. As Excel Funds Management Inc. of Canada put it in an article entitled "Reasons to Invest in China," "China has one of the fastest growing middle classes in the world, which is driving an increase in demand for cars, housing, leisure activities, education, and health care." Yahoo! China conducted a survey of three hundred thousand middle-class residents (their definition was three-person family annual incomes in the 60,000–500,000 RMB range) in Beijing, Shanghai, Guangzhou, Nanjing, and several other key cities, called "An Investigation of the Dreams of the Middle Class."[27] Chinese consumers not only aspired to possess the following general consumption goods but named particular brands: cell phone—Motorola V3 or Nokia 7280; notebook computer—IBM Thinkpad; credit card—the Construction Bank Dragon Card or the Bank of China Great Wall Card; travel destination—France, East Africa, or Northeast Asia; automobile—Audi A4. In a 2005 lecture at the Wharton School of Business at the University of Pennsylvania, I tested out this preference list on thirty Chinese executives; they generally agreed with the rankings, though they wanted even newer models. Indeed, by 2006 China had become the world's third-largest consumer of luxury goods at 12 percent of global sales, growing from 1 percent five years earlier.[28] The same year, China was the third-largest market for Rolls Royce vehicles, and Audi sales jumped 40 percent.[29]

One of the key issues germane to the middle class is its presumed role in political change. While this topic is addressed in chapter 6's discussion of the vulnerabilities of the current system, there is a general expectation abroad that a growing middle class creates pressures for political change in a democratic direction. The tendency of Western analysts to view the middle class as an agent of political change contrasts somewhat with the prevailing Chinese elite's expectation that the emerging middle class on balance will be a force for stability, at least for the short and medium terms.

Concisely, for international (and domestic) investors, the rapid growth of a middle class hungry to consume is alluring news, though there is a nagging fear that class polarization and lack of opportunities for political participation could destabilize the country and increase risk.

OVERSEAS CHINESE

The so-called Chinese Diaspora has been very significant to Chinese growth through remittances, investment, the provision of know-how and technology, and the provision of marketing and trade networks. Overseas Chinese have played variable but important roles in China's economic, educational, and social life for a very long time. While analysts and commentators ought not exaggerate the cohesion of the approximately thirty to thirty-five million ethnic Chinese living outside the PRC and Taiwan, in 1972 Stephen Fitzgerald wrote about the importance of overseas Chinese remittances to local communities in the PRC, particularly up through 1957.[30] And while the capital flows of the 1950s and the 1960s were very significant for Guangdong and Fujian provinces, those resources have been dwarfed by the financial, managerial, intellectual, and marketing resources that ethnic Chinese living outside China have brought to the PRC's modernization since the late 1970s. By year-end 2003, of the cumulative total of more than $500 billion in overseas FDI, 65 percent was accounted for by overseas Chinese.[31] As Singapore's ambassador to the United States Chan Heng Chee put it, "There is no doubt China's strategy for its modernization and rapid growth relies heavily on the participation, support, and investment of ethnic Chinese overseas."[32] In a September 2003 ceremony in Beijing, the PRC awarded "honor medals" and certificates to one hundred key overseas Chinese invested enterprises, noting that at that time "overseas Chinese account for more than 70 percent of the total number of overseas-funded enterprises in China and more than 60 percent of the total actual overseas investment in China."[33]

Hong Kong, Taiwan, and Singapore have funneled enormous investment into China, accounting for about 54 percent of utilized FDI going into the mainland in the first eleven months of 2004 alone, if one includes funds flowing through the British Virgin and Cayman Islands.[34] PRC sources assert that 85 percent of the population on Taiwan traces its origin to Fujian Province and that globally "the overseas Chinese of Fujian origin top 10 million. . . . And investment from Fujian's overseas Chinese has reached US$42.5 billion, making up more or less half of the total foreign capital inputs [into Fujian]. They had set up more than 20,000 enterprises throughout the province [by year-end 2003]."[35]

Chinese immigrant communities pool talent and capital and develop networks founded on entrepreneurship. Networks of overseas Chinese not only contribute capital to China's growth but also are significant in the transfer of hard and soft technology, with Chinese students studying abroad serving as one part of this complex process.[36] Overseas Chinese scientists often return for periods of time to the PRC to help build science there. A 1999 study by AnnaLee Saxenian, distributed by the Public Policy Institute of California, reported that "Chinese or Indian immigrants led 24 percent of all Silicon Valley firms" and that the "foreign-owned firms accounted for approximately 14 percent of the region's total employment."[37] This large, foreign-born Asian presence partly reflects the fact that between 1990 and 2000 the number of Chinese immigrants to America rose from 529,837 to 988,857, constituting 3.2 percent of the immigrant population in the United States according to the 2000 Census. The National Science Foundation estimated in 2001 that China was "among the top six countries of origin of foreign-born scientists and engineers employed in the United States."[38]

These immigrants and long-term residents, in turn, build connections back to their home countries and in some cases eventually return, creating interpersonal, intellectual, technological, financial, and corporate networks. Hong Liu reports that of the more than 2,600 new Chinese migrants who had gone abroad (half of whom had PhDs) and attended a technology fair in Guangzhou at the end of 2001, "28.8% of them planned to return [to the PRC] to set up enterprises and 34% intended to seek domestic partnership."[39] Saxenian concluded: "The 'brain drain' from developing countries such as India and China has been transformed into a more complex, two-way process of 'brain circulation' linking Silicon Valley to select urban centers in India and China. . . . The professional and business links between California and these distant regional economies are developing quickly."[40]

POLICY CONTINUITY AND POLICY CONTENT

For a brief period after the 1989 Tiananmen violence, it seemed conceivable that Beijing might reverse its policies of economic openness and reform. But after Deng Xiaoping's 1992 "southward journey" *(nanxun)* to rekindle reform, China never looked back. Thereafter FDI took off and in the next dozen years rose from a cumulative utilized investment total of US$34.36 billion (at the end of 1992) to US$563.8 billion by the end of 2004 and $618 billion in 2005.[41]

Beyond investment, however, the IMF has undertaken research that shows that policy continuity, and the content of that policy, have driven productivity increases in China that are even more important than raw capital accumulation. "By the early 1990s, productivity's share of output growth exceeded 50 percent, while the share contributed by capital formation fell below 33 percent."[42] The basic story of China's opening and reform era has been liberalization and marketization starting in the countryside, then moving to the cities, and now moving to the inland belts, all the while increasing the percentage of the economy outside the state sector. While there has been enormous political struggle at each step along the path of reform, the continuity and productivity-enhancing character of policy is impressive.

By 2005, "purely private firms account[ed] for between 20 to 30 percent of non-agricultural GDP"[43] and employed about one-third of the total urban workforce.[44] If one uses the broader definition of *nonstate firms* (which includes the "collective" sector), close to three-quarters of economic output and employment occurs in an essentially private-like work and productivity environment.[45] Additionally, there has been an increasing reliance on market signals to allocate resources, more authority has been granted to enterprise managers, land use rights are becoming progressively more predictable (widespread and destabilizing land grabs aside), and a commercial legal system is gradually developing, despite massive problems in areas like intellectual property protection. In addition, the quality of human resources has steadily improved.

In the trade system continual decentralization has occurred (there were twelve trade corporations in 1978 but thirty-five thousand in 2001, and by 2004 any company could be authorized to engage in trade).[46] Barriers to foreign trade (licenses, quotas, and tariffs) and impediments to economic competition have steadily diminished, thereby incrementally driving the domestic economy to improve. Foreign exchange use has been steadily liberalized, and Beijing has employed tax policies to promote trade and investment.[47] As a result, by 2004 trade had grown to 79 percent of GDP (by some estimates), with the Chinese government stating in late 2005 that "foreign trade accounts for over 70 percent of China's economy."[48]

Other features of this supportive and rather steadily evolving policy environment have been relatively low variability in the inflation rate (since the mid-1990s), rising (though still low) R&D spending, relatively low urban and enterprise tax burdens, declining entry and exit barriers, and increasing labor market flexibility.[49] In short, the content of Chinese national policy has been consistent in terms of strategic direction and has contributed to productivity growth. As the IMF put it: "While capital investment is crucial to growth, it becomes even more potent when accompanied by market-oriented reforms that introduce profit incentives to rural enterprises and small private businesses."[50]

Significant problems remain (addressed in greater detail in chapter 6), among which are persistently low levels of consumption, excess capacity in key industries, a still fragile banking/financial sector, environmental deterioration, great variation in local business environments, corruption, widespread violation of intellectual property rights, inadequate infrastructure, and a judicial system that lacks independence. Nonetheless, the perceived opportunities and macroeconomic environment are so positive that, when these are combined with the generally favorable policy direction, investors discount current severe operational problems that they confront.

THE EXPRESSIONS OF ECONOMIC POWER

Like other forms of power, economic power expresses itself in several ways: as the power of the *buyer*, the *seller*, the *investor*, the *development assistance provider*, and the *innovator*. Although China has varying strengths in each realm of economic power, its capacity in each is expanding. Economic power is the form of power China is emphasizing most in its overall strategy.

THE POWER OF THE BUYER

Flying into Shanghai's Pudong International Airport, one sees a terminal designed by a French architect. At Guangzhou's international airport the facility is of American design, with a Singaporean air traffic control tower and Danish boarding gates.[51] At both airports one sees cheek-to-jowl Boeing and Airbus planes, aircraft themselves assembled with components coming from a global supply chain—including China. At all airports, your taxicab is likely to be a non-Chinese nameplate vehicle; 90 percent of the cars bought in the PRC are foreign brands.[52] As in the United States, where subcontractors for building weapons systems are strategically selected from a multitude of key states and congressional districts, in China the practice of buying from a multitude of other nations gives those nations a stake in the PRC's continued success. Whether this has occurred by accident, by design, or out of fear of dependence on one supplier is uncertain.

China's economic strategy has given the rest of the world a piece of the action. This is an interesting contrast to Japan's economic development strategy. One comparative measure of this is Chinese and Japanese trade-to-GDP ratios. In 2003 China's ratio of trade in goods (exports plus imports) to GDP was 56 percent, with imports and exports close to balance then; Japan's trade-to-GDP ratio was 11 percent that year.[53] Imports constituted nearly 35 percent of China's GDP a year later.[54] According to Chinese trade figures, from 1980 China's imports grew at an annual average rate of more than 15 percent, making China the world's third-largest importer after the United States and Germany by 2004. In 2003, China accounted for 32 percent of Tokyo's export growth, 36 percent of Seoul's, 68 percent of Taipei's, 28 percent of Berlin's, and 21 percent of Washington's.[55] And China has allowed inward-bound FDI on a scale never dreamed of in Japan, investment being made in significant measure to produce goods for sale in China itself. In 2003, the PRC's FDI-to-GDP ratio was 35 percent, while Japan's was 2 percent.[56]

China's developing mass market and its willingness to buy from others gives Beijing power—this ability of "bolstering other countries' economies with its vast purchase of their goods and services."[57] One PRC report in 2005 estimated that three to four million jobs in South Korea were related to trade with China.[58]

Buying strengthens China in another way that one Wal-Mart official explained. By allowing large-scale foreign retail, consumer product, and service providers like Wal-Mart and McDonald's to sell domestically, Beijing enlists multinational firms in the development of China's manufacturing and agricultural supply chains. Retailers on the scale of Wal-Mart and McDonald's want to source as much as possible locally. These companies become drivers forcing the PRC's manufacturing and agricultural industries to become globally competitive through supply chain development. India lags behind China in manufacturing for many reasons, but one is that India allows virtually no foreign penetration by large-scale retailers.

Multinational production chains (in which China is often the last stop) also invest outsiders in PRC success. China has become a buyer of much of what Asia sells in commodities and intermediate manufactured items. In some areas, such as silicon chips, China is becoming an increasingly important supplier itself. This is reflected in the once close correspondence between China's trade surplus with the United States and its trade deficit with Southeast Asia.

Where these economies previously exported to the United States or Japan, they now increasingly export to China. Between 2001 and 2004, for example, China's commodity imports from the Philippines increased 366 percent; from Thailand, 145 percent; from Singapore, 173 percent; and from Malaysia, 193 percent.[59] This helps account for the noticeable change in perceptions of China in the late 1990s and in the first years of the new millennium. Whether one is in Singapore, Malaysia, Australia, or Indonesia, the perceptual change is characterized in almost identical words—a change in China's image from "enemy" to "engine of growth." There are worries about China throughout Asia, but the predominant regional sentiment has shifted toward a recognition of opportunity. As Singapore's ambassador to Washington put it in 2005: "Initially, ASEAN viewed China's economic rise as a threat, but increasingly they are seeing opportunity aside from the challenges. The rhetoric has changed. Trade is booming."[60] The Sino-Japanese relationship does not entirely fit this pattern; economic relations are "hot," but political/security ties fluctuate between "cool" and "cold," as elaborated in chapter 5.

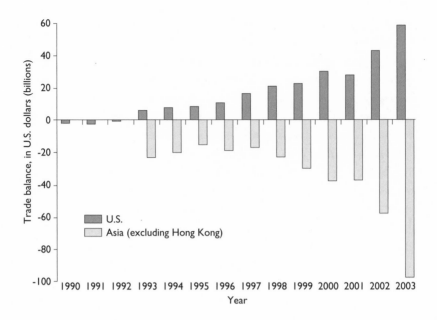

FIGURE 5
China's trade surplus with the United States mirrored its deficit with Southeast Asia.
Source: Centennial Group, using CEIC Database and WTO data, cited in Manu
Bhaskaran, "The Economic Impact of China and India on Southeast Asia," in
Southeast Asian Affairs 2005, ed. Chin Kin Wah and Daljit Singh (Singapore: Institute
of Southeast Asian Studies, 2005), pp. 62–81.

The power of the buyer seeps through the social and political fabrics of trade
partners. Beijing's capacity to choose among these national export competitors gives
hungry foreign firms (and their local and national governments) the incentive to
cooperate with the PRC, particularly given that China is the fastest-growing new
market for many of them. This is most obvious in key sectors—aircraft, nuclear
power, and raw materials. In both the United States and Europe, the aircraft and
nuclear power industries are concentrated in a few large firms with numerous suppliers. In the United States no new nuclear power plants are currently on the drawing boards (though this may change), but China plans to build thirty-two by 2020.
Boeing and Airbus are fighting over about $200 billion in anticipated aircraft sales
to China by 2025. Approximately $4 billion in Boeing sales were announced in con-
nection with President Bush's late 2005 visit to China, followed almost immediately
by Premier Wen Jiabao's trip to France, where, in exchange for Airbus promises to
look into setting up an assembly line in China (a joint venture deal that was con-

cluded in June 2007), Beijing agreed to purchase $5 billion in aircraft. As one Airbus official put it, "It's the market where you have to be."[61] If the leading firms in the aircraft and nuclear power industries—firms like Westinghouse, AREVA, Atomstroiexport Company, Mitsubishi, Atomic Energy of Canada, Boeing, and Airbus Industrie—want to stay competitive in the Chinese market, productive relations with Beijing are key, at both the company and national levels. If these firms do not have the production efficiencies of scale that big sales to China permit, their overall global competitiveness will decline.

Governments compete globally for manufacturing jobs and are partners with "their" companies. Megadeals can be complex and can cross sectors. For instance, China wants Russian oil (as does Japan), and Moscow wants to sell Beijing nuclear power plants (as do Paris and Washington). When Russian presidential aide Victor Ivanov was in Beijing talking about oil in April 2005, he stated that "the parties at the talks in Beijing had expressed their willingness to develop cooperation on atomic energy."[62] In short, China's thirst for oil may put it in a supplicant role vis-à-vis Russia, but its ability to decide where to buy nuclear power plants may put it in the driver's seat. This brings us to China's hunger for natural resources.

China's reach for raw materials, energy, and agricultural commodities is evident in Latin America, Australia, the Middle East, Central Asia, and Africa—areas in which China's clout historically has been modest. Though Chinese demand for these imports certainly will go up and down with economic cycles, from 1995 to 2003 China accounted for 68 percent of global demand growth for oil; 82 percent of steel; 100 percent of copper; 100 percent of aluminum; and 73 percent of nickel.[63] Significantly, in 2003 China became the world's largest importer of iron ore, a major component of steel, a development reflected in Beijing's interest in the iron-rich countries of Latin America, Southeast Asia, and Australia. Commodity-exporting countries compete for Chinese investment and long-term contracts, evident in Argentina's welcoming of President Hu Jintao's November 2004 visit, during which Beijing raised expectations for $20 billion in investment over the following ten years.[64] With respect to uranium, "China is expanding its nuclear power and Australia has [perhaps] half the uranium oxide in the world,"[65] so the Australian connection has become even more crucial. When interviewing a senior diplomatic official in Australia, I asked him, "How would you begin to describe your country's [Australia's] interests with respect to China?" His succinct yet striking answer was "Wools, alumina, iron ore, coal, and educational services."[66]

In 1993 the PRC became a net oil importer, and it has since reached oil and natural gas deals in Africa, Iran, Central Asia, and Latin America (e.g., Cuba and

FIGURE 6

Australian Prime Minister John Howard and Chinese Premier Wen Jiabao at the June 2006 opening ceremony of the Guangdong Liquefied Natural Gas Project Phase I in Shenzhen. The multibillion-dollar project reflects the rapidly growing economic and resource relationship between China and Australia and the PRC's hunger for energy. Liu Jin/AFP/Getty Images.

Venezuela), often with regimes that have deficient practices regarding human rights and proliferation and that represent political risk from the perspective of Western governments and potential investors. For these regimes, China's interest in long-term economic relationships is very attractive. For instance, about 87 percent of Colombia's oil resources are unexplored, and during Hu Jintao's April 2005 visit there President Alvaro Uribe Velez told him that "as long as China invests, there would be great potential [for making deals for exploration and production]."[67] For Russia's oil industry, China's growth is an opportunity, even as Moscow avoids becoming export dependent on Beijing by playing Japan and China off against each another. As the Russian media put it, "Today, oil is the principal item of Russian export to China. . . . In expert opinion, its need for energy resources will continue to grow and Russia may become their main supplier."[68]

Being a major buyer of strategic commodities (from Brazil, Russia, Australia,

Vietnam, India, Mongolia, Pakistan, Chile, Canada, Papua New Guinea, and much of Africa and Latin America) brings with it influence over suppliers, as well as two less welcome side effects from Beijing's perspective: vulnerability to supply interruption (and volatile prices) and the resentment of suppliers who believe that they are being exploited. There are the ever-present dangers of nationalistic reaction, instability in the supplier state, price volatility, and transport interruptions from distant locations. Moreover, because (as Li Xiaobing, the deputy director of the West Asian and African Affairs Division of the then Chinese Ministry of Foreign Trade, put it in 2004) "we import from every source we can get oil from,"[69] there is the danger that one of China's risky suppliers will run afoul of Washington (e.g., Iran over proliferation, Sudan over human rights, or Venezuela over political relations). Beijing may get caught between the United States, key resource suppliers, and its own mounting domestic requirements. Hu Shuli, the editor of *Caijing* (Finance) magazine, cautioned compatriots, writing: "We must remember, most major known reserves are claimed and tapped into. This, more than anything else, explains Sinopec and PetroChina's active engagement in countries like Sudan and Iran. And it is these countries' very hostility towards western oil firms that leaves opportunities for Chinese players. . . . But the strategy as we know it tends to focus excessively on laying our hands on the oil and gas, without adequately considering the political consequences."[70]

Then there is the other problem—resentment. Countries such as Brazil or Mozambique wish to sell their resources but simultaneously resent simply being materials suppliers who do not capture value added. This is true in Russia too. In the late 2006 Zambian presidential election mentioned above, the challenger attacked the incumbent administration, saying, "If Levy wants these [Chinese] investors, let him take them at his farm. And Saki, please tell those investors cutting down trees in Western Province that the Lozis are supposed to cut down trees for the Chinese to buy. Have we ever gone to China to cut down trees?"[71] In Russia, particularly in its far east, there is resentment of Chinese legal and illegal loggers hauling off natural resources and suspicion that the Chinese are occupying strategic border regions by stealth.[72] Another problem was clearly illustrated in June–August 2005 when CNOOC Ltd. (China National Offshore Oil Corporation) made a bid for the modest-sized U.S. oil company Unocal and the U.S. Congress adopted an amendment to an energy bill that lengthened the time necessary for the U.S. government to evaluate the offer. This maneuver effectively killed the deal. The underlying congressional fears were resource shortages and PRC control of strategic materials, as well as presumed subsidized financing. Of course, fear-mongering made for good domestic politics as well.

Beyond strategic materials, China is assuming importance as a purchaser of agricultural commodities. Though PRC agriculture has historically been highly protected and Beijing has been wary of dependence on foreigners for food, China currently is the world's largest soya and wheat importer (and Brazil is the world's largest soya exporter), a fact not lost on wheat exporters from Kansas to Kazakhstan or soya growers from America to Brazil. Beijing University Professor Lu Feng pointed to what farmers in the United States, Canada, Australia, Argentina, Brazil, and elsewhere already know: "In the long term, it is natural that China becomes a net importer of grain, due to its limited land resources." In 2004, China had an unprecedented agricultural trade deficit. Politically, this invests powerful farm lobbies around the world in stable relations with the PRC and gives Beijing another tool in its diplomatic arsenal. So when China launched its "early harvest initiative" that substantially opened its own domestic fruit and vegetable market to Thailand in 2003 (then to Myanmar in 2004 and to the Philippines in 2005) and promised struggling farmers in southern Taiwan similar access in 2005, this was an intelligent use of Chinese muscle. When Vice Premier Wu Yi visited the United States in April 2006 to clear the way for President Hu Jintao's visit later that month, her mission agreed to purchase in excess of $15 billion of agricultural goods, aircraft, and machinery. The same kind of "buying mission" preceded the U.S.-China "strategic economic dialogue" of mid-2007.

In the Doha Round of the WTO negotiations Beijing has sided rhetorically with countries hurt by industrial country agricultural import barriers but has not taken a leadership role in pushing the agenda of these nations in the Group of 20. China's economic position as an agricultural buyer gives it potential ideational (or normative) power (discussed in chapter 4) by allowing Beijing to promote the interests of struggling agricultural nations disadvantaged by the agricultural protectionism of the wealthy, but Beijing fears pushing too hard and alienating developed countries, and it has its own agriculture to protect. Other contradictions were demonstrated in 2004 when China was contracted to take delivery of large volumes of soybeans from Brazil but the global price dropped by around $50 per ton between the contract and delivery dates. The PRC refused to accept very large shipments (suddenly imposing a zero tolerance policy for fungicide residues), in hopes of renegotiating the price as the food deteriorated while it was waiting to be delivered. This move angered the Brazilians: "Some shipments did in fact contain seeds treated with fungicides. But that was also the perfect excuse for Chinese to renegotiate prices. . . . China will continue to use this type of commercial strategy because it has enormous purchasing power."[73] As one former Brazilian minister in the economic area put it to me, "Yes, that was not fair. They [the Chinese] used health standards, fungus, as the excuse."[74]

In Africa, China's buying power is often a mixed blessing, and the exercise of that power is creating the specter of the "ugly Chinese"—a nation on the prowl for resources, cutting deals with often corrupt elites, and having no concern for the general social welfare or sustainable development in the selling nations. In my presence one European former foreign minister told a Chinese ambassador in Europe in 2006 that, in Africa, "India is mostly driven by business issues with modest strategic interests. China has a different package. . . . It used to be that Taiwan drove China, but now fewer countries recognize Taiwan; now oil drives China, and timber. Now there is a projection of power. . . . China is after markets and acquiring strategic interests to acquire parity with the United States. Is China prepared to be a responsible power? Arms to Zimbabwe or Sudan without regard, helping people destroy the economy of their country like Zimbabwe. An attitude of looking the other way. Is this the way?"[75]

All this reveals how types of power overlap, how contradictions arise, and how attractive power can easily morph into a political liability when the power to buy is used coercively. Beijing can exercise the power of economic attraction as a buyer but exercise coercive power when it refuses to buy or buys without reference to consequences for the selling nation's people. Moreover, the reassuring buyer of one commodity is the coercive seller of another, as we see below. China, like the United States, will find that its power wins *and* loses friends.

Buying power is two-edged in another way—one can buy so much that one loses the freedom to sell. As of January 2006, Beijing possessed $818.9 billion in foreign exchange reserves (excluding gold), a near-second to Japan ($846.9 billion). In February of that year, the PRC (with $853.7 billion) surpassed Japan (with $850.1 billion). By mid-2006 China's foreign reserves totaled a staggering $941.1 billion, and by early 2007 the PRC had passed the $1 trillion threshold. This gives Beijing significant influence over global interest rates but also makes the PRC vulnerable to fluctuating foreign exchange rates. Beijing has said that it commonly holds 60 to 70 percent of these reserves in dollar-denominated assets,[76] particularly U.S. Treasury notes and agency debt, which have been growing very rapidly.

Periodically, when holders of U.S. dollars become jittery concerning U.S. fiscal policy or Washington's mounting trade deficit, markets look for early signs that Beijing and other holders of U.S. debt (for example, Tokyo and Seoul) are selling or changing their portfolio allocation ratios when purchasing new debt. Statements by a Chinese bank governor such as "We have long attached importance to the hold-

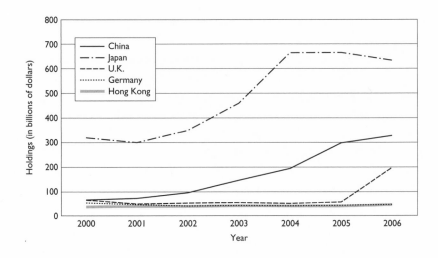

FIGURE 7

Major foreign holders of U.S. Treasury securities. Source: U.S. Department of the Treasury's Treasury International Capital System, www.treas.gov/tic/.

ing of a certain amount of euro assets," have assumed an unprecedented importance in today's global markets.[77] A big buyer that threatens to become a big seller has leverage, though it simultaneously can reduce the value of its own remaining holdings by rapid liquidation. Were China to quickly move any significant fraction of its dollar assets into holdings denominated in other currencies, this would probably push the U.S. Treasury to pay more for its borrowings, which would push U.S. interest rates higher. Increased interest rates, in turn, would be bad news for American consumers, U.S. politicians, and Chinese exporters. Beijing and Washington are two scorpions in an economic bottle, each with an incentive not to sting the other.

THE POWER OF THE SELLER

While China's power as a buyer is underappreciated, its power as a seller of vast quantities of manufactured items has produced an exaggerated sense of its underlying strength, particularly in the United States. A common perception is that everything is "Made in China," but underlying realities differ. The U.S. share of global industrial output as measured by real value added rose between 1990 and 2002 (from 20.7 percent to 23.3 percent),[78] mainly because of increases in American manufacturing sector productivity. While America has enhanced its global share of industrial output value added (as distinct from employment in manufacturing), other countries in the same 1990–2002 period lost share of global industrial output value added, including Japan, Germany, Italy, the United Kingdom, Brazil, and Russia.

Although China's global share of industrial output as measured by real value added went up in the same period (from 2.2 percent to 6.6 percent), the "Made in China" *label* does not mean that an item was actually made in China. Lucrative parts of globalized production chains have, thus far, remained outside China, leaving the lower-value-added final stages of the manufacturing process in the PRC—the "label" gets added at the end, but many of the more expensive components of a product are made elsewhere, though this is changing and other manufacturing nations should not be complacent. Manufacturing value added per capita in the United States in 2002 was more than fifteen times that of China.[79] Ironically, China gets 100 percent of the political heat for being the last link in the production chain while contributing only a modest percentage of the value added. This pattern produces the paradoxical result that in 2005 over 30 percent of the PRC's GDP was exports,[80] creating the illusion of a stronger China than the underlying production capabilities warrant.

According to the PRC's Ministry of Commerce, in 2005 foreign-invested companies operating in the PRC accounted for 57.3 percent of China's total exports.[81] About 85 percent of high-tech products made in the PRC are controlled by foreign enterprises.[82] In 2004, 88.6 percent of high-tech product exports from Shanghai's Pudong were produced by foreign-invested firms.[83] Indeed, Taiwan-invested firms manufactured over 70 percent of the electronics produced in the PRC in 2002.[84] The economist Lawrence Lau estimates that the value added by the PRC to its overall exports is approximately 30 percent,[85] meaning that the other 70 percent of export value from China accrues to others, such as foreign component makers, brand holders, distributors, marketers, packagers, transporters, and other service providers. This reality is reflected in the fact that in 2004 China had only one company (Haier, in white goods) among the world's top hundred recognizable brands. This partially accounts for PRC firms' purchase of brand names like IBM PC, Schneider, and Thomson and their attempts to secure others like Maytag. Overall, according to Morgan Stanley's Andy Xie, "On average, each dollar the U.S. pays for imports from China retails for $3–$4 in the U.S. Adding value on Chinese imports may account for 3–5 percent of the U.S. GDP. Four to eight million jobs in the U.S. could be associated with adding value in the China trade."[86]

This is a good example of the distinction drawn in chapter 1 between "power" and "impact." *Power* is the ability to achieve one's goals, whereas *impact* is the ability to affect others without having control over content and/or consequences: certainly attracting global attention as a job snatcher while garnering a modest share of the valued added was not Beijing's intention. Since the PRC needed to keep large employment-generating state-owned enterprises in business for a considerable period and wanted to boost exports while bringing new technologies and management practices into the country, it kept subsidizing state-owned enterprises as it simultaneously provided incentives for foreign firms to first use the PRC as an export platform and then create competition in the domestic market as well.[87] The result has been that foreign firms "now control the bulk of the country's industrial exports, have increasingly strong positions in its domestic markets and retain ownership of almost all [high-end] technology."[88] As of spring 2007, for instance, 90 percent of digital controls for machine tools were made by foreign companies, prompting a senior Chinese industry official to say, "If manufacturers continue to rely heavily on key component imports, the country's economy and national defence will be stunted."[89] This implies that the current U.S.-China economic relationship with China as the seller is more favorable to U.S. interests than is generally recognized. The Chinese Academy of Engineering put it this way in March 2006: "We should face the shortcomings as well. China's electronic information industry ranks second in the world in scale, but its core technologies are basically controlled by others. In the first ten months of 2005, the profit ratio of the one hundred most powerful electronic enterprises in China was merely 1.8 percent, less than one-tenth of that of Microsoft, Intel or Samsung. China ranks third in world trade, but only 10 percent of its exported goods have independent brands or independent property rights, so the profit margin is very low."[90]

China's weakness as a seller is also seen in its 2005 efforts to sell significant minority shares of its major banks (the China Construction Bank, the Industrial and Commercial Bank of China, the Bank of Communications, the Bank of China, and several municipal banks) to foreign financial institutions. This reflects these banks' needs for injections of skills in risk assessment and modern banking practices that must be rapidly acquired if PRC financial institutions are to survive as protections against international competition are reduced.

Competitors abroad should not draw too much comfort from these weaknesses, however. China will become more innovative, developing its own technologies and brands (the 2008 Olympic Games will help with the latter), and will move up the value-added chain, probably with unanticipated speed. This will occur as more sectors of the PRC economy have dynamic nonstate players and invest abroad and will accelerate if Beijing can continue reforming the financial system to allocate capital with increasing efficiency to nonstate enterprises. China is likely to develop innovation strategies even if it does not develop many transforming technologies and products anytime soon (see chapter 4). And as China gradually becomes a developer of proprietary technologies, processes, and products, its market size will enable it to establish standards to which others wishing to sell in the PRC must conform. But these are future prospects, not current realities, and many obstacles must be overcome in the interim.

There are areas in which China currently is a competitive superpower in terms of sales—footwear, textiles, and apparel, for example. By 2005, China annually exported six billion pairs of shoes, about one pair for every person in the world. The PRC's competitive power derives from disciplined (often Taiwanese) management in factories, efficient global distribution networks, and a deep reservoir of relatively skilled labor. Globally, EU footwear exports, the next largest export source after China, reached only 192.6 million pairs, or 3.8 percent of China's 2003 export volume by pairs. By the first quarter of 2005, the EU footwear industry was facing the reality that while the number of pairs of Chinese shoes imported into Europe had increased only 2.8 percent year on year, the value of those imports had jumped 30.8 percent—a clear indication that China was quickly moving up the value-added chain, alarming the high-fashion footwear centers in Italy, Spain, and Portugal.[91] In September 2004 in Spain, two Chinese footwear depots were burned and a march against "yellow competition" was banned for fear of violence.[92] As for the EU Commission's attempts to come up with a policy on Chinese (and Vietnamese) shoe exports to the Continent, as of 2006 the commission seemed hopelessly divided between member countries making shoes and the rest who were consumers with an interest in low prices. In textiles and apparel the picture is similar, with the power of the Chinese export machine apparent even before the Multi-Fiber Arrangement quotas expired in January 2005. In 2003–4, total U.S. imports of textiles, textile products, and apparel from China grew 22.2 percent (by dollar value). In the first five months of 2005 (after textile quotas were briefly removed on January 1 and before Washington reimposed surge protections in May consistent with the terms of China's WTO accession agreement), U.S. imports in these same categories jumped 53.6 percent. In specific categories of imports, the leaps were 261.8 percent in non-woven fabrics, 606.5 percent in tire cords and fabrics, and 192.4 percent in male underwear and nightwear. In anticipation of restrictions on its textile exports to the United States, PRC textile manufacturers and exporters began to locate textile and apparel marketing and research and development centers in the United States so they could more effectively compete in the U.S. market, capture value added, and develop their own brands.[93]

These developments must be viewed comparatively—Chinese textile exports were only 8 percent of total U.S.-China trade in 2004. Moreover, as the economist Daniel Rosen points out, the United States exported "just over 4 billion pounds of U.S. grown cotton in 2003 and is one of the world's largest exporters of yarns and fabrics. Textile exports (including cut pieces of U.S. fabric) last year [2004] totaled over $14 billion."[94] Regarding U.S. industry charges that China subsidizes its textile exporters, it is appropriate to observe that U.S. cotton growers received $4.7 billion in government subsidies in 2004—for twenty thousand farmers (amounting to $235,000 each).[95]

For other textile-producing economies (e.g., Mexico, the Philippines, Cambodia, South Africa, and Malaysia), however, Chinese textile power is almost coercive. In September 2005 I asked a group of China scholars from Mexico what was on their minds with respect to the PRC. They responded, "Lots of our manufacturing [has been] lost to China—clothing, toys; it has cost [Mexico] a lot of industry." "Many enterprises are angry. Medium and small enterprises are not competitive [because of] labor costs. Mexico opposed China's entry into WTO very strongly [till the end], but the Mexican government can do nothing because of low Chinese wages."[96]

One Australian analyst explained, "Cambodia fears it will hemorrhage textile jobs—two hundred thousand textile jobs they fear losing with textile quotas off."[97] Other textile-exporting developing nations saw declines in their U.S.-bound exports, showing that once comparative advantage determines production they will suffer from Chinese competition. Research by John Weiss of the Asian Development Bank Institute shows that Malaysia, Thailand, Indonesia, and the Philippines face a broad-based export challenge from the PRC that has resulted in their consistent loss of market share in many manufactured goods to the United States and Japan, even as their exports to China have increased.[98]

The South Koreans, who had seen their steel exports to China grow 26 percent monthly between 2002 and early 2004, saw the rate slow to 5 percent in 2004 as China's own domestic production soared 22 percent that year, reflecting Beijing's sizable investment in its own steel industry. By early 2005, the vice-chairman of Dongbu Steel Company, Kim Jeong-il, was saying, "We have hitherto been exporting a large portion of our steel products to China, but we now face a situation where we will have to compete with China in the global market. . . . The bigger threat is that a large amount of Chinese steel can come into the domestic market."[99]

Though the perception of China as a "buyer" is often positive globally, China as a "seller" creates anxieties that Beijing seeks to assuage. Again we see that all forms of power have multiple expressions—in specific areas of labor-intensive production, China's economic power can appear coercive while China as a buyer presents the visage of an attractive remunerative power. Of course, Chinese counter that their exports keep inflation and consumer prices lower than they otherwise would be. Finally, China has become a mammoth exporter so rapidly that its internal regulatory structures cannot guarantee the quality and safety of many exported goods, some critical components in global supply chains. Likewise, in importing nations the regulation of import safety has proven inadequate.

THE POWER OF THE INVESTOR AND DONOR

Since many of China's most externally active firms have close financial and policy links to the state, the distinction between "private" business and state purposes often is blurred. Consequently, PRC outbound investment and foreign aid are considered together here. The mandate of the PRC's Ministry of Commerce includes regulating inward FDI, working out "administrative measures and specific policies guiding China's overseas investment," and "providing aid to foreign countries and regions."[100] China is pursuing what it calls its "going global" strategy, first sanctioned in general terms by President Jiang Zemin in 1992,[101] solidified in 2001, and accelerated considerably in 2004 when the Ministry of Commerce and Ministry of Foreign Affairs issued guidelines for domestic firms investing abroad.

When President Hu Jintao visited the Philippines in April 2005, for example, "China extended loans and investments worth a combined 1.62 billion dollars," including a $950 million investment by Baosteel and the China Development Bank to redevelop a nickel company; a $500 million loan to extend the rail system to light industry centers; Huawei Technology's agreement to provide $27 million in equipment to Philippine Telecommunications; and a framework agreement for about $10 million in investment for oil and gas exploration.[102] Similarly, in Gabon in February 2004, President Hu Jintao signed three economic accords with Libreville: an oil investment, a grant for agriculture, and a no-interest loan for construction. In oil-rich Nigeria, Chinese rice growers train Nigerians to cultivate the crop, Chinese telecom interests are building communications systems, and Chinese are teaching the Chinese language to Nigerian officials and businesspersons.

Beijing's apparent ability to coordinate foreign aid, state-owned enterprise investment, "nonstate" investment, tariff and other trade policies, debt relief (e.g., $1.3 billion in Africa), and even weapon sales (as in Zimbabwe) would seemingly make it a relatively effective competitor; it seemingly has the potential to act as a coherent aid and business player in a way that other, more pluralized societies do not. Though Beijing also has its bureaucratic struggles over aid policy, the capacity to act relatively cohesively is generally welcomed by the elites of many developing nations. After having been promised a $500 million loan, trade increases, and tariff reductions from Beijing in late 2003, President Musharraf of Pakistan gushed: "The past belongs to Europe, the present belongs to the United States, and the future belongs to Asia."[103]

On the other hand, the easy cooperation of many local elites with Chinese investors and the PRC government can alienate broad swaths of society in developing countries. One influential businessman from East Africa put it this way: "The Chinese come in, build a building, give a government building, an auditorium, a bridge, to the elite and they then make a deal.... Chinese companies came to Mozambique, a team, a disaster. Take timber—export. Not plantations. No value added. Our friends in China need to add value, to build sustainable forests. To add sustainability for the future."[104]

In short, Chinese economic power is not exempt from the political version of Newton's Third Law of Motion—"For every action, there is an equal and opposite reaction." When a great power comes in, makes deals with local elites, has little regard for spillover effects, and uses its own workers rather than local manpower, it creates resentment.

Outbound Investment   According to PRC statistics, as of May 2006 Chinese enterprises were in 160 countries and regions, predominantly in Southeast Asia, with growing numbers going to North America and Europe, and some investments even farther afield. In Singapore, Chinese companies were incorporating at the rate of one hundred per year in the 1993 to 2002 period; in 2003, that rate jumped to two hundred per year.[105] One Wenzhou merchant who is investing in Pyongyang's largest department store said, "This is a great time to get in on the ground floor!"[106] Thomson Financial and Lehman Brothers reported in 2006 that announced Chinese cross-border merger and acquisition activity (where the PRC was the acquirer or global target) was $2.6 billion in 2003, $5.8 billion in 2004, and $9 billion in 2005. China's International Chamber of Commerce reported in late 2005 that about 23 percent of responding firms intended to increase outbound investment over the next year, with larger firms more active than smaller ones, nonstate firms more active than state firms, and the most activity in firms focused on trading, manufacturing, and extractive industries. In December 2006, the China Council for the Promotion of International Trade and the Asia Pacific Foundation of Canada reported that 53 percent of the respondent Chinese firms intended to increase substantially or moderately their outward direct investment within the following two years.[107] By mid-2006, with the establishment of the China Council for International Investment Promotion, Beijing announced that the outward investment of Chinese firms totaled $55 billion,[108] an amount smaller than even a single year of the PRC's inward-bound FDI but a large increase from the total of $7.6 billion at the end of 2000. China's outbound FDI grew 27 percent in 2004 for a yearly total of $3.62 billion, of which $2.51 billion was new funds and $1.11 billion reinvested profits abroad.[109] The following year, 2005, PRC outward FDI reportedly reached a yearly total of $11 billion.[110] Friedrich Wu argues that China's Ministry of Commerce figures understate actual PRC outward FDI.[111] Whatever the absolute size of PRC FDI in 2005–6, it probably will jump dramatically in the future because of a growing private sector, looser control of foreign exchange, and the 2007 creation of a government-controlled investment arm.

Motivations for this external investment include increased foreign competition in China's domestic market (motivating PRC firms to seek markets abroad and get inside protectionist barriers); the search for strategic materials abroad; excess domestic production capacity; risk diversification; the acquisition of brand names; and the quest for technology and skills abroad. These motivations suggest the dominance of commercial, as opposed to political, considerations in PRC outbound FDI decisions; Hong and Sun report that "in terms of key actors, central government has given way to local government and, now, to enterprise-led activity."[112]

As of the end of 2003, 80 percent of China's nonfinancial overseas direct investment was in Asia (and three-quarters of that was in Hong Kong); 14 percent was in Latin America; and small percentages were in the United States, Europe, Africa, and Oceania.[113] This distribution and the scale of investments began to change in 2004 with more investment in Africa, particularly Sub-Saharan Africa. In April 2006 President Hu Jintao signed an oil deal in Nigeria involving $4 billion in investment.[114] Much of this initial drive to invest abroad derived from China's appetite for resources, something somewhat unsettling to other resource importers and contrary to Beijing's general desire to keep a low profile.

Chinese direct investments are also potentially important to Americans, particularly in areas losing employment (like Camden, South Carolina, where Haier Group opened a $30 million plant making refrigerators in March 2000). In Ardmore, Oklahoma, as of 2007, there were uncertain plans to build a Chinese joint venture to run an MG auto plant that would employ about 550 people.[115] This latter deal reflects China's determination both to control its own global brand names and to strategically invest around the world, thereby giving other societies a vested interest in keeping trade channels open through providing employment in importing countries. As an article in the August 2006 issue of *Caijing* (Finance) magazine put it, "An effective and long-term solution [to China's image problem in the United States] is to build a factory or to set up a company on the soil of the United States. This means hiring American employees—their influence over the congressmen from their constituency is much stronger than any foreign institution or enterprise."[116]

Chinese investment is important to other countries and localities as well. Brazil has sought massive funds for its steel, iron, and transport industries. In Britain, a study by GLA Economics on London's receipt of FDI from the PRC, Hong Kong, Taiwan, and Singapore showed that though the average employment per project is small, the number of PRC investment projects going into London is growing faster than those from Taiwan, Singapore, and Hong Kong and that among investment projects since 2002 those from China and Hong Kong are the most numerous.[117] The prospect of additional Chinese investment and trade is motivating London (and much of the EU) to cultivate Beijing, with the mayor of London, Ken Livingstone, noting, "I have taken the decision to open offices of the Mayor of London first in Beijing and then in Shanghai to strengthen London and the UK's economic and cultural links with China."[118]

Russia also is actively seeking Chinese investment to develop its resources, particularly in its far east, though its citizens in the region are leery of a significant Chinese presence. With Chinese investment in Russia totaling $500 million in 2003, the Russian trade minister announced in June 2004 plans to lease Russian forests for ninety-nine years and invited PRC participation. Also in 2004, a Chinese company in Heilongjiang leased a Russian coal mine in Sakhalin for forty-nine years, contracting to restore roads, electricity networks, and machinery in the bankrupt enterprise. And in 2005, Sinopec acquired Russian oil assets west of the Ural Mountains by purchasing a stake in Udmurtneft. Beijing is making the same demands on Moscow for a favorable investment climate that foreigners have long made on China itself. In 2004 meetings with Russian officials, the head of the State Development and Reform Commission, Ma Kai, said, "We'll increase the number of licenses [for investment] if we're convinced that Russia's regional and federal authorities do their best to create [favorable] conditions for China's capital."[119]

If one considers China's financial holdings abroad, including $327.7 billion in U.S. Treasury securities (as of June 2006), China's investment abroad is very large. Increasingly Chinese financial institutions such as insurance companies and the National Social Security Fund are assessing where they can most profitably place their assets abroad.[120] In 2006 the Chinese government permitted individuals to legally take investment funds ($20,000 per year) out of the country and was developing rules whereby domestic securities firms could raise private funds for investment abroad.[121]

In this investment activity China is using three levers—the power to generate employment, the power (through acquisition of U.S. debt in particular) to influence global interest rates, and the provision of capital itself. While one should not exaggerate these effects, each is increasing. It is becoming important, for example, where China places its enormous foreign exchange reserves and which countries' tangible assets Beijing acquires. Beijing increasingly would like to hold productive, growing U.S. assets, as opposed to being invested so heavily in low-yield debt instruments. Indeed, then U.S. Treasury Secretary Robert Rubin advised the Chinese in 1997 that they would be better off using their large U.S. debt holdings more productively.[122] As they do, the employment effects of China's investments will grow for the United States and everywhere Chinese assets are located. This will set off competition among potential recipients of investment. To the extent that the United States permits the PRC to acquire vast quantities of U.S. dollars through its own bilateral trade deficits and simultaneously refuses to sell China tangible assets, it generates resentment in Beijing.

At the same time that these outbound investments give China attractive power, in some domains (particularly strategic resources and high tech) they create anxieties, as seen in U.S. congressional reaction to CNOOC's already mentioned attempt to buy Unocal and earlier concerns with the sale of IBM's PC division to Lenovo in 2005. In mid-2007, some concerns were expressed in the U.S. Congress and elsewhere about China's plans to make a $3 billion investment in the American private-equity group Blackstone; the U.S. Treasury said the deal did not merit a national security investigation. As one senior Australian explained about Chinese FDI in general: "We ask ourselves, how soft is Chinese soft power? FDI is growing and welcomed by recipients. But in contrast to other FDI, as distinct from the ROK, Taiwan, and Japan, it is state enterprise driven. In other countries it is private sector. So Chinese FDI is subject to administrative control."[123] A global business entrepreneur in Indonesia put it this way when discussing FDI in the energy field: "If an oil field is worth 100 to Exxon-Mobil, it is worth 110 to China. There is a major difference. To China, oil is a strategic interest and CNOOC represents this state strategic interest, so they are willing to pay for their interests. Exxon-Mobil doesn't have this dimension of strategic interest."[124] Brazilian and Argentinean negotiators for Chinese investment in 2004 saw a linkage between fund commitments and their designation of Beijing as a "market economy," which would make it difficult to impose antidumping penalties on the PRC.[125] Editorial writers at the *Toronto Star* reacted to Chinese attempts at acquiring a Canadian mining firm, Noranda, by asking what it would mean for Canada's ability to speak out on human rights: "Do we want Beijing making political demands of us, while holding Canadian jobs hostage?"[126] And because Chinese multinational corporations often receive financing from PRC governmental entities, the issues of subsidization and unfair advantage attach to some potential investments, as was the case in CNOOC's attempted Unocal acquisition.

Promises of FDI hold other dangers for China. In November 2004 President Hu Jintao visited several Latin American countries, including Brazil and Argentina, and promised $100 billion to the region over the next ten years. These promises were well received, given that the region as a whole had experienced declining FDI since 2000. Yet by 2006 there already were grumbles in the region that actual investments were not matching Beijing's promises.

Development and Humanitarian Assistance   In the 1960s China was a significant aid donor, particularly in Africa, using assistance as one tool in its struggles against the Soviet Union and the United States. Given the small size of its GNP at that time, Beijing's foreign aid represented a significant burden on a nearly destitute economy.[127] Construction on the Tanzam Railroad started in 1970 and was the largest showpiece project of that era. In the 1980s and 1990s, however, China concentrated on its own development problems, entered the Bretton Woods Institutions, and began to receive large infusions of Japanese overseas development assistance (ODA), initially for infrastructure development and subsequently for environment-related projects. Nonetheless, over time, China has received diminishing development assistance—$2.456 billion in 1998 and only $1.325 billion in 2003.[128] And with respect to the net financial flows from multilateral institutions (the World Bank, the IMF, and regional development banks), the PRC had a net outflow in 2002, a somewhat bigger net outflow in 2003, and a small net inflow in 2004.[129]

While China is not such a large recipient of aid funds any longer, neither is it a major donor-player in development and humanitarian assistance, though precise statistics are absent. Of the fourteen official tasks that the Ministry of Commerce enumerates in its mission statement, the first ten relate to regulation and development of China's domestic commerce, foreign trade and related issues, and inward foreign investment. Only the eleventh task deals with foreign aid.

Though development assistance is generally limited, it is increasing, and Beijing

FIGURE 8

In November 2004, President Hu Jintao visited several Latin American
countries, promising investment and enhanced economic and space cooperation. During this journey Hu also visited Cuba for two days. Presidents
Hu and Castro met on November 22, 2004, in the Palace of the Revolution
in Havana. It is perhaps significant that Castro had his fist clenched and arm
raised in a revolutionary gesture, body language that Hu did not duplicate.
Claudia Daut/Reuters/Corbis.

is starting to recognize the soft power gains to be made through development assistance and humanitarian efforts, along with military aid. While Chinese capabilities
to rapidly and massively introduce aid and humanitarian assistance were limited in
the aftermath of the tsunami disaster of December 26, 2004, Beijing began to move
in several new directions (such as sending limited military and medical personnel to
the region) that signaled its intention to gradually play a more prominent role in the
region. Beijing pledged $65 million to tsunami relief, plus another $18 million in private relief funds for a total of $83 million, though the amount seems small in com-
parison to Japan's $500 million and Washington's $950 million (plus 13,000 U.S.
troops promptly dispatched to disaster-stricken areas, and perhaps $1 billion in pri-

vate donations).[130] The PRC leadership was stung by the comparison between its efforts and those of Washington and Tokyo during the tsunami disaster. A PRC ministerial-level official told me that

> China's response to the tsunami is not equal to the United States and others. This is our first time, we are not so experienced. . . . In the beginning, China did not have such a precise assessment of the tsunami, we mentioned a small sum, but in two days we increased the sum of relief. . . . So actually, in the initial stage, the U.S. criticized us for donating too little. . . . If compared to the U.S., China has twenty to thirty million poor. The Chinese population is poorer than the international average, and the tsunami countries have not yet put forth their demands. . . . So now we don't have a clear action plan and we need close consultations according to needs.[131]

It will take time for China to become a major provider of global development aid and humanitarian assistance, though the PRC now is transitioning from net recipient to net donor. It is a significant player in Africa, where since 2000 Beijing has written off over \$1 billion in bilateral debt for various countries,[132] and in late 2006 it pledged to double its aid for Africa by 2009.[133] China's participation in the UN's World Food Program (WFP) is emblematic. The WFP was slated to make its last donation to China in 2005 after having helped for thirty years. Looking forward, the WFP hopes Beijing will become a significant donor, with the organization's director, James Morris, saying, "I'm hoping over time China will become more supportive of our work in Africa. . . . I think we'll see over the next 25 years, China will become one of our most important friends."[134] Indeed, in mid-2006 the WFP announced that for 2005 China had donated 576,582 metric tons of food to twelve countries: the principal recipient was North Korea, and small amounts went to Liberia, Guinea Bissau, Sri Lanka, and others.

China's foreign aid policy has two characteristics: it is interest based, and it comes without the political, human rights, and environmental conditionality that many recipient regimes find troublesome. Beijing generally asks little of aid recipients other than that they recognize the "one China" principle and that they be important to China's economic and/or strategic interests. What Peter Van Ness told us in the early 1970s remains true. "In this regard, communist internationalism to the contrary notwithstanding, the CCP's primary constituency—one is tempted to say its only constituency—is the 750 million people of China; and the task of creating, developing, and defending a viable society within the boundaries of the People's

Republic is the overriding first priority."[135] As one diplomat from Benin put it when Hu Jintao passed up a visit to his long-friendly country in early 2004 to go to oil-exporting Gabon, "This tells me that China has no friends but rather only interests."[136]

The Chinese modus operandi often is welcome, an approach that then vice minister of foreign affairs Zhou Wenzhong laid out plainly in 2004: "Business is business. . . . We try to separate politics from business. . . . You [the West] have tried to impose a market economy and multiparty democracy on these countries, which are not ready for it. We are also against embargoes, which you have tried to use against us."[137] China's growing investment in, trade with, and aid to neighboring Myanmar have weakened U.S. sanctions against the country, for example, and in early 2007 Beijing and Moscow joined together to veto a U.S.-backed resolution in the UN Security Council proposing to condemn political persecution by the regime. Western donor and investing nations, multilateral development banks, and members of the U.S. Congress all fear that Beijing's lack of conditionality reduces their leverage to secure good governance and human rights in Myanmar and worldwide. Sierra Leone's ambassador to China, Sahr Johnny, put it crisply: "They [the Chinese] just come and do it [give aid and build projects]. We don't start to hold meetings about environmental impact assessments and human rights and bad governance. I'm not saying that's the right thing to do. I'm just saying Chinese investment [and aid] is succeeding because they don't set very high benchmarks."[138] The head of Nigeria's Investment Promotion Commission said, "The U.S. will talk to you about governance, about efficiency, about security, about the environment," but "the Chinese just ask, 'How do we procure this license?'"[139]

Not making investment and aid conditional on conformity with politically onerous external standards can itself be a powerful idea, a form of ideational power (discussed in the next chapter) bound up with concepts of sovereignty and self-determination. On the other hand, extending aid to elites alienated from their own people and widely perceived as odious is at odds with the overall thrust of China's foreign policy, which is to be viewed as a responsible stakeholder in the international system. Against the backdrop of this dilemma, it is noteworthy that in early 2007 Beijing at least wanted to appear somewhat more proactive in using its leverage on the Sudanese government to peacefully resolve the problems of mass killings in Darfur.

Providing aid does not always give the donor much leverage; indeed, it sometimes reflects the absence of other power options. This is what one finds in Beijing's relations with North Korea. Realist that it is, Beijing provides aid to Pyongyang to secure fundamental interests such as avoiding the North's collapse, preventing war on the peninsula, and preserving a buffer state. When I asked one Chinese intellectual why Beijing provided so much aid to a regime that repeatedly has compromised PRC interests, he answered (paraphrase): "To take something away [from North Korea], you first have to give them something." This logic partly accounts for China's supplying of North Korea with a large percentage of its energy needs and then having a "technical problem" with the oil pipeline in early 2003, using the supply interruption to create pressure on Pyongyang to join multilateral talks about its nuclear efforts. This is power of a very peculiar sort. Beijing is not buying good behavior but hoping to procure less bad behavior from Pyongyang.

The case of North Korea underscores two paradoxes of power. First, though Beijing is far stronger than Pyongyang, North Korea has parlayed its weakness and destabilizing behavior into a near-extortion game, knowing that the PRC is committed to stability on the border and that it prefers a divided Korean peninsula to a unified and stronger state under the potential sway of another power(s). Weakness can be strength. Second, while one normally considers aid to be an attractive expression of remunerative power, it can be coercive when Beijing uses the interruption of that aid as a threat.

Mongolia has experienced this type of coercion—a curtailment of rail transportation by Beijing in retaliation for a late 2002 visit to Ulan Bator by the Dalai Lama. Subsequently, Mongolia was reluctant to accept a June 2003 aid offer from visiting President Hu Jintao. Mongolian Prime Minister Tsakhilganiin Elbegdorj explained that "this is the heart of [our] policy"—"not to be too dependent on one country." "Mongolians are concerned that after [paying the Russian debt] we could also become a debtor to other countries, to China." The velvet glove of economic power can obscure the brass knuckles of coercion.[140]

THE POWER OF THE INNOVATOR

Because innovation has its roots in the realm of ideas, the topic is treated in the following chapter. Suffice it to say here that innovation is a multifaceted phenomenon: it includes development of transformational technologies (invention); process innovation, whereby products are made ever more efficiently; the capacity to put old components together in new ways; and the capacity to find new applications for current technologies. China is not yet a force in developing transformational technologies, but it has more immediate potential to be an innovative force in application, process, and productivity enhancement. Innovation is an important component of ideational power and an attractive asset.

ECONOMIC POWER AND CHINA'S REGIONAL ROLE

While in the 1980s and 1990s China eschewed an international "leadership role," since the turn of the millennium it has been converting its power as buyer, investor, and assistance provider and its position as a key link in global production chains into a regional leadership role that it now embraces, along with increasing power in international economic institutions such as the IMF. Here we focus on China's regional clout.

Vientiane, Laos, and November 29, 2004, are a place and a date to remember in terms of China's ascent as a regional leader. Chinese Premier Wen Jiabao delivered an extraordinary speech at the eighth leadership summit of ASEAN plus China, Japan, and the Republic of Korea ("10 + 3"). In remarks larded with talk of "win-win" cooperation, reassurance that integration would be a "long-term process," and calls for "openness, transparency and inclusiveness," Wen proposed a protracted process of deepening regional cooperation and integration in which ASEAN would be a driving force and China, South Korea, and Japan would be partners. This process was to culminate in a (vaguely defined) East Asian Community. Initially the process would build upon the foundation of the ASEAN Economic Community, through the development of individual bilateral free-trade areas (FTAs) between ASEAN and China, Japan, and South Korea. Concurrently, China, Japan, and Korea would examine the possibility of bilateral FTAs among themselves. Moreover, against the backdrop of the 1997–98 Asian Financial Crisis, the premier said in this speech that "priority should be given in East Asia to using the rich foreign exchange reserve[s] and capital within the region, improving the investment and financing environment and building risk prevention and control capacity in the financial sector"—for example, financial and trade crisis management. Wen also included security, calling for an expansion of "security dialogue" and cooperation on other transnational issues.[141] In one stroke Beijing painted a picture of increasing economic and security cooperation from Southeast Asia to East and Northeast Asia, with the 10 + 3 unit of the ASEAN Secretariat playing a key role, culminating in an "East Asian Community."

Beijing is using its allure as a buyer and investor as the catalyst for such cooperation. One obstacle to 10 + 3 cooperation is the complex tensions among China, Japan, and South Korea. Another impediment is the wish of China's smaller neighbors such as Indonesia and Singapore to have a unit of cooperation that includes the United States and/or some of its allies, such as Australia, New Zealand, and perhaps India. Two issues underlie this tension: How do China's neighbors look at the prospect of a more powerful China in an increasingly integrated region (examined in chapter 5)? And what implications does this have for America? Beijing prefers a more closed regionalism than many of its neighbors, defining the "region" in such a way as to maximize its own sway. In the run-up to the East Asian Summit of December 2005, China and Thailand took the position that ASEAN + 3 was the "core" and that they did not want the mention of a wider community, fearing that efforts to draw into the community other nations such as India, Australia, and New Zealand were designed, in the words of *People's Daily*, to make those nations "serve as a counterbalance to China."[142] As one senior Chinese diplomat put it in February 2005, "We don't need to invite the U.S. into all regional organizations. . . . To be offended is unreasonable."[143]

The region is ambivalent because most of China's neighbors see opportunities and challenges in China's growing economic and security roles. They generally have adopted the Gulliver strategy—entangle China in a web of interests and constraints that collectively keep its range of motion limited. They have few illusions about China. While recognizing the coercive dimension of China's economic power, most neighbors also see potential advantages, sharing the views of one well-placed Singaporean analyst. "We see China making impressive strategic advances using the economic card. They are more confident in multilateral forums, they are trying to get in the driver's seat to get their objectives. . . . China's free-trade area proposal, and later including Japan and the ROK, all represent recognition of the importance of soft power. They have adroitly handled border disputes with India and the South China Sea. . . . China's efforts are beginning to pay off—[the region is] signing on with China as a growth engine. . . . This has boosted China's confidence."[144]

IMPLICATIONS FOR THE UNITED STATES

Americans need to keep two contradictory thoughts in mind: first, Chinese power and influence in East Asia are growing, but this does not necessarily foretell American decline unless Washington misplays its cards; and second, Asian nations both need and want U.S involvement in the region but do not want this involvement to be too intrusive. The United States remains Asia's principal end market, and this gives America leverage to win reciprocal access in the region. As for the security dimension, Asian nations generally trust a distant America to be the regional military balancer more than they trust one another. They want an unobtrusive U.S. security presence that is not provocative.

Washington must be skillful. It is extraordinary that neither Japan nor Australia could induce Malaysia, the convening nation (with the backing of China), to include Washington in the East Asia Summit held in Kuala Lumpur in December 2005, a meeting that included the 10 + 3 as well as India, Australia, and New Zealand—every U.S. ally in the region. It is even more sobering that all the attendees at the summit had to first agree to sign the 1976 Treaty of Amity and Cooperation, which includes a renunciation of the use or threat of force and a pledge not to threaten the sovereignty and territorial integrity of contracting parties. This creates additional ambiguity about how U.S. allies would respond to a Washington-Beijing conflict in the Taiwan Strait.

A similar tussle over U.S. involvement on China's periphery occurred in July 2005 when the SCO agreed to ask Washington to withdraw its forces from Central Asia by a date certain. This posed problems for Washington, which needed these facilities to efficiently prosecute the war in Afghanistan; U.S. forces ultimately were withdrawn from Uzbekistan. While the impetus for the move probably came more from Uzbekistani leader Karimov's fallout with Washington (and Beijing blames Russia in conversations with Americans), Beijing was not averse to Karimov's moves. Whether or not China's total investment of $1.6 billion in SCO countries as of 2003, and $19.7 billion in trade that year,[145] made the Chinese inclination more potent is open to debate.

From Beijing's perspective, promoting Asian regional integration that keeps the United States at arm's length helps create an environment that constrains Washington. To offset this effort, the United States has many resources in Asia, but it must use them skillfully. Washington cannot simply seek to strengthen ties with India, Japan, the Republic of Korea, and central Asian states as an explicit offset to rising Chinese power and then be surprised when Beijing plays the same game. Countries such as India and South Korea do not wish to be viewed as pawns in the strategic games of others. Much of China's leverage derives from its economic strength. However, the more Beijing tries to exclude America from surrounding areas, the more motivated many in these areas become to keep Washington in the picture—Beijing has to play its cards carefully too.

Continued, high-speed economic growth is likely to continue in the PRC for a considerable period measured in decades. It would be a strategic misstep to assume otherwise, given the powerful drivers of growth at work. China is a continent whose eastern edge is the only region that is comparatively developed. Like America in the nineteenth century, the PRC has to move developmentally across a very large expanse. This will not only take time but also drive growth.

Strengthening its economic power and building what Beijing hopes will be a stabilizing middle class is the foundation of China's national grand strategy. Economic power is the most convertible form of power, giving Beijing remunerative strength, coercive options, and normative attraction in a world that respects this power. Though China's neighbors are somewhat anxious about its growing strength, they simultaneously hope that the strategy of enmeshing the PRC in a network of constraining relationships and interests will serve to reap the benefits of economic cooperation while keeping the PRC's coercive strength at bay. At the same time, both China's neighbors and more distant nations in Latin America and Africa are antagonized when the PRC throws its economic weight around with little regard for local needs. Though Beijing's economic strength affords opportunities to forge new relationships and exercise influence, its misuse can elicit hostility.

The PRC's mounting economic strength also is altering U.S. relations with its post–World War II allies. As the Chinese economic juggernaut has moved forward, NATO, the Republic of Korea, increasingly Australia, and others such as Thailand and Israel have emphasized economic opportunity in China, while America and Japan have been more concerned about the security implications of China's rise.

Interdependence increasingly is creating a situation in which the outside world cannot be indifferent to either China's successes or its failures. Any major economic failures in the PRC will quickly become world problems (as seen in the early 2007 contagious effects of the Shanghai stock market's decline on markets globally), and China's successes will bring many positive contributions to global welfare. With respect to possible failures, Paul Speltz, the U.S. economic and financial emissary to Beijing for the George W. Bush administration, put it this way: "China is not an island unto itself anymore; China has succeeded so well that if you sneeze here [Beijing], it's felt in Tokyo, Seoul and London, immediately."[146] With respect to successes, as the PRC occupies its natural economic niches by capitalizing on high savings, relatively educated, healthy, and abundant labor, and a large domestic market, other nations will need to adjust by finding new niches and moving up the value-added chain by increasing R&D, boosting productive investment, expanding their pools of highly educated and skilled personnel, and lowering the relative costs of social overhead. The costs that these adjustments impose will be unwelcome to many and will ignite political conflict within and among societies. How China manages and regulates its own economy will continue to be a subject of international debate, as seen in international criticisms of China's banking system, investment policies, and weak regulation of export industries.

The PRC's economic strength is grounded more in its roles of "buyer" and "investor" than in its role of "seller." The role of seller often generates fear, while the roles of "buyer" and "investor" provide leverage and appeal. Though the money China earns from the export of goods and services is fundamental, its roles as buyer and investor are what wins the PRC influence that a more import- and FDI-closed Japan, for example, has not enjoyed. Beijing has given outsiders an interest in its success.

China's economic power has advanced several national objectives: keeping the regime in power, promoting human welfare at home, and bringing China the international status it has so long sought. The PRC's economic attraction has fostered an environment of reduced threat around its periphery, thereby permitting Beijing to remain focused on domestic concerns and keeping defense spending within tolerable bounds. China's economic power attracts U.S. allies and friends globally, reducing the support Washington could expect were it to pursue a confrontational course with the PRC. As one Australian official put it in talking about the need for the United States to manage ties with Beijing carefully—"We will go up a hill with you but not march over the cliff."[147] In August 2005 Singapore's Lee Kuan Yew underscored this point: "South Korea today has the largest number of foreign students in China. They see their future in China. So, the only country that's openly on America's side is Japan. All the others are either neutral or friendly to China."[148]

In appreciating Beijing's growing economic sway, however, one should not imagine an eight-foot giant. Chapter 6 examines the myriad ways in which progress could be disrupted. China faces huge obstacles that are central features of its current situation. A principal reality of China is that when one looks at it in aggregate terms it is huge, but when it is seen in per capita terms it is still poor. China is strong and weak, rich and poor, all at once.

Moreover, economic power has some self-limiting characteristics. Excessive and unbalanced selling elicits protectionist responses. The export of dangerous products generates fear and export restraints. Attempts to buy sensitive assets abroad produce counter-reactions. Even when one acquires foreign assets, what it means to "own" and "control" them remains uncertain, and as China locates manufacturing capacity abroad to get inside protectionist walls, this too may elicit counter-reactions. Finally, with China's global economic strength and involvement have come ever-higher degrees of interdependence and vulnerability, vulnerabilities that lead Beijing to diversify partners and sources, acquire more coercive power, and maintain and safeguard the common international infrastructure.

In the nineteenth century national success was ensured by controlling (occupying) resources and markets. In the twentieth century, three empires (Germany,

Japan, and the Soviet Union) sought to continue and expand this practice, efforts that generated two world wars and a global cold war. In each case the aggressor collapsed or was destroyed. China's leaders explicitly refer to the lessons of the twentieth century, and indeed in 2006 the Chinese Academy of Social Sciences released an eight-disc DVD educational film entitled "Consider Danger in Times of Peace—Historical Lessons from the Fall of the CPSU." Lessons of history aside, the interdependencies and weaknesses described above suggest that the strategies available to rising powers in the nineteenth century and the first half of the twentieth century are not available to China today. Beijing's range of motion is limited, not least by the decades-long task of domestic modernization that lies before it.

The world must plan for a China with more economic strength and more options. Nonetheless, the PRC is increasingly tethered to a global economic system that naturally keeps it from exercising unbridled power. The current defining characteristic of Chinese foreign policy is the desire to minimize friction with almost everyone. This brings us to "ideational power," or the power of minds.

Through international competition Chinese enterprises
have improved themselves. Some say the world is a
global village because of the information revolution—
this is true. But in this village you find rich and poor
and not everyone is happy. For example, in U.S.-China
competition, we are not equal in position because of U.S.
science and technology. We don't have complaints; that
is the reality. Competition will bring us forward—we
have been closed too long.

NATIONAL PEOPLE'S CONGRESS CHAIRMAN LI PENG,
August 2000

They [the Chinese] have negative soft power—it
[Beijing] doesn't nag about human rights and good
governance, and that goes down pretty well in the
region. Soft power, movies, culture do exist, are part
of the scene, but it varies by country. China is setting
up Confucian Institutes, like the Goethe Institutes, and
this resonates well in Asia—twenty years ago [China
was] seen as subversive. The Olympics has the potential
to leverage it all. They are just being China.

AUSTRALIAN OFFICIAL, June 2005

Interviewer: What surprises you most about America?
Jack Ma: Five years ago, what really surprised me—the
    passion, the innovation. Today I see that in China.

JACK MA, Chinese founder of Alibaba.com
Corporation, 2006

We only export computers, not revolution.

ZHENG BIJIAN, chairman of China Reform Forum,
November 2005

Outside observers, particularly Americans, are likely to be surprised by China's ideational power. Since 1978 China's ideational power has gained strength from the success of its rapid economic development and in turn has fostered that economic growth both directly and indirectly. China's fourth-generation leaders have made a clear decision to strengthen their nation's ideational power, or what others somewhat differently term "soft power."[1]

Ideational power is that form of power that does not rely primarily upon material ("money") rewards or coercion ("might") but rather derives from the intellectual, cultural, spiritual, leadership, and legitimacy resources that enhance a nation's capacity to efficiently define and achieve national objectives. Much like Joseph Nye's "soft power," ideational power rests on attraction. When Amitai Etzioni defined "normative power," he had in mind the capacity to motivate using ideas and social approval—creating group norms with which individuals wish to identify. These are key dimensions of what I call ideational power. However, ideational power is broader because it includes leadership, human resources, innovation, and culture. Nor is ideational power identical to "soft power" as Nye defined it,[2] though it is also close. Ideational power is broader inasmuch as it explicitly embraces innovation and considers political and diplomatic leadership. Like Nye's soft power, ideational power has its wellsprings in a nation's culture, political values, and external policies—its potential for intellectual attraction.

Ideational power is not manifest simply in ideological attractiveness ("The Shining City on the Hill") and the ability to create national unity based on shared belief. What a nation "stands for" can be a great source of national power, as it has often been for America, but so also can be what one "stands against." Moreover, some cultures reinforce modernization efforts and attract others, thereby enhancing their national capacities. China's traditional culture has great attractive power; Mao Zedong's efforts to eradicate "the four olds" (old customs, habits, culture, and social thought) denied China an important dimension of national power and influence. Today's leaders in Beijing seek to capitalize on this previously latent resource.

The caliber of a nation's leadership (including its diplomats) is another key component of ideational power, inasmuch as leaders are central to defining national objectives and strategies to achieve them and efficiently implementing policies. Along with leadership, however, legitimacy must be considered. The brittle legitimacy of the PRC's regime in the eyes of its own people is among its greatest disabilities in this third realm of power.

Ideational power is a very useful face of power; Chinese since Sun Tzu have attached particular importance to some, but by no means all, elements of it.

Ideational power can be the most economical face of power, often requiring less output of financial, material, and human resources: often it is more cost-effective to achieve people's compliance by instilling a wish to behave in the desired fashion or the belief that such behavior is "right" than by bribing or coercing them. Ideational power also is critical because in its innovative dimensions it is essential to realizing economic development and improved standards of living. In its diplomatic expression, ideational power, particularly as Beijing is seeking to use it, is reassuring. Reassurance is central to Beijing's national strategy because reassuring both near and distant states about the future use of its growing coercive and economic strengths is central to securing more breathing space for internal development.

Although China is strong along some dimensions of ideational power, it remains weak along others. On the whole, however, one should not underestimate China's current and future capacities in this realm. In terms of broad national strategy, Beijing is emphasizing economic and ideational power. If the United States responds to this power mix by overinvesting in coercive power instead of expanding its own economic and intellectual capabilities, it will be making a monumental strategic mistake.

LEADERSHIP AND HUMAN RESOURCES

Leadership and human resources are fundamental to ideational power. This is particularly true for China, with its Confucian heritage in which the cultivation of leaders to guide the population is a central state function. In two separate interviews with senior PRC officials I was struck by their respective assertions: "I believe that the most treasured thing for China is Chinese leaders"[3] and "We train the best leaders in the world. Our cadre training system is such a big system; there are many tests [in a career]."[4] Lee Kuan Yew has similarly claimed that "the quality of people in charge of China is impressive. . . . They have capacious minds, analytical and quick on the uptake."[5] One Singaporean economist put it this way, "The good thing is that they [Beijing's leaders] learn so fast—they learn faster than we do. The CCP [Chinese Communist Party] is extraordinary—not weak—look at the leadership renewal. There is a system that grows good young people and guides them to power in corporations, the military, and government. This is a smart system, though more rigid than I would like. It shows intelligence. I am not one of those who see a coming collapse. . . . This is not a low-grade system."[6]

Deng Xiaoping, who died in early 1997, nearly two decades after launching reform in 1978, is in a leadership league of his own. His central contributions as a leader fall into three categories: (1) redefining the goal of political and national life from class struggle to economic growth; (2) staking China's future on global integration; and (3) cultivating and institutionalizing a technocratic elite. These ideas set the PRC on a course of sustained development. The resulting performance has attracted the interest and investment of the rest of the world to China.

Leadership is the act of defining goals, devising strategies and tactics for their achievement, matching resources and ambitions, motivating followers to work for the specified goals, and overseeing a complex process of implementation. Deng Xiaoping possessed these capacities. During a meeting in the early 1980s with Robert McNamara, then World Bank president, Deng made it clear that he wanted to work with the World Bank to transform China. McNamara recounts that meeting:

> Twenty-five years ago [as president of the World Bank] I spoke with Deng Xiaoping about his objectives. They were to quadruple the Chinese GDP by 2000 and to expand the welfare of his people. People in the U.S. don't understand this accomplishment. He accomplished clear objectives. . . . He required senior executives to assume responsibility for moving toward the objectives. Deng Xiaoping required all senior people in his cabinet to read the summary volume of the eight-volume World Bank assessment that had been made of the Chinese economy. And officials all knew the main social welfare indicators on poverty reduction nationwide over time. His priorities were the military in the last place. He provided incentives. The result was 8 percent growth in agriculture—unheard of.[7]

At almost every turning point since 1978 Western analysts have underestimated what Chinese leaders could accomplish. Perhaps this was understandable in 1978: those who came of age during the Cold War, the "Great Leap Forward," and the wave of political campaigns culminating in the decade-long (1966–76) Cultural Revolution would have found it almost impossible to envision the changes that the transition from Mao Zedong to Deng Xiaoping foretold. After the 1989 Tiananmen tragedy, when the slow-motion transition from Deng Xiaoping to Jiang Zemin began in the 1990s, most Western analysts labeled Jiang as a weak, "transitional" figure and underestimated his staying power and the change that occurred during his long tenure in office (1989–2002)—the PRC's entry into the WTO being one example. Then, as Jiang headed for the sidelines in 2002, his successor, Hu Jintao, was seen as a gray bureaucratic climber who would take a long time to consolidate power, if he could do it at all. Yet within two years of Hu's assumption of the top position, he was in a much stronger position than anticipated and initiating policy departures, though not the political liberalization so many Westerners hoped for.

The contours of change are clear. Since the late 1970s, when Deng moved into the role of supreme leader, the average age of senior leadership in China has dropped and the average educational level has risen dramatically. The initial leadership group, which was mostly from the cosmopolitan coastal regions, is now being leavened under Hu Jintao with more appointments from inland areas. The educational backgrounds of the leadership have become progressively more diverse below the Politburo. In the country's supreme decision-making body, the nine-person Politburo Standing Committee selected at the 2002 Sixteenth Party Congress, all members were engineers, most were from coastal areas, and most spoke a foreign language. At this same party congress it was decided to formally allow "entrepreneurs" to join the Communist Party. Regarding military leadership, younger officers moving up the ranks are more educated, more technically and professionally proficient, and somewhat more cosmopolitan. The dimension of political leadership that remains largely unchanged is the very small role women play at the most senior levels.

If one wants to anticipate what tomorrow's Chinese central political elite will look like, the best single place to search is in the pool of today's provincial leaders.[8] Governors in the United States provide a reservoir from which U.S. presidents have often been drawn; a similar process is at work in China. Of the year 2004 Politburo members, 83 percent had served previously as provincial chiefs or their deputies, and many Chinese provinces are bigger than most European countries.[9] Of the sixty-two top provincial leaders in China that Professor Cheng Li studied in 2005, the oldest was sixty-six years old and the youngest fifty, with the average age being fifty-nine. Six had PhDs, fourteen had MAs, and almost all had at least a college education, with a few having graduated from junior colleges. Twenty of these provincial leaders had graduated in engineering and thirteen in economics.[10] There was only one woman among the sixty-two leaders.

The new provincial chiefs appointed in the 2004 Fourth Plenum of the Sixteenth Central Committee were a group that presumably reflected Hu Jintao's priorities for future promotion. Most of these relatively young leaders had received education in economics and management, a high percentage had advanced degrees, most served in inland areas or the northeast, *none* came from high-ranking families ("princelings"), and most had long-standing close ties to Hu Jintao through the Chinese Communist Youth League.[11]

With respect to civil-military relations and the characteristics of military leadership more narrowly, the situation has changed dramatically from one in which almost all of the most senior civilian leaders had military experience (1978) to one in which the senior civilian political leaders have none. Another important contrast is that in the military those now leading the PLA have risen through the ranks, with the exception of the chairman of the party's CMC, Hu Jintao. In today's PLA, appointments and promotion are driven largely by institutional procedures and professional criteria. The CMC is largely composed of military leaders—those responsible for the military's central bureaucratic structures and service branches. Reflecting the movement of PLA doctrine away from conventional land warfare, leaders from the air force, the navy, and the second artillery have assumed more importance, particularly since the fall of 2004.[12] This evolution of military leadership is associated with some fundamental changes in the PLA that David Shambaugh catalogs: "Recruitment into the PLA is now based predominantly on technical criteria. The military's mission today is almost exclusively external, to protect national security, rather than internal security. The role of ideology is virtually nil, and political work has declined substantially. . . . In place of the earlier informality and personalization of command and control, the military is now also subject to a large number of laws and regulations."[13]

To understand leadership in today's China, however, it is insufficient to simply analyze the predominantly middle-aged to older men on the Standing Committee of the Politburo, the Politburo, the Central Committee, and the CMC. Nor is leadership simply about staffing the PRC's enormous state and territorial bureaucracies—thirty-one provincial-level administrative units (twenty-two provinces, five autonomous regions, four municipalities [Beijing, Shanghai, Tianjin, and Chongqing]); two special administrative regions (Hong Kong and Macau); 333 divisions at the prefecture level; 2,861 units at the county level; 44,067 units at the township level; and 625,000 villages. Increasingly an evaluation of leadership must include an assessment of those responsible for directing China's rapidly growing key state and private enterprises. As the role of private enterprises continues to grow and absorb many of China's most talented people, these individuals are clearly influencing the political system in many ways, though, as the works of Bruce Dickson, Margaret Pearson, and Kang Xiaoguang suggest, these individuals may make corporatist common cause with the current party elite rather than struggling against it in ways likely to rapidly produce a "democratic" outcome.[14]

One of the most important phenomena in China is the character of emerging leadership in both state and private enterprises and these leaders' movement into the Communist Party. At the Sixteenth Party Congress in 2002, for example, "a total of

24 entrepreneurs from large state-owned enterprises, collective firms, joint ventures, and commercial banks were selected to serve on the 356-member 16th Central Committee as full or alternate members."[15] In 2004, 34 percent of private enterprise owners were CCP members.[16] Jae Cheol Kim's research shows that increasing numbers of entrepreneurs are joining the party, people's congresses, and political consultative congresses at various levels.[17] And in the first half of 2007, two persons who were not members of the Communist Party were appointed ministers: Chen Zhu as minister of public health and Wan Gang, a former auto engineer at Audi, as minister of science.[18]

The research of Cheng Li on the CEOs of China's top hundred enterprises (ranked by revenue in 2004) gives us an idea of the aggregate characteristics of China's emerging business-corporate leadership.[19] Of the top hundred firms only ten were based inland, with about three-quarters of the total concentrated in Beijing, Shanghai, and Guangdong. Fourteen of the top hundred firms also were ranked in the 2004 Global 500. The average age of the CEOs from the top hundred firms for whom data were available was 49.8 years; nearly 55 percent held postgraduate degrees, including over 10 percent with MBAs. Most had worked themselves up in the company or industry (not transferred in from the government), and all of these CEOs were male, except one; four were non-PRC citizens.[20] One illustration of the emerging willingness of Chinese firms to recruit management internationally is that in September 2005 Mengniu Dairy (Group) Co. announced that it was advertising in *Business Week* as a part of its effort to look globally for a new president. The company's chairman explained that "an international company needs a president with a global perspective."[21] In 2005 Jiangsu Province advertised abroad for general managers on more than twenty occasions.[22]

The effort to train and recruit corporate and business talent does not stop with top firm leadership. The Shenzhen government signed a contract with a firm in India (Zensar Technologies Ltd.) to train one thousand software project managers to turn the Shenzhen Software Park into China's principal software outsourcing location. The program's purpose was for the trainees to learn etiquette, negotiating skills, communication, and international business standards. The Chinese project director explained that the program was being instituted because Chinese enterprise leaders in the software outsourcing area were "not sure how to run projects successfully."[23]

These are promising directions in Chinese management, but a fascinating survey that is a part of the GLOBE (Global Leadership and Organizational Behavior Effectiveness) project points to four limiting "tensions" in PRC conceptions of executive leadership: a tendency toward autocratic style rather than empowerment of employees; a tendency toward in-group bases of trust rather than mechanisms of "formal trust"; a tendency toward reliance on the government rather than oneself; and a tendency toward defining "Chinese traditions" as a higher-order goal than worldliness.[24] Changing corporate or business culture is difficult, as is changing political culture.

The development of education in China is the foundation upon which future political, business, and intellectual leadership rests. In the years ahead, the PRC is likely to surprise outside observers because of the investments it now is making and the return of talent from abroad. Between 1990 and 2003 the percentage of secondary school–age children enrolled in China rose by over one-third, and since 1991 the percentage of China's population in tertiary education has more than quadrupled.[25] In 2003 more than half of undergraduates were enrolled in natural sciences (science, agriculture, and medicine) as well as engineering.[26] Cadre training is provided by CCP schools throughout the country; the Central Party School is at the apex, with a curriculum that has become increasingly cosmopolitan since the 1990s. China has built an increasingly thorough and multistage leadership education program within both the party and the military.

With respect to training and education abroad for Chinese students, nearly sixty-two thousand Chinese students matriculated into American institutions of higher education in 2003–4. In contrast, Nye notes that "in the 1950s, only 40 to 50 college and graduate students from each country [the United States and the Soviet Union] participated in exchanges" with each other,[27] and even in 2004–5 China had twelve times the number of students enrolled in U.S. institutions of higher education as Russia.[28] China also has sent enormous numbers of "scholars" abroad to work after graduation (many teaching and conducting research), accounting for 18 percent of all such foreign individuals in the United States in 2003–4.[29] As of 2002 China had almost twice as many students enrolled in OECD universities as India.[30] What one sees across a very broad base is a concerted effort to train and recruit globally competitive talent. In 2004 China's Ministry of Education reported that "77 percent of the presidents and 80 percent of academicians in the Chinese Academy of Sciences and the Chinese Academy of Engineering have an overseas education background."[31] According to UNESCO, between the 2000–2001 and 2002–3 academic years, the number of Chinese students in Australia rose 246 percent; in France, 248 percent; in Germany, 121 percent; and in Japan, 62 percent.[32] Presumably, to some unknown extent, these increases reflect the difficulties that many foreign students have had since 9/11 in obtaining U.S. visas in a timely manner.

While thus far only a modest (but uncertain) percentage of students trained abroad have returned to China, the return rate is rising as the PRC is increasingly perceived as a land of opportunity compared to more mature economies in Europe, Japan, and the United States. The OECD reports that as of 2006 more than ten thousand returned PRC overseas graduates had established about four thousand firms.[33]

An important subset of leadership and human resources in international affairs is a nation's stock of skilled diplomats. In the case of China, a rising power, skilled diplomacy is particularly important because, in the words of Joseph Nye, "A rising power must avoid creating fear and countervailing coalitions. It wants to create a bandwagon, not produce balancing [offsetting] behavior."[34] The concept of "peaceful rise" or "peaceful development" is aimed at this end. As discussed in chapter 1, it seeks to assure neighbors and other big powers that China's primary tasks and interests are to accomplish internal change; to make no major changes in the international status quo; to build the PRC into the globalized international economic system; to take no part in alliances directed at third parties; to keep military spending within prudent bounds; and to never seek hegemony.

During interviews for this book I was struck by the frequency with which well-placed observers and policy makers throughout Asia mentioned the quality of the PRC's representation abroad. In Jakarta a senior Indonesian NGO official mentioned that "the young diplomats [of China and] the deputy chief of mission of the Chinese Embassy in Indonesia [born in Surabaya] speak excellent English and Indonesian. We [Indonesians] have sixty diplomats in Beijing, one speaks Chinese; here [at the Chinese Embassy in Jakarta], of all their diplomats, only the ambassador doesn't speak Indonesian."[35] In Canberra, almost every Australian official and individual I met in 2005 spoke of China's Ambassador Fu Ying in admiring and respectful tones—one of her predecessors, Zhou Wenzhong, went on to be ambassador to Washington. One former senior Australian government official recounted how in mid-2005 Fu was dealing with the touchy case of a defecting Chinese consular official [one of her subordinates then] who was seeking asylum in Australia and publicly charging that the PRC had a spy network of one thousand informants there. These charges created much anxiety among Australian citizens of Chinese ancestry, not to mention other Australians. "She [Fu Ying] made a joke recently about not getting to dinner parties because she was so busy managing her spy network. The main thing she is doing with this humor and reasonableness is reassuring the Chinese residents in Australia. She is very effective. She is very open to the media. We have never before had an authentic public diplomat [from China]. . . . She is a bit of a public figure. She does the hard-edged talk shows."[36] In 2007 Fu was named ambassador to the United Kingdom.

In the United States, ever since the posting of Ambassador Li Zhaoxing to Washington, DC (1998–2001), Chinese ambassadors have seized opportunities to appear on live, national news programs, hoping to speak directly to the public. In the past, Chinese diplomats saw their work as less public. Not long ago they would have been hesitant to accept offers of broad, uncontrolled public exposure. In September 2005 at a black tie gala in New York City, both China's ambassador to the United States and its ambassador to the United Nations were at the head table listening to Deputy Secretary of State Robert Zoellick deliver a major foreign policy address that contained some critical comments about China. In an earlier era, the Chinese ambassador to the United States would have felt compelled to excoriate the criticisms. However, when his turn came to address the audience, Ambassador Zhou Wenzhong briefly responded, saying that he "could be more positive" than Zoellick in his remarks, thereby making clear his disagreement without becoming disagreeable himself.

Reflecting this increased sophistication in dealing with the media and public relations, Chinese diplomats increasingly seek to put a human face on China. The resumés of Chinese leaders that were once devoid of information are now somewhat more fulsome. On the Web site for China's embassy in the United States, one is instructed to "Make Friends with the Ambassador." This increasing openness is also true in China itself. Foreign Ministry diplomats occasionally speak of their online interactions with nationalistic citizens who feel that the ministry does not represent China's interests with sufficient backbone—the cutting criticism being that Chinese diplomats lack calcium in their diet.

Before the mid-1990s, diplomacy in the PRC was conceived largely as meeting with the host government's executive branch to resolve issues. Dealing with legislators was considered far afield—host governments were to manage their own legislators. This has changed, at least in the United States. The legislative liaison section of the Chinese Embassy in Washington has grown in staff and sophistication, particularly since the 1990s with the need for China to influence the annual congressional debate over continued most-favored-nation (normal trade relations) treatment for the PRC and to win entry for China into the WTO. PRC diplomacy has adapted to the need to deal with whole governments and whole societies, not just executive branches. Hence China's ambassador, Zhou Wenzhong, traveled to Iowa in 2005 "because this is where America's political battles are settled"—and, he might have added, where farm votes in the U.S. Senate are to be found.[37]

Chinese Ambassadors, a book by the former PRC foreign-service officer Xiaohong Liu, is instructive. She says of the fifth generation of PRC diplomats (in the late 1990s):

They are now in their forties [and early fifties], but many have already assumed responsible positions at divisional and departmental levels. [This generation] . . . includes perhaps the most accomplished foreign-service officers the MFA [Ministry of Foreign Affairs] has ever produced. Politically, they are freer and bolder. . . . Professionally, they are the first generation trained not only as language students but also as students of social sciences. Many of them have obtained graduate degrees abroad in international relations, thereby gaining new perspectives and instruments for understanding of world affairs. The international community can expect from them rationality, collegial courtesy, professional disposition, and shared practice following the norms of the international system. At the same time, they are tough and skillful negotiators and representatives on behalf of the Chinese government and Chinese national interests.[38]

China's most senior diplomats in critical ambassadorial posts in 2005, the diplomats that Beijing sends abroad (and about whom we have information), are predominantly from cosmopolitan coastal areas, university graduates; one-third of those examined had attended prestigious foreign universities and professional schools. At China's embassy in Washington, DC, for example, Dr. Su Ge was minister counselor for governmental affairs and congressional liaison from 2003 until mid-2006. Before coming to Washington, Su was an academic focusing on U.S.-China relations, professor and vice president at the Foreign Affairs College, and vice president at the China Institute of International Studies. After coming to the Chinese Embassy in Washington, his congressional section grew in size and improved in quality of personnel and sophistication of action. Likewise, when Ambassador Zhou Wenzhong assumed his post in the United States in 2005, he had completed studies at the London School of Economics and the University of Bath and had been posted to America four times previously (as third secretary in Washington, deputy consul general in San Francisco, consul general in Los Angeles, and minister at the embassy in Washington).

China's diplomats are reinforced by national leaders who travel to countries important to national interests. Phillip Saunders reports, "The total number of days spent abroad by top leaders in 2002–2004 increased significantly."[39] The PRC's top four leaders visited thirty-four countries in 2004, and in that same year twenty-nine heads of state and twenty-three heads of government visited the PRC.[40] In the third quarter of 2005 alone, Premier Wen Jiabao met with foreign or multilateral organization leaders on at least twenty-nine occasions, and President Hu Jintao met with such leaders on at least fifty-eight occasions at home and abroad.[41] From 2003 into November 2005 Hu Jintao traveled to thirty-five countries.[42] One U.S. NGO officer in Indonesia contrasted the Chinese approach with that of the George W. Bush White House: "The respect that the Chinese show Indonesia is great. Premier Wen Jiabao came to Indonesia with seventy persons in his delegation, business leaders, and they stayed six days. [George W.] Bush stayed eighteen hours and he was scared to leave the airport. The Chinese did business and didn't talk terrorism. The Americans go out of their way to say how bad the business environment is and [point out the] weak enforcement of contracts—the Chinese don't harp."[43] When President Hu was in Indonesia for the Bandung Conference Golden Jubilee in 2005, he stayed an extra day to go to Jakarta and put his signature on a "strategic partnership" agreement.

Suffice it to say here that the quality and professionalism of China's representation abroad have greatly improved in the reform era and that Beijing posts representatives who increasingly see their job as dealing with whole societies and whole governments. PRC diplomats are becoming more adept at using the mass media in their host nations. China's capacity to articulate and disseminate its central foreign policy ideas is going up, and the approach is designed to be as attractive and reassuring as possible.[44]

INNOVATION AND RESEARCH

In this era of globally competitive and linked markets, the capacity to undertake the research upon which much innovation rests is a critical dimension of ideational power. Innovation (which includes both invention and novel refinement and adaptation) is fundamental to improved standards of living, international competitiveness, and reduced dependence on other nations in key areas, and in many respects it is attractive to other nations. PRC leaders are serious about enhancing national innovation capacity. Premier Wen Jiabao himself chairs the State Leading Small Group on Medium and Long-Term Planning for the Development of Science and Technology. A science and technology plan was approved in 2003 with goals through 2020, although some scientists both inside and outside China believe that the plan, and the mentality on which it rests, may, in fact, slow innovation because it inherently represents rigidity rather than flexibility. In January 2006 President Hu Jintao delivered a speech entitled "Adhere to a New Path of Innovation with Chinese Characteristics and Strive to Build an Innovation-Oriented Country." In his remarks he called for a dramatic rise in R&D spending to reach 2.5 percent of

GDP by 2020; increased effort to attract foreign R&D facilities to China and establish Chinese R&D facilities abroad; and more linkages between business, academe, and government research organs.[45]

In the preceding chapter we deferred discussion of innovation, saying simply that it has many dimensions—from new technology creation and development, to the utilization of existent technology in new ways and in new products, to developing and refining processes used to manufacture products more efficiently. China is better positioned to be innovative along some dimensions than others.

Many considerations are enabling China to improve its innovative capacities. Factors inside China include increased (though still modest) domestic R&D expenditures; expanding and more research-oriented higher education at home and training abroad; the infusion of more "human resource input to R&D" than any other country except the United States, growing 77 percent in the 1995–2004 period;[46] an improving science policy structure and a more nimble system of moving applied research into production; and, perhaps most important of all, a growing private sector. External factors enabling China to increase innovative potential include the development of global production chains and technology flows within them; the PRC's involvement in epistemic communities (transnational communities of professionals) that facilitate the global transmission of information; and the increasing movement of foreign research facilities into China and the PRC's establishment of such centers abroad.

All this argues that, while China may not become a comprehensive innovator quickly,[47] its capacity to compete globally in the military and economic realms will continue to grow with a speed unanticipated by many. A former very senior official of the CIA summed it up in this way: "When I was at the CIA we had experts in technology out [to the headquarters in Langley] to ask about development of technology and science in China. In technology it is not so important to invent it; it is more important whether you can apply it, integrate it—China will pass Germany and France and challenge the United States in these respects."[48] The Germans already are worried, with *Der Spiegel* asking Senior Mentor Lee Kuan Yew in August 2005, "How afraid should the West be?" His reply was informative: "In 50 years I see China, Korea and Japan at the high-tech end of the value chain. Look at the numbers and quality of the engineers and scientists they produce and you know that this is where the R&D will be done. . . . We have to face that. But you should not be afraid of that. You are leading in many fields which they cannot catch up with for many years, many decades. In pharmaceuticals, I don't see them catching up with the Germans for a long time."[49]

The fascinating work of Dieter Ernst and Barry Naughton helps disaggregate the notion of "innovation" into analytically useful subcomponents and helps explain how innovation capacity grows. According to Ernst, "There is a well established literature that demonstrates that, as industrial latecomers, Asian economies do not have to proceed *sequentially* from imitation to innovation along a linear trajectory similar to that used by the already advanced countries."[50] Ernst and Naughton have elaborated a typology in the IT industry that has broader application. They define four basic "types" of innovation (incremental, modular, architectural, and radical), with the types differentiated by the degree of change in the overall architecture of the system or item and the degree of change of the components that constitute the system or the item.

> "Incremental" innovations take the dominant component design for granted, but improve on cost, time-to-market and performance. With "modular" innovation, new component technology is plugged into a fundamentally unchanged system architecture. "Architectural" innovations use existing component technology, but change the way components are designed to work together. Architectural innovations build on a company's familiarity with market trends and user requirements to specify an electronic system, but use existing component technology that is available on the market to implement this design. Finally, "radical" innovations involve both the use of new component technology and changes in architectural design.[51]

This typology can be portrayed in a fourfold table (table 2).

From Ernst and Naughton's typology, I conclude several things relating to innovation in China. To start, assessments of current Chinese capacities and future potential depend on what kind of innovation one is considering. Next, currently and for the near and middle future, the PRC has the greatest potential for architectural and incremental innovation. China can be expected to be most innovative in using the components developed elsewhere and putting them together in ways that best meet its markets' preferences and needs—"architectural innovation." This is the area where much current Chinese R&D spending is going, and this is one reason that increasing numbers of Western R&D facilities are being located in China (more below).[52] A good example of this kind of innovation, in which a concept from abroad is adapted to the local market with impressive results, is Jack Ma's develop-

	Components of System	
Architecture of System	Unchanged	Changed
Unchanged	Incremental	Modular
Changed	Architectural	Radical

TABLE 2   Types of Innovation

ment of Alibaba.com, a soaring, multifaceted Asian online business.[53] Ma has practically put eBay out of business in China by adapting the online auction concept to concrete Chinese circumstances, as he tells the story.

> I think eBay is one of the companies I respect the most in e-commerce. They are really so successful. But in China, I think they are gone. This game is over. They have made so many mistakes in China. We are lucky. . . . There are several mistakes that they made. For example, they believed too much that their business model in the U.S. will work in China. . . . [I]n China the credit card system is bad and Internet infrastructure is no good. . . . Second is the technology platform. They think that eBay needs a global technology platform, so they put the China site on their global technology platform. It sounds great, like a Boeing 747 flying is great. But if the airport is a school yard, you cannot land. Even if you want to change a button, you have to report to 14 guys. . . . I'm afraid of nobody. For years, I competed with China Telecom. EBay is very scary, too. Now I think I do my job and they do their job. There's no life-long friends and there's no life-long competitors. Who knows?[54]

With regard to "incremental innovation," given the rate at which the PRC is moving up the manufacturing learning curve, and given its educated, disciplined, and still relatively inexpensive workforce, it ought to have many advantages in innovations associated with enhancing the efficiency of the manufacturing process, improving the item's performance, and shortening time to market. Much of China's innovation is centered on manufacturing. These advantages are apparent, according to *Industry Week* and Cleveland's Manufacturing Performance Institute: "The survey found that Chinese manufacturers' on-time delivery rate is 99%, compared with 96% for U.S. manufacturers, and 98% of Chinese manufacturers' products meet specifications on the first try, compared with 97% for U.S. manufacturers."[55] Of course, some of this superior performance reflects the fact that in some areas China's capital equipment is newer than that of U.S. competitors—91 percent of U.S. plants in 2006 were more than a decade old, while in China the figure was 54 percent. *Industry Week* also reported survey results revealing that while 54 percent of PRC manufacturers surveyed cited innovation as a primary goal, only 26 percent of U.S. respondents did so.[56]

China will still lag for some time in the development of entirely new components (modular innovation) and in innovation involving the development of entirely new systems with entirely new components (radical innovation). This discussion leads us to data on the issuance of patents, copyrights, and academic citations in China and abroad as indicators of potential for radical and modular innovation. The data reveal a country moving up but doing so gradually.

> By the year 2000, China ranked eighth in the world in terms of the number
> of scientific papers contributed by Chinese authors. . . . This is a considerable
> improvement from just five years before, when China ranked only 15th in the
> world. . . . The number of Chinese patent applications and certifications also
> show[s] continued steady growth, although most are not for inventions but
> for designs or utility models. . . . Between 1995 and 2000, the total number
> of patent applications certified in China more than doubled, and approved
> patents for inventions grew more than three-fold. But the rise in PRC patents
> overall is in part due to foreign applications, which have been outpacing
> domestic patent applications for inventions in recent years.[57]

The U.S. Patent and Trademark Office reported that South Korean inventors filed for 21,685 applications for utility patents in 2006 and that Japan filed for 76,839. In contrast, Chinese inventors applied for 3,768 in 2006, though that figure is up from just 469 in 2000. Although the OECD reports data differently, the story is the same—China is moving up from a low base.[58] To put all this in perspective, however, 221,784 utility patent applications were filed in the United States in 2006 by U.S. entities. Another indicator of innovation is the Science Citation Index (a multi-disciplinary searchable database with author abstracts that covers the principal scientific journals). UNESCO reports that in 1991 China accounted for only 1.4 percent of the world's scientific publications while India accounted for 2.2 percent and Japan 9.4 percent.[59] By 2001, China had risen to 4.1 percent, India had fallen to 1.9 percent, and Japan had risen to 10.8 percent. Most dramatically, the U.S. share from 1991 to 2001 declined from 39.4 percent to 32.7 percent (table 3).[60]

The PRC's current low ranking notwithstanding, most analysts expect its position according to these indicators of innovation to continue rising as its universities

TABLE 3   World Shares of Scientific Publications,
1991 and 2001 (in %)

	1991	2001	Change
USA	39.4	32.7	−6.7
India	2.2	1.9	−0.3
China	1.4	4.1	+2.7
Japan	9.4	10.8	+1.4
Developed countries	92.3	87.6	-4.7
Developing countries	10.3	17.3	+7.0

Source: UNESCO, *UNESCO Science Report 2005* (Paris: UNESCO, 2005), p. 9.

develop, as new research facilities open, as the country makes its intellectual property regime more effective, as it recruits more talent globally, and as its entrepreneurs and inventors recognize the value (through licensing) of patents. However, now and in the near future, China will be a modest innovator in terms of patent grants, applications, and citations. The intellectual property regime will take considerable time to build, as will the habits of academic honesty and research teamwork—plagiarism and other academic misconduct is a problem. The president of Chinese Science and Technology University, Zhu Qingshi, told domestic and foreign university heads in China in July 2006 that "overall academic ethics have hit rock bottom."[61]

Nonetheless, the PRC is making progress, as seen in the case of the gene therapy called Onyx-015, a product employing a genetically modified virus to kill cancer cells while leaving normal cells unharmed. The original work on this was conducted by Onyx Pharmaceuticals in California. But after publishing its research (in 1996) and getting a U.S. patent (but not a Chinese patent), the firm switched its efforts to another drug in 2003. A Chinese enterprise, Shanghai Sunway Biotech, read the research, utilized it, made marginal improvements, and paid Onyx for worldwide licensing rights, and the drug was approved in 2003 in China. The cofounder of Onyx, Frank McCormick, said: "I was a bit shocked at first. . . . But since we haven't been able to find anyone in the U.S. to support the project, it's better than having it die on the vine. Over all, I'm actually delighted."[62]

If China has comparative advantages in architectural and incremental innovations, other countries, particularly the United States, must develop their comparative advantages in radical and modular innovation. (These two forms of innovation require large R&D expenditures, a well-educated workforce, and supportive public policy.) This is the challenge that China presents: more advanced economies must focus on more sophisticated forms of innovation as China (and India) progress. This is part of what makes primary and secondary school deficiencies (particularly in big cities), inadequate basic research funding, and the overall dearth of interest in the physical and mathematical sciences in the United States a pressing challenge.

Because China has comparative advantages as a site for certain forms of innovation, many major foreign firms (including those in Taiwan) are locating portions of their R&D efforts in the PRC—firms like SONY, Accenture, STMicroelectronics, Samsung, Siemens, Caterpillar, Microsoft, DuPont, Ford, General Electric, General Motors, IBM, Intel, Lucent Technologies, Nokia, Motorola, Rohm and Haas, DaimlerChrysler, Toyota, Philips, and Areva. While figures for both expenditure and numbers of such centers are fragmentary, the trend since 1990 (particularly since the mid-1990s with the surge in FDI in China and the mid-1995 State Council "Decision on Accelerating Scientific and Technological Progress") has been clearly upward. In 1994 U.S. R&D expenditures in China were about $7 million, but by 2000 that number topped $506 million, according to the National Science Foundation, making the PRC the eleventh-biggest recipient of U.S. R&D expenditures abroad. Even more interesting, U.S. firms devote 9.2 percent of their investment in China to R&D while the percentage for U.S. affiliates worldwide is 3.3 percent.[63] By 2002, according to the OECD, "R&D expenditures by U.S.-owned subsidiaries in China" were $650 million.[64] In early 2005 Commerce Minister Bo Xilai asserted that "foreign investors have set up more than 700 research and development centers distributed mainly in electronic and communication equipment manufacturing industries, etc."[65] And by February 2006 the Chinese government was saying there were 750 such centers in the PRC.[66] Total foreign R&D investment in China was estimated to be $4 billion as of mid-2004.[67]

Many factors drive increased R&D investment in China: a WTO world of reduced economic barriers; provision of financial and other incentives in the PRC to attract foreign R&D; the diffusion of skilled researchers globally and the return to China of skilled personnel from abroad; lower labor costs in developing nations;

the ability to adapt products to local markets closer to the consumption point; the availability of high-speed, high-volume data lines globally; the desire of multinational firms to stay abreast of technological innovation in the host society; a declining role of the U.S. government in R&D and a greater (relative) role for the private sector; and firms' competitive strategies. With respect to the latter, a Samsung spokesman explained, "In the Chinese market, we are increasingly doing R&D design work locally, hiring local people in the top management. So that way, the Chinese consumers feel as if it's their own brand."[68]

Thus foreign R&D funding is growing in China and in many advanced economies as well, as Kathleen Walsh observed by noting that foreign-funded research in the United States quadrupled between 1981 and 1999.[69] At the same time that China is the recipient of foreign R&D investment, it also is investing abroad in R&D capacity; in late 2005 it was announced that about 3 percent of the PRC's overseas investment was in R&D centers.[70] When China-based Lenovo purchased IBM PC in May 2005, research facilities in Raleigh, North Carolina, were included. Lenovo, founded in Beijing originally as Legend Computer, also had an R&D facility in Silicon Valley as of 2003. When Shenyang Machine Tool Group bought the bankrupt German company Schiess in 2004, the parent firm planned to use the new acquisition as "a foreign base for training and research."[71] As of mid-2005 Huawei telecom and networking company had R&D centers in the United States, India, Russia, and Sweden.[72] Haier Group has eighteen design centers abroad.[73] And ZTE Corporation (Zhongxing Telecommunications) also has an R&D facility in Sweden.[74] R&D is globalizing for everyone.

Many of the research centers being established in China by foreign firms are wholly owned undertakings. In such enterprises care is taken to keep the resultant intellectual property within the foreign firm. Therefore, developments in these centers do not necessarily translate into one-to-one increases in Chinese national capabilities. In the most careful study on the subject, Kathleen Walsh concludes that "on balance, although foreign R&D centers are contributing to China's impressive recent high-tech growth and increasing competitiveness in ICT [information communications technology] industries, they are contributing as much or more . . . to foreign companies' high-tech development and production capabilities and, thus, to the U.S. economy."[75] The same ambiguity and mutuality of benefit exist with respect to the numerous Chinese science, technology, and engineering graduate students in the United States. They have become critical to many frontier university-based research programs, a development that will eventually increase PRC capabilities but is also immediately strengthening American capabilities.

Though total R&D spending in China doubled between 1995 and 2000,[76] and there is some debate over these expenditure figures, the proportion of GDP amounted to only slightly more than 1 percent in 2000 (and 1.3 percent in 2002),[77] while in the OECD countries throughout the same period it exceeded 2 percent.[78] Viewed in absolute terms (measured in PPP), Chinese R&D spending in 2001 came in fourth, behind the United States, Japan, and the European Union.[79] Between 1995 and 2004 China's R&D spending grew fivefold.[80] The EU is worried that the PRC will catch up by 2009–10, given the current rate at which Chinese R&D expenditures are increasing. Between 1998 and 2002 Chinese R&D spending rose 18.5 percent annually, while during the same period the increase was only 6.47 percent in the EU, 5.83 percent in the United States, and 6.19 percent in Japan.[81] The figures on the annual growth in R&D expenditures as a percentage of GDP ("research intensity") tell the same story: an average 10.91 percent in China in the 1998–2003 period as compared to only 1.48 percent in the EU-25, 1.28 percent in the United States, and 1.41 percent in Japan.[82]

Nonetheless, the absolute amount of R&D funding in China still remains low, is concentrated in eastern China, and is constrained by budgetary considerations, poor intellectual property (IP) protection for both foreign and domestic IP developers, and a poorly developed venture capital industry. Finally, in the realm of China's science policy there still is a legacy of state domination and "plan thinking" despite strides in this area since the 1980s.[83] In November 2004 Beijing authorized the Ministry of Science and Technology and the Chinese Academy of Sciences, along with the local government in Anhui Province (one of China's poorest provinces but with a history of scientific work), to build a "science city" in Hefei, the provincial capital. As Cheng Biding, an expert in regional development, put it, "It is a great move for the Chinese government to promote its innovation ability by building a city gathering scientific and technological research centers and high and new technological industries, just like Silicon Valley of the U.S."[84] Yet this model is at variance with the more interactive, university-industry, entrepreneurial, venture capital–driven nature of Silicon Valley's development and the more market-oriented features of China's own science and technology reforms.

On the other hand, now in China the majority of R&D is done by enterprises and universities (as opposed to government institutes), and this shift should gradually produce more innovation. Moreover, retailers in the United States that are big but too small for their own new product development and design facilities are encouraging their Chinese suppliers to be innovative so that the U.S. retailer can have new products with which to compete. One owner of an American megastore chain put it this way: "We welcome Chinese innovation because we can't afford to design our own products. We are not like Wal-Mart."[85]

Consequently, China will move up the value-added curve faster than many expect. South Koreans are keeping a wary eye on their big neighbor. As of 2004, South Korean research reported that "the technological gap between Korea and China in the 99 fields designated by the Korean government as core technology, including telecommunication and future energy, has been narrowed to [an] average of 2.1 years. For 10 major growth engine industries, including the next-generation semiconductor, the technological gap between the two countries was shortened to 2.5 years on average."[86] In turn, South Korea is 5.8 years behind the United States, 4 years behind the EU, and 3.7 years behind Japan according to these measures. While these data are only suggestive, if China is only a bit behind South Korea, and South Korea is only somewhat more behind the United States, the growing capacities of China described above should only continue to narrow these gaps in the years ahead if the United States does not increase its exertions.

All of the above notwithstanding, open and free societies enjoy an inherent advantage in innovation that China does not currently possess by virtue of its legacies of plan economics, authoritarian politics, and Confucian culture. Moreover, China is a nation in a hurry, so there is less systemic patience for the long gestation periods required for fundamental research; there is much more interest in applied inquiry. Xu Tian, a scholar who works at both Yale University and Fudan University in Shanghai, explained to a reporter in 2005 that China is a "system that teaches people to follow the rules, not be an innovator." China, he said, would have to overcome thousands of years of tradition "that has always avoided exploring different ways of thinking and exploring, and has emphasized staying within the system."[87] The degree to which this remains true will be the degree to which the PRC will lag in innovation, particularly radical innovation. This brings us to culture as a component of ideational power, simultaneously a tremendous power resource along some dimensions, while a drag along others.

CULTURE

The most fundamental strengths that societies can possess are the ideas, concepts, and norms that animate their peoples and reinforce cooperative and entrepreneurial activity at home and prove attractive abroad. Liberty, individualism, and associational activity are such animating values in America. In China, one such idea is material and intellectual self-improvement. In the course of my interviews throughout Asia I was struck by how observers of China view the character and culture of its people and how Chinese view their own cultural values and premises. Chinese culture is an asset that in many ways enhances its leaders' capacities to achieve national objectives. The cultural values that foster entrepreneurship at home and create the expectation for success abroad are attractive to outsiders, and this, in turn, provides an inducement for others to cooperate. One Asian entrepreneur summed it up this way: "Chinese people are committed to improving their lot. If they get ten square meters [of housing], this is an improvement toward which they strive. Chinese are small business specialists; they keep turning [inventory], knowing that even small margins add up. You have to compliment the people running China— they face tremendous challenges. All these people, and they [the leaders] need to keep the standard of living for all of them rising, even if not at the same rate for all. All the Chinese people need to be going up because all Chinese set out to better themselves."[88]

The economist Martin Wolf put it in more academic terms: "Some poor countries possess within them a stock of values, behaviors and institutions that are better adapted to running a modern economy than others. It is not surprising to find that China, until just a few centuries ago the world's most advanced economy, is among them, as was Japan in an earlier generation. In the right policy environment, such countries are likely to grow rapidly and accumulate physical and human capital more quickly than others."[89] Here Wolf points to the need for conjunction between culture and policy. A population with an intrinsically productive set of cultural values can fail to realize its potential in the wrong policy framework or external environment. This is what happened under Mao Zedong's long rule and also helps explain why things could turn around so rapidly once Deng Xiaoping restored congruence between culture and policy. Mao was working against fundamental cultural values that are focused on self-improvement and material advancement (as well as respect for education); Mao's external policies compounded these problems, and the Western world was unwilling to cooperate. Deng Xiaoping engineered a realignment of Chinese culture and policy and simultaneously contributed to an improved international environment more supportive of PRC efforts.

Conversations with PRC officials and scholars reveal a belief that meeting popular desires for material advancement is key to regime survival. As one Chinese official explained in an interview,

The rise of China is a dream of the Chinese people; [they have] been dreaming [of it] over the last several decades. When [they] look to the outside world—Japan and the United States—they [would] like to live like that, a better life, to drive cars and not ride bikes, [to have] a color TV, not black and white, to send their kids to schools at home and abroad—Harvard and Johns Hopkins. [There is] no way to persuade Chinese people otherwise. [There is] a strong desire to develop, [even] among farmers and peddlers. To earn money, to get rich, nothing can stop that.[90]

Though culture can be an asset and an important dimension of ideational power, some elements of Chinese culture have proven less conducive to reform at home and less appealing abroad. We already have mentioned the culture's (retarding) effect on radical innovation capacity. Another dimension damaging to new ideas is the political culture. By *political culture* I have in mind the politically relevant values and attitudes of citizens and political leaders along the following dimensions: civic obligation; orientation toward (and expectations of) government; levels of interpersonal trust among citizens or subjects; social capital—the ability of citizens to cooperate and organize productively; and deeply abiding ideas about the relationship between those governing and those governed. Whether the people and elites consider the general population as "subjects" (passive receptors of policy) or "citizens" (active participants in governance) is key too. The balance between the "duties" of citizenship and the "rights" of citizens is another central consideration. Deeply held values such as these influence regime legitimacy and system durability and affect external appeal.

A central dimension of ideational power that is a net positive for China consists of the work, investment, and aspirational elements that we associate with Chinese culture. Yet simultaneously one of China's greatest vulnerabilities resides in an authoritarian political culture that is constantly under assault by the pluralizing forces of modernization.

Cultural explanations for a nation's economic or political performance have their weaknesses and critics, although social capital theorists are trying to revive culture as part of the explanatory toolbox. Beyond the fact that defining and measuring distinctive cultural attributes is difficult, "culture" is a multidimensional phenomenon and provides a plethora of potential variables from which competing explanations can be fashioned. If Confucianism, with its emphases on family, education, frugality, mutual obligation and networks, and achievement, is so important in explaining current development success, why did China lag for much of the nineteenth and twentieth centuries when these elements of culture were no less present? Since the early 1800s, Confucianism and its presumably rigid hierarchical character were used to explain China's backwardness. Now much of China's success is attributed to discipline, the propensity to save, an ethic of mutual obligation, the value attached to education, and the ability to network—all continuous features of Confucian thought and society. One is driven to ask: "How can the same Confucian values hold a society back from modernization for hundreds of years and then propel it into amazing levels of growth over a few decades?" The intuitive sense that culture is central, along with the realization that its content is so elastic that it is difficult to define or measure, has created controversy for decades. Additionally, part of the answer is that culture interacts with other variables such as domestic policy and international contexts.

The importance of culture is not limited to the role it plays in creating the conditions for material advancement and national cohesion. Some cultures constitute resources for winning support and cooperation abroad. There is much in Chinese culture that foreigners find admirable (and enjoyable)—values of discipline, respect, and education; the role of food in Chinese society; artistic endeavors of all descriptions; and the intricacy of Chinese history and society. The PRC is beginning to systematically promote Chinese culture abroad for reasons of pride, influence, and revenue. Chinese culture can contribute to China's capacity to win cooperation, which contributes to its capacity to achieve objectives. This is power. Culture in international affairs is discussed later in this chapter.

Values, ideology, patriotism, and nationalism are closely related to culture and are important aspects of ideational power.

IDEOLOGY

The word *ideology* conjures up the notion of a tightly integrated set of economic and/or political beliefs guided by theory and values that are widely shared and provide a basis for group solidarity and action. Ideology, when it is widely shared, binds together the individual, group, and society in a sense of common endeavor. Beyond culture, materialism, and nationalism, today's China does not have an ideology or set of transcendent shared national values that bolster domestic integration or generate widespread external appeal. One senior former official in Singapore put it bluntly: "You should make a huge distinction between science and technology, where China will make huge strides, and ideology. The Chinese model is not an export. The Chinese know their political system has to change. They envy the U.S. system, and few Americans envy their system."[91]

Nonetheless, this may be too narrow a lens through which to view both the influence of China's domestic development model and Beijing's vision of an international order. In terms of a development model, the Chinese approach that features high growth and gradual political change has more attraction than many Americans wish to accept, as Joshua Cooper Ramo somewhat excessively argues in his *The Beijing Consensus*.[92] Interviewees in Vietnam, a country extremely wary of Chinese power (as we will see in chapter 5), freely concede the attraction of the Chinese model compared to the failure they associate with Soviet/Russian reform efforts and the threat of Western models. Indeed, from this perspective, even the modest political change in China is progressive. At one meeting with social science researchers in Vietnam's south, the following remarks were made: "China provides some useful lessons though we are an independent country. The Three Represents, [which include bringing 'advanced social productive forces' and entrepreneurs into the Chinese Communist Party, were a useful innovation,] and in the future we'll have more political reform, democracy. The government will represent the people more. . . . The market economy in the direction of socialism is similar to China, and we adopted the Chinese model. Economics first. . . . We are trying to learn how to reform the political system of Vietnam by looking at China."[93]

Beijing's domestic policy, which emphasizes legal development, greatly circumscribed civil rights, gradual systemic reform, and opening to the world, has its attractions to many in the developing world, not least to Central Asia and perhaps to much of the Middle East. I was struck by a 2005 editorial in the *Daily Star* of Lebanon.

> The Prophet Mohammed, in conveying the divine word to Muslims, commanded them to search for knowledge "even though it be in China," calling such a pursuit a "duty" for the faithful. Ironically today, we should be learning a lot from our friends in the Far East. There has been a recent push for the application of a certain knowledge in China that would be useful to the survival of regimes in the Islamic world. In the past few years, China has made great strides to define and develop a justice system that will protect and uphold the legal rights of its citizens. . . . While China is enjoying the development of a society built upon the rule of law, our societies are stagnating under the strangling grip of security regimes.[94]

My guess is that this view finds resonance in much of the world, particularly nondemocratic societies and societies in which citizens perceive themselves to have suffered under "the Washington Consensus" (of capitalism, democracy, rule of law, and the tough love of the IMF).[95] People who have not enjoyed political and social order and desire a more promising economic future seek to learn from those who have overcome these disabilities.

VISION OF THE WORLD ORDER

In terms of the international order, Beijing is promoting an alternative vision of the role of big powers to the United States' post-9/11 stance—"harmony without uniformity." It is doing so while trying to maintain productive relations with a Washington that takes democracy promotion seriously. Beijing wins support at home and abroad not by articulating lofty aspirations but rather by identifying itself with the resentments of those who resist an ideologically assertive America. This is evident in a speech that China's respected foreign policy spokesman, the former vice premier and foreign minister Qian Qichen, delivered in mid-2004 and that was subsequently published by *China Daily* (on the eve of the U.S. presidential election in November 2004).[96] Although Beijing was embarrassed that the timing of the statement's release suggested that it wanted George W. Bush to lose the general election (which was not true), the PRC government never distanced itself from Qian's remarks. Indeed, most PRC citizens with whom I spoke agreed with Qian.

The remarks promoted a vision of a more institutionalized, rule-based, and less force-driven international system than that promoted by Washington. The indictment of post-9/11 U.S. foreign policy (the "Bush Doctrine") was a response to the redeployment of U.S. forces around the world; the creation of U.S. bases in Central Asia; the attempt to produce democratic political change throughout the Middle East; and aggressive, sometimes preemptive efforts to halt proliferation (e.g., in Iraq). The core elements of Qian's indictment were:

- "Washington's anti-terror campaign has already gone beyond the scope of self-defense." "The philosophy of the 'Bush Doctrine' is in essence force. It advocates the United States should rule over the whole world with overwhelming force, military force in particular."
- With respect to the Iraq War, "Washington opened a Pandora's box, intensifying various intermingled conflicts, such as ethnic and religious ones."
- "The Iraq War has made the United States even more unpopular in the international community than its war in Vietnam."
- "It is now time to give up the illusion that Europeans and Americans are living in the same world, as some Europeans would like to believe."

- "The Iraq war was an optional war, not a necessary one, and the preemptive principle should be removed from the dictionary of the US national security."
- "Mounting hostile sentiments among the Muslim world towards the United States following the war have already helped the al-Qaeda terrorist network recruit more followers and suicide martyrs."
- "The US' call for help from the United Nations (UN) for Iraq's postwar reconstruction work once again shows that in the current world, unilateralism is not appropriate in solving international affairs."
- "The troubles and disasters the United States has met do not stem from threats by others, but from its own cocksureness and arrogance."

These views resonate with Russians, Europeans, and South Koreans, to mention but a few. Beijing has managed to assume a relatively nonconfrontational profile in controversies about the UN's role in Iraq and nonproliferation policy as it pertains to Iran, knowing that the views of many American allies and friends create constraints for Washington without the necessity for Beijing itself to openly and persistently resist the United States directly. Americans were stunned when a September 2003 Gallup poll in South Korea indicated that nearly as many citizens there saw George W. Bush as "threatening to peace in Korea" (38 percent) as saw Kim Jong Il in that light (42.1 percent).[97]

The PRC's foreign policy is more than passive opportunism, however. One could go back to the mid-1950s' "Five Principles of Peaceful Coexistence," which argued for equality, noninterference, and mutual benefit in interstate relations, and to the post-1996 "New Security Concept" to see that a recurrent theme of Chinese foreign policy has been that big powers should minimize the use of force and intervention in the affairs of others. This idea has widespread appeal globally. Chinese leaders often say that Washington ought to conduct its international relationships with the same respect for diversity that it practices at home.

Most recently, in its articulation of "peaceful rise" *(heping jueqi)* or "peaceful development" (analyzed in chapter 1), Beijing promotes a vision of how it can grow stronger in ways that do not threaten the existing international order. This too has been a set of ideas that nations around China's periphery applaud, though there are skeptics to be sure, as will be shown in chapter 5. It certainly puts a new face on Chinese foreign policy to have a former official, Zheng Bijian, say in a prominently featured article for the fall 2005 issue of *Foreign Affairs* entitled "China's 'Peaceful

Rise' to Great-Power Status": "The most significant strategic choice the Chinese have made was to embrace economic globalization rather than detach themselves from it. . . . In pursuing the goal of rising in peace, the Chinese leadership has strived for improving China's relations with all the nations of the world."[98] As we see below, international public opinion data suggest that this posture confers more legitimacy on the PRC than many Americans perceive or wish to concede.

Therefore, it may be conceited to believe that China's normative attraction pales in comparison to that of the United States, at least under the conditions prevailing in the second half of the first decade of the new millennium. American values, to the rest of the world, often conflict with Washington's behavior. The Chinese are drawing comparative attention to U.S. and Chinese actions, not declaratory values. As discussed below, comparative international opinion surveys conducted by the Pew Research Center on the People and the Press (and others) demonstrate that it is U.S. behavior (what America "does"), not U.S. values (what America "is"), that creates international dissatisfaction.

NATIONALISM

Nationalism is closely related to ideology, and both are central aspects of ideational power. In the case of China, nationalism is one dimension of ideational power that is troubling to most observers of its foreign policy, particularly its neighbors. As one interviewee in Indonesia put it to me when speaking of his military's concern about China, "The problem the [Indonesian] military has isn't that China is communist, it is that China is nationalistic."[99]

Regime legitimacy in China currently rests on two pillars—rapid economic growth and vigorous defense of nationalistic values. While nationalism can be a prop strengthening the legitimacy of a regime, it also can become a spear that the populace aims at leaders who are perceived to be weak in the face of external challenge. When economic growth requires globalization, and globalization to some extent affects "self-determination" and "economic sovereignty," contradictions can arise between a populace fearful of globalization and an elite that sees such growth as critical to its own, and the nation's, survival.[100] Modern Chinese history provides numerous examples of the dual character of nationalism.

At the start of the twentieth century, the Empress Tz'u-hsi (Cixi) fanned the embers of the Boxer Rebellion, thereby using antiforeign nationalism to increase support for her waning Qing Dynasty. Nationalism was a powerful force uniting students and intellectuals against Japan in the early twentieth century, and, as anti-

Japanese student and popular demonstrations in the 1980s and in April 2005 indicate, this impulse remains a powerful force in today's PRC. Chalmers Johnson described the role of peasant nationalism in helping Mao's communists come to power in the context of the Japanese occupation and the subsequent civil war. And Americans will remember Chinese nationalism on display in popular anti-U.S. reactions to the mistaken bombing by U.S./NATO aircraft of the Chinese Embassy in Belgrade in 1999 and the collision of a Chinese jet fighter and a U.S. reconnaissance plane in 2001.[101]

Anti-Japanese nationalism has remained a particularly potent force. Chinese riot police were called out in spring 2005 to control Shanghai citizens shouting "Japanese pigs get out!" and inflicting damage on Japanese consular facilities, restaurants, and stores in reaction to Prime Minister Koizumi's visits to the Yasukuni Shrine and Japanese textbooks that were perceived to understate Japanese crimes during World War II. More harmlessly, in late 2005 municipal authorities in Kunming, Yunnan Province, forced property developers to rename the Ginza Office Tower.[102] And showing that anti-Japanese nationalism born of the industrial age can find its full expression in the cyber age, in 2005 the Chinese Communist Youth League announced that a PRC online gaming technology firm, PowerNet Technology, had cooperated with the league to develop a new online game called Anti-Japan War Online. "'The game will allow players, especially younger players, to learn from history. They will get patriotic feeling when fighting invaders to safeguard their motherland. . . .' Players are able to play simulations of key battles, but will only be able to play as the Chinese side. Players will also not be allowed to kill other players in the game. In addition, fighting in the game between Japanese and Chinese soldiers will be shown only in miniature, so as to reduce the violence level of the game."[103]

These episodic displays support a generalization made by John Mearsheimer—that in a world where many states have not enjoyed sovereignty and independence, the attraction of nationalism in the face of assertive outside powers can be far more powerful than the appeal of democracy. Mearsheimer raises the cases of the wars in Vietnam and Iraq as evidence for his proposition.[104]

This observation leads to two additional generalizations about nationalism as ideational power in the PRC. First, nationalism can be a potent deterrent to other states' policies and actions, creating apprehension among foreign decision makers that their moves could generate an uncontrollable backlash. Second, perceived intervention in Chinese internal affairs and strident attempts by Washington or others to foster political change in China can actually increase popular support for the regime, even among those groups one presumes would be the greatest beneficiaries of such

FIGURE 9
Nationalism worries China's neighbors and others. This photograph of a large demonstration in Beijing was taken May 10,
1999, in the immediate aftermath of the tragic and mistaken
bombing of the Chinese Embassy in Belgrade by U.S./NATO
forces. Xie Jiahua/China Features/Corbis.

change. This nationalism was one effect of post-June 4, 1989, Western, particularly
U.S., sanctions. Sohu.com carried a *Huanqiu Shibao* (Global Times) poll in March
2005 showing that those areas in which Chinese most expected conflict with the
United States in the future were issues with the most nationalistic content—
Taiwan (60.5 percent of respondents) and human rights (17.7 percent). Almost 57

percent of the respondents in the poll believed that the goal of the United States was to "contain" China.[105]

One Chinese professor at China Youth College for Politics in Beijing conducted a survey on how students viewed foreign and domestic policies.

> Students hold some [common] views in international affairs but divergent views on internal [to China] affairs. International questions are abstract and not related to their interests, hence views are affected by the mass media [in China] and they are inclined to accept nationalist values. In comparison to traditional ideology here in China, other ideologies are not that familiar. As we all know, the Chinese government has certain controls of the mass media, and as a result the media have a uniform viewpoint on international affairs. Because of mass media characteristics, student viewpoints are quite similar to each other. For most students domestic problems are totally different; they pay more attention, it has a closer relationship to their own interests. Of course the media affect views, but there are friends, relatives, life experiences, and these play a bigger role in shaping the view of domestic problems. Different life experiences, different views on domestic politics. When analyzing problems, appeal to nationalism in international affairs and pragmatism in domestic politics. In contrast, the traditional ideology of China has been relegated to second place.[106]

Because China still has unresolved territorial issues (such as Taiwan, the South and East China seas, and borders with India), Chinese nationalism and military strength present a threatening visage to neighbors. The potential of China's nationalism to become quickly strident creates anxiety among PRC neighbors and is one reason that many want Washington to remain involved militarily in the region. So Chinese nationalism is a great source of legitimacy and strength for Beijing, a potentially lethal weapon that its citizens can aim at the regime's heart, and a source of anxiety to foreigners, particularly neighbors.

Not all nationalism, however, is the same, as Allen Whiting and Chen Zhimin remind us. Whiting identifies three types of nationalism, one that is generally constructive, one that is malignant and will lead nations to bandwagon against China, and one that can go either way. *Affirmative nationalism* "fosters patriotism and targets attitude"; it "centers exclusively on 'us.'" Here we see an essentially constructive patriotism directed toward inward change and constructive international participation. This reflects the completion of the first stage of nation building: building a national identity. People see an obligation to make sacrifices for the good of the larger national community. Many failed states are nowhere near having this kind of strong, unifying collective identity—Iraq comes to mind. *Aggressive nationalism* "arouses anger and mobilizes behavior." According to Whiting, "This is the form of national feeling that most concerns China's neighbors. It is focused on 'them.'" Finally, *assertive nationalism* has the potential to become either "affirmative" or "aggressive" nationalism because it "adds 'them' as a negative out-group referent" to the "us" of affirmative nationalism. "To the degree that it places greater emphasis on an external challenge and increases this over time, it may foreshadow aggressive nationalism."[107] The essence of the problem is that China's neighbors cannot be sure when assertive nationalism may mutate into its aggressive cousin; they cannot be certain that enhanced Chinese capabilities will not produce new goals and capabilities to act upon old grievances.

This brings us back to our main theme—each power form, whether coercive, economic, or ideational, has multiple expressions, consequences, utilities, and dangers. Nationalism can enhance domestic legitimacy while undermining Chinese action abroad. Nationalism that can at one moment strengthen domestic legitimacy can at the next become a delegitimizing force for a government seen as weak in defending national dignity and interests. While Chinese nationalism creates anxieties in the regional and global systems, Beijing has expended considerable effort in assuaging worries, with some effect. And recent research by Alastair Iain Johnston offers the empirically grounded observation (based on Beijing survey data) that the PRC's emerging "middle class exhibits a greater level of nascent liberalism than poorer income groups,"[108] a trend offering the hope that a richer China might be more moderate.

THE WORLD LOOKS AT CHINA, ITS POLICIES, AND ITS FUTURE

An important dimension of a nation's ideational power is how others in the international community view that state's goals, current condition, future prospects, and impact on others. The more favorable the external perceptions, the more willingly others cooperate. Cooperation enhances a state's ability to achieve its purposes efficiently. Stephen Walt has written about how unfavorable international views of a nation hinder its capacity to win compliance with its policies and how widespread unfavorable views of a nation's policies can lead others to balk at, oppose, or build coalitions against that state.[109] For instance, a 2005 report of the Pew Global Attitudes Project indicated that as a result of negative European attitudes about the United States, "Europeans surveyed want to take a more independent approach from the

U.S. on security and diplomatic affairs."[110] In light of this connection between the cooperation a nation can expect and the view others hold of it, a 2007 BBC World Service poll showing a progressive increase in the percentage of those surveyed in twenty-five countries who view the "United States' influence" in world affairs as "mainly negative" (from 46 percent in 2005 to 52 percent in 2007) is sobering.[111]

How does the rest of the world perceive the PRC? Are U.S. views of China convergent with or distinct from the perceptions of others in the international system? Are Chinese capacities to shape external views growing, and what is the PRC doing to increase its capacities? What are the implications of these perceptions and capacities? And, as Chinese power grows, how must Beijing be careful?

Americans have a decidedly less favorable view of China than the people of most other countries that have been surveyed—often by a considerable margin, though as China's economic and military power have grown, wariness toward Beijing has grown elsewhere as well.[112] In a 2006 survey conducted by the Chicago Council on Global Affairs, American attitudes toward the PRC were markedly less favorable toward China than those of U.S. allies and close friends in the region—Australia, South Korea, and India.[113] The same survey reported that "the Asian countries surveyed all have warm feelings toward China, though Americans give it a cool rating." Only 43 percent of the Americans polled by the Pew Research Center for the People and the Press in May–June 2005 viewed China "favorably," compared to 65 percent of people polled in Great Britain. Indeed, by mid-2005 Pew reported that "China now has a better image than the U.S. in most of the European nations surveyed,"[114] though by mid-2007 European enthusiasm for the PRC had cooled somewhat.[115] Vice-President Cheney's response to this news was "I frankly don't spend a lot of time . . . reading polls."[116] While Canadians have anxieties about China, the Ipsos-Reid poll released in June 2005 reported that Americans were more wary: "Anxiety about China's emergence as a superpower is unsettling to many in North America: Fifty-four percent of Americans and 40 percent of Canadians agree that 'the emergence of China as a superpower is a threat to world peace.'"[117] Perhaps most startlingly, in June 2006 a *Harris-Financial Times* poll reported that 36 percent of those surveyed in Britain, France, Italy, and Spain identified the United States as "the greatest threat to world stability," as opposed to 30 percent who so identified Iran and 18 percent who so identified China.[118]

In the already cited Pew and Ipsos-Reid polls, two more dimensions of world attitudes toward China are clear. First, there is considerable anxiety that China's growing economy could negatively affect other societies, but this anxiety coexists with a sense of opportunity. "The [Pew] survey finds that while China is well-regarded in both Europe and Asia, its burgeoning economic power elicits mixed reactions."[119] The Ipsos-Reid study put it this way: "Most Canadians (61%) and half of Americans (50%) would describe China's economic growth as an 'opportunity.'"[120] Second, countries worried about China in either the economic or security domains nonetheless often see it as a useful offset to Washington's power. "There is considerable support across every country surveyed, with the notable exception of the U.S., for some other country or group of countries to rival the United States militarily."[121] While Europeans are against China's becoming a military rival to the United States, in most Muslim countries, including Turkey, "most people think a Chinese challenge to American military power would be a good thing."[122] While Canadians worry about Chinese economic competition, "seven in ten Canadians (68%) think expanding Canada's trade relations with China is a good idea because it will help reduce dependence on trading with the United States."[123]

Another 2005 global attitude survey, conducted for the British Broadcasting Corporation (BBC) World Service, reinforces the Pew and Ipsos-Reid findings. The poll director, Steven Kull, said of the results, "It is quite remarkable that with its growing economic power, China is viewed as so benign, especially by its Asian neighbors. However, this cordial view . . . does appear to depend on China's re-straining itself from seeking to convert its burgeoning economic power into a threatening military presence."[124] In seventeen of the twenty-two nations surveyed, more respondents thought China had a "positive influence" than a negative influence, and evaluations of China were on average higher than those of the United States. "Indeed China, at 48%, is almost on a par with Great Britain, which scored 50%."[125] As Steven Kull remarks, "Even more striking is the fact that, despite the country's [China's] incredible economic clout, when asked about the prospect of China's becoming more powerful economically, 16 [of 23] countries view that as a welcome trend."[126] Finally, when in late 2003 the Kasikorn Research Center in Bangkok asked Thais what country they considered their "closest friend," 76 percent chose the PRC, while only 9 percent selected the United States, Thailand's current ally.[127] It is essential to underscore, however, that as China's power, particularly its military strength, has grown, apprehensions have grown too, particularly in South Korea, India, Russia, and Japan.[128]

The above data suggest that Washington is prone to policy miscalculation because it presumes that its negative evaluations of the PRC are shared by other nations, some of whom are U.S. allies. Americans (particularly congressional staff) are perceptually predisposed to underestimate Chinese appeal elsewhere and to assume that our traditional friends (such as Australia and Canada, not to mention EU countries) accept U.S. values, assessments, and policies.[129] Gallup poll data show that for a decade after June 4, 1989, American attitudes toward China remained consistently unfavorable, despite the advances of Chinese reform after the Tiananmen tragedy.[130] Only by February 2005 had there been any significant increase in favorability rating of the PRC in the United States, and even then it came nowhere near the positive sentiment that had existed in the United States before Tiananmen. Data from polls conducted by Zogby International in 1994 and again in 2004–5 document the same trend; by 2005 Americans' "favorability" rating of China had improved, rising from 46 percent to 59 percent in 2004–5 among the general public, but the favorability rating by congressional staff was at a rock bottom 19 percent.[131] According to a joint Council on Foreign Relations and Pew Research Center poll comparing May 2001 and October 2005 data on how the American general public assessed China as an emerging power, in 2001, 51 percent reportedly viewed China as a "major threat," and in 2005 the figure was 52 percent.[132] As one former senior Australian government official put it, "We all worry a bit about U.S. policy. . . . Australia is much more accommodating [to China than the United States is]. There are elements absent in Australia. The ideological aspect is missing, [as it is for] the Europeans. We don't feel compelled to make China democratic. [We don't have the] idea that there should be a key determinant—[we] like case-by-case analysis."[133]

The Cato Institute's annual report *Economic Freedom of the World* provides added, and perhaps slightly more objective, perspective.[134] The report ranked the Hong Kong SAR of the PRC number one in the world in terms of economic freedom in both 2004 and 2005, a determination that is noteworthy in light of the widespread concerns regarding rule of law and individual rights after Hong Kong's reversion to Chinese sovereignty in mid-1997. In the 2005 annual report the United States was tied for third, along with New Zealand and Switzerland, with a score of 8.2, while the PRC was ranked 86th with a score of 6.0 on a scale of 1 to 10 in which 10 was the highest, and Hong Kong scored 8.7. The PRC ranked slightly lower than Mexico, slightly ahead of Brazil, and considerably ahead of Russia. The report notes that "the impact of economic freedom on whether states fight or have a military dispute is highly significant [statistically,] while democracy is not a statistically significant predictor of conflict. Nations with a low score for economic freedom (below 2 out of 10) are 14 times more prone to conflict than states with a high score (over 8)."[135] These data suggest that China has significant economic freedom and is not overly prone to conflict but that it has much room for improvement in economic freedom. The data seem more compatible with world public opinion of China than with the predominant U.S. sentiment toward the PRC.

The PRC's current image in the world is not nearly as negative as Americans are predisposed to think, and congressional staff opinion tends to be measurably more skeptical than that of the general U.S. public. The United States will not find Asia, Europe, and much of the rest of the world disposed to put pressure on Beijing as frequently or as much as the United States might wish. Instead, much of the world (including China) is looking for ways to offset American preeminence, though, as Yanzhong Huang, Bates Gill, and Sheng Ding point out, "The idea of having China as an alternative military power challenging the U.S. is not favored by the general public in the Western world."[136] A former senior Singaporean diplomat summed up global public opinion with brutal frankness: "There is rising anger against America. It is against American indifference to their problems. The Chinese are capitalizing on this brilliantly. I was in Australia, your [the United States'] deputy sheriff. When I finished my talk in Melbourne, all thirty people there attacked me for being too soft [on the United States]. A public poll there indicates people there see the U.S. as a bigger threat to world peace. If you look at South Korea, they are worried about who is less predictable. North Korea is predictable in its own way. Your talk of regime change—who will pay the price?"[137]

The core aspects of Chinese foreign policy are intended to reassure the world through talk of "peaceful rise," "peaceful development," and "the New Security Concept." The PRC buys and invests abroad and acts multilaterally. These policies are a reasonable response to the mélange of fear and optimism that characterizes foreign views of China. The degree to which Beijing projects a reassuring image augments China's capacities to win cooperation and minimizes the likelihood that the United States or others could form a countervailing coalition. This relatively positive image, along with the economic opportunities described in the preceding chapter, has made China attractive both economically and diplomatically, insofar as Beijing provides an alternative model of how big powers should relate to others— the essence of Nye's "soft power." The area in which China is least reassuring to others is that of transnational spillovers from its headlong rush for economic growth—product safety in the global supply chain, environmental effects, and resource competition, phenomena discussed in chapter 6.

VEHICLES FOR SPREADING
CULTURE, POLICY, AND IDEOLOGY

China's leaders, particularly those in the diplomatic, education, and propaganda fields, are thinking systematically about the vehicles for effectively projecting ideational power. I was struck by the 2005 remarks of the president of the Foreign Ministry's Foreign Affairs University, Wu Jianmin, about how China must improve its ability to express itself internationally:

> It is also necessary to learn how to engage in exchanges in the process of communicating with the outside world. . . . After becoming president of the Foreign Affairs University, the lesson I most wanted to give students was that [lesson] in "exchanges," because China is still very weak in this respect. In order to better face society and the future, the university has now established a course in the "study of exchanges." This is a newly emerging science on the international scene; we are not talking about dull theory; instead, through a great number of vivid and concrete examples and classroom simulations, we are urging the students to combine theoretical study with their personal practice, and enhance their ability in oral and non-oral exchanges, cross-cultural exchanges, and handling of relations with the media, thus cultivating a good attitude and ability among the students in carrying out communications.[138]

FOREIGN STUDENTS IN CHINA AND
CHINESE STUDENTS ABROAD

Since about 2000, Beijing has increasingly facilitated foreign students' study in the PRC and developed special programs and support systems for them. Although students from Taiwan (or from the Hong Kong and Macau SARs) are not considered "foreign" by Beijing, they have been affected by the policy changes. From 1985 to 2000, the total number of students coming to China from Taiwan for undergraduate education numbered 2,895 (averaging 193 per year throughout the period); in graduate studies they numbered 864 (averaging about 58 per year). From 2000 to 2004, those total corresponding numbers were 2,875 (719 per year) and 2,766 (692 per year in MA and PhD programs), a sharp increase over the prior period's average.[139] In a January 2005 group meeting, Premier Wen Jiabao said, "There are eight thousand students from Taiwan here."[140] Whatever the exact number, Beijing planned to accelerate this trend, and in August 2005 it announced that students from Taiwan who were studying in mainland institutions of higher education would be charged the same tuition as local students, with tuition losses for PRC schools made up by the central government.[141] As of this writing, Taipei is reluctant to recognize the course work and degrees obtained by its students on the mainland. In a subsequent conversation that I had with a senior Taiwan official involved in cross-Strait relations, he described a fear among educational authorities on the island that

Beijing's growing educational capacity would draw students away from island institutions. In late 2006, breaking the ice somewhat, six PRC universities agreed to a small undergraduate student exchange program with National Taiwan University.

In Hong Kong as well one sees growing numbers of Hong Kong university-bound students going to the PRC, in some cases because the opportunities for study there are broader, in some cases because the perceived prestige of China's top universities is greater than available alternatives, and in some cases simply because they can get in.[142] Interestingly, as Hong Kong students are exposed to the Chinese educational and political systems, they become more critical of the problems of those systems, such as inflexibility, poor English-language instruction, and corruption.

With regard to enrollments of students of other nationalities, the Ministry of Education reported that in 2003 there were 77,715 foreign students in the PRC—almost 82 percent of them from Asia and 45 percent from South Korea alone.[143] For 2004 the ministry reported that China had 110,844 overseas students, up over 42 percent from the preceding year,[144] and the target was to have 120,000 foreign students enrolled by the end of 2007.[145] Compare this to the figure of over 565,039 international students in the United States in 2004–5. Students from the United States in the PRC numbered 7,000 in 2004 (up from 4,703 the year before), while those from Europe totaled 6,000. Indeed, some Chinese institutions are becoming selective about which foreign students they accept—in mid-2005 Fudan University administered its first entrance exam for foreign student applicants, with the number of available slots considerably fewer than the number taking the test.[146] In December 2003, to encourage good students from around Asia to come to China, retired Asian statesmen initiated the Education Forum for Asia, and the China Scholarship Council was given responsibility for administering scholarships to be awarded to one or two students nominated by their home countries throughout Asia. The first entrants into Chinese universities with this support began study in fall 2005. A primary purpose of coming to the PRC for foreign students is language study. China's economic power and prospects attract foreign students' interest, which in turn enhances China's cultural influence. Beijing reported that 2,563 Indonesian students were granted visas for study in 2003, up 51 percent over the previous year.[147] In 2004, 1,000 Mongolians were studying in China, reflecting the fact that in Mongolia Chinese and English have become the preferred foreign languages, surpassing Russian.[148] Singapore's government sends as many students to China and India as to America. One Singaporean student returning from the PRC explained, "People looked down on China. Now there is a 180-degree change. In the past, experience in the United States was important; now experience in China is just as good."[149]

Chinese graduate schools now are establishing special programs targeting foreign students in areas where they are competitive, such as China studies. In September 2005, for example, Fudan University's School of International Relations and Public Administration began an all-English-language MA program in Chinese politics and diplomacy. Students from twelve countries enrolled; three were from the United States. Students who matriculate will pay $12,000 a year in tuition.[150] Also in 2005, People's University in Beijing announced a master's degree program in contemporary China studies, to be taught all in English by Chinese professors. The point is that Chinese "exports" gradually will come to include the provision of intellectual and cultural services in areas where America has heretofore been dominant. Until China has free access to information and less constrained expression, however, it will be disadvantaged.

There are two reasons for Beijing's drive to boost the number of foreign students—influence and revenue. With respect to influence, the Ministry of Education declared that "more than 30 of the students who returned to their home countries from China now are holding ministerial-level posts. Over 10 have returned as ambassadors to China while another 30 are holding other high positions in their countries' embassies here. About 120 are professors or associate professors, and hundreds are project managers or commercial deputies in cultural, economic and trade entities of their countries engaged in activities with China."[151] With respect to revenue, the ministry noted in 2004 that 90 percent of the foreign students provided their own funding.

While many are receptive to China's drive to attract foreign students, there is resistance in some countries. Notably, some of the resistant countries are on China's periphery and have a deeply engrained fear of Chinese cultural domination, even when Chinese cultural legacies are everywhere apparent. Vietnam is a striking example. "Do Vietnamese students go to China to study?" I asked the members of one Vietnamese academic organization. As one participant simply shook his head "no," another replied, "China wants this, and what I say is not based on official sources, but [China is] not a major destination for Vietnam. Australia and New Zealand are preferred, Europe and North America. We are sending one researcher to Shanghai University—they send no one here. We are survivors, we have defined our independence over a thousand years."[152] Or, as one U.S. government official put it, "More Vietnamese study in California than all of China."[153]

The PRC also sends numerous students abroad, though as its own education system grows in size and quality there is a somewhat diminished need to do so. In Australia and Thailand, Chinese students (including students in secondary school) have become important for their provision of both talent and money; as Hu Jintao noted in his October 2003 speech to the Australian Parliament, "China is now the biggest source country of foreign students in Australia."[154] One senior Australian official acknowledged their financial importance by saying they were "the largest student population [in Australia], sixty thousand, one-half of whom are in secondary schools to feed into the universities. One-half are undergraduates. All are fully paying."[155] In the late 1990s there were only fifty PRC students at Assumption University in Thailand, but in 2004 there were eight hundred, most paying their own fees.[156] In U.S. graduate schools, Chinese graduate students have been important to hard science research and teaching programs for a long time: in the 2003–4 academic year there were 61,765 matriculated Chinese students in American institutions of higher education.[157] The number of Chinese students has also been rising dramatically elsewhere—in South Korea, for example. In the academic year 2003–4, 47,740 Chinese were studying in the United Kingdom, up 35.8 percent from the previous year,[158] and for the entire EU that year the number was estimated to be 100,000.[159] Perhaps the most significant development has been that since about 2002 the rate of return for PRC students who studied abroad has increased, with the overall rate of return from 1978 through 2002 having been about 26 percent.[160] There are many reasons for rising rates of return, but perceptions of increased economic opportunity are primary.

Bridging the gap between conventional student exchanges and the building of cultural centers abroad (discussed below), in 2005 the Chinese and Egyptian governments announced the creation of an "Egyptian Chinese University" slated to enroll nine hundred students for the 2006–7 academic year. This institution would be "the first Chinese university to be set up in the Middle East region" and would be home to a Confucius Institute.[161] Also in 2005, for the first time a foreign university was allowed to set up a representative office in Beijing "to promote academic exchanges between Tokyo University and Chinese universities and research institutes."[162]

CHINESE CULTURAL CENTERS
AND RELATED INSTITUTIONS

Chinese language study is becoming more popular in many parts of the world. Beijing is establishing cultural centers abroad that offer foreigners multiple ways to learn Chinese language and to be exposed to Chinese culture and views. This effort draws on the experiences of the Goethe Institute, the Maison Française, the Spanish Cervantes Institute, and the British Council, as well as Fulbright Commissions. The

PRC Ministry of Education's National Office for Teaching Chinese as a Foreign Language (charged with "promoting the Chinese language and helping other countries acquire a better understanding of China") is establishing "Confucius Institutes" around the world, institutions that teach the Chinese language, as well as promote Chinese movies and television programs, facilitate foreign study in China, offer library services, and "fuel research work in the field of China studies."[163] PRC plans in 2005 called for one hundred such institutions worldwide by 2010; institutes in Seoul, Korea, and at the University of Maryland were formed in November 2004 and subsequent institutes were under development in 2005 at the University of Western Australia, Stockholm University, the British Columbia Institute of Technology, Nanyang Technological University in Singapore, the Université de Liege in Belgium, the University of Auckland, the University of Melbourne, Ritsumeikan and Obirin Universities in Japan, Nairobi University in Kenya, and one institution in Uzbekistan. According to one report, in the program's first year, Beijing established twenty-seven such institutions and had a budget of $200 million to teach foreigners the Chinese language.[164] In April 2007, Beijing announced that there were 140 institutes in fifty-plus countries and regions.[165]

The Confucius Institute Project headquarters in Beijing specifies the various kinds of arrangements pertaining to the creation, governance, and operation of branch institutes abroad: "A 'Confucius Institute' can be built with direct investment from the Headquarter, partnership between the Headquarter and a local institute, or franchise authorized by the Headquarter. Currently the 'Confucius Institute' will be built mainly through partnering with foreign institutes."[166] The guidelines make clear that it is a prerequisite that institutes "accept operational guidance from the Headquarter and follow relevant teaching standard[s]."[167] Like Fulbright Commissions established around the world, bodies that have binational membership and close ties to U.S. embassies, Confucian Institutes are the leading edge of Beijing's public diplomacy effort, which draws on the experiences of the United States, Taiwan, and others.

China is building or participating in other cultural centers as well. In 2003 the Thai royal family supported the construction of such a center, one that received substantial PRC support. That year centers were also established in Egypt, France, and Malta. In Kathmandu, Nepal, in July 2004 a nongovernmental organization called the Chinese Information Center was established that regularly shows Chinese films. It is difficult to assess the impact of these institutions, but they are part of a new, systematic effort to increase China's attractiveness and influence through language and culture.

In an example of linguistic foreign aid, China has agreed to pay 50 percent of the estimated $1.35 million cost to help develop the Advanced Placement Chinese Language and Culture course for U.S. high schools—work that involves scholarships for Chinese teachers and the actual creation of exams, teacher training materials, and a preparation regimen. The number of primary and secondary school students studying Chinese in the United States is already growing, having tripled from 1995 to 2005, though from a low base. In Chicago, where Chinese language classes in the public schools are being promoted, Mayor Richard Daley said: "I think there will be two languages in this world. There will be Chinese and English."[168] In 2003 Beijing was asserting that thirty million persons abroad were learning Chinese and that one of its most successful book export areas was textbooks for learning Chinese.[169]

TOURISM

Tourism is an indicator of attractive capacity and a vehicle of spreading influence and hence ideational power. It also contributes to economic muscle and therefore overlaps with economic power. Beijing knows that other countries compete for the rapidly growing numbers of mainland tourists who are surprisingly big spenders abroad, with each traveler on average spending about $2,400 in 2003: 90 percent of the 250,000 Chinese travelers to the United States went to Las Vegas.[170] When President Hu Jintao visited Mexico in September 2005, the one thing he could offer Mexico City that held out the prospect of compensating to some extent for Mexico's gaping trade deficit with the PRC was a promise to allow large Chinese group tours to go to Mexico.[171] As one senior Chinese Foreign Ministry official put it, "True, ten years ago people were suspicious of China, but now we are promoting trade, cultural cooperation, and tourism. So more and more countries want China to designate them as an approved destination for tourism."[172] As of February 2005 China had approved travel to sixty-three countries for Chinese tour groups.[173] In 2006 the First Ministerial Conference of the China-Pacific Island Countries Economic Development and Cooperation Forum was held in Nadi, Fiji, with the host and Vanuatu calling for more tourism and investment from China. The Chinese report of the meeting stated that "so far, all countries in the Pacific region having diplomatic ties with the People's Republic of China have become destinations for Chinese tourists,"[174] an explicit linkage between tourist revenue and diplomatic ties, meaning derecognition of Taiwan.

In 2003 China surpassed Japan as the leading source of Asian tourists (20.2 million people, spending $48 billion). The World Tourism Organization predicts that by 2020 Chinese will be taking one hundred million trips abroad annually;[175] 34.52 million PRC citizens traveled abroad in 2006. Countries wishing to receive large numbers of Chinese tourists must develop an infrastructure and at least minimal language capacity and cultural sensitivity to attract and accommodate the visitors. One Chinese tourist in Paris complained about the lack of hot drinking water, saying, "They need to think about catering more to Chinese tastes. . . . We don't drink cold water."[176] The need for countries seeking to lure Chinese travelers to adapt to Chinese needs represents one form of influence. Indeed, the power of Chinese tourist dollars (an estimated six hundred thousand tourists visited France in 2005) prompted the French government to publish a guide recommending that those hosting Chinese tourists avoid sensitive political topics. Tourism Minister Leon Bertrand reportedly explained that the goal was to make sure that the Chinese returned on subsequent visits.[177]

In Singapore (with 880,000 tourists from the PRC in 2004, exceeded only by the 1,765,000 from Indonesia that year), tourism has become an important part of the economy.[178] Other important destinations for PRC citizens are Japan, Vietnam, South Korea, Russia, Thailand, and the United States. In Macau, while figures are almost impossible to verify, about 70 percent of the money passing across gambling tables is of PRC origin. On landfill connecting two islands in Macau, "The City of Dreams" is under construction to expand and capture the flow of bets.

As for tourists coming to China, the number of inbound travelers has grown at an average annual rate of 20 percent since 1978; Beijing expects to be the world's most popular tourist destination by 2014 and became the world's fourth-largest tourist destination in 2005, supplanting Italy.[179] As He Guangwei, director of China National Tourism, put it, "China is on its way to becoming one of the world's most powerful tourism nations."[180]

ESTABLISHING THE INFRASTRUCTURE FOR GLOBAL MASS COMMUNICATION

Beijing could not be clearer about its determination to break the U.S. and Western global media monopoly. In the words of *Renmin Ribao* (People's Daily), "The United States, on its part, not only possesses the world's largest political and military hegemony, but also has in its hands the biggest media and cultural hegemony. The 'soft strength' of Western news media far surpasses its economic 'hard strength.'"[181]

The Chinese space program is part of the PRC's effort to break U.S. media domination and includes ambitious plans to develop a comprehensive satellite communications system that would enable China to have a real-time, twenty-four-hour global television and mass communication capability under national control by 2010.[182] In February 2005 China inaugurated satellite television service in Asia, making its "Great Wall TV Package" of eleven channels with programs in English, Mandarin, Cantonese, and Min dialect available in Vietnam, Thailand, South Korea, Myanmar (Burma), Hong Kong, Macau, and Taiwan; this package had been launched the preceding October in North America. Li Jian, president of the China International TV Corporation, said, "We are looking to launch our Great Wall satellite service in Europe, Africa and Oceania in the future to serve Chinese around the globe and overseas audience."[183] In a September 2005 conversation with a CCTV employee I was told that their figures were not reliable but that the network believed that the Great Wall package was available in forty to sixty million households. Just to give an idea of potential, according to the U.S. Census Bureau, Chinese is the second (albeit a distant second) most spoken foreign language in the United States after Spanish. With regard to English-language radio broadcasting in China, reports indicate that in late 2004 China Radio International was broadcasting twenty-four hours daily in English, while Voice of America was slated to cut back to fourteen hours daily.[184]

This global communications capacity connects the Chinese Diaspora discussed in the preceding chapter to China and partially accounts for the rising nationalism among overseas Chinese communities documented by Hong Liu. "Through such intermediaries as Chinese-language newspapers, websites, and TV programs, they form a borderless and imagined greater China that is bound by *both* the ideas of sovereignty and transnational culture. From the mainland, a series of policies relating to the Chinese overseas facilitate the connections between China and its population overseas, thus providing a potential ground for the revival of overseas Chinese nationalism. The rise of China as potential world power further prompts such a trend" (emphasis in original).[185]

In the area of film, Beijing's Culture and Propaganda ministries and nongovernment producers, often in partnership with firms in Hong Kong and elsewhere, are seeking to broaden the reach of Chinese movies. Drawing on data from *Screen Digest*, David Hancock shows that while the English language has a "global weight" of 16.4 percent, English-language films draw 54.2 percent of the global box office (tickets sold); the Chinese language, while also having a global weight of 16.4 percent, only draws 1.6 percent of the global box office. As Hancock puts it, English is "punching movie tickets above [its] linguistic weight" while Chinese-language films punch below their linguistic weight.[186] Nonetheless, PRC firms and governmental organizations are trying to increase audience share. In late 2004 Warner Brothers set up a joint venture with China Film Group (state owned) and Hengdian Group (a private Chinese firm) called Warner China Film to "produce, market and distribute Chinese-language feature films, TV movies and animation."[187] In 2004 China had the fastest-growing total of film box office revenues in the world, though it still accounted for only 0.9 percent of total global revenues—the United States accounted for 45.8 percent.[188]

China's entertainment and publication industries are developing export products both to earn revenue and to embed Chinese views abroad. The PRC Press and Publication Administration uses financial and tax policies to encourage Chinese publishing enterprises (all four hundred thousand of them) to expand overseas. In late 2004 the Press and Publication Administration announced, "China will organize [a] publishing and distribution corps to increase international competitiveness."[189] While the Propaganda Ministry plays a major role in this outward thrust, it has virtually no sense of what foreigners are looking for; occasionally Chinese firms have developed products favorably received abroad through joint ventures.

Overall, however, China's cultural export industry is weak, as reflected in the fact that in publishing "the export of China's copyrights are only one-tenth of the imports, or 5,362 over the past nine years."[190] One interviewee involved with this industry said that, despite the ineffectiveness of many current efforts, in a decade or two foreign publishers were going to be surprised by what Chinese competitors had learned. The days are gone when the Chinese were passive, hoping that someone in America would understand and articulate their point of view for them.[191] In 2003 it was reported that the U.S. and Canadian circulation of Hong Kong's Beijing-oriented *Ming Pao* was growing at 7 to 10 percent annually.[192] Nonetheless, while the desire to enhance Chinese cultural exports and media influence is there, these efforts will be retarded until political penalties for free expression are diminished.

The PRC is also exploiting new information technologies. The number of Chinese-language-speaking Internet users was second only to the number of English-language users in late 2005.[193] With respect to cell phone technology, in spring of 2005 China's state-run news agency, Xinhua, signed an agreement with a subsidiary of Fujitsu whereby the two parties would provide Japanese cell phone subscribers online information over the Internet, including news, photos, and economic data. The report of this transaction concluded by noting that Xinhua had "products in seven languages for domestic and overseas markets."[194]

Besides building the systems to convey culture, data, and ideas globally, the PRC has been encouraging neighboring countries to use more Chinese programming. In late 2004 South Korea's deputy minister of culture and tourism, Bae Jong-sin, reported that "the Chinese Minister of Culture Sun Jiazheng, explaining the rapid expansion of the 'Korean Wave' in China, asked for cooperation so that a 'Chinese Wind' could blow in Korea as well." Sun reportedly stated that "European culture had led the world for the last 500 years, but the era in which Asian culture should lead global culture has come."[195]

Culture, educational exchange, tourism, and communications infrastructure are part of a nation's ideational power as well as its economic base. While the Chinese have a powerful culture that is attractive in many respects and the PRC infrastructures for public diplomacy and international diffusion are improving, capabilities are not yet robust. Nonetheless, in the satellite, cable television, and the Internet era, English-speaking populations can be unaware of developments in the parallel universe of Chinese language diffusing all around them.

The best available net assessment of China's use of ideational power was provided by Singapore's ambassador to the United States, Chan Heng Chee, in remarks in 2005:

> China's new soft power engagement [in Southeast Asia] in recent times has created reactions never thought possible before. For example, for the last four decades, hardly anyone of Chinese blood in Southeast Asia publicly identified with China. There were Chinese clan associations and Chinese business networks throughout Southeast Asia, but apart from those in Malaysia and Singapore, most kept a low profile. Now they are positively flourishing. Studying *putonghua* [standard Chinese] is trendy again. Thai PM [Prime Minister] Thaksin Shinawatra tells Premier Wen Jiabao, "I am Chinese too, brother." Indonesian President Megawati declared that Chinese Indonesians can celebrate ethnic Chinese holidays. This was a new democratic Indonesia talking, but it was also the rise of China. Malaysian Prime Minister Abdullah Badawi, Thai Prime Minister Thaksin Shinawatra, and President Gloria Arroyo of the Philippines paid their first visit outside of ASEAN to China.[196]

To return to the level of China's grand strategy and the interlocking and mutually interacting character of the three types of power, Chinese leaders since Deng Xiaoping have given pride of place to the acquisition of convertible, economic power. Economic power has contributed to the growth of ideational strength in several ways. Economic success itself is attractive and suggests to other developing countries a way forward. Moreover, economic power is convertible, providing the wherewithal for the development of communications infrastructure, international exchange, education, and R&D. These factors have all contributed to the growth of ideational power and facilitated the creation of an external environment that offers the most resources and fewest threats to China as it modernizes. Beijing also emphasizes the acquisition of ideational power to drive economic growth by cultivating leadership talent and innovation capacity.

China has strong assets along some dimensions of ideational power while remaining weak in others. In terms of international legitimacy and conventional diplomacy, the PRC shows increasing strength. In education, cultural exchange, and communications infrastructure, its progress has been striking. Research and innovation capacities are increasing but still not robust. At the same time, China has its weaknesses, notably in mass cultural products and broader political system attractiveness.

One difficulty is that Beijing faces what Joseph Nye calls the "two audience problem"—its message often plays better in poor, autocratic, and sometimes Asian societies than in Western liberal democracies. Moreover, China's attempt to reassure others in the international system with ideational power will be effective only as long as its coercive and economic faces are also reassuring. If one considers where China was in terms of ideational power in 1978, what has been described above represents a revolutionary departure from Maoist policies. Aggressive and confrontational ideology has been replaced by the vocabulary of multilateral diplomacy and interdependence. Intellectual autarky has been replaced by scholarly cross-fertilization. China's diplomatic face to the world, once that of ignorant revolutionaries, is now that of cosmopolitan diplomats, technocrats, intellectuals, and businesspersons. A country that used to be both unwilling and too economically and intellectually impoverished to travel, to engage in meaningful cultural and educational exchange, or to participate in international competition in the realm of ideas is now active in all domains. Though these developments create competitive challenges for outsiders, they are expressions of Chinese ideational power that are essentially constructive. The last genuine hurdle to be overcome is creating the kind of intellectual and political society in which heterodox thinking stimulates even more rapid growth in all forms of power.

We now turn to the utilization and effect of the three faces of Chinese power in its neighborhood.

FIVE · China and Its Neighbors

> The water far away cannot put out the fire nearby—
> China is the nearby fire and the United States is the
> distant water.
>
> VIETNAMESE SCHOLAR,
> Ho Chi Minh City, 2006

> Australians look at a map and say, how isolated we are—
> we are alone and we need friends—the United States.
> New Zealanders say, look how isolated we are, no one is
> going to bother us and we don't need friends—no one
> will bother.
>
> SENIOR AUSTRALIAN OFFICIAL, 2005

> Our worst fear is to get two simultaneous phone calls,
> one from Washington and the other from Beijing, asking
> us to take sides in a conflict.
>
> SENIOR SINGAPORE OFFICIAL, 2005

> Our dream is to move to another place, but [this is] not
> possible, so we have to live with China.
>
> VIETNAMESE NGO OFFICER, 2006

Contemporary Chinese leaders employ the nation's coercive, economic, and ideational power across an ever-larger geographic expanse. As Beijing's interests and capabilities expand, the periphery of concern will correspondingly enlarge. The Middle East, Latin America, and Africa loom larger in Chinese thinking than ever before.

Nonetheless, pacifying the nation's close-in periphery and exerting sway over its neighbors have traditionally been the first preoccupations of Chinese statecraft; these purposes remain very important today.[1] In the thirteenth century China was occupied by Mongols; in the seventeenth century it was again occupied, this time by the neighboring Manchus; and in the twentieth century the weak Republic of China was overrun by the Japanese. In the 1950s the PRC was embroiled in bloody conflict with America and its UN allies on the neighboring Korean Peninsula. Sino-American friction over Taiwan and Vietnam (where the French were fighting) in the 1950s, along with fears of China's nuclear development effort in the early 1960s, produced explicit and implied nuclear threats directed against Beijing. When the Soviet Union considered preemptive strikes against PRC nuclear facilities in the late 1960s, the proximate cause was border conflict. When Washington wanted to subvert the Chinese communist regime during the Cold War, it operated, in part, along the frontiers of Tibet in the southwest. And there were border conflicts along the boundaries with India in the 1960s and Vietnam in the 1970s.

The central lesson for China from this long history of conflict and at times occupation by peoples on its periphery has been that correctly managing relations with its neighbors is essential to forestall threats, whether the origin of the peril is near or far away. China fully trusts none of its neighbors—it has no Canada along its vast boundaries, and it is predisposed to see hostile distant powers operating through nearby proxies. The Russians have tried to use India, Afghanistan, Central Asia, and Korea as leverage over China at various times. The Americans have threatened China from Korea, Taiwan, Vietnam, and bordering Himalayan states. Consequently, Beijing always scrutinizes U.S. and other foreign-power dealings with China's neighbors for clues to intentions toward the PRC itself.

From the perspective of its Asian neighbors, China's attentions have been at times coercive and at times soft, using the seduction of economic inducement and the attractive features of culture. Whatever the instrument, China's neighbors have to varying extents been wary for a very long time, employing a broad repertoire of means to constrain Chinese behavior or adapt to the Middle Kingdom's strengths. Their tools have ranged from active resistance to deterrence, alliance or balancing with other powers, entanglement of China in multilateral agreements and relationships, and submission (feigned or otherwise). Today globalization, regional economic integration, China's growing military and diplomatic strength, and its cultural reach (including growing numbers of tourists) all combine to make Beijing increasingly salient to its neighbors.[2] As a then foreign minister in an Asian capital told me, "Imagine that you are watching a very large gorilla on TV and it suddenly jumps from the box into your living room and says, 'I want to be your friend.'"

If you visit Hanoi, the first public monument you are likely to see is a statue of Ly Thai To, who lived from 974 to 1028 CE and founded a stable Vietnamese dynasty in the area of the Red River Delta, a polity sufficiently strong to resist Chinese encroachment for two centuries. Ly founded his dynasty after nine hundred years of subordination (in the northern part of today's Vietnam) to China by building a bureaucratic edifice and hydrological infrastructure (skills at which the Chinese had long excelled). These regime pillars provided a relatively stable basis for governance and the economy, while at the same time revealing both the influence of China on the Vietnamese people and the enduring Vietnamese desire to resist Chinese control. More than a few city streets and landmarks in today's Hanoi are named after martyrs in the cause of resisting Chinese occupation and pressure, including one avenue named after the Trung sisters (Hai Ba Trung), who lived around 40 CE and committed suicide rather than surrender to the northern oppressors.[3] The city's central lake, Ho Hoan Kiem, "the lake of the restored sword," is associated with the fifteenth-century defeat of Ming Dynasty invaders. Thus it should not be a surprise that even today much of what the Vietnamese do in the realm of foreign affairs takes China into account.

Because of these types of memories and contemporary asymmetries of power, how China deals with its neighbors will be taken as an indicator of how it will employ its growing strength more broadly. China's neighbors are the proverbial canaries in the mine for the rest of the world. For the PRC, how other powers behave in its neighborhood will be a litmus test of their intentions toward China.

When outside powers frame their dealings with China's neighbors as a means to constrain PRC power, they feed Chinese suspicions. Crude attempts by Washington or others to use Vietnam, India, or other Asian countries to explicitly balance Beijing are ill advised, and China must similarly be careful about how its dealings in Central and South America will look to U.S. observers, as Beijing is beginning to realize.[4] Even if the United States or other powers attempt to balance certain neighbors of China against Chinese power, this will not be an easy task—China's neighbors are proud and unwilling to be cast as any nation's pawn. Surviving with China and seizing the opportunities it provides require that the PRC's neighbors act with discretion and subtlety. Everyone in the region, including the Chinese, understands the eternal necessity to seek balance but understands that this must be done "tacitly," in the words of Cheng-Chwee Kuik.[5] As one eminent academic of ethnic Indian origin living in England put it, "But the U.S. ganging up with India is a danger, and India needs to be careful, and Asia, not to get entangled in American problems."[6] And as one very senior defense official in Australia told me bluntly, "I was in India ten days ago. They [the Indians] are pleased with the recovery in India-China relations and more so with relations with the U.S., but they don't want to be seen as encircling China, at least not be seen to be doing so. India is conflicted."[7]

This chapter will describe the dominant understanding in Beijing of its neighborhood; discuss the diverse instruments that Beijing employs to pursue its regional and more distant interests; and turn to how China's neighbors view Beijing's intentions and actions and what strategies they pursue in light of that understanding. Thereafter it will examine four countries in the Pacific Rim neighborhood (Australia, Singapore, Indonesia, and Vietnam) and conclude by looking at China's interactions with its closest big-power neighbors (Japan, Russia, and India). The selected cases provide a glimpse of the varied circumstances, dilemmas, and policies China confronts in the region.

DIPLOMATIC GEOGRAPHY FROM BEIJING'S PERSPECTIVE

China lives in a tough and complicated neighborhood. Among its fourteen contiguous land neighbors, four have nuclear weapons (Russia, India, Pakistan, and the DPRK), and others nearby have the theoretical potential to acquire them relatively quickly. Beijing has fought armed conflicts of some significance with (and/or in) four neighboring states since 1949 (India, the Soviet Union, Vietnam, and Korea), not counting its periodic displays of force toward Taiwan and its involvement in the Afghan insurgency against Moscow in the late 1970s and 1980s. This history of conflict with (and within) its neighbors, combined with contemporary circumstances, creates an implicit matrix in the minds of PRC policy makers.

The central axes of this matrix are the "importance" of a particular state to PRC national interests[8] and the perceived intentions of that state's leadership toward China—running from "friendly" to "hostile." A neighbor's location in the resulting matrix can change over time, and different policy-relevant Chinese actors may differ over how to categorize individual nations or societies at any given moment. Obviously, this categorization is subjective inasmuch as a state's "importance" and "intentions" are subject to multiple interpretations. A state's importance in one issue area or circumstance may not be the same in another. Further, different relationships energize different networks of bureaucratic and social interest in the Chinese polity. Maintaining good relations with North Korea, for example, is more important to China's Korean War veterans than it is to younger Chinese, who often view Pyongyang as a retrograde, ungrateful drag on China's quest for modernity, respect, and security.

Placing China's neighbors in this hypothetical matrix produces several conclusions. To begin, China has very few neighboring relationships that are both highly important and reliably friendly. Pakistan appears to be an exception, though Beijing is not sure how long Muslim fundamentalism may be held at bay in Islamabad.

Today's cooperative relations with Vietnam, Russia, and Indonesia, for example, could quickly sour. Conversely, China's current rather troubled ties with Japan could improve or deteriorate further. China has few low-maintenance relationships.

Second, allies of the United States (Australia, South Korea, Philippines, and Thailand) are more likely to be in China's "somewhat friendly/important" category than in the "somewhat unfriendly/important" category. Washington, therefore, needs to keep in mind that its allies and Beijing have a bigger investment in positive bilateral relations than it may realize. Containment of Beijing is not a realistic policy option for the United States—as long as the PRC acts reassuringly.

Third, the most difficult big-power relationship Beijing currently has is with a regional neighbor, Tokyo. This is a major problem not only for China and Japan but for Washington too, given the U.S.-Japan alliance. Also in the highly problematic category are Beijing's ties with Pyongyang, a relationship China detests but fears to rupture.

Yet for Beijing, at the same time and despite all the challenges, the current external environment is the least hostile it has been in hundreds of years.

OBJECTIVES AND TOOLS IN DEALING WITH NEIGHBORS

OBJECTIVES

In chapter 1 we described the broad current consensus in Beijing concerning the need to maintain relatively stable external relationships in order to provide conditions for sustained focus on China's enormous internal problems, challenges discussed at greater length in the following chapter. Now (and for the next several decades) Chinese leaders and people are predisposed to increase comprehensive national power, secure the homeland, increase national status, and establish a plausible foundation for eventual "reunification" with Taiwan in the indeterminate future. As Beijing's economic resources grow, its armed strength will increase. Chinese generally view this process as one of regaining the place they have occupied throughout most of recorded human history rather than achieving an unfamiliar status. They see their growing role not as destabilizing but as restoring a global equilibrium that was shattered by the industrial revolution and the rise of the West and Japan.

For its neighbors, however, the concept of restoring an equilibrium in which China played a leading role is mixed news. For Japan, a country with its own sense of greatness, distinctive culture, global economic importance, and democratic politics, the news of a rising China has its distressing aspects. For the smaller nations, societies, and peoples near the PRC who in the past have felt Chinese coercive power (e.g., Korea, Mongolia, and Vietnam, not to mention the special case of Taiwan), the prospect of restoring a past equilibrium is anxiety inducing. At the same time, these smaller societies see the advantages that can be derived from trade and finance and from the ability to play big powers (e.g., the United States, PRC, and Japan) off one another.

In the foreseeable future, China's objective in the region is not to dictate outcomes so much as to prevent others in the region from undertaking activities that threaten core Chinese interests. Beijing, for example, does not wish to see U.S. naval bases in nearby states, just as it does not wish to see Japan and Washington speak of their "common strategic objectives" in relation to Taiwan's security (as they did in the "two-plus-two" talks in early 2005 and thereafter). Neither does Beijing appreciate Tokyo and Washington's cooperation on antimissile defense technology that could undermine the credibility of its missile deterrent. The ultimate question for Washington is, therefore, Can the United States live with a China that does not seek to control Asia, or expel America from it, but rather seeks to prevent actions that are contrary to its own core national interests? I think that the United States can live with such a China and that the PRC's neighbors increasingly will demand that Washington do so, even as they want the United States to remain a major presence in the region.

China's neighbors find themselves in a delicate balancing act—they seek the "water far away" (the United States) to help manage the "fire nearby" (China), all the while preserving all their positive economic interests with both America and China. Beijing knows these sentiments exist and tries to short-circuit the propensity of its neighbors to seek external balancers and arm themselves by engaging in reassuring diplomacy and other activities, to which we now turn.

TOOLS

China now participates in regional and global multilateral organizations to a degree that is striking. Beijing is most active multilaterally when it sees the opportunity to constrain other powers and/or to greatly influence a multilateral organization. So, for example, China favored an East Asia Summit in late 2005 that effectively excluded Washington from participation. Beijing has been a driver of the SCO, which at its mid-2005 summit adopted a declaration calling for the "respective members of the antiterrorist coalition" (read the United States and its allies) to "set a final timeline for their temporary use of the above-mentioned objects of [military-related] infrastructure and stay of their military contingents on the territories of the

SCO member states."[9] Richard B. Myers, then chairman of the U.S. Joint Chiefs of Staff, accused the PRC and Russia of "trying to bully" their Central Asia neighbors into this move.[10] Beijing promotes an ASEAN free-trade area (FTA) and ASEAN + 3 mechanisms to offset the North American Free Trade Area and the EU as well as to create forums for discussion in which Washington is not present. The FTAs that Beijing proposes also put additional pressure on Taipei to improve relations with the mainland if it wishes to gain the benefits that such arrangements presumably would confer. At the same time, Beijing avoids engaging in bilateral conflicts with the United States.

Nonetheless, it is easy to discern Beijing's enduring preference for bilateral relationships, particularly with its smaller neighbors. As one Vietnamese researcher working on the greater Mekong River system put it, "By emphasizing bilateral negotiation they [China] can restrict others in the region. For example, go bilateral with Thailand; give a grant to Cambodia—$400 million. These create discriminatory treatment. Laos [was given] a very modest $100 million. In our point of view, Thailand, China, Vietnam should cooperate. Each side's policies, the three should harmonize so all members can benefit. We should build a consensus rather than a more fragmented approach."[11]

In its bilateral dealings Beijing uses a rich repertoire of means to promote its interests and can create realities that compel the smaller party to cooperate. In September 2004, for example, the Philippine National Oil Company and the China National Offshore Oil Company (CNOOC) signed an agreement for joint seismic surveying of energy resources in "certain areas" (contested by Hanoi) of the South China Sea.[12] Beijing's ability to win agreement with Manila reflected not only China's comparative military weight but also its ability to produce rapid trade growth, reduce agricultural tariffs, increase development assistance, dangle the prospect of an FTA in front of the Philippines, and even provide some limited assistance to its military.[13]

In the face of this agreement between Beijing and Manila, Hanoi had the unpalatable choice of either belatedly joining this seismic survey agreement or confronting the possibility that the two parties would begin tapping the field's energy, thereby potentially siphoning off resources from Hanoi's own fields or fields in contested areas. The Vietnam Oil and Gas Corporation signed an agreement on March 14, 2005. The Vietnamese were not happy with this maneuver but had no choice, as one Vietnamese scholar explained, with some agitation: "I must admit that sometimes we have to let the Chinese get what they want. For example, they made some initiative to explore the South China Sea [with the Philippines] and we had to accept this."[14] A member of the Vietnamese National Assembly put it even more bluntly: "Our Philippine friends were not very wise. China likes bilateral negotiations—the smaller party is fragile and vulnerable."[15] For its part, China frames the agreement of the three parties to survey South China seabed resources as an "important step" that will "help narrow differences between China and the countries concerned so as to further enhance the cooperation and development."[16]

Similarly, by virtue of its location uppermost on the Mekong River, Beijing creates new realities simply by moving ahead with dams on its territory, then using economic leverage over smaller downstream nations like Laos by buying their cooperation with relatively modest aid. With its headwaters on the Tibetan plateau in the PRC, and nearly a third of the Mekong's total flow originating in Yunnan Province, China has big plans for dam construction, navigation, and resource exploitation on its section of the river. Since it is the most upstream nation, the five downstream nations have to hope, in the words of the then head of the Laotian National Mekong Committee, that Beijing will "consult."[17]

Military coercion has also been used, most notably in establishing claims in the South China Sea (the Paracels in 1974 and the Spratly Islands in 1988), and land border claims, most notably involving Vietnam in 1979. In the latter instance, China also used force to pursue its geostrategic interest in weakening Vietnamese domination of Cambodia and to lessen Hanoi's support for what Beijing viewed as a Moscow-dominated Asian security system. In then secret conversations with President Jimmy Carter, on the morning of January 29, 1979, Deng Xiaoping told the American president that "Vietnam is 100 percent the Cuba of the East. . . . There is a nation of 50 million people and has a large military force. You have had much contact, and we have had an even longer contact with Vietnam. . . . The Soviet Union is attempting to build two positions of strength in the East and in the West linked by the sea. The situation is analogous to a bar-bell."[18] After Deng asked President Carter his opinion of a punitive strike against Vietnam, the president thought it over that night and the next day (January 30) read his handwritten letter to Vice Premier Deng stating that a punitive strike "would be a serious mistake." The president enumerated his reasons and concluded with "The United States could not support such action and I strongly urge you not to approve it." President Carter pointedly did not say that his administration would oppose such a move in any vigorous way—and Washington did not.[19]

With respect to economic coercion, in early 2003 China announced "technical difficulties" with its oil pipeline to North Korea, thereby exerting pressure on Pyongyang to enter the Six-Party Talks on its nuclear program(s) with China, Japan, South Korea, Russia, and the United States. Subsequently, in mid-2006, Beijing froze DPRK assets in the Macau Branch of the Bank of China.[20] Unsurprisingly, these were uses of China's coercive power that Washington not only welcomed but wanted more of.

Washington's willingness to sometimes acquiesce or endorse Beijing's strong-arming of smaller neighbors is the genesis of those neighbors' periodic fear of a U.S.-PRC condominium, improbable as that sounds to contemporary American ears. I was jolted, for example, when speaking at the Institute of International Relations in Hanoi in March 2006, to be asked whether Beijing and Washington would seek to exercise some form of regional "condominium" that would be adverse to Vietnam's interests. When I responded by asking why this perception would exist, the reply was that Washington had acquiesced to Chinese seizure of the Paracels in the mid-1970s and had turned a blind eye to the Chinese attack on Vietnam in the late 1970s.

China also employs positive inducements, as chapter 3 illustrated. While China can withhold resources from North Korea, Beijing's preferred strategy has been to buy tolerable behavior through food and energy supplies. As one Chinese scholar explained, if you are to take something away from Pyongyang, you first have to give them something that subsequently can be withheld. Another salient manifestation of the PRC's growing economic attraction is that by 2008 China will have become Southeast Asia's number one trade partner, and it is already the leading export market for Taiwan, South Korea, and Japan. For ASEAN-5 (Singapore, Malaysia, Indonesia, Thailand, and Philippines), trade with the PRC from 1993 to 2003 increased on average by 15 percent annually.[21]

Because the Chinese economy is becoming increasingly central to its neighbors in so many ways, the reality of increasing economic interdependence gives China positive leverage while simultaneously constraining Beijing. For example, in 2006 Vietnam planned to purchase 1.1 billion kilowatt-hours of electric power from China, since China's southern provinces are rich in hydropower potential and Vietnam's northern provinces are power short. As early as 2004, Dao Van Hung, the general director of electricity in Vietnam, said that by late 2006 the "national grids of Vietnam and China will be linked together."[22]

Finally, in its dealings with neighbors, particularly members of the former Soviet bloc, Beijing believes that because it blazed a path from plan to market with phenomenal economic performance and without political collapse it provides a pow-

FIGURE 10

Indicative of China's more active diplomatic role regionally and globally has been Beijing's hosting of the Six-Party Talks since 2003. The talks concerning Pyongyang's nuclear program(s) involve North Korea, Japan, China, Russia, South Korea, and the United States. State Councilor and former Foreign Minister Tang Jiaxuan is shown meeting with the negotiators on February 26, 2004, in Beijing. The talks did not forestall a nuclear test by Pyongyang in October 2006. Greg Baker/Pool/Reuters/Corbis.

erful model. China has used its dramatic economic progress amid relative political stability with particular effect in its relations with Vietnam and, to a lesser extent, North Korea. On at least four occasions between 2000 and January 2006, Kim Jong Il made visits to the PRC that included tours of special economic zones and advanced enterprises, not the least the GM Buick factory in Pudong and the Shanghai Stock Exchange in January 2001.[23] Chinese scholars and diplomats straightforwardly say that the only peaceful way out of the dilemmas on the Korean Peninsula, and the only way China itself can stop pouring money into the Pyongyang sink, is to get North Korea on the road to economic and social reform, a path similar to that taken by the PRC since 1978. After his January 2001 China visit Kim seemed to accelerate domestic economic reform.[24]

Although the Vietnamese have their security and cultural apprehensions about China, they also appreciate that the PRC has the only political economy initially similar to their own that has succeeded in moving well toward the market while keeping the Communist Party in power. There is great attraction in, and desire to learn from, the Chinese model, not as a sign of subservience to Beijing, but as the best available means to strengthen the country in the face of growing international economic competition, mounting domestic demands for economic and political betterment, and rising Chinese power. One Vietnamese social scientist put it this way:

> China's experience has been very useful to us. . . . Reforms in agriculture and industry had strong impact on Vietnam. We also had borrowed the *hukou* [household registration system from China] to control migration, to pursue industrialization. So when China reformed agriculture, this was very supportive of our learning and our *hukou* is breaking down too. . . . It seems that Vietnam is behind China about ten years; we try to learn, but what we do is sometimes wrong.[25]

Though it may be disconcerting to some Americans, the Chinese model has its attractions, both politically and economically, to even some relatively liberal elements in Vietnam. These people see opportunity in China's moves to incorporate new social and intellectual elites into the Communist Party, and they hope their own party follows suit.

In short, Beijing's means are varied:

- Use multilateral organizations to reassure other nations, to constrain the big powers acting in the region, and to achieve other objectives best obtained through cooperation.
- Dominate bilateral interactions when possible.
- Provide economic inducements through trade, finance, and assistance.
- Emphasize ideational power.
- Use the Chinese model to produce change in peripheral countries favorable to China's interests (e.g., North Korea).
- When all else fails, be willing to use coercive measures.

If these are the tools Beijing employs to pursue its interests in its own neighborhood, what are the strategies of the PRC's neighbors? These states have a critical mass and enough resources that, when they join forces and when powers at further distances constructively engage with them, they generally are able to defend their vital interests.

NEIGHBORS DEAL WITH CHINA:
FOUR DAVIDS AND ONE GOLIATH

China's neighbors have diverse reactions to the mainland's growing power, depending on the character of the historical and contemporary bilateral relationship, geographic proximity, perceived gains versus risks, and third-party relationships. All of China's neighbors make risk-reward calculations. Beijing's growing power weighs far more heavily on the minds of some than others. For Thailand, relations with Beijing are distinctly positive and the risks are generally perceived to be manageable. Indeed, given Thai anxieties about Vietnam, PRC power is viewed as a restraint on Hanoi. Others, such as Japan, show a much more discernible apprehension about Chinese power despite a growing and mutually beneficial economic relationship. And in another distinct example, the city-state of Singapore, ever determined to maintain a balance of forces in the region, has good relations with Beijing while seeking the comprehensive involvement of the United States. A senior Australian defense official put it this way: "There are four types of countries in the region [in terms of dealing with China] beyond those that blow with the wind like Laos and Thailand. There are those who tend to resist—Vietnam, Korea, and Japan. There are those that seemingly welcome China's rise—Malaysia. There are those who are fearful—Indonesia. And there are those like us who work both sides and for whom being forced to choose is a disaster."[26] To some degree all countries in the region have adopted mixed strategies that rely on a combination of economic integration, acquiescence to Beijing in certain areas, deterrence, and soft (Indonesia) or hard (Japan) external balancing.

Below, a more detailed examination of four of China's regional neighbors (Australia, Singapore, Indonesia, and Vietnam) shows a range of evaluations on a continuum from China as threat to China as source of opportunity. Simple proximity to China does not dictate a sense of anxiety, for nearby Thailand is more relaxed than distant Indonesia, but those who are close remain more focused than those who are distant. All these societies have diverse views within their own polities, all wish to have productive relations with Beijing, and all see a wholly confrontational approach as contrary to their fundamental interests.

At the positive end of the continuum of economic and political relations with Beijing we have Australia, which, as a commodities exporter to a ravenous PRC, sees boundless opportunities. Canberra is also relatively confident about its ability to move up the value-added ladder in global production chains in the face of Chinese competition, and its historic experience with China has not been perpetually traumatic—the Cold War and the conflicts in Korea and Vietnam certainly are remembered, but more as history than as statements about current reality or future prospects. In addition, the alliance with Washington is a source of security, and Australians, like Singaporeans, want to maintain regional balance in the face of PRC growth. At the other end of the continuum, Vietnam occupies much the same economic (low-cost labor) niche that the PRC occupies, and Hanoi's distant and recent history with China has not been particularly happy. In the more mixed category lies Singapore (closer to Australia on the spectrum): it must remain attuned to shifting power balances in the region, but it has great capacity to move up the value-added ladder as Chinese economic capabilities increase. Singapore has capital in search of productive investment and is doing well providing services and high-tech intermediate goods to the PRC. Finally, there is Indonesia. As a commodity exporter, Jakarta sees tremendous opportunities in a PRC that needs energy and minerals. On the other hand, its troubled history with China argues for circumspection. Indonesia, like Vietnam, occupies a low-cost labor niche in which China is an ever-present competitive challenge.

AUSTRALIA

As one senior Australian official described his country's attitude toward China compared to that of other neighboring nations, "The Thais are at one end of the spectrum of allies and countries in the region, and Vietnam is at the other. We share views with Singapore—their [Singapore's] level of comfort and discomfort with the Chinese." A realism derived from history shapes Australian views, a sense that "China's influence is a natural part of the order in human history. . . . We now find ourselves in a region moving back to the historical pattern."[27]

Developments in Australia-China relations display many of the features of ties with the PRC throughout East and Southeast Asia, including both perceived opportunities and not-so-latent anxieties. Currently, the principal instruments of Beijing's influence are economic and cultural. Australian security worries vis-à-vis China coexist with considerable concern that Washington will mismanage its relations with Beijing and drag the entire Pacific Rim into unnecessary conflict. Even though Australians share core American values, they wish to focus on economic relations with Beijing rather than dwell on ideological disagreements. As one very senior official put it to me: "By the way, democracy is not traveling well out here."[28]

Canberra is of the opinion that economic growth in the region is stabilizing, particularly in Indonesia, a country of considerable security concern to Australians. China has become an engine of regional growth, and Canberra wants to keep it humming. As one former senior defense official told me: "We are a country next to Indonesia in an amazing dynamic region. We don't know what to make of it. We are simultaneously optimistic about economic opportunity, a lucky break, but how do we hold our place where force is important but there is no regional structure? The UN is not going to rescue us. India registers less than China."[29] This underlying anxiety helps account for the March 2007 agreement between Tokyo and Canberra to develop a closer defense relationship with respect to disaster relief and peacekeeping.[30]

There is an overwhelming determination in Australia to avoid having to choose between the United States and China. In paraphrase, one senior Australian official put it this way: "It will be a failure of policy if we have to choose between you and China, and in that unfortunate case our choice is clear—the U.S."[31] This desire to avoid choice springs not only from security calculations and economic interests but from domestic politics too. Domestic, often local, political considerations in Australia's China policy were clarified when I was informed that about 10 percent of the constituents in Prime Minister Howard's constituency in 2005 were of Chinese ethnicity.[32]

Two features of Canberra's evolving relationship with Beijing and its implications for Washington deserve elaboration. The first is security—Australia's reluctance to have Beijing treated in ways that reduce its cooperation and increase its perceptions of threat and Australia's desire to avoid entanglement in the Taiwan issue. The second feature concerns economics.

Australians paying attention to these matters perceive U.S. policy toward China as an unwelcome uncertainty. They wonder whether parts of the administration of George W. Bush are not inappropriately (and certainly prematurely) consigning Beijing to an adversarial status and crudely trying to use Japan and others as cudgels to beat China. When George W. Bush assumed office in January 2001, and during the election campaign immediately preceding his victory, he and his subordinates telegraphed a predisposition to view the PRC as a "military competitor."[33] Writing as early as 2000, Condoleezza Rice (who later became the president's advisor for national security affairs and thereafter his secretary of state) said: "It is important to promote China's internal transition through economic interaction while containing Chinese power and security ambitions. Cooperation should be pursued, but we should never be afraid to confront Beijing when our interests collide."[34]

Taiwan is another area of concern for Australians. In late April 2001, President Bush indicated he would do "whatever it took" to help Taiwan defend itself, a declaration preceded by approval of an enormous weapons sales package to the island, much of which, as of this writing, Taipei has declined to purchase.[35] Deputy

Secretary of State Armitage visited Australia in August of that year to remind Australians of their alliance with Washington and U.S. expectations of assistance if conflict occurred in the Taiwan Strait.[36] This set off criticism in many quarters of Australia, the net result of which was that Canberra subsequently encouraged restraint on Washington's part (and in Taipei) with regard to cross-Strait relations.

A widespread sentiment in Australia is that Americans should relax a bit on Taiwan—"Don't worry about Taiwan as a problem because the Chinese don't want to waste money on rockets raining down on Taiwan and they need Taiwan to make money."[37] Another very senior government official put it this way: "China is in almost all respects a status quo power—this is the case with respect to the DPRK [North Korea] and Taiwan. The Chinese are very conservative."[38] This elite view is reflected in a relaxed popular view of China as a potential security problem; in 2005 only 35 percent of Australians saw China as a threat.[39] Moreover, the political elite in Australia saw that Taiwan President Chen Shui-bian took the Bush administration's expressions of support as a security backstop that enabled him to challenge Beijing on the one China policy, thereby decreasing regional stability. As one Australian official put it, "If we are put in the position of having to choose, the losses of being on the wrong side of China are growing. What this means [is], we have even greater interest, a bigger interest in not mismanaging this [the U.S.-China and China-Australian relationships]. The U.S. has done pretty well managing this; the stakes are higher. Bush initially took his eye off the ball, but he rebuked Chen Shui-bian publicly [in December 2003], and the message got through to Taipei."[40]

The Australian security perspective differs from that of elements in the George W. Bush administration in another way as well. There are many ethnic Chinese residents, students, and tourists in Australia; about sixty thousand students alone are from the PRC, approximately the same number as in the United States. "So working with Chinese is a part of daily life," I was told by a former senior defense official, "unlike with Japan. . . . And, we haven't had a world war with China. . . . If the Australian government announced a land force exercise with China next week, there wouldn't be a peep [from the Australian public]. You'd have an interesting reaction if there were one with Japan."[41]

Australians have several economic security concerns vis-à-vis China, one being that much of China's economic interest in Australia is commodity related. PRC state-owned enterprises (SOEs) dominate Chinese activity in this area, with one corporate leader from Melbourne saying, "COSCO [China Overseas Shipping (Group), formerly China Overseas Shipping Company] has about four hundred ship calls per year hauling this island away to China bit by bit."[42] Although Australians express enthusiasm for the economic gains, beyond environmental worries they also are concerned that much of the FDI coming into Australia from China is government controlled. These investments have a state character that makes some Australians nervous. Paraphrasing one senior official in Canberra, "FDI [from the PRC] is growing and welcomed by recipients. But in contrast to other FDI, as distinct from the ROK, Taiwan, and Japan, it is SOE driven. In other countries it is the private sector. So Chinese FDI is subject to administrative control."[43]

This brings us to the second important dimension of the Australia-China relationship—economics. The two economies are complementary, as mentioned in chapter 3, though Beijing would like easier access for its goods and Canberra enhanced access for its services. And one can see why if one considers what China buys, what Australia sells, and the fact that investment is pouring into Australian resource and other projects. Just in the first months of 2006 PRC entities acquired Australia's largest ethylene producer (Qenos) and the world's largest animal nutrition supplement producer (Adisseo). China-related investment is driving substantial growth across the continent.

Asian demand for commodities (mostly Chinese demand) surged in 2005 through the first quarter of 2006, with base metals prices rising 11.4 percent in the first three months of 2006 alone. With China's economy growing 10.3 percent in the first quarter of 2006, "Australia's exports to China soared 42 percent in the 10 months to April 30 [2006] from a year earlier."[44] For comparison, at the same time, Japan's economy was growing at a much slower pace of 1.9 percent after a sustained period of relative stagnation. Major actors in the Australian economy, Rio Tinto Group and BHP Billiton ore exporters, for example, were expanding their mines in Western Australia (to the tune of $2.65 billion) in 2006; Woodside Petroleum Ltd. (oil and gas) announced on June 1, 2006, that it had $10 billion in projects over the next four years. Overall, Australian trade with China jumped 33.6 percent in 2005 over the previous year.

These economic ties and interdependencies create a reciprocal relationship in which Australian policy reflects a balance struck among domestic interests, Chinese interests, and American policy preferences. American preferences do not always trump the symmetry of Chinese and Australian needs and interests. Australia, for instance, was the second developed country (after New Zealand) to extend "market economy status" to Beijing, even though the United States was nowhere near this point in 2006. Similarly, though Washington (and various domestic groups in Australia itself)[45] had anxieties about Canberra's export of uranium to China for power generation (Australia accounts for about 30 percent of global uranium oxide deposits),[46] Canberra and Beijing signed a deal in April 2006, though it would be several years before actual exports occurred, barring future problems.[47] All this means that Canberra often is in an uncomfortable bridging role—trying to reassure Beijing that its alliance activities with Washington (and security-related activities with Japan) "shouldn't be interpreted as an act of conspiracy against China" while simultaneously seeking to reassure Washington of its steadfastness as an ally. This dilemma was apparent in the March 2006 "Trilateral Strategic Dialogue" (between the foreign ministers of Australia, Japan, and the United States), when before the talks the U.S. secretary of state indicated that China and its military growth would be an important item of discussion.[48] This aroused Beijing's suspicions, which (in the wake of the talks) Australia's foreign minister, Alexander Downer, sought to assuage, saying:

> It's not for China to feel that we're ganging up on China, or that Australia is suddenly changing its policy on China. Most of the time critics say we are too close to China, we're not robust enough in criticizing China. So we certainly don't have a policy of, well, containment. Clearly we don't—of trying to constrain China or working with other countries against Chinese interests, or anything like that—we certainly don't. This is a very natural relationship—it's a very natural thing for Australia, Japan and the United States to meet together periodically, to talk about global and regional issues—and shouldn't be interpreted as an act of conspiracy against China. Of course it's not.[49]

While it is not accurate for Americans to construe China's growing influence to mean that the United States is "getting pushed out of Asia," it does mean that U.S. preferences increasingly compete with the preferences of others who have their own needs and influence. It means, as the former Australian diplomat Milton Osborne said, that "China has now established itself as the paramount regional power in Southeast Asia."[50]

SINGAPORE

In his book *From Third World to First,* Lee Kuan Yew describes Singapore's fundamental strategic challenge as "Surviving without a Hinterland."[51] In the late 1950s and 1960s this small city-state (which even in 2006 would have a population of only 4.5 million) did not enjoy a resource base, possess a market of sufficient size, or have friendly neighbors that were conducive to economic growth and national security. Consequently, it followed a clear three-part strategy. First, it would "leapfrog the region" and build economic ties with America, Europe, and Japan. Singapore would cast its lot with globalization.[52] Second, it would be better organized and more modern than any of the surrounding societies—"If we were only as good as our neighbors, there was no reason for businesses to be based here."[53] Finally, while it had political and other differences with America, it would turn to the United States as the preferred regional balancer.

> Singapore is a densely populated, tiny island located in a turbulent region, and it cannot be governed like America. However, these are small differences compared to the value of U.S. presence in Asia, which has ensured security and stability and made economic growth possible. . . . Americans have become as dogmatic and evangelical as the communists were. They want to promote democracy and human rights everywhere, except where it would hurt themselves as in the oil-rich Arabian Peninsula. Even so, the United States is still the most benign of all the great powers, certainly less heavy-handed than any emerging great power. Hence, whatever the differences and frictions, all noncommunist countries in East Asia prefer America to be the dominant weight in the power balance of the region.[54]

Singapore is one of the few places in the contemporary world where there is an identity between the vision of its still living founding leader ("the Senior Mentor") and the national strategy. Officials from the top to bottom of Singapore's foreign policy, defense, and intelligence structures seemingly, and I believe genuinely, share a vision of a small society that survives by dint of its people's skills in global business and a realistic approach to security. They do not believe they have the luxury of what many there consider American idealism disconnected from the realities of survival in a tough region.

Singaporeans want the United States in the region not because they agree with it but because they need it. They admire what America has achieved in its own development and world security, but this admiration coexists with worries that America has gone soft morally at home and has become a political evangelist abroad. So how do leaders and officials in this city-state predominantly view China and the other powers in the region? What are Singapore's fundamental policies?

From my interviews and discussions with officials, government analysts, and academics in Singapore in mid-2005, a clear gestalt emerged:

> We are not as anxious [about China] as Rumsfeld [who had just been in Singapore a few days earlier]—but we don't see it as a pussycat either. China has

historical baggage, it is not a status quo power, but it is now involved in a set of relationships that give it powerful incentives to work with others. . . . China now realizes that soft power is useful. China sees itself as a weak power, but the question is how that might change with more power. . . . They [the Chinese] seem to be thinking of moving beyond coastal defense, they need to ensure access to oil and other materials, and this provides incentives to move forward with naval development. But they also have a big interest in ensuring that nothing disrupts [their domestic policy and development].[55]

Several observations underlie Singapore's broad assessment of China's intentions and methods. For one thing, Beijing has settled its boundary disputes with many of its neighbors and is handling remaining disputes with India and in the South China Sea more adroitly than in the past. China has also improved ties with the Philippines and Indonesia, states that traditionally have regarded it with suspicion.

According to these officials and analysts, the PRC's highest foreign policy priority is good relations with the United States, and while it would like to see regional integration proceed with a reduced American role, Beijing will not compromise relations with Washington to achieve this. In terms of PRC security, the Chinese "are concerned about the U.S. troop realignment in Asia, [and] there are increased concerns that the U.S. [is] trying to tighten the noose. Hence, China is more interested in the noose."[56]

Beijing would like to improve relations with Tokyo, I was told, but this was hard to do when Japanese Prime Minister Koizumi continued to go to the Yasukuni Shrine. "The problem in Chinese-Japan relations is fundamental on both sides— both governments are quite weak [domestically]. . . . He [Koizumi] wants to keep the pot boiling to strengthen his position [at home]. In China, the regime is not strong enough to tell its people not to be too emotional, and all this is not helpful to China's long-term interests."[57]

According to my interviewees, a trend toward increasing domestic disturbances in China is making Beijing more cautious. Tight control will not end soon, though PRC leaders "know they need an appealing issue" to increase domestic legitimacy.[58] When all is said and done, however, the PRC is nowhere near collapse, and it has exceeded expectations at home and abroad.

China's good economic and diplomatic performance, I was told, owes a great deal to the quality of the leaders from Deng Xiaoping on. Chinese economic power is proving attractive throughout Asia because of the PRC's willingness to import, open its economy, invest, and allow large numbers of its citizens to go abroad as tourists ("the biggest, most sought-after spenders"). China will not grow in a straight line—there will be booms and busts. "It is nonsense that they [China] will eat our lunch, dinner, and all the snacks in between. It is impossible because of comparative advantage."[59] Thus the United States, as well as countries in the region, should promote PRC membership in as many multilateral security, economic, and other regimes as possible—"it at least ties them down" and is "a cheaper way to bring them in line than with arms."[60]

Because China is increasing its influence and Washington is anxious, Singaporeans feel that countries throughout Asia have the opportunity to play the two off against each other. "For example, Indonesia is worried about the United States. . . . It is not that they [the Indonesians] see it [China] as an ally; rather, they see it as a card to use against an overbearing U.S. There is no running away from the rise of China, [or from situations where] countries [are] forced to choose, but most countries in the region don't want to choose. They take into account the stabilizing role of the U.S., and most countries want to have their cake and eat it too."[61]

The widely shared Singaporean view is that the George W. Bush administration initially came into office in 2001 with an excessively confrontational view of Beijing and then became distracted from the region in the wake of 9/11 but that it "has lots of cards to play if it pays attention."[62] Singapore's core strategy is to cooperate with a Washington that is constructively involved in the region, all the while reaping the security and economic benefits to be realized from building cooperative relations with Beijing and building the PRC into regional multilateral structures. For Singaporeans in the business, government, and intellectual elite, Washington's tendency to place the promotion of democracy and human rights near the top of the U.S. agenda is ineffective and counterproductive. There is a palpable feeling that the United States has double standards: "The U.S. criticizes China's defense spending without saying anything about its own—as if the U.S. had a birthright; and why can't the U.S. accept the rise of other countries? It doesn't go down well."[63]

In the final analysis, Singapore has a three-part strategy toward the PRC: develop mutually beneficial economic ties; make sure that American coercive power is never very distant; and involve Beijing in as many constraining multilateral arrangements as possible to create mutual interdependence. In terms of the economic dimension, in 2004 the tiny city-state was the eighth-largest foreign investor in the PRC.[64] With respect to the balancing component of policy, Singapore picked up the slack by providing services to the U.S. Navy after Washington vacated Subic Naval Base and Clark Air Base in the Philippines in the early 1990s. In January 1998 Singapore announced it would construct new harbor facilities that could dock U.S.

aircraft carriers, and these facilities now exist at Changi Naval Base. Before that, Singapore had already provided access for U.S. military ships and planes and provided a home for a small U.S. logistical contingent. And with regard to multilateral diplomacy, Singapore not only wants Chinese participation in regional organizations but also seeks to make sure that PRC sway over them is diluted by others more closely aligned with Washington. So, for example, in the debate over whom to include in the emerging East Asian Summit structure in late 2005, Singapore pushed to include Australia, India, and New Zealand, despite Beijing's posture of wanting only ASEAN plus China, Japan, and South Korea.[65] The PRC feared that the others would use the summit to promote human rights and "to build up U.S.-Japan-centered western dominance."[66] Singapore's ambassador to Washington, Chan Heng Chee, clearly explained ASEAN's view of the utility of multilateralism and interdependence: "ASEAN's approach to China has been to bring Gulliver to shore, . . . to tie him down with many strings of engagement, in multilateral fora, protocols and declarations. Gulliver seems not at all to mind, and, never being asleep, is also tying a few strings round ASEAN. We will be enmeshed with each other just as the region is enmeshed with Japan and the U.S."[67]

Like China's other neighbors, Singapore is concerned that Beijing will be unable to control (or that its leaders may find it expedient to unleash) xenophobic nationalism. When the then deputy premier Lee Hsien Loong went to Taiwan in 2004, for example, Singaporeans were surprised at the depth and extent of the Chinese official and popular anger at his trip. Similarly, in the spring of 2005, when Chinese violence and anger were directed at Japanese because of textbooks that allegedly "whitewashed" Tokyo's World War II behavior in Asia, it was clear to Singaporeans that as much as one might hope for China's peaceful rise, it is not assured.

INDONESIA

Why Indonesia—populous, large, and distant from China—has significant concerns about the PRC and its own citizens of Chinese ethnicity calls for some explanation. In part, the answer goes back to the Dutch East India Company and its founding in 1602.[68] The Dutch used local aristocrats and the Chinese residents to derive revenue from the archipelago, and the Chinese played a significant role thereafter in taxation, agriculture, and money lending, particularly in Java and Sumatra. Later, under the Japanese occupation in the twentieth century, some ethnic Chinese locals cooperated with the occupiers and were losers in the nationalistic revolution thereafter. As Kahin put it, "Many of these [Indonesian] peasants tended to identify the Chinese with the old colonial order and to see the revolution as directed against them as well as against the Dutch."[69] Thus the Chinese presence in Indonesia has a long history.

These historically derived and more contemporary perceptions and concerns have periodically produced brutal attacks on ethnic Chinese living in the archipelago (e.g., in the 1950s and 1965). As recently as 1998, substantial popular violence was directed at ethnic Chinese living in Indonesia, with a thousand or more persons killed and countless women raped as the Suharto regime fell and Indonesians felt the economic distress of the Asian Financial Crisis.[70] The 1998 incidents produced demands and public protests in the PRC (e.g., in Beijing) and among overseas Chinese (e.g., in Los Angeles) for Beijing to do something. While in the 1950s and 1965 Beijing had sent ships to rescue ethnic Chinese from the violence, in 1998 all the PRC could do was issue protests through official channels. The 1998 case of anti-Chinese violence put the limitations of PRC power in bold relief. Had Beijing even contemplated intervening in some forceful way to secure the rights and safety of ethnic Chinese living in Indonesia, it would have aroused anti-Chinese nationalism and fear of PRC military power throughout the region.

Indonesian trepidation about China as a country (and the separate but related periodic spike in concern about ethnic Chinese living in Indonesia) has several sources. One frequently encountered assertion is that about 3 to 4 percent of Indonesians who are ethnic Chinese control "70 percent of the corporate wealth."[71] This presumed concentration of wealth in an ethnic and cultural minority makes the group an easy target for the resentments of the majority, particularly since, until 1980, Beijing's policy was that an ethnic Chinese born anywhere was considered a Chinese national. As Singaporean ambassador to the United States Chan Heng Chee explained, this "fueled anti-Chinese feelings domestically, opening the minority to suspicions of disloyalty and being a potential 'fifth column.'"[72]

This long-existing state of affairs was compounded by China's own revolutionary evangelism of the Cultural Revolution era (1966–76) and the structure of power during the Suharto years (1965–98) in Indonesia. In the "New Order" of military strongman General Suharto, his closest and most well-rewarded business partners often were of Chinese ethnicity, and corruption was widespread. As the Suharto regime underwent its death throes in 1998 amid the Asian Financial Crisis, with ethnic Chinese already under attack, it was predictable that a besieged military would direct popular hostility toward Chinese and away from itself. Suharto's son-in-law, General Prabowo Subianto, added fuel to the fire of popular resentment by claiming that "traitors" (meaning Chinese) were spiriting their money abroad.[73]

Indonesians' view of the Chinese has had an ideological dimension as well. For much of the Cold War until well after Mao Zedong's death, the Indonesian military feared Beijing's attempts to export communist ideology using the vehicle of the Indonesian Communist Party (PKI). In 1965 a coup against the revolutionary leader Sukarno produced widespread lethal violence directed against leftists, and many Chinese suffered or were killed in the ensuing mayhem. The "New Order" regime of Suharto that emerged promptly aligned itself with Washington and the West in the Cold War. In August 1967, at the height of the Cultural Revolution in China, Red Guards ransacked the Indonesian Embassy in Beijing. Consequently, the Indonesian military was able to run what one expatriate development officer living in Indonesia called a "protection racket." The military used the Chinese threat as a basis to garner popular support and maintain social cohesion, while "protecting" the affluent parts of the Chinese population from the popular resentments that the military did little to discourage and sometimes fanned.[74] An Indonesian strategic analyst echoed this analysis, saying, "The military does charge the Chinese protection money."[75]

Something deeper in Indonesian self-identity than the differences between the Muslim majority population and the predominantly non-Muslim Chinese population creates anxiety about China, particularly a rapidly growing China that has competing offshore claims with Jakarta.[76] Indonesians conceive of their country as a cultural (indeed civilizational) equal to China and Japan.[77] It has a rich and diverse cultural and religious heritage. It has, for instance, more persons of the Islamic faith than any other country in the world. Yet Indonesia is the weakest and most strategically vulnerable of the three countries/civilizations, given its fragmentation across a vast island chain. The Indonesian state, particularly its military, worries about this weakness and fragmentation, resents intrusion, and wants to keep a regional balance that maximizes its own room for maneuver. A senior Indonesian strategic analyst put it this way in June 2005:

> There is still a difference between the [Indonesian] Foreign Ministry and the military on this [the PRC]. The Foreign Ministry is open and seeking to bring China into a web of interaction. But for the military, the question is how in twenty years China will use its power. The problem the military has isn't that China is communist, it is that China is nationalistic. They [the PRC] still look at the map, and that is still not resolved—[e.g.,] the Natuna Islands. . . . But at the same time there is the sense that China is an opportunity but that it will make life miserable as an economic competitor. . . . ASEAN believes in interdependence, but we really believe in balance. Japan has always been a candi-

date to balance, but it isn't easy for Japan to play this role. . . . The elite in Indonesia are more comfortable with Japan than China—[after] forty years of overseas development assistance [from Tokyo].[78]

As to what Indonesians want the United States to do about all this, this strategic analyst said: "Keep in the area, just not my house, but please stand in the street in front of my house, or stay in someone else's house. China should not be left alone [in the region]."[79] Indonesians worry that in the wake of 9/11 the United States has become distracted—a concern because Jakarta, like Singapore, looks to Washington to be the ultimate balancer. Jakarta is worried about China's inroads into Burma, its quest for port rights on the Indian Ocean, and it is anxious about what this may mean for Beijing's capacity to project force. As the same source put it: "If the U.S. is going to leave you to Chinese mercies, then make friends with China,"[80] which is what happened in Jakarta in April 2005 when the Chinese and Indonesian presidents agreed to a declaration entitled "Building of Strategic Partnership."[81]

This partnership was driven by Indonesians' desires to reap what economic gains were to be had from Beijing and to get Washington's attention rather than by any abiding faith in common strategic interests with the PRC. A decisive point in moving toward a more constructive relationship with China was the onset of the Asian Financial Crisis (1997–98). Beijing's commitment of stabilization funds through the IMF for Thailand and Indonesia and the PRC's rising imports thereafter helped lift the Thai and Indonesian economies. China seemingly moved from military threat to economic salvation in the popular imagination. As one U.S. NGO leader living in Indonesia put it in March 2005, "It is all China, all the time, in Indonesia."[82]

Indonesia, like almost every other country, wants to export more, receive more FDI, and reap the employment that goes with both. In 2005, Indonesian exports to the PRC grew 44.69 percent from the preceding year. Indonesian exports to Japan, by contrast, grew "only" 13.07 percent that year, though Japan remained far ahead of China in total imports from Indonesia.[83] With respect to FDI, Beijing is most interested in investing in natural resources, and this means SOE investment rather than "nonstate" Chinese investment, a fact that creates some anxieties among Indonesians about the degree of PRC government control (which, as we saw above, is also true among Australians).

Concisely, the magnetic pull of China's rapid economic growth and security accommodation impelled Jakarta toward some degree of "partnership," as it impels most of China's neighbors. This does not mean Asia is becoming Sino-centric. The

United States and Japan remain huge markets for Indonesia. But Indonesia is emblematic of the reality throughout Asia of growing interests with the PRC, the need to balance opportunities and threats, and the need to balance each country's interests with China against those with America and other big powers.

This reality unsettles some in the United States. In March 2006 U.S. Secretary of State Rice visited Indonesia, in part to try to diminish the sense that Washington was distracted and disengaged. As part of that effort, the secretary acknowledged that the United States was increasing its military links to Indonesia after having abandoned these as retaliation for human rights abuses. The secretary also sought to jump-start educational exchange and some development assistance. In this sense, perhaps Indonesia's advances to Beijing did increase U.S. ardor.

But as one Indonesian strategic analyst explained, Jakarta had underlying motives for improved ties with Beijing and also saw limits to such gains: "Things [with China] can be nice on the surface, but if economic cooperation doesn't benefit the natives, then we can sacrifice relations with China to get domestic support. One issue we are worried about is that domestic politicians here might use the economic wealth of the Chinese here. Talk has begun that when the PRC wants to invest, instead of hiring natives, better hire Indonesian Chinese. They hire all these people [Indonesians of Chinese ethnicity]. Now, this is true to a degree."[84]

How does Jakarta acquire and maintain its room for maneuver and seek to constrain and use the big powers, particularly China? Like Vietnam, Indonesia promotes multilateralism, seeking strength in numbers and bringing China into constraining regimes that protect the weaker party. "The behavior of states can be restrained not only by military [force] but politically induced by multilateral organizations. . . . Using the military to do it is very dangerous."[85] This predisposition reflects the modest assets of Indonesia's military. It has a small budget ($1.3 billion in 2004, or about one-sixth of Taiwan's 2005 defense budget),[86] and it is stretched thin from having to exert at least nominal control over about seventeen thousand islands stretching across 3,200 miles of ocean; domestically the security apparatus must deal with several centrifugal forces; and democratic change in Indonesia since the late 1990s means that now, unlike before, the armed forces must compete for scarce resources and leadership attention.

All suspicions aside, the coming of democracy to Indonesia in 1998 brought more civility and less overt anti-Chinese behavior to the country. This has been reflected in developments such as the observance of the Chinese New Year as a national holiday; the emergence of four Chinese-language newspapers and "a nightly Chinese segment TV news bulletin";[87] and the first-ever appointment of an ethnic Chinese person as a cabinet minister. Dr. Mari Pangestu, who has a PhD from the University of California at Davis in economics, was appointed minister of trade.

Along with these internal developments, the PRC has become more sophisticated and sensitive in its diplomacy and use of ideational power, as described in chapter 4. All of this has contributed to considerably improved Sino-Indonesian relations. As one expatriate development organization leader put it, "China and Indonesia is the soft power story. . . . People are proud to study the Chinese language. Democracy has had an effect in allowing China to exert its soft power. The military had a Chinese = Communist = PRC formula, but now people are converting to Buddhism. . . . The Chinese, PRC, are really savvy, not heavy-handed. The PRC had wanted to normalize relations with Indonesia long before Indonesia was willing to do so. The respect that the Chinese show Indonesia is great."[88]

Further bolstering Chinese influence is an increasing flow of Indonesian tourists to the PRC, though the preferred destinations are still in the West and Australia. For their part, growing numbers of Chinese tourists journey to Bali, Medan, and historic sites on Java. As for study abroad, some students do go to the PRC, but Indonesia's young prefer the United States, Australia, and Malaysia. "There is a language barrier in China, and the quality of education is better elsewhere. If Indonesian students go to a Chinese place it will be Hong Kong or Singapore."[89]

In a nutshell, Indonesia deals with China in hopes of reaping economic benefits but seeks security in regional multilateralism and other big-power military and economic involvement regionally. One interviewee put it with admirable clarity: "We don't want to be caught between the United States and China. We can't afford it, and we try to exploit the situation. . . . Be friendly with everyone if you can't be sure who the problem is."[90]

China's diplomacy has been remarkably effective, but underlying suspicions remain, and there is a danger that Beijing's promises of big investment in Indonesia will not materialize, thereby feeding Indonesian disillusionment, a danger that the PRC also faces in Latin America and Africa. Beijing can easily lose what confidence and goodwill it has painfully built up.

VIETNAM

The Socialist Republic of Vietnam (SRV) is culturally proud and anxious.[91] One Vietnamese Foreign Ministry official explained (when asked about the appeal of Chinese popular culture to Vietnamese youth), "If you don't have culture, you lose the nation."[92] Moreover, Vietnam has no reliable big-power backer(s)—the Soviet Union is gone, and relations with Washington, while improving, are ambivalent. Hanoi knows that throughout the entire post–World War II period Washington has viewed its interests in Vietnam as derivative of its larger geostrategic calculations. The Vietnamese were not surprised, for example, that U.S. Secretary of Defense Rumsfeld visited Hanoi in June 2006 to raise relations with its military to a new level just as the U.S. Department of Defense was focusing on the growth of PRC military power. While this creates suspicion in Hanoi (and Beijing), Vietnamese have their own interests in improving ties with Washington, though not at the cost of falling out with Beijing.

Economically, China is Vietnam's leading trade partner (at the US$8.7 billion level in 2005), with Vietnam running a significant deficit.[93] While the Vietnamese see some areas where their economy is complementary to China's (e.g., high-quality finishing work, seafood, and raw materials), and while they see opportunities in rapidly growing Chinese tourism, particularly casino activity in Halong Bay, they are also anxious. They worry greatly about head-to-head competition in textiles, footwear, and other labor-intensive manufacturing where China excels. Vietnamese also see Chinese exports "flooding" their market (e.g., motorbikes against which Hanoi has thrown up some arguably protectionist barriers such as "safety standards").

At the same time, with labor costs rising in some of China, and with foreign investors diversifying investments away from overreliance on the PRC, Vietnam is gaining significant FDI. For the government in Taipei (as distinct from Taiwan businesspersons), Vietnam is a preferred investment site, and Taiwan was the biggest external investor in the country as of early 2006.[94] When businesspersons in the southern part of Vietnam speak of "Chinese investment," they often have in mind money from Taiwan, Hong Kong, Singapore, and Chinese communities elsewhere in the Asia-Pacific region. Two 2006 reports put PRC FDI in Vietnam at about US$2 billion,[95] though the Vietnam Chamber of Commerce and Industry reported the figure at about $700 million in early 2006;[96] *Xinhua* reported in late 2006 that China ranked fifteenth as an investor in Vietnam.[97] One of the largest Chinese investments (reportedly $1 billion) is in bauxite in the Central Highlands.[98]

Hanoi is employing a diversified set of instruments to deal with these insecurities and opportunities. Its primary decision rule is not to offend core PRC interests if possible. On occasion Hanoi acquiesces to Chinese moves, as it did in 2005 to the seismic survey in the South China Sea agreed to by Beijing and Manila. As one very senior U.S. official in the SRV put it to me, "[W]hen push comes to shove, the

Vietnamese go with China. If China objects to a U.S. proposal, Vietnam does not sign on. The Vietnamese are not going to challenge China, they don't want to antagonize; there is a long history of that. If there is open conflict it goes against the development strategy. There will be no alliance with a country that threatens [China]—no alliance with the United States. No foreign troops on Vietnamese soil. No deviation from the line on Taiwan. These are the main red lines, and the Vietnamese try to avoid opposing China."[99] Nonetheless, Hanoi is not supine. As China and the Philippines were presenting Hanoi with their fait accompli on the seismic survey, Hanoi solicited tenders from foreign oil companies to bid for exploration rights in the Phu Khanh Basin in the Spratly Islands, a move that Beijing vigorously protested.[100]

Second, Hanoi is simultaneously improving relations with Washington, since it hopes not to see excessively intimate ties between Beijing and Washington. As one Foreign Ministry official in Hanoi said when asked what kind of U.S.-China relationship he would like to see: "We want both competition and cooperation. Condominium [between Washington and Beijing] is too much cooperation. But if you are heading toward conflict we don't like that because it hurts peace and stability. We want a middle way for small and medium-sized countries."[101] Hanoi desires improved relations between itself and Washington at the same time that it welcomes moderate tension between Washington and Beijing: friction that does not escalate to a lethal cross fire.

Third, Vietnam seeks to embed itself in ASEAN and international multilateral institutions and to build regional east-west infrastructure and economic links (with Laos, Cambodia, Thailand, and Burma). By doing so, it seeks strength and safety in numbers and hopes to avoid overreliance on north-south linkages, meaning dependence on China.

Finally, Hanoi wants to minimize the degree to which it is drawn exclusively into the Chinese cultural orbit. Perhaps one manifestation of this hope is that fewer Vietnamese students were studying in China in 2006 (around two thousand) than in America (four thousand), Australia, Britain (five thousand), and the rest of Europe,[102] though the number going to the PRC for technical training is significant. Very few Chinese (fewer than one hundred) were studying in Vietnam in 2006.[103] As one U.S. official in Saigon (Ho Chi Minh City) put it, "Down here [in Ho Chi Minh City] [it is] a much tougher sell to move Chinese soft power than in Singapore. What is true in Southeast Asia is not happening here. The overwhelming number [of students going abroad] here want to go to the U.S., Australia, and the U.K. [There are] English [English-language] schools every few feet. Here 3,500 student visas are issued per year to the U.S. It is starting to rival Malaysia. Increasing numbers are going to Australia."[104]

A more detailed look at key elements of the Vietnamese strategy is warranted.

Multilateralization   When its occupation of Cambodia ended with the Paris Agreements in October 1991, Hanoi improved the prospects of joining what was then the six-nation regional grouping of ASEAN (Brunei, Indonesia, Malaysia, Singapore, Philippines, and Thailand). ASEAN was formed in 1967 (Brunei joined in 1984) to resist the export of communist revolution and improve the economies of the member nations. From 1993, when it became an ASEAN observer, Hanoi actively sought full membership, a goal reached in July 1995. Vietnam's sights were set on improving relations with its neighbors; gaining support to substitute for benefits that had disappeared with the USSR in 1991; avoiding discriminatory tariff treatment as ASEAN built free-trade arrangements; and building a counterweight to Beijing. At the time of the SRV accession to ASEAN the Australian Parliamentary Research Service's Frank Frost noted that "ASEAN membership will also increase Vietnam's sense of confidence as it handles relations with China, whose power is growing rapidly."[105]

At the same time that Hanoi sought entry into ASEAN, it laid foundations for normalization with Washington, a move that was critical if it was to enter the principal international multilateral economic and development institutions. In September 1993 the United States ceased to object to Hanoi's joining the World Bank and the Asian Development Bank; in January 1994 the first halting steps were taken to restore contact between the Vietnamese and U.S. militaries; and the next month President Bill Clinton lifted the trade embargo against the SRV. In July 1995 formal diplomatic relations were established between Hanoi and Washington, and in December 2001 the two countries signed a Bilateral Trade Agreement. These moves were a reflection of the changed post–Cold War geostrategic environment, globalization, and the *Doi Moi* (renovation) reforms launched in Vietnam in 1986.

Amid this activity, Hanoi applied for membership in the WTO in 1995, began negotiating with Washington bilaterally in 2002 on U.S. requirements for such membership, reached basic agreement on accession terms in late May 2006, and entered the WTO in January 2007. Like China before it, the SRV sought to use the WTO as a driver for internal economic reform and hoped that WTO membership would offer protection against the restrictive practices (such as antidumping and textile quotas) of stronger economies. Along the way, in late 1998 Hanoi joined the Asia-Pacific Economic Cooperation forum (APEC), yet another step in integrating itself into the regional economy and joining multilateral organizations that would be helpful in their own right and assist in balancing China.

Diversification   A second aspect of Hanoi's strategy is diversification of economic relationships. This is reflected in an effort to build economic ties to the countries to its west (Laos, Cambodia, Thailand, and Myanmar/Burma). The SRV does so, in part, to avoid being drawn into an exclusive PRC economic orbit. Vietnamese officials and scholars with whom I spoke in March 2006 mentioned their desire to strengthen regional east-west economic linkages by building communication lines to countries to their west. As early as the mid-1990s, Don Weatherbee noted that the construction of transport infrastructure from the PRC's southwest through Southeast Asia to the Indian Ocean would provide a pathway for Chinese commercial penetration and strategic influence; China is actively building this infrastructure in Southeast, South, and Central Asia.[106] Building transport and communications networks in different directions than the Chinese pathways diversifies Vietnam's lines of influence and reduces its dependence on its big neighbor to the north.

This impulse to forge stronger east-west regional ties with its neighbors, in part, leads Vietnamese to criticize Western human rights—motivated sanctions against Burma: they fear that its isolation merely drives Myanmar further toward China. The Vietnamese see Burma's growing military cooperation with the PRC and call for the West to engage Burma, as it has done with China and Vietnam itself. One senior National Assembly official implored, "Please pay attention to the west-east economic corridor idea supported by Japan and the Asian Development Bank—the highway from Thailand, through Laos, and Vietnam to Danang. You Americans should pay attention to what is happening in Burma. Engagement with Burma would have rub-off effects. You and Europe are wrong on Burma."[107]

Military Links to the United States   Hanoi's balancing efforts also include walking the tightrope of increasing military cooperation with Washington without alienating Beijing. The process began in January 1994 with the visit of the commander in chief of the Pacific Charles R. Larson to the SRV, followed in March 2000 by U.S. Secretary of Defense William Cohen (the first post–Vietnam War secretary of defense to do so), followed in November 2003 by the return visit of the Vietnamese defense minister to the United States and the port call in Saigon of the *U.S.S. Vandegrift.* The 2003 port call was followed a year and a half later by the *U.S.S. Gary*'s visit to Saigon. U.S. Secretary of Defense Donald Rumsfeld's June

2006 visit to Vietnam made it clear that U.S.-Vietnamese military relations were moving toward allowing small numbers of SRV military personnel to study in U.S. military language and technical schools.[108] Immediately following the secretary's trip, two U.S. naval ships visited Ho Chi Minh City in July. In explaining this elevated attention to Hanoi, former U.S. ambassador to Vietnam Raymond Burghardt explained:

> [W]hile the U.S. had been distracted with Afghanistan and Iraq, China's regional influence had been increasing at America's expense. Vietnam's leadership authoritatively conveyed its concerns about America['s] inattention to Asia during Deputy Prime Minister Vu Khoan's visit to the United States in early December 2003. Khoan alluded to these concerns in his public remarks and was even more forthright in his private meetings with Secretary of State Powell and National Security Advisor Rice. . . . In a policy of hedging relations with China, Vietnam, with its long history of troubled relations with its huge neighbor, is an obvious partner. . . . In private and even some semi-public meetings, authoritative Vietnamese officials specifically raised the Chinese angle in their newfound enthusiasm for the U.S. As one important foreign policy official put it to me, "The triangle is out of balance." . . . Over the past two years [2004–5], Vietnamese officials and think tank experts have expressed regular concern over China's rapidly deepening ties with Cambodia, Laos, Burma and Thailand. . . . Vietnam will value America's role as a strategic balance but will resist being seen as part of a containment policy against China. . . . Hedging is not containment.[109]

One sees the strengths and weaknesses of China's regional position in its ties with Vietnam. PRC economic power is welcome to the degree that it invests and buys Vietnamese goods but is resented to the degree that it presents competition. Culturally, even though Vietnam owes China a great debt, its people are fiercely resistant to Chinese cultural domination. And militarily, the concept of "friend" or "enemy" is less salient than the belief that big powers oppress small ones and that the destiny of the smaller people is to play big powers off against one another.

For the Chinese, managing the relationship with Vietnam is not easy. In describing the visit of Politburo Standing Committee Member Jia Qinglin to Hanoi in early March 2006, *Viet Nam News* used language more befitting a friction-laden relationship than interparty fraternalism: "The two sides stressed on [sic] the need to enhance friendship and mutual trust, boost comprehensive cooperation, and implement agreements effectively."[110]

BIGGER NEIGHBORS: JAPAN, RUSSIA, AND INDIA

It may seem odd to devote relatively less space to an analysis of China's relations with its bigger neighbors given the attention accorded smaller players above. This allocation, however, reflects a principal point—if the smaller states around China can secure their interests using a variety of means (multilateralism, soft or hard balancing, economic interdependence and diversification, deterrence, and occasionally concessions), this is even more true of larger neighbors. Each of the three nations examined below (Japan, Russia, and India) has a web of common and divergent interests with the PRC. Each seeks to minimize frictions and enhance cooperative factors.

Not only do Japan, Russia, and India each have more resources to defend their interests than smaller societies, but each also has some core interests that diverge from China's. Beijing seeks cooperation with these larger nations, takes prudent measures to hedge against a possible future breakdown in ties, and attempts to address current sources of friction. These relationships require constant management. Failure to manage them effectively would adversely affect a broad range of Chinese interests. Beijing cannot dictate outcomes with these big states. Even within the framework of basically cooperative relations with a country such as South Korea, occasional incendiary issues have arisen, such as the historical treatment of the ancient Kingdom of Koguryo (37 BCE–668 CE) that lies within the current boundaries of the PRC or the treatment of undocumented North Korean refugees in the PRC.[111] One South Korean think tank leader suggested in November 2004 that his countrymen's views of China's intentions varied by generation. "There is a China fever among young Koreans who do not have historical understanding. . . . In time these young people will be shocked at China."[112]

Washington often is in an advantageous position in key bigger-power triangles (U.S.-Japan-China, U.S.-Russia-China, U.S.-India-China). First, in each of the above triangular relationships, Washington is for the other two parties the distant power without ambitions for territorial control. Second, America remains the biggest source of final product demand for what they all have to sell, despite increasing volumes of intermediate goods flowing through China in global production chains. Finally, the United States can often influence events in favor of one party or another.

Despite Beijing's anxieties, the security environment for China today is as good as it has been in centuries—a fact that lies at the core of the PRC's national strategy. This does not mean, however, that there are no problems. Beijing was somewhere between amazed and aghast when in June 2005 then U.S. Secretary of

Defense Rumsfeld told an international audience that "no nation threatens China."[113] This is not how Beijing understands its situation.

JAPAN

China pays the most attention to the big powers and to its neighbors, and Japan is both.[114] In this first decade of the new millennium, Sino-Japanese relations are not sound, reflecting a gradual souring of public opinion in each society toward the other and a fundamental strategic mistrust between the elites of the two countries, a distrust that sometimes is starkly manifest and at other times lies just beneath the surface. This strategic mistrust extends to the Korean Peninsula, where Beijing values stability more than Tokyo, who views Pyongyang as a threat.

Many developments converged in the last years of the twentieth century and the first years of the new millennium to motivate Japan to play a bigger, more "normal" security role: North Korean missile tests in 1998 and 2006 and Pyongyang's October 2006 nuclear test; the advent of the global war on terrorism, Washington's search for helpful members of its "coalition of the willing," and an overstretched United States needing Tokyo's security help in Asia and elsewhere; the incursion of a Chinese submarine into Japanese territorial waters in November 2004; a Washington worried about Japan's constitutional and material ability to help should conflict break out in the Taiwan Strait; and the desire of a new generation of Japanese to leave the legacy of World War II behind in security and diplomatic terms (emblematic of which was the election of Shinzo Abe as prime minister in September 2006). All this helps account for Tokyo's late 2004 shift toward a more assertive defense policy.

Public opinion polls in Japan conducted in October 2005 and released by the Cabinet Office showed that nearly two-thirds of Japanese were "not feeling good about China" and that almost three-quarters felt that "Sino-Japanese ties were not in good shape."[115] In 2004, the Cabinet Office reported that "affinity toward China" had fallen 10 percent from the previous year.[116] Also in 2004, when a *Sankei Shimbun* poll asked, "Is China a threat to Japan?" 51.8 percent of respondents said, "Yes."[117] In China in late 2004, a little over 40 percent of respondents were willing to say they "disliked" or "quite disliked" Japan.[118] Chinese and Japanese view one another with what Masaru Tamamoto referred to as an "unstable mix of respect and condescension."[119] Almost identical percentages of respondents to a late 2006 poll in each country viewed the other "unfavorably" (70–71 percent).[120] Professor Pang Zhongying of Nankai University explained the range of Chinese attitudes toward Japan, one of which was "We don't see this much smaller country as being worthy of comparison with us."[121]

Strategic thinkers in China believe they see an America distracted by wars in the Middle East and Central Asia, simultaneously concerned about China's rise, and consequently driven to deputize Japan as its hedge against Chinese power in Asia.[122] Tokyo's leaders and the Japanese public see China as a strategic challenge, view its growing military power as a risk, and believe that China has not given Japan much credit or gratitude for its tremendous development assistance to the PRC over recent decades (US$31.7 billion).[123] Then there is the history of World War II aggression: the Japanese are tired of apologizing for that era, and the Chinese uniformly believe their contrition has been insufficient. Against this backdrop of mutual frustration, leaders in both Tokyo and Beijing periodically appeal to their nationalistic political bases, thereby compounding frictions with one another. What Peter Gries calls "Internet nationalism" has given extreme elements in China an open forum for their expressions of hostility, in turn intimidating nervous intellectuals and government officials in the PRC from exercising a moderating influence, even if that were their inclination.[124]

Japanese Prime Minister Koizumi's annual visits (from 2001 up through 2006) to honor war dead at the Yasukuni Shrine (where some war criminals also are interred) were particularly combustible in both China and Korea.[125] Even the U.S. Congress declined to invite the prime minister to address a joint session in summer 2006, and upon the occasion of his August 2006 visit to the shrine Prime Minister Koizumi gratuitously added that he would have gone there even if President George W. Bush had asked him not to do so.[126] Japanese, who for six decades after World War II have, in their own view, atoned for Japan's aggression in Asia (including the October 1992 visit of the emperor to China and a 1993 apology in the Kono Statement about the exploitation of "comfort women" throughout Asia) and been responsible global citizens and economic actors, have had enough of apologies and wish to play a more significant global role. And some incidents, such as the summer 2004 Chinese displays of anti-Japanese sentiment at the Asia Cup soccer games in the PRC and the intrusion of a Chinese submarine into Japanese waters later that year, have left lasting impressions on Japan.

In October 2006 Shinzo Abe made his first trip abroad as prime minister to the PRC, where he met with President Hu Jintao and his senior colleagues and, among other things, agreed to a joint history study. Chinese ambassador to Japan Wang Yi characterized this trip and a subsequent meeting in Hanoi as "healing the political stalemate."[127] These were good steps, but much suspicion and resentment must still be overcome, and Abe's parallel domestic moves making Japan's Defense Agency a full-blown defense ministry, increasing the patriotic content of national education curricula, and backing away from Tokyo's prior admission of guilt for "comfort women" in World War II work in the opposite direction.

Some in America who worry about growing Chinese power seek to draw Japan even more closely toward the United States as a security partner, a move that only intensifies Chinese suspicions. Further fueling Chinese distrust is what seems to be Japan's gradual acquisition of military power-projection capacity, ongoing debates about the wisdom of amending Japan's "peace constitution," the possibility that Japan will acquire nuclear weapons, and a 2006 discussion in Japan about whether a preemptive strike against North Korean military sites might under some circumstances be justified. Among the many notable things said in Japan's various internal debates were remarks by Liberal Party leader Ichiro Ozawa in April 2002: "If [China] gets too inflated, Japanese people will get hysterical. . . . It would be so easy for us to produce nuclear warheads. We have plutonium at nuclear power plants in Japan, enough to make several thousand such warheads. . . . I told that person [a Chinese] that if we get serious, we will never be beaten in terms of military power."[128]

A broadened Japanese security role is reflected in Tokyo's sending ground troops out of the region for the first time, 550 troops to Iraq as part of the "coalition of the willing." Tokyo also is cooperating with Washington on missile defense R&D and subsequent production[129] and has agreed to allow the siting of ABM interceptors in Okinawa in the wake of the July 2006 North Korean missile launches.[130] Moreover, Tokyo has shored up agreements with Washington on how to cooperate in a regional conflict, and in 2004 it began to actively seek permanent membership on the UN Security Council. Chinese were so outraged after the Yasukuni Shrine visits, textbook issues, and other security and territory-related frictions that more than twenty-two million of them reportedly signed a petition of opposition to UN Security Council membership for Tokyo.[131] The Chinese government openly stated its opposition to Japanese membership, saying, "We also believe that if a country wishes to play a responsible role in international affairs, it must have a clear understanding of the historical questions concerning itself."[132]

For its part, Tokyo has been seeking to enlarge the East Asian Summit structure (as Singapore, India, and Australia also have been doing) to create a membership that is less easily overshadowed by Beijing and more responsive to democratic values. To this end, for example, Prime Minister Koizumi traveled to Canada in mid-2006, urging that Canada seek to play such a role.[133]

Despite their disagreements, Tokyo and Beijing share many interests, the most apparent of which are economic. Sino-Japanese trade is growing rapidly, with Japan's exports to China expanding 8.8 percent in 2005 and imports from China growing 15.8 percent.[134] In 2005 Japan was China's second-largest trade partner and China's number one import supplier,[135] and in 2005 China (including Hong Kong) was Japan's largest trade partner. Despite rocky political relations in 2005, Japanese FDI in the PRC grew 19.8 percent, partly because Japan keeps many of its exports competitive by off-shoring labor-intensive tasks to the PRC.[136] In short, we have two business-minded societies, both of which desperately need but also deeply mistrust each other. It is testimony to the power of common economic interests that even as public opinion has mutually soured since 1998 (when President Jiang Zemin made his ill-starred trip to Japan), economic relations have become progressively broader and deeper. This deepening is in turn reflected in the growing number of Chinese students studying in Japan, reportedly sixty thousand in 2002.[137]

Nonetheless, unless Washington drives Beijing and Tokyo together, it is unlikely that they will be able to comprehensively cooperate to America's disadvantage. The two see themselves as competitors for influence in Asia, and many of the spillover effects from China's development (e.g., environmental impacts) hit Japan—and the Korean Peninsula—first. The more genuine problem for America is how to keep tensions between Beijing and Tokyo in check so that their frictions do not cause regional instability and prevent regional cooperation to resolve pressing transnational issues. The areas where Sino-Japanese competition could get out of control include offshore island and natural resource claims (Diaoyutai/Senkaku and the Chenxiao gas fields), mutually reinforcing nationalism in both countries, interrelated anxieties about energy and sea-lane security, and military modernization in both China and Japan.

Then there is the danger that a conflict in the Taiwan Strait could embroil Japan. Because of Japan's pre-1945 colonization of Taiwan, along with Tokyo's twenty-first-century economic and security interests in the island, Beijing is suspicious of Japanese involvement there. Were conflict to break out in the Taiwan Strait, Washington would expect Tokyo's assistance in a variety of ways as a treaty ally. When Washington and Tokyo declare shared "common strategic objectives" with regard to the island and regional security (as they did in early 2005), this feeds suspicions in Beijing further,[138] as do efforts to agree on a joint course of military-related action in the case of hostilities in the Strait.[139] These sorts of actions probably do not make the Taiwan issue more manageable.

Despite the frictions, both Beijing and Tokyo have ample reasons to try to realize gains from their common interests. There is a reasonable prospect that they will be able to do so. The Chinese will "walk on two legs" in their Japan policy. As Professor Shi Yinhong of People's University put it, "China must unswervingly take steps to balance relations with Japan, including preventing the Japanese public from forming a prolonged image of a 'hostile China.' While making those efforts, the Chinese government must persist in accelerating the building of its own power and be prepared to strengthen its own military power."[140] The dilemma is that doing the latter will reduce the likelihood of achieving the former. It is by no means clear that Tokyo's policies will be much more productive.

RUSSIA

Sino-Russian political relations remained satisfactory in the first part of the new millennium.[141] In 1997 Beijing and Moscow agreed to a "Strategic Partnership." Russian President Putin reaffirmed the "strategic partnership" of his predecessor Boris Yeltsin as soon as he gained power in 2000,[142] and Russia was the first foreign country that President Hu Jintao visited after his 2002 elevation to the position of general secretary of the CCP. A major driver of this partnership is a common dissatisfaction with a distribution of international power in which the United States is so dominant.

The last territorial issues between China and Russia were "thoroughly settled" in 2005,[143] and in the summer of 2005 the nations' two militaries cooperated in joint exercises in the Yellow Sea and Shandong Province, maneuvers that involved 10,000 personnel, 1,800 of whom were from Russia.[144] As described in chapter 2, Beijing's (along with India's) purchases of Russian armaments and related technology have been crucial to Russia's capacity to continue producing modern weapons systems and have helped the PRC acquire capabilities that the United States has refused to sell (and actively discouraged others from selling), such as aerial refueling tankers.[145] Beijing and Moscow also cooperate in the context of the SCO, with a shared objective of keeping the U.S. military presence and influence in Central Asia to a minimum, as well as enlarging regional economic cooperation and confronting terrorists. Russia and China "insist on a dominant role for the UN in the search for and use of political, diplomatic, economic and even military levers for influencing the international situation."[146]

Economically, Sino-Russian relations are growing; in the 2001–5 period, bilateral trade grew three times, from US$10.67 billion to $29.1 billion, a volume of trade that made Russia the PRC's number nine trade partner in 2005.[147] Even this expanded trade, however, represented only 2.05 percent of China's total trade and 6 percent of Russia's.[148]

Yet beneath this layer of cooperation lie tectonic plates of divergent interest, one of which is Russian resentment at becoming a "raw materials tributary" to China and others.[149] One need only look at demographic, resource, and administrative maps of the Sino-Russian and Sino-Central Asian border regions to understand the origin of some of these instabilities. The most basic fact of life is that Russia and China now share a 4,300-kilometer-long border (it had been 7,000 kilometers long prior to the implosion of the Soviet Union). This border is only a thin membrane separating seven million Russians in the Siberian-Russian Far East region (a population that was nine million in 1991) spread across 6.2 million square kilometers from about one hundred million Chinese in the PRC's three northeastern provinces. Illegal immigration, corruption, fears of economic domination, and ethnic conflict all are features of the interaction across this membrane. With the dissolution of the Soviet Union territorially, three new independent Central Asian states appeared along the PRC's border (Kazakhstan, Kyrgyzstan, and Tajikistan), meaning that both Beijing and Moscow had new regimes over which to compete for geopolitical influence, trade, and resources. In the context of the SCO, for instance, Russia wants to go slower on regional economic integration than China, fearing that the more dynamic PRC economy could come to overshadow Russia's in the region.[150]

With respect to energy, China is a consumer and Russia increasingly a supplier, meaning that Moscow seeks to use its supply relationships to maximize its geopolitical influence. In thinking about where to run oil and gas lines in the Russian Far East, for example, Moscow has hesitated to have pipelines go solely into China. Were that to happen, it would give the PRC leverage and reduce Russian marketing options that Moscow prefers to keep open. Russian President Vladimir Putin made clear his decision criteria on the eve of his fall 2004 visit to the PRC, saying, "We must proceed from our own national interests."[151] The CEO of Lukoil, Vagit Alekperov, explained his company's decision criterion when his company took from Yukos the responsibility to supply China—"If it is profitable we will continue supplies, but if it is 5 cents more profitable to ship crude to another destination, we will ship it to the other destination."[152] Russia also seeks to use its ability to play China and Japan off each other to extract maximum investment from both.[153] In late 2004 President Putin welcomed Beijing's expression of interest in making US$12 billion of investments in Russia but said he would like them "directed primarily towards progress in high-technology fields." Russia isn't interested in being just a commodity supplier to an industrial China or just a recipient of cheap PRC products.[154]

Strategically, Russia's armed forces must have a defense industrial base that develops new technologies, and this requires scales of production that are possible only with foreign sales (including large purchases by China), so the Russian military worries. It worries about the transfer of military capabilities to a dynamic society that is growing rapidly, with a huge population in search of resources, right next to its own vast natural wealth situated in sparsely populated territory. Consequently, Moscow has held back on selling some key military and technology items to the PRC.[155] As Paradorn Rangsimaporn put it, "Despite being the 'backbone' of the strategic partnership, MTC [military-technological cooperation] causes latent fears of a Chinese threat even among government officials who support the policy. The issue seems to create incongruence between official policy statements and actual beliefs. The impetus to MTC cannot thus be seen as a conscious result of the Kremlin's strategic calculus but rather as a case of economic interest dictating policy."[156] In this context some Russians looking ahead are strategically worried that if the EU ended its arms embargo against Beijing, as was being discussed in late 2004, the competitive pressures would force Moscow to acquiesce to more Chinese technology transfer demands, including possible joint development of new military aircraft.[157]

Leaders in Moscow also worry that the Russian Far East is many time zones removed from the capital and that this area is managed by local administrations not always responsive to central authority. Often corrupt local authorities make deals with Beijing and local PRC authorities of which Moscow does not approve. Illegal trade in timber is a prominent example.

In sum, while a shared opposition to a major U.S. security presence in Central Asia, a desire to dilute U.S. sway globally, and some shared economic interests foster Sino-Russian cooperation, there also are sources of friction that make cooperation tenuous and impermanent, even in the economic area, where cooperation is most evident. Russia is unhappy about some Chinese protectionism such as antidumping duties on some imported Russian steel.[158] Moscow, like many others, is dissatisfied with its volume of exports to the PRC. For their part, Chinese are frustrated with Russian bobbing and weaving on energy deals and their strategic opportunism.

Like their neighbors in the Mekong watershed, and like Japan and Korea with respect to wind-borne pollution, Russia must worry about spillover effects from China's modernization. A striking example of this was the late 2005 chemical spill in the Songhua River, the news of which was delayed for more than a week as the toxic slick moved toward Khabarovsk.[159]

INDIA

The core of wisdom on Sino-Indian relations is that these are two civilizations, not just two countries.[160] Each is proud and displays a tendency toward "moral self-righteousness."[161] Each hopes that past grandeur will be reflected in future greatness.

Neither wants to be a pawn of any other great power, much less of each other. The two share, and are profoundly separated by, the world's highest mountain range, a physical feature that each would like to dominate but cannot. Economically, there are areas where cooperation is feasible (e.g., China's Huawei Technologies had eight hundred persons in its Bangalore development center) and some areas in which competition is inevitable (labor-intensive production). These are two societies, each on its own trajectory, with some common interests and some mutual concerns.

Economic cooperation between the PRC and India is growing rapidly from a low base, having exceeded the US$10 billion threshold for the first time in 2004, at which point the volume of Sino-Indian trade ranked next after Thailand-China trade among Asian countries—US$13.6 billion in 2004.[162] As of 2007 the two sides seemed to be making gradual progress at managing, if not resolving, conflicting territorial claims along their border. In addition, Beijing has accepted India's nuclear status as a fact of life (knowing that its deterrent is aimed at both Pakistan and China), and Beijing and New Delhi are improving relations with each other even as China keeps its long-standing ties with Pakistan in good repair. Finally, India, China, and Russia, singly and together, "have been searching for ways to create a multipolar or polycentric international system in which they can ensure their autonomy in making foreign policy."[163] New Delhi, like Moscow, has a "strategic partnership" with Beijing, one consummated in April 2005 during Premier Wen Jiabao's trip to India. India, China, and Russia, for instance, have been collectively concerned about imposing economic sanctions on Iran for its nuclear energy endeavors, to the consternation of Washington.

Underneath these cooperative dimensions, however, lie fundamental and mutual suspicions beyond those deriving from their different political systems and ideologies. Among these anxieties and frictions are:

- Chinese efforts to drive to the sea using port arrangements and development in both Pakistan and Burma (Myanmar).
- India's significant naval power astride shipping lanes along which China's rapidly growing energy imports travel.[164]
- The fact that India provides a home for the Dalai Lama and the Tibetan government in exile (even as New Delhi since 2003 has explicitly recognized Beijing's sovereignty over the Tibet Autonomous Region).
- India's resentment at China's having helped Pakistan acquire nuclear weapons and missile capabilities as well as uncertainties about possible current and future cooperation in these and related domains.

- The ongoing dispute (under discussion) over the eastern and western sectors of the border, the latter being a chunk of real estate about the size of Switzerland and the former the size of two Taiwans.[165]
- Challenges of economic competition and perceived lack of reciprocity, with Indian manufacturers fearing Chinese competition, the PRC resenting that in 2006 two thousand Indian-invested projects were under way in China, initiated by 150 Indian companies, while only 50 Chinese companies were operating in India;[166] and both countries competing for resources, often in countries such as Myanmar, Iran, Nigeria, and elsewhere that face rebuke in much of the Western world.

These frictions, however, are unlikely to break into severe conflict any time soon because both nations emphasize domestic reform and stable external relations.[167]

In 1946 Jawaharlal Nehru described his thinking, which I believe has endured in India, about India's future security role in Asia. His words make clear where some of the underlying tensions with China lie: "[India] is potentially a Great Power. Undoubtedly, in the future she will have to play a very great part in security problems of Asia and the Indian Ocean, more especially of the Middle East and Southeast Asia. Indeed, India is the pivot round which these problems will have to be considered. . . . The importance of India to any scheme of Asian security is vital."[168]

Beijing must constantly manage ties with New Delhi. As Harry Harding suggests, the prospect is for a "shifting triangular relationship" such that the United States, China, and India variously align with one another, issue by issue, as interests and expediency dictate.[169] Certainly the March 2006 agreement between the executive authorities in the United States and India to move ahead in civilian nuclear cooperation is important, but tenous. The agreement has implications for the global nonproliferation regime and further feeds Beijing's suspicions about U.S. objectives in encircling China. But that agreement does not alter the underlying reality of India's independent role regionally and globally. India will not permit itself to be the instrument of another's will. As its minister of defense Pranab Mukherjee stated in January 2005, India has "two fundamental principles" on national strategy: maintain "an equitable strategic balance," and "engage all players both bilaterally and collectively through institutions such as the ASEAN Regional Forum."[170]

Military coercion has a limited role to play in Beijing's strategy at this time. Economic and ideational power are more effective means to achieve PRC aims.

China's neighbors, however, cannot be certain that a stronger future China will not reintroduce coercion more prominently into the equation.

The essence of Beijing's regional strategy is to reassure through economic benefit, use military strength in reassuring modes to the extent possible, and exert and increase Chinese influence through cultural and other soft instruments. The PRC hopes that this will minimize the incentives for the United States and/or Japan to boost coercive capacities in the region, reduce the incentives for others in the region to respond themselves or seek a muscular U.S. presence to offset mounting Chinese capacity, and allow Beijing to focus on its own development while securing needed markets and resources to sustain its rapid economic growth. All the while Beijing will steadily improve its military capabilities.

It is not easy living next door to China. For Beijing, it is not easy to manage its complex relations with so many surrounding societies that embody such a broad range of interests and circumstances. China is surrounded by nuclear and near-nuclear states, and history has not bequeathed PRC rulers trusting relationships in any direction. If Beijing sought to dominate one or more of its neighbors through crude means, it would complicate its relations with almost everyone else on its periphery, not to mention some big powers at greater distances. Given the primary importance that the PRC elite and citizenry attach to domestic development, it is obvious why Beijing seeks to reassure.

The security and welfare of these neighbors do not solely depend on Beijing's solicitude; these countries also possess the means to secure their own futures. Though none of China's neighbors are in a position to completely ignore Beijing's preferences, they are not now, and are not likely to be in the future, entirely supine in the face of PRC demands. These countries have resources China needs but cannot coercively grab; they have the capacity to align with other big powers; and they have the ability to join with others in the region and to participate in multilateral organizations to seek safety in numbers.

The biggest challenge China's neighbors face is not the malevolent use of growing PRC power but the spillover effects from its rapid modernization. Countries downstream from China (whether Laos, Cambodia, Thailand, Vietnam, North Korea, or Russia) or sharing the same coastal waters (such as the Koreas, Japan, and Vietnam) will face challenges derived from water pollution, fisheries, and related concerns. Countries downwind from China will face air pollution, as Japan and South Korea already do. There also will be countless other dimensions of spillover, including illicit commercial deals (e.g., timber resources), illegal immigration, trafficking of all sorts, insufficiently regulated exports affecting the global supply chain and consumers around the world, and just the economic competition unleashed by 1.3 billion dynamic people entering the global workforce. Effectively addressing these challenges requires cooperation, something that the fractured history of Asia does not make easy—perhaps not even possible.

Asia is becoming a place where Chinese interests cannot be ignored, but at the same time Chinese interests alone will not be determinative. Asia is not becoming Sino-centric. If America plays its cards skillfully, it will remain decisive in Asia's future.

We turn to the challenges Beijing faces as it attempts to keep the juggernaut moving forward at a sufficient rate (and with sufficient equity) to maintain domestic order.

SIX

A Precarious Balance

The Chinese are very conservative. They fear China
itself. They say that the threat is in China, not outside.
The security map of China is not red arrows pointing
into the map. Rather, it is the map that shows the number
of incidents and crimes. Blokes robbing banks—red
dots all over, it's the aggregation; coal mines, strikes,
bloody stuff; 1.3 billion people. Thus far it [the disrup-
tion] is local, not concentrated. This is what scared them
about Falungong.

SENIOR AUSTRALIAN DEFENSE OFFICIAL, June 2005

Among China's 100 wealthiest counties in 2004, 92,
including the whole top 10, were located in the coastal
region. In 2003, the average revenue of the 8,477 towns
in the east coast region was 28.3 million yuan, in contrast
to only 4.8 million yuan on average for the 5,748 towns
in the western region. . . . The ratio of GDP per capita
between Shanghai and Guizhou increased from 7.3 in
1990 to 13 in 2003. In contrast, the ratio of GDP per
capita between the highest and lowest of the 24 regions
of the European Union (EU) was 2.4 in 2002, a statistic
that produced an incentive for the EU to act to reduce
the gap.

CHENG LI, "New Provincial Chiefs:
Hu's Groundwork for the 17th Party Congress," 2005

Speaking of ideas, what did the new leaders give us? Sun
Yat-sen at the critical moment [in the late nineteenth and
early twentieth centuries] pointed the way. Hu [Jintao]
and Wen [Jiabao] are thinking of stability to preserve
the one-party system, not a multiparty system. Americans won't help us keep order. So Hu is right, stability
overrides [everything else]. But if you are a great leader,
[you need] great ideas. What is the idea that can move
us beyond physical wealth? The core value is stability,
but stability for what?

SENIOR CHINESE SCHOLAR IN SHANGHAI, 2004

China and its people confront internal and external challenges that could disrupt the nation's continued, rapid acquisition of coercive, economic, and ideational power. This chapter draws its inspiration from the observation of a former deputy director of the Central Intelligence Agency who, when discussing China's development, stated, "Linear projections of current performance are dangerous. A number of considerations could dramatically alter linear projections in China: SOE [state-owned enterprise] debt, Taiwan, corruption, demographic changes, and energy demand."[1] To this list I add abrupt changes in the international economy, leadership fragmentation, and relations with the big powers—the United States and Japan in particular.

Chinese leaders seek to achieve a precarious balance between rising demands of all kinds and their society's and government's limited institutional capacities to meet them. The growing economic power described in chapter 3 is the most important aspect of their effort to maintain system balance because economic power is the most convertible form of power and rising standards of living are central to regime legitimacy. But ideational power also has an important role to play by helping reassure the outside world that it need not take preemptive measures to make China's modernization more difficult than it already is. And although, as described in chapter 2, the growth of Chinese coercive power is essential for deterrence and basic national security, if it is too rapid the world will quickly turn hostile and resources better used for modernization will be diverted.

The governance tasks confronting China's leaders are immense—one wonders how they have the courage to get out of bed in the morning. Unless Chinese leaders are deflected, they have a domestic agenda that will occupy them for decades to come.

A DEVELOPMENTAL PERSPECTIVE ON THE CHALLENGES FACING CHINA

Throughout Chinese history there has been a belief that as internal conditions deteriorate, external forces seek to take advantage of that weakness to pursue their own goals and exploit a supine China. The Chinese formulation is *nei luan, wai huan,* a relaxed translation of which is, "When there is turmoil within, the barbarians from without inflict disasters." Or, as the scholar-general Zeng Guofan put it positively in the mid-nineteenth century, "If you can rule your own country, who dares to insult you?"[2]

The PRC confronts two overriding challenges to maintaining domestic stability while achieving economic growth. The first is that development processes are a sequence of problems that systems confront and must manage or resolve. The rapidity with which these development challenges have presented themselves and the scale of the problems make China distinct. The second broad development challenge is to maintain a balance between the demands being placed on the system by the populace and the international community and the system's institutional capacity to meet those demands. Beijing must address these two sets of development challenges with a per capita physical resource base well below the world average in almost every single category. Moreover, as the PRC confronts internal development challenges, the outside world is making demands on it to conform to a variety of international "norms" that did not exist when Europe and the United States developed.

The comparative politics and development literatures are helpful in understanding the dimensions of the challenges facing Beijing.[3] Development is a succession of political/economic challenges or "crises" confronted and (hopefully) resolved or managed. I use the framework of Gabriel Almond and G. Bingham Powell, who identify four such crises for development: those of *state building* (establishing state authority and creating the institutions to extract resources, regulate activity, provide security, articulate and aggregate societal interests, and distribute benefits); *nation building* (creating identity as a nation and loyalty among subjects and/or citizens); *participation* (in which citizens demand greater say in the operation of political institutions); and *distribution* (in which new patterns of participation create demands for altered division of benefits).[4]

For a state to modernize it must resolve or effectively manage these crises over time, with the resolution of one challenge often setting the stage for dealing with the next. The sequence in which crises present themselves, and the pace at which they must be addressed, vary. With respect to sequencing, for example, in the United States national identity either preceded or developed in tandem with the formation of state institutions, while in Chad, for example, state institutions exist but there is virtually no national identity among the state's putative citizens. With respect to the pace at which crises are confronted, the American development pattern was characterized by a relatively leisurely spacing of development challenges—nation and state building in the period around 1776–1865; participation from 1861 to 1968; and the ongoing distribution challenge from 1932 to the present. The one period of U.S. history where the nation, state, and participation crises bunched up for the United States was that of the Civil War (1861–65). This admittedly heuristic and imprecise periodization suggests that generally speaking America has had the relative luxury of confronting its challenges sequentially over a protracted period of time. Moreover, it did so with a relatively large per capita resource base and in a circumstance where two oceans protected it from external threats.

China's current situation is different. While the nation-building challenge has been substantially addressed (except along China's enormous periphery, where concentrations of non-Han peoples live under PRC jurisdiction in Tibet, Mongolia, and Xinjiang, not to mention the special case of Taiwan), China still seeks to construct appropriate and functional state and civic institutions within its borders. Beijing simultaneously faces increasing popular demands for political participation as successful economic growth produces ever-more-vociferous calls for more equitable distribution. Beijing faces a compression of development crises that its leaders must address without the geographic buffers or resources that America enjoyed. Instead, powerful actors in the international system are adding to the pressure by pressing the PRC for painful changes in governance and international behavior. China's system is hovering on the brink of overload, it is under-resourced, institutional capacity is anemic, and isolation is not an option.

Henry Rowen's research provides a complementary perspective from which to view China's development. His core insight is that there is a high correlation between per capita GDP level and political liberalization.

> When will China become a democracy? The answer is around the year 2015. Some might think such a prediction foolhardy but it is based on developments on several fronts, ones inadequately reported in the American media. There are, indeed, unmistakable signs of important positive changes in China. These changes are undoubtedly related to China's steady and impressive economic growth, which in turn fits the pattern of the way in which freedom has grown in Asia and elsewhere in the world. . . . China's per capita GDP [in exchange rate terms] will be between $7,000 and $8,000 (in 1995 dollars) by the year 2015. This figure is very significant. Several scholars have suggested that the transition to stable democracy correlates with mean incomes between $5,000 and $6,000, and becomes impregnable at the $7,000 level.[5]

Though I am skeptical that such numerology will prove to be a precise predictor, I am more convinced by the underlying logic, namely that economic growth creates new social groups (a middle class), new levels of societal awareness, and an increasingly complex and pluralized society that becomes difficult to manage by central fiat. The economic growth that Beijing requires to maintain minimal legitimacy eats at the foundations of the authoritarian regime. China's elite recognizes this and is endeavoring to manage the situation. Indeed, many Chinese in and out of government suspect that the economic income threshold for system change may be lower than Rowen suggests. According to one such thinker, "International experience shows that a society faces a high risk of instability when its annual per-capita gross domestic product is between $1,000 and $3,000. China is right in the middle of the 'high risk' period."[6] Indeed, the Fourth Plenum of the Sixteenth Central Committee in 2004 explicitly acknowledged this danger period, as did the Sixth Plenum in October 2006.[7]

For our purposes, Samuel Huntington's core insight is most central: sociopolitical change is a dynamic process involving the relationship between social mobilization/political participation (*demands* on the system) and the institutions through which political participation can be expressed and productively channeled (*institutional capacity* of the system).[8] The goal of development in this perspective is to maintain balance between the level of demands and institutional capacity. If demands far outstrip institutional capacities, political instability is likely to result. Conversely, if institutional strength is so great as to overshadow the capacity of citizens to participate or make demands, then one has some form of an autocratic system in which the state dominates society without necessary social feedback mechanisms, and repression and often irrational policy result. China's elite desperately seek to create and maintain a situation in which the level of demand remains at or below the level of institutional capacity, for they have learned from the Soviet Union's collapse what the costs of failing to do so can be—regime change, social disorder, and conceivably economic and social retrogression.

A concept similar to Huntington's is that of Ian Bremmer in his book *The J Curve*.[9] Bremmer postulates a relationship between "stability" and system "openness" over time. In the initial stages of development, very closed states tend to be highly stable (e.g., North Korea), but as they open up to the outside world they can quickly become less so. A high degree of stability (system equilibrium) is regained only when system openness has been matched with a new set of institutions appropriate to the new penetrable and fluid environment in which the state must now operate. Francis Fukuyama, in his *State-Building*, makes a point that resonates with both Huntington and Bremmer but is distinct—that the "strength of the state" (institutions) must be able to handle the "scope of state functions."[10] Each theorist, in his own way, asserts that sustainable development requires a balance between institutional capacity and demands.

THE NEED FOR INSTITUTIONS

INSTITUTIONAL DEFICIENCIES

As the PRC has moved from a planned toward a market economy, it has sought to construct market-appropriate regulatory and welfare institutions—everything from a strong central bank to an effective food and drug authority, a reliable social safety net to catch those who fall through the holes in a market economy, and an effective export control system that can implement and enforce its policies.[11] China has moved more quickly toward the market than it has constructed institutions appropriate to regulate and cushion it. The results of this disconnect are pathologies from adulterated (sometimes fatal) drugs and products such as baby formula, liquor, and antibiotics, to corruption and misappropriation of public property, to the weakly regulated export of weapons and related technologies. In turn, popular unrest is energized by the injustices of unregulated raw market power and a social safety net with many large holes. Even when nominally regulatory institutions are created at the national level, they often prove ineffective as their edicts filter through distorting bureaucracies at the provincial, municipal, county, and township levels.

In addition, China's people have urbanized rapidly, and this trend will only continue. When Deng Xiaoping's reforms began in the late 1970s, Chinese urban residents constituted 17.92 percent of the total population; in 2004, their percentage was 41.76 percent; and, in 2005 the United Nations Development Programme estimated that an additional two hundred million rural dwellers would move to Chinese cities by 2020.[12] Such a titanic rural-urban migration creates a huge demand for infrastructure, services, and regulation that are simply not a part of agrarian life.

Moreover, as Beijing has moved away from the one-man rule of Mao Zedong, his successors increasingly have found that they cannot micromanage individuals, enterprises, or institutions. In the place of direct control and shared moral precept, effective legal and regulatory systems now are required. Yet legal and regulatory systems take time to develop, become effective, and become part of the practice of daily lives of both leaders and citizens. In today's China, the institutions through which popular demands can be effectively articulated and grievances adjudicated (meaningful legislatures and independent courts) are weak in the face of a much stronger executive or Communist Party authority.

The PRC also has a dearth of appropriate social organizations (what the Chinese call *shehui tuanti*), a particularly important lacuna given the rapidly mounting societal demands described below. These societal demands are being driven by past

FIGURE 11

In the 1930s and 1940s Mao Zedong's revolution found sanctuary from the "counter-revolution" and Japanese imperialism in the caves of Shaanxi Province, but today there is no refuge from the communications revolution even in those same caves. Modern telecommunications reach the most remote geographic corners of China, bringing its poor areas awareness of improved conditions elsewhere in the country and world and creating uncertainties about future political stability. Photograph date: October 2006. Liu Liqun/Corbis.

progress ("rising expectations"), increasing information availability (one indicator of which is the explosion of the Internet, with 137 million reported users in mid-2007), a rising middle class that wants to participate and protect its growing material assets, and the demands of others in the international community. Civic institutions, which in theory could lift some of the load from the government's shoulders and give constructive voice to discontents, are weak and generally kept that way by a government fearful that they will become vehicles for radical opposition rather than means by which to solve problems.

Another area of concern is the cohesiveness of the Chinese political elite. Many political demands are being made on China's creaky institutional structure, the stakes are high, and this remains a substantially personalized system at its upper reaches. Everything we know about Chinese politics suggests that high-stakes decisions, affecting large populations, in circumstances where there are many policy alternatives with unclear long-term effects, produce conflict. If China's elite fragments in the course of addressing these enormous issues, the PRC could experience the kind of intraelite paralysis and resulting mass mobilization that contributed to widespread social conflict in 1989, not to mention the Cultural Revolution decade in the mid-1960s to mid-1970s.

In the afterglow of a relatively smooth succession between Jiang Zemin and Hu Jintao in the 2002–5 period, it is easy to forget that the challenge of leadership renewal and succession is ongoing and is next scheduled for 2007–8. China still has no constitutionally embedded succession process, though the norms of peaceful succession seem to be taking root. Nonetheless, it is premature to be fully confident of the succession process, and the Chinese worry, as one official essay explained in August 2006: "The recent successions in [the] CPC and State leaderships have demonstrated a de facto pattern of limiting terms. But there was never a written clause stipulating [that] a CPC or State leader should leave after serving his or her term of office."[13] Without confidence in the succession process, sociopolitical stability cannot be assumed.

Of all the important institutional deficiencies, none is more decisive than the weakness of the central government's capacity to extract and redistribute resources and the financial footing of local governments nationwide. This makes it hard to address inequalities in income, health, and education. The central government and local governments across the country have insufficient revenues to discharge their core (and growing) responsibilities. The needs for redistribution are huge, and as the PRC scholar Hu Angang points out, there is not simply one China; instead there are four "worlds" internally, each differentiated by income. While far less than 10 percent of the national population is in "first China" (predominantly along the coast in Shanghai, Beijing, and Shenzhen), with incomes higher than in "moderately developed" nations, more than 50 percent of the population is in "fourth China," with incomes characteristic of the world's low-income countries.[14] How does one transfer resources (or change the distribution of investment and subsidies) from the first to the fourth China?

From 1978 to 1995 total revenue for government at all levels (excluding off-budget resources, which were significant, running to "61.6 percent of the [total] fiscal revenue" in 1995),[15] fell as a percentage of GDP, dropping from a high of 31.2 percent in 1978 to a low of 10.7 percent in 1995.[16] This drop was leading to a situation in which "approximately half of the expenditure of the central government had to be financed by borrowing from banks," according to the Chinese economist Jinglian Wu.[17] Since then, total government revenue has been capturing a progressively greater share of GDP, passing 20 percent in 2004.[18] Moreover, from 1981, when the central government (as distinct from subnational governments) captured 57.2 percent of total government revenues at all administrative levels, the central share fell in 1993 to a low of 33.4 percent, excluding revenues derived from debt issuance.[19] Following the budgetary reforms of 1994 that established "a tax-sharing system based on a reasonable division of authority between the central and local governments,"[20] the central government increased its share of total government revenues (54.6 percent in 2003),[21] but central resources remain inadequate to meet local government needs for transfers, particularly in poor areas.

This inadequacy of central resources has driven the central government to place ever more unfunded responsibilities on local governments, even though local governments have inadequate taxing authority and revenue sources to meet their ever-enlarging responsibilities. "Particularly in rural areas, the supply of funds to carry out state-mandated programs such as education, local infrastructure, and poverty alleviation has never been adequate."[22] Corruption is an inevitable result as local officials raise funds by hook or crook, and local government insolvency is widespread. To deal with insolvency, local governments, particularly townships, take on increasing debt (loan) burdens from individuals and banks, with investments gone sour adding to debt burdens. As Jing Jin reported in her study of fiscal federalism in China, "For all the 26 townships in the county under investigation [in southern Jiangsu Province in 2001], 25 of them have an average accumulated debt ranging from 1,194,000 [yuan] to 38,456,700 [yuan]." The only township in the county without debt was the poorest one—no one would lend it money![23]

Further, local investment has been nearly half financed from extrabudgetary resources largely under the control of local governments, meaning that localities with enterprises generating such monies can invest while localities without such resources cannot.[24] In China's more prosperous localities, taxes remitted to local governments from foreign-invested enterprises and their employees are a significant fraction of local revenue, thereby giving localities throughout China incentives to attract foreign investment for both their revenue and their employment effects. Tax revenues derived from trade and foreign-invested enterprises have become extremely important for both the central and local governments. In January 2005 China's Minister of Commerce Bo Xilai reported that "the import and export tax revenue accounts for about 18 percent of the nation's total. The tax revenue of foreign-related enterprises makes up over 20 percent of the national total. The number of employees working in the field of foreign trade has topped 80 million and the processing trade has become the export of labor service provided within China."[25] This is a sign of the weakness of the domestic taxation and redistribution system.

In short, China is underinstitutionalized: it does not have fully appropriate institutional capacity to justly manage an increasingly marketized, urbanized, and globalized system. The problem with China's government and institutional structures is not that they are too strong but rather that often they are too weak. The Chinese polity is on the edge of having a surfeit of demands while being saddled with only partially appropriate institutions to address and manage them.

THE CHARACTER OF THE POLICY PROCESS

China is not nearly as centrally capable as popular conceptions in the West would have it. The PRC has what Kenneth Lieberthal and I have called a "fragmented authoritarian" or "bargaining" system.[26] Most issues, most of the time, must be addressed through a complex process of consensus building and bargaining involving a large and fluid array of territorial and functional actors. Because the legal system is weak it is unable (and often not allowed) to resolve many disputes. Consequently, leaders at the top are called upon to do so, and they become overloaded as lower levels kick difficult problems up the political hierarchy. It takes time to address issues. Legal predictability takes a back seat to political power. Finally, once a decision is made, it must be implemented through a complex process in which every level of the system (center, province, municipality, county, township, and village) may deflect the central government's policy from its initially intended course. The central government's oversight capacities are limited, and often it is of more than one mind itself. Beijing's original policy intentions can be radically deformed by the time they reach the grassroots level.[27] A good example is seen in birth control policy, where wealthier areas, villages, and households have had the option of paying fines "for excess births" while more draconian means have been used in impoverished areas, villages, and households. A great deal of implementation varies according to who is in charge locally, their own objectives, and the competing priorities of the moment. At the apex of the political hierarchy, by way of example, the bureaucracies in Beijing germane to the making of energy policy are so numerous (thirteen by one count) that a Chinese scholar Kong Bo has written, "The way energy institutions are structured and operate in China predisposes the country toward a series of loosely connected policies that are inconsistent, short-sighted and ad hoc, precluding them from producing any coherent and long-term national energy strategy."[28]

The preceding suggests a very different view of the Chinese system than that implied by popular discourse about a Chinese behemoth striding the world stage. The Chinese institutional and decision-making system has great weaknesses, it confronts challenges of enormous scale under conditions of time compression, and Beijing's drive to achieve economic growth to maintain legitimacy erodes the authoritarian system. China's strength abroad will ultimately depend upon its strength at home.

A CASCADE OF CHALLENGES

If one half of the political equation is institutional capacity, the other half is the level of demand placed on institutions. The demands placed on government at all levels are tremendous. Some emanate from within the system and others from outside, or, as Vice President Zeng Qinghong put it when he explained the 2004 Fourth Plenum's efforts to strengthen the CCP's ability to govern, "We still face pressure from developed countries," and "Certain significant contradictions and problems persist in China's economic and social development."[29] In theory, one might distinguish between short-term and long-term problems, but in reality all of the challenges of developmental significance in the PRC are long term in character. Below, they are categorized as internal challenges, specifically those of demographics, equity and equality (in income, health, and education), and participation (new actors, new issues); challenges bridging the internal and the external, specifically those of nationalism and Taiwan; and external challenges, specifically those of international dependencies and wary international actors.

INTERNAL CHALLENGES

Demographics　　In the late 1970s Beijing launched its one-child policy, a controversial project at home and abroad. This policy has undergone modifications over the years, sequentially exempting some groups and then others, but it still applied to about 63 percent of China's people in 2005.[30] While there is debate over how much of the post-1970s slowing of population growth to attribute to the policy and how much to other influences (such as urbanization, two adults working, education, and the reduction of implicit subsidies for childbearing that existed under Mao Zedong), there is agreement on the current characteristics of the Chinese population and what they portend for the future:

- In 2005 fertility in the PRC was below the replacement level, though there is uncertainty over the exact number because of unreliable birth data.

- The skewed sex ratio (the number of males born divided by the number of females born) in China has become dramatically more unbalanced since the late 1970s, reaching 119.2:100 in 2000 and 118:100 in 2005 (even though it is necessary to note that many female births go unreported as a way around the one-child policy).[31] Beijing reports that in some areas (e.g., Guangdong and Hainan) the ratio is 130:100.[32] This male-to-female imbalance reflects sex-selective abortion, infanticide, and mortality differentials. Parenthetically, gender imbalance is also a problem in India.[33]

- China's huge population is aging. In the mid-1980s the PRC population sixty years of age and over was 7.6 percent of total population, with 4.9 percent above age sixty-five. By 2000 the corresponding numbers were 10.5 percent and 7.1 percent.[34]

- China's urban population is aging faster than its rural population, in part reflecting the lower urban birth rate.

How do these facts create demands on Chinese institutions and affect resources available to build system capacity? The sociologist Wang Feng estimates that there will be 45.6 million persons over sixty-five years of age in China's cities and 128.2 million in the country's rural areas in 2025, for a total of 173.8 million persons—almost 60 percent of the 2005 U.S. population.[35] Moreover, many Chinese males will be in search of nonexistent females to wed—China's National Population Development Group predicts that by 2020 there will be thirty million more men than women aged twenty to forty-five.[36] These two developments already are having profound social and economic consequences that will become more adverse over time.

To start, the worker-to-dependent ratio will become increasingly adverse, with each working-age Chinese having to support more elders. Jackson and Howe report that by 2040, 28 percent of the Chinese population will be at or over the age of sixty; the corresponding figure for the United States is projected to be 25 percent.[37] Assuming that there is an effective social security system in place by then (and today this system does not exist even in the cities, much less the countryside), such a system would impose an increasing economic burden on the working-age population. According to the United Nations Development Programme (UNDP) in China, at the end of 2004, "Pension coverage is much broader for urban residents, with basic pension insurance currently covering only urban workers; farmers have virtually no access to such insurance."[38] If an effective social security system is not constructed and funded by about 2015, the regime will be confronted with the problem of an enormous number of impoverished elders. The most important change in living arrangements and associated mores has been the ongoing change in household size, which was 4.5 persons in 1985 but is projected to be 2.7 persons by 2015.[39] There simply are going to be fewer children available nearby to take care of aged parents, a trend that will be exacerbated by geographic mobility. Further, as people age, they require increasingly costly medical procedures and drugs, and as the costs of medical care rise, the expense of caring for China's increasingly numerous elders will also mount sharply.

Regarding the sex imbalance, it is hard to imagine a more destabilizing phenomenon than large cohorts of mostly rural, poor males without marriage prospects. In its 2005 report, the UNDP reported that for China "recent research indicates that child mortality rates are rising at .5% a year for girls while falling at 2.3% a year for boys."[40]

China's remarkable economic performance, therefore, has to some extent occurred in a window of demographic opportunity that is closing. Now there is an enormous population of working-age people who are saving at a remarkable rate. As China ages, workers (people aged fifteen through fifty-nine) in proportion to the elderly (aged sixty and over) will drop, going from 6.4:1 in 2000 to 2:1 in 2040.[41] The costs to each worker of maintaining elders will mount. This portends societal stresses that will be compounded by an inevitable slowing of red-hot economic growth as the Chinese economy gets larger. All these changes are unavoidable. The only questions are: How fast will these problems become apparent? How rapidly might China's leaders change birth and other policies such as retirement age? And how financially sound and universal a social safety net will be created? No other society has ever dealt with these problems, on this scale, with this time compression, having such meager resources. Creating a viable social safety net is an institution-building job that may take more time than Beijing has.

Equity and Equality: The Distribution of Essentials   An equitable situation is one in which individuals have equal opportunities for success, though there is no guarantee of equal outcomes. Equality speaks to the distribution of outcomes. China has three sets of political problems that derive from considerations of equity and equality. First, with respect to equity, there is the problem of "unjust" distribution of opportunities. When some groups, such as the politically advantaged, gain access to opportunities denied others, resentment grows because of the absence of equity, or procedural justice.

With respect to equality, the problem is outcomes, or substantive justice. Even on a level playing field, which does not exist in the PRC, some individuals and groups will do much better than others. One of the principal problems is that the distribution of income, education, and health services has rapidly become more unequal, though this does *not* mean that large numbers of persons are becoming absolutely worse off. Indeed, generally speaking with respect to income, most boats have been rising in China, but some much faster than others. Under Jiang Zemin, China's leadership recognized the problem of mounting inequality, but it has fallen to the post-Jiang leadership to focus more seriously on this challenge.

The third problem is how to weigh economic "efficiency" (or high-speed growth) against both equity and equality. This issue has set off intermittent, intense political debates, the most recent of which was waged in 2005–6. Some leading social scientists, such as the economist Liu Guoguang, argue that relatively more attention needs to be paid to equity and equality than to high-speed growth, while other party officials, such as Zhou Tianyong and Zhou Ruijin, have argued that China must take advantage of the national window of opportunity to amass aggregate wealth as rapidly as possible and worry about distribution later.[42]

In April 2005 Nita Lowey, a member of the U.S. House of Representatives from New York, asked Premier Wen Jiabao about these issues. The premier described how he viewed inequalities and the protracted nature of China's developmental struggle, noting in passing that these issues disturbed his sleep.

NITA LOWEY: I am aware of inequalities in education and health care, especially in rural areas.

WEN JIABAO: You have raised the question I am most interested in and also something I think about even in my dreams. China is very big and also very unequal. There is uneven development—inequalities among cities and between east and west. GNP per capita is $^1/_{20}$th that of the U.S., so it is still an uphill journey. There are 250 million people in urban areas, 24 million of whom are looking for jobs and only 12 million can be successful. . . . We have successfully lifted 250 million from poverty, but still 30 million are in absolute poverty. . . . We have to work 50 years to reach the level of a moderately developed country. To catch up with the modern countries we have to work for generations, tens of generations. This leaves us with no choice but to follow the peaceful road to development. . . . We have a dream, and our government is making efforts to realize these dreams, that from last year to next year, three years, we will relieve farmers from agricultural taxes and there is a special $90 billion fund for this. Also, there are other policies. By about 2007, nine years compulsory education in poor areas [will be realized], in 592 poverty stricken counties, students get exempted tuition, books, and subsidies for dorm expenses. We also have a plan for the road network to link townships to county towns by 2010—asphalt roads. Last year we provided [jobs for] 8.9 million unemployed [people] and this year there will be 10 million. Gradually we are addressing health care in the cities—expensive, hard to see a doctor. I have a dream.[43]

The ultimate questions are: Will the premier's dreams be adequately funded or implemented? Will palliative steps be enough to preserve tolerable stability? Let's look at each of these areas of inequality.

INCOME   The most basic fact about the PRC is that it is a poor, developing country. Even with a rather dramatic 16.8 percent upward revision of China's GDP figure for 2004 to adjust for undercounting the growing service sector, per capita (exchange rate–calculated) GDP was only $1,490 that year.[44] According to the World Bank's cross-national comparisons, China's GDP expressed in per capita PPP terms was $4,980 in 2003, well below the world average of $8,190, though above Malawi at $590, Kenya at $1,030, Bangladesh at $1,870, Bolivia at $2,490, and Venezuela at $4,750. Yet this meager per capita GDP obscures enormous inter-regional and urban-rural disparities.

Beijing aims for an "olive-shaped" wealth distribution—a bulging middle class and relatively small low- and high-income groups. However, income distribution is becoming progressively more uneven, with a Gini coefficient that reached .39 in 1999, near the international warning level of .40, and was at .465 by 2004, getting quickly closer to the threshold of "high income inequality" of .50.[45] By 2002, China had worsened in twenty years by 50 percent in terms of inequality measured this way, giving the PRC a rank of 90th out of 131 countries.[46] As time has progressed, different studies have produced different precise figures, but the story remains the same—rising inequality. In its 2006 report, the Chinese Academy of Social Sciences reported that the Gini coefficient had reached .496.[47]

The story behind summary indicators is that tremendous gains coexist with enormous problems. Real, annual disposable income grew about 7 percent per year between 1990 and 2005.[48] The percentage of rural population living in poverty in 1978 was 30.7, while in 2004 that number had dropped to 2.8, according to Chinese measures (which set a poverty line that is hard to fall below).[49] If one applies the international standard of "absolute poverty" (US$1/per capita/per day), in 2004 there were 85 million rural poor, or about 6.5 percent of the entire national population.[50] With regard to annual income, in 2003 the average urban dweller received US$1,045 while the average rural dweller received $323.[51] Between 1990 and 2003 the differential in rural and urban incomes rose by more than 600 percent.[52] The average wage of migrant workers coming from more isolated areas to work in larger urban areas was about 80 percent of the amount (without many benefits) earned by local urban workers, according to a 2005 UNDP report: only 55 percent of migrant workers in cities had access to sanitation, and less than 2 percent had full or partial unemployment insurance;[53] in spring 2007 only 13.4 percent of the migrant worker population had work injury insurance.[54]

Though one should not ignore growing numbers of urban poor, the concentration of poverty in remote rural areas and the widening urban-rural income gap account for the focus of the Third Session of the Tenth National People's Congress (March 2005) on reducing the agricultural land tax, increasing subsidies for laid-off workers, providing free textbooks to rural students, and controlling the (often corrupt) conversion of agricultural land to other uses, a phenomenon so large that at least forty million and perhaps as many as sixty-six million farmers lost land to urban expansion and "other reasons" between the 1970s and 2005.[55] The Fifth Plenum of the Sixteenth Party Congress (October 2005) focused on this same set of issues as it considered the Eleventh Five-Year Plan (2006–10). Inequalities of such magnitudes are a major challenge to keeping order.

HEALTH   There have been important public health gains in China during the reform period—infant mortality reportedly dropped from 38 per 1,000 live births in 1990 to 30 per 1,000 in 2003.[56] Life expectancy increased by eight years between 1975 and 2005, with China's life expectancy now six years higher than the average for developing countries.[57] In the 1983–97 period, the annual number of malaria cases in China fell from 265,000 to approximately 27,000.[58] However, rural infant and maternal mortality rates in 2001 were both more than twice as high as in urban areas,[59] and the average life expectancy for a Chinese rural dweller in 2000 was 5.6 years less than for an urban resident.[60] About 45 percent of urban residents had "social" medical insurance in 2003, while less than 5 percent of rural residents were said to have such coverage.[61] In addition, the level of coverage and the quality of medical facilities accessible to rural residents were greatly inferior to what was available to urban residents. Consequently, Beijing is again experimenting with "rural cooperative health care," one of the better-conceived Cultural Revolution efforts to promote equality and equity, although this policy also had its severe problems.

The state of the public health system in China is precarious, a vulnerability that became dramatically apparent in the five-month-long SARS crisis that started in November 2002 (see chapter 2). When discussing that crisis, one retired PRC military officer called it "stonewalling, bad information, and even a reluctance to acknowledge the serious nature of the problem."[62] The SARS crisis demonstrated two important points. First, adaptive and virulent infectious diseases can move swiftly, having great impact, both domestically and globally, before national authorities can (or do) respond. Second, the SARS challenge showed that the Chinese government (once the extent of the danger became obvious and there was the political will to act) still possesses impressive capacity to implement an almost Mao-style mobilization campaign that, in this case, helped to effectively isolate the disease. That the PRC was successful in 2002–3, however, is no guarantee that this always will prove true, since the early-warning and reporting systems are deficient and since the capacity of the health system to appropriately handle a jump in the number of sick is questionable.

Many of the same risks exist with respect to HIV/AIDS. A 2002 UN-sponsored report was entitled *HIV/AIDS: China's Titanic Peril*. A study by the U.S. National Intelligence Council warned: "Even if adult prevalence rates rose only to two percent by the end of the decade, China would have about 15 million infected people by 2010—surpassed only by India."[63] In 2001–2 UN and other foreign observers estimated that China had between 1.5 and 2+ million cases,[64] a number considerably higher than the official Chinese estimate. In October 2005 China's Ministry of Public Health reported a 42 percent increase in the number of new HIV cases between 2004 and 2005,[65] but in January 2006 the Chinese authorities and the World Health Organization (WHO) reported a number that was 190,000 lower than the official 2003 Chinese figure of 840,000 cases nationwide—that is, 650,000.[66] Some other independent scholars have much higher infection estimates, usually derived from extrapolating presumed infection rates in problem areas to the entire nation. Whatever the specific numerical baseline for the disease, the dynamic under way is worrisome[67]—the mounting rate of infection is being propelled by internal migration, prostitution and unsafe sex practices, substance abuse, and criminal practices in the blood plasma industry. Injection drug use and homosexual and commercial sexual transmission account for the great majority of cases; the disease is spreading from rural, western areas into urban and coastal areas and is moving out of the tra-

FIGURE 12

The 2002–3 outbreaks of severe acute respiratory syndrome (SARS) produced deserted streets in some major Chinese cities, led some villages to throw up barricades to keep out "outsiders," and led to widespread public health mobilization. The outbreak, which killed 774 persons globally, alerted China and the world to the economic, public health, and public order consequences that epidemic diseases could have, simultaneously highlighting some of the PRC's institutional weaknesses. This photograph was taken at a Beijing bus stop in May 2003. Reuters/Corbis.

ditional high-risk groups. "Eighty percent of those HIV positive do not know their status and the government does not know who they are."[68]

After initially downplaying the disease, then seeing the spread of the disease in India, Africa, and some parts of Southeast Asia, China's central leaders have encouraged international community involvement and promised free testing and drug treatment for the infected. China's leaders are worried, with officials estimating in late 2005 that HIV/AIDS-infected individuals could number ten million by 2010 if effective measures were not taken.[69] Speaking of other even higher estimates a year earlier, the China National Development Research Center stated, "This is by no means an alarmist talk."[70] As with so many aspects of public policy in China, however, the real issue is the effectiveness of implementation and money, not simply principled central intention—under 2006 regulations, financially starved local governments were responsible for picking up the cost of the central government's good intentions.[71] As Zhao Pengfei, WHO program officer in Beijing, put it: "The key to an adequate AIDS response in China lies in three changes: from policy to action, from pilots to scaling-up program implementation, and from health response to societal involvement."[72]

A Chinese government that fails to skillfully handle a serious disease outbreak will see its own competence called into question domestically and internationally, with consequences for regime legitimacy. One retired Chinese military officer made the risks clear in recalling the SARS crisis:

> The disastrous implication of the disease is not so much the death tolls it had brought to the nation but the extremely negative psychological effect it had on the minds of the average people. Everyone seemed to be scared and at a loss as what to do since the exact cause of the sudden eruption of the epidemic remained mysteriously unidentified. In the peak of the disease, Beijing and many other major cities looked like deserted cities. That led to the high risks of serious dysfunction of the whole society. Meanwhile, the Government's initial poor performance invited criticism from world opinion. By many, China was regarded as the source of the problem. The credibility of China's new leadership was being seriously questioned.[73]

Demonstrating how hard it is to say that "systems have learned lessons," in 2006 the WHO publicly let it be known that it did not have high confidence that Chinese authorities were providing timely data on H5N1 influenza virus infections and deaths.[74] It often is unclear whether senior PRC officials know and are hiding the truth, are unsure of the situation throughout the vast continent they nominally rule, and/or fear setting off social panic.

Other aspects of public health concern the Chinese workplace and the natural environment. At the Seventh China Economists Forum and International Forum of late 2005, Huang Yan reported that in each of the years from 2001 to 2004 more than 130,000 workers perished in workplace accidents; 2002 was the worst year, with 139,400 deaths. The estimate for 2005 was 130,000 deaths. Coal mining was the most dangerous occupation;[75] the UNDP reported that in 2003 China accounted for 80 percent of the world's coal mining–related fatalities and only 35 percent of global coal production.[76] In 2005, 5,986 persons died in 3,341 coal mine accidents.[77] In a scathing report, one Chinese publication stated, "There have been major mining accidents in China, but the first move by the local government involved is to block

FIGURE 13

While China's coastal and urban areas are in "first" and "second" China, half or more of the nation's population lives in "fourth China," a land of material hardship and manual labor. Coal mining is a major contributor to total workplace deaths and injuries in the PRC, and coal mine deaths constitute a very disproportionate percentage of global coal mine mortality. Bob Sacha/Corbis.

the news, then secretly try to resolve problems arising in the aftermath. As a result, the same type of accident happens again and again, and the situation grows worse."[78]

The UNDP also reported that two hundred million Chinese had been diagnosed with "work-related illnesses" in 2004 and that sixteen million businesses handled "poisonous and harmful substances" with insufficient safety controls.[79] In *China: 2020* the World Bank estimated that as much as 3 to 8 percent of GDP per year was lost due to air and water pollution and that "as many as 289,000 deaths a year could be avoided if air pollution alone were reduced to comply with Chinese government standards."[80] A decade later, in 2007, another World Bank study that was only partially released reportedly "found that about 750,000 people die early every year in China because of the filthy air and water."[81] Elizabeth Economy cites estimates that the total annual costs to GDP of environmental degradation may run to 12 percent.[82] The Development and Reform Commission's deputy director Zhu Zhixin, in speaking of the Eleventh Five-Year Plan in 2006, said that the annual economic losses from environmental pollution and biological environment destruction totaled 14 percent of GNP.[83] These enormous losses in terms of mortality, morbidity, wasted natural resources, and foregone economic growth generate social instability and cumulatively reduce the pool of resources necessary to build stronger institutions.

China's total government expenditures on public health and medical care have been paltry over the years, generating a certain surprise at how well the system has done given those meager expenditures. The PRC *Blue Book of Chinese Society 2002* reported that "in 1999 the average total health expenditure per individual in China [from all sources] was only 332 *yuan* [or US$40.98 by exchange rate calculation], which ranked 144th [of 191 countries] in the world. Of this per capita expenditure, the Chinese government contributed 51 *yuan* [US$6.29], or only 15 percent, individuals contributed 59 percent, and society [outside government] 26 percent."[84] World Bank data for 2002 provide a similar picture, with health expenditures said to constitute 5.8 percent of total GDP and with the public sector accounting for about one-third of total health expenditure—most remaining health expenditures were private. Total average health expenditures per capita in 2002 were reported to be US$63.[85] The UNDP *Human Development Report 2005* reported that "in effect, health financing has been privatized."[86]

With such a high fraction of health expenditure coming from individual and non-governmental resources, wealthy and urban areas have more to spend on health care than poor and rural areas, with 67.7 percent of government health spending going to hospitals (located generally in cities) in 2002.[87] According to a 2001 PRC government report, 60 percent of rural dwellers stayed away from hospitals because of cost.[88] Since physicians and hospitals are concentrated in wealthier urban areas, and since the supply of both doctors and hospital beds has stayed the same, rural and remote areas are in a precarious, and certainly unequal, public health and medical position. The number of doctors per 1,000 persons hardly changed at all between 1990 and 2004 (from 1.5 up to 1.6), and the number of hospital beds per 1,000 persons showed little change during the 1990s and up to 2002.[89] China's rural residents, 60 percent of the population, have access to only 20 percent of these medical resources.[90] To strengthen these basic systems, state finance at all levels needs new priorities, according to economist Jinglian Wu. State finance "should also gradually withdraw from ordinary competitive fields, reduce its financial aid to business development projects and applied research projects in enterprises, and increase its input in education, science and technology, health care, public security, social security, and infrastructure construction."[91] By early 2006, Beijing was promising that central and local government medical care subsidies "in rural areas will increase 'by big margins.'"[92] Time will tell.

Although China's medical and public health system is not in the condition of the poorest countries (such as Chad, Eritrea, or Ethiopia), its characteristics place it in a category of countries inconsistent with a superpower image. In terms of percentage of population with access to improved water sources, for example, China in 2002 was at 77 percent, up from 70 percent in 1990—very close to the figures for Burundi, Bangladesh, Georgia, Haiti, and Indonesia. In 2002, only 44 percent of China's population had access to improved sanitation facilities, up from 23 percent in 1990 but still putting the PRC in a category with Cote d'Ivoire, Kenya, Malawi, and Papua New Guinea.[93]

Two measures of Beijing's seriousness in dealing with public health and medical challenges will be whether government spending goes up dramatically and whether that spending finds its way to rural areas. A public health fiasco cannot be ruled out, and were this to occur it could have enormous effects on social stability and legitimacy. Indeed, the Ministry of Public Health keeps statistics on violence directed at medical personnel and facilities. Looking at the longer term, as China's population ages, the medical system (and public finance) will face ever more chronic, expensive, and debilitating disease. China is not moving fast enough, particularly in rural areas, to prepare for this tidal wave.

EDUCATION   In Chinese education, while there has been great progress in the reform era, enormous problems persist, and inequities and inequalities are growing.

The percentage of school-age population enrolled in primary school in the year 2000 was 11 points above the developing world average; the percentage of Chinese youth who were literate was 13 points above the developing world average; and university enrollments in the PRC more than tripled from 1995 to 2003.[94] Nonetheless, adult illiteracy is growing nationally, the rate of illiteracy in Tibet was almost seventeen times higher than in Shanghai, and 50 percent of migrant worker children did not attend school in 2005.[95] The State Council's Development Research Center and UNDP report that the PRC spent 3.4 percent of GDP on education in 2002, while even "Third World" nations averaged 4.1 percent. The report also noted that the Chinese central government paid only 2 percent of rural compulsory education costs, with townships (which, as noted above, are often broke) "footing as much as 78 percent of the bill."[96] In affluent Shanghai, the central city district of Jing'an annually spent 11.3 times as much per pupil as the suburban rural county (in Shanghai) of Fengxian.[97] Given weak redistribution capacities and the shortage of resources at the local level, remedying these problems will be difficult.

Political Participation: Actors, Arenas, and Issues   Participation in politics assumes many forms, ranging from peaceful articulation of interests through established channels to violent protest, involves many potential different kinds of actors, and can be driven by new or old issues. Often preexistent institutions are incapable of dealing with newly aroused actors demanding redress with respect to new issues.

ACTOR: THE MIDDLE CLASS   A key issue germane to middle classes is their role in political change and governance. Westerners generally expect a growing middle class to push for political change in a democratic direction. Henry Rowen's research (discussed earlier) even provides a GDP per capita range that he argues marks a rough point of no return on the trip from authoritarianism to more pluralistic and participatory governance—US$5,000 to US$7,000. The tendency of Western analysts to view the middle class as an agent of political change contrasts somewhat (but not entirely) with the dominant elite view in China.

China's elite has focused on the middle class as a force for creating social stability, not as a Trojan horse for political change. *China Daily* hopefully noted that "the moderate and conservative ideology of the middle stratum tends to be accepted as the mainstream ideology of a society and thus helps safeguard social stability by forcing out extremism."[98] *Xinhua* quoted the sociologist Lu Xueyi saying: "Socially or economically speaking, the middle income class is the most stable one in a society. They generally enjoy a well-off life, hav[e] stable jobs, hold [a] positive attitude toward the society and policies, and are loyal consumers."[99] China's fourth-generation leaders have bet their rule and China's future on the development of a middle class that they *presume* will remain patient and stabilizing, perhaps a middle class something like what they conceive the one in Singapore to be—economically and socially active but not politically aggressive. Though this is a bet that Beijing's current elite could lose, in a mid-2005 urban/suburban survey of Chinese citizens by the Pew Organization, respondents reported themselves "optimistic about the future and confident that the growing opportunities they have experienced in recent years will continue to expand." Sixty-eight percent of respondents asserted that "other countries think positively of China," and China topped the list of sixteen surveyed nations in percentage of respondents expressing "satisfaction" with national conditions.[100] While the reliability and comparability of such results are questionable (and rural opinion largely is ignored), these findings should shake the certitude of those who simply assert China's regime lacks legitimacy. In other, more differentiated research, Professor Anthony Saich finds that citizens report higher satisfaction with higher levels of government than with local levels, and citizens in major cities report higher satisfaction with local government than those living in villages.[101]

Most foreign and Chinese research shows that the country's middle class has reached an implicit bargain with the Communist Party, reflected in the fact that one in three private business owners in the PRC is a member of the party and that "the percentage of CPC members among large private companies is even larger."[102] The most forceful PRC proponent of this argument is Kang Xiaoguang, and the most articulate Western analyst has been Margaret Pearson, who says, "Ultimately, then, there is reason to be skeptical that the business elite in the PRC will either emerge as a strong independent force or that it will be at the center of a more progressive form of state-society relations."[103] As Kang Xiaoguang put it, "The ruling clique's alliance is with the economic elite and the intellectual elite. . . . The foundation of support for the government has now shifted from workers and agricultural people to the economic and intellectual elites."[104] The CCP's Organization Department announced in mid-2006 that the party then numbered 70.8 million persons and that the number of college students entering the party in 2005 grew by 734,000, a rate of expansion twice that of overall party growth. Twenty percent of Tsinghua University's undergraduates were in the party, as were half of the graduate students.[105]

This utility-driven alliance, however, should not be considered an eternal feature of the political landscape. Members of China's private business elite are becoming more politically involved to secure their own personal interests and to institutionalize the rights of a private sector.[106] In two remarkable articles on "corporate political activities in China," two researchers from Huazhong University of Science and Technology note the many avenues by which business influences government (including trade associations and standard setting):

> [Being a] Congressman in China is a part-time job. Congressmen [in the National People's Congresses] come from every strata and every walk of life including business circles. Therefore, there is a very different and unique phenomenon in China—businesspeople participate in politics directly as Congressmen. . . . And the government decisions that firms want to influence are decisions in which firms can exert their influence and derive benefits, such as getting land and credit loan approval to do certain projects, changing certain by-laws, quick monetary returns, beating competitors, and so on. Firms do these within a cost-benefit framework. This means that firms take action only when the benefit to influence government decisions exceeds the relevant cost.[107]

As the private sector gains more stakes and autonomous resources, and as its preferences begin to diverge from those of other parts of the elite coalition, conflict may result. More broadly, as Samuel Huntington observed long ago, the middle class, amid the reform from which it benefits, often becomes the catalyst for deeper political change. In this regard, for example, growing numbers of college-educated youth with all the dissatisfactions and aspirations of youth can become an unstable element, as seen in 1989 throughout China and again in 2006 with student disturbances in Jiangxi Province.[108]

One other aspect of the middle class calls for discussion—the likelihood that it will become stridently nationalistic. In fascinating but nondefinitive survey research conducted in Beijing, Professor Alastair Iain Johnston has found a tendency for middle-class urbanites to hold more liberal, internationalist views when it comes to global economic issues, military spending, nativist thinking, and attitudes toward "others" and the United States.[109] Even if true, this does not mean nationalism is not a danger, but it does suggest that a growing middle class may be supportive of more restrained international behavior.

ACTORS AND ARENAS: ELECTIONS, INCIPIENT PARTIES, MEDIA, AND SOCIAL ORGANIZATIONS   Pressures for increased political participation are also apparent along other dimensions. Beyond the establishment of elections for villagers' committees throughout much of rural China, there is steady pressure to move elections up to townships, counties, urban districts, and beyond. Additionally, there are steady pressures to establish multicandidate selection processes in village, party, and National People's Congress elections. In July 1998, the China Democracy Party was founded, an effort that was almost immediately squashed. And increasingly, commercialized media push the boundaries of the politically permissible. As each new political space opens, popular desires to expand participation, and the leadership's fear of it, may produce conflict.

In the realm of social organizations, in the late 1980s Beijing was drafting a "social organization law" to guide and shape the formation and operation of nongovernmental (more properly, quasi-governmental) organizations. Since then many regulations and provisional regulations have been issued. Nonetheless, the legal identity for such organizations is not solid, and they are subject to the vagaries of shifting party attitudes at both local and national levels. The authorities worry about the uses to which such organizations could be put. Despite the impediments, however, Chinese official statistics released in 2004 indicated that there were 262,000 local "NGOs," with outside observers saying the actual number was much higher.[110] After the World Bank's president journeyed to China in fall 2005, the bank estimated that the PRC had somewhere between 300,000 and 700,000 civil society bodies "delivering services from legal aid to environmental protection and at the village level . . . building playgrounds for children and sharing technologies in smallholder agriculture."[111] And in late 2006 Chinese officials said there were 315,000 NGOs, of which 2,768 were environmental.[112]

Since 2000 there has been dramatic growth in property owners' associations, medical and welfare-related organizations, and environmental NGOs. Property owners' associations in urban areas are increasingly common and often engage in heated conflict with local governments and property-managing agents. In Beijing there are at least a dozen NGOs providing medical assistance to migrant workers; there is a fine line between helping destitute migrants and being advocates for them. Likewise, nongovernment schools are springing up throughout Chinese cities to meet the needs of the children of migrants. While many environmental NGOs have very close financial and leadership ties with government agencies, those with more tenuous ties are multiplying. In November 2001 it was announced that nationwide there were more than two thousand environmental organizations, with over a million volunteers, and that the largest group had more than one hundred thousand members. In 2003–4 many domestic and foreign environmental NGOs joined to try to stop a dam project on the Nu River (Nujiang). In early 2004 the project was at least temporarily suspended; the director of the Tsinghua University Research Center on NGOs commented, "The 2003 campaign marked a turning point for

China's environmental organizations, as they began to affect the process of the government's decisions on public issues."[113]

ACTORS: WORKERS AND PEASANTS   In an April 2002 group meeting between Premier Zhu Rongji and some members of the U.S. Congress, the premier paid particular attention to labor unrest and its origins:

> In the last few years of reform, China has been deepening reform of the state enterprises. Without these efforts it would have been impossible for China to have such great economic success. In the restructuring, it is inevitable that some plants are closed, that workers are laid off. Even the famous oil field of Daqing has declining production, so our only choice is to reduce the workforce—there is no other choice. I think if we simply show no regard for workers or use violence against workers we betray our ideas—we are the Communist Party. Therefore, we are trying to establish social security and to meet their needs. However, because we are poor, it is impossible to have benefits like the Western or Nordic countries, so active workers have more benefits than laid-off workers. This current period is one of transition from the plan to the market. Before we emphasized egalitarianism, but now they [the workers] feel disoriented, and that is why they take to the streets. It is inevitable. . . . The problem is that they [laid-off workers] think that they have made great contributions [to China] in the past, and they think [ask,] Why should they have less than current workers now? I think that although these laid-off workers with poor education [will always be] labor heroes, their skills are not appropriate to the new economy, even with retraining. It is inevitable that large numbers will be laid off, provided with social security, but it is impossible to avoid troublemaking. But development of the market economy will lead them to have "rebalanced thought."[114]

Workers from China's old state enterprises and former villagers already in the cities are not the only people that need to be considered. In March 2005 the Chinese economist Fan Gang described the population affected by restructuring and internal migration: "After twenty-five years of opening, 150 to 200 million rural workers already [have been] relocated—a big achievement. Still, there are 200 to 300 million rural workers waiting to come out [of the countryside into the cities]. People who have jobs in the cities, their wages can't go up, so all of them are very vulnerable. This is a fundamental problem. The whole world is talking about jobs going to China, but we are talking about where to get another 200 to 300 million jobs."[115]

If one considers the 38.91 million SOE workers laid off between 1997 and 2004, and the many more since then (though at a slower rate),[116] and the twelve to thirteen million rural dwellers moving to cities annually (a phenomenon that is likely to continue for decades),[117] it is remarkable that there has not been more tumult. Nonetheless, a domestic economic downturn, especially one concurrent with problems in the international economy and leadership disunity at home, could spell serious problems. Thus far, the regime has been able to stop the formation of labor bargaining units independent of the party-sponsored All China Federation of Trade Unions (ACFTU), and, given the backlog of cheap labor, the situation may remain the same for some time, even though some urban wages were rising in thriving coastal areas in 2006–7.

The story of China's contemporary peasant population deserves several books. The problems confronting the still rural population are enormous: capricious land expropriation, destruction of the rural environment through the unregulated construction of rural industry and urban sprawl, pollution of irrigation and drinking water, forced relocation of communities to make way for big projects, and abysmal education and health care funding are all everyday issues. Then there are the local petty potentates who ignore unwelcome instructions from Beijing and often rule their localities with an iron fist. All this begins to account for a rising tide of rural incidents and violence.

In short, though we are early in the process, we are seeing the gradual emergence of new political spaces and new actors. Whether or not China's government and people can build the array of social and government institutions sufficient to peaceably manage rising demands will be a central determinant of China's future. In addition to the actors driving demands are specific issues that do the same thing. Several issue areas currently are central drivers of increased demand, including the environment, corruption, and corporate governance.

ISSUE DRIVER: THE ENVIRONMENT   Environmental deterioration is driving demands for political participation, and China's regulatory and political institutions currently are inadequate to the challenge. In Changxing County's Meishan Township in Zhejiang Province, for example, local residents closed down the Tian Neng Battery Company because its neighboring residents complained that their children (58 percent of those tested) had highly abnormal levels of lead in their bloodstreams, though China had no national blood level standard for lead (instead relying on U.S. standards). In August 2005 violence ignited, police were beaten, vehicles were destroyed, and the torch was put to the plant itself. The violence was quelled only after the local government promised to cover all medical costs and determine the source(s) of the contamination.[118] Similarly, in Xinsi, Gansu, it is reported that "there's not one person in this village without lead poisoning."[119] And showing the effectiveness of new technologies in environmental activism, after about a million text messages opposing plans for a chemical plant in Xiamen had been sent, the project was put on indefinite hold in June 2007.[120]

Take water as another example. In the early 1980s I undertook research on China's water problems. Upon returning from the field I wrote an article for the Joint Economic Committee of the U.S. Congress in which I observed that "China's serious water problems for today will become increasingly burdensome constraints in the future. . . . Some Chinese already are arguing that the 'water crisis' is bigger than the country's widely acknowledged energy woes."[121] Since then the PRC's water problems (scarcity, floods, waste, and pollution) have only worsened, with water shortages causing 2.5 times as much economic loss as floods.[122] In Xinchang (near Shanghai) in July 2005 an estimated fifteen thousand people defiantly massed to protest a pharmaceutical plant's pollution of the area, particularly water pollution. The factory's alleged ties abroad also were targets of the protest. One demonstrator said, "They are making poisonous chemicals for foreigners that the foreigners don't dare produce in their own countries."[123]

In late 2005 and early 2006 a succession of large toxic river spills affected multiple provinces and left entire cities without safe water for days. A dramatic case occurred in the Songhua River in November 2005. A chemical plant explosion in upstream Jilin Province contaminated the river with about one hundred tons of toxic benzene, which flowed downstream to Heilongjiang Province, curtailing tap water for four days in Harbin, and then moved into the Amur (Heilong) River, creating hazards for Khabarovsk in Russia. At the end of 2005, another spill, this time of cadmium, polluted the Bei River in Guangdong Province, affecting drinking water. And in January 2006 two large spills occurred in the Yellow and Xiang rivers, with the Yellow River spill in Henan Province moving downstream to Shandong Province. After varying periods of silence, denial, and/or obfuscation, the central and local governments were put under such domestic and international pressure that an array of local and national officials were dismissed, compensation and ecological investments were promised to affected areas and river basins domestically, and compensation was offered to the Russians. In addition, new central crisis management regulations were issued (on January 8, 2006) requiring prompt notification of accidents and the ongoing provision of information to the public.[124] Yet these efforts are but a drop of clean water in an otherwise polluted ocean—42 percent of all water in China's seven principal river systems has a quality index of 3 or lower ("unfit for human consumption").[125]

In Taiwan, Eastern Europe, and some parts of the former Soviet Union, environmental organizations took the lead in challenging authoritarian regimes.[126] The increasing number of environmental-related organizations that Elizabeth Economy describes in her work entitled *The River Runs Black* poses dangers for Beijing's capacity to control social mobilization. Nonetheless, an overburdened and stretched government increasingly seeks societal cooperation in solving problems, as Economy explains: "This trend in inviting greater political participation in environmental affairs represents a much more widespread phenomenon in state-societal relations: the emergence of nongovernmental associations and organizations to fill roles previously occupied by national or local governments and state-owned enterprises. . . . China's leaders therefore have been careful to circumscribe both the number of NGOs and the scope of their activities. Yet there is evidence—nascent still—that the Chinese leadership will prove no more adept than the East Europeans at managing reform while avoiding revolution."[127]

ISSUE DRIVER: INJUSTICE AND CORRUPTION   When institutional capacities are inadequate and when systems are transitioning from one set of principles and structures to another, corruption often multiplies, filling the ethical and legal voids. Personal connections and trading favors among the influential become ways of distributing scarce resources and opportunities when law, standard operating procedures, and ethics do not guide behavior. Moreover, in transitional eras bureaucracy often grows because new organizations and functions are added faster than old ones are subtracted. The proliferation of bureaucrats, officials, and state agents multiplies the seekers of what Xiaobo Lu calls "rank" (status and authority) as well as "rent" (the use of discretionary approval power for personal gain). In 1978 at the start of reform, China had 4.67 million government personnel; by 1992 it had 11.48 million.[128] Minxin Pei believes that official figures on the number of state agents are substantially understated because local officials wish to conceal the degree of overstaffing.[129]

Because of corruption's very nature, there are no firm figures on the economic toll that it imposes, much less its legitimacy costs. However, Hu Angang and Minxin Pei have been trying to get some approximation of the economic magnitude. In his 2001 book *China: Fighting against Corruption,* Hu estimated that four categories of corruption (rent seeking, the underground economy, tax evasion, and corruption in investment and public expenditure) accounted for between 13.3 and 16.9 percent of GDP in 1999.[130] Pei gives considerably lower estimates of the economic toll, 4.79 percent of GDP, but he goes on to point out that the effect of this corruption is to retard the development of public and private industry, reduce tax revenues, retard development of public goods, and weaken the financial system. Phenomena such as the widespread selling of official posts and the diversion of grain purchase funds traditionally have been associated with periods of dynastic decline and contribute to a loss of legitimacy.[131] On the eve of the June 1989 Tiananmen violence, the Chinese economist Hu Heli was making estimates of the total sum of rents in the PRC economy that ran to between 20 and 40 percent of GDP.[132] The well-known Chinese economist Jinglian Wu reports that in the mid-1990s "selling and buying official positions [had] quietly become a common practice in some parts of China."[133]

Both official corruption and popular rage against it are driven by the recognition, among both the corrupt and the citizenry, that the odds of meaningful sanctions being imposed on transgressors are slight. This is particularly so if one is a high official at the county level or above. Pei reports that "official data would indicate a consistent increase in both the scope and the level [amount of money per case] of corruption. The share of corruption cases characterized as 'large' (involving large sums of money) doubled from 1990 to 2002." But of the cases in 2002, only 6.1 percent were said to involve officials at or above the county level (up from 1.7 percent in 1990), suggesting that while it was somewhat more likely for a high-level official to be investigated in 2002, overall it still was not very likely. And even when this small percentage of ranking officials is investigated, prosecuted, or punished, most receive party discipline, with only a small percentage being eventually sentenced according to criminal law.[134] In short, the higher your rank, the more protected you are: corruption generally pays.

In the memorable April 2002 conversation with Zhu Rongji cited above, Senator Paul Sarbanes of Maryland referred to a quotation attributed to the premier:

SARBANES: You said, Prepare one hundred coffins—ninety-nine for the corrupt officials, and one for yourself!

ZHU: I understand your meaning and thank you for your goodwill. All party and government leaders stand strongly against corruption. I can't take credit for all this, but I speak frankly, and the people like my speeches. The fight against corruption is a long-term task and still a serious task; [in part the] reason is that there is no full-fledged legal system. I have never said one hundred coffins, one for myself.

I know of this widespread rumor. But one hundred coffins are not enough for all the corrupt officials!

Corruption feeds the sense of inequity, inequality, and procedural injustice that fuels popular rage. The Tiananmen demonstrations of 1989, energized in significant measure by rage against corruption and inflation, provide an inkling of this issue's capacity to generate demands that the system finds difficult to meet.

ISSUE DRIVER: FINANCIAL SYSTEM REFORM AND CORPORATE GOVERNANCE   Problems in China's financial system and corporate governance system are related to one another and, in some ways, to corruption, as demonstrated by state auditors' mid-2006 revelation that the Agricultural Bank of China had improperly handled $1.8 billion in deposits and made $3.5 billion in illegal loans.[135] The economist Jinglian Wu put the more general problem bluntly. "The root cause of the Big Four's [China's major banks'] problems lies in their poorly defined relations of property rights and lack of proper governance structure. Although they are nominally state-owned banks, the owner is actually absent. . . . [T]hey not only lack a strict system of board of directors in a real sense but also have no normalized procedure for the appointment and dismissal of their presidents. As a result, without pressure from the government, no one really cares about the financial risk and economic efficiency of state-owned banks."[136]

Within the broad category of financial system problems, the most salient issues are bank nonperforming loans (NPLs) and unfunded pension liabilities. With respect to the latter, because of the combination of failing state enterprises with large implicit and explicit pension obligations, large numbers of laid-off workers in manufacturing, a rather low retirement age, a still largely pay-as-you-go system, and the graying of the population, various foreign and domestic estimates for 1997 put these liabilities in the range of 30 to 145 percent of GDP.[137] As Naughton put it in 2005, "Today, the national social security system is scarcely reflected in budgetary figures at all. The lack of funding of the pension system matters because implicit pension liabilities are quite large."[138]

With respect to NPLs, Chinese banks frequently are unqualified to assess the degree of risk that individual prospective borrowers represent, and they are not politically empowered to turn down loans to the powerful or economically important (often local state enterprises). More to the point, banks and their officers can be personally enriched by making what turn out to be "bad" loans. Historically there has been no downside attached to loan default for either the lender or the borrower.

Estimates of the size of the national inventory of NPLs vary over time, but in 2002–3 they constituted above 20 percent of GDP, according to Chinese reports that may well understate the scale of the problem.[139] In 2005 one of China's most well-known economists told a group of U.S. congressmen that Beijing had reported that NPLs were about 30 percent of GDP, while he believed the figure was closer to 40 percent.[140] Charles Wolf Jr. and colleagues at RAND believed that the true figure in 2003 may have been closer to 60 percent.[141] Indeed, since the late 1990s there have been periodic, large-scale government capital infusions into the principal state banks to address this problem.

The banking system's poor track record in making sound loans has been papered over by the high savings rate discussed in chapter 3. Chinese savers pour money into banks that, to a considerable extent, make imprudent "loans" to SOEs. Anything that dramatically lowers the propensity to save and/or causes rapid withdrawals from banks will cause grave instabilities until the banking system is put on a sound footing. But for this to happen, as Naughton explains, Chinese leaders must "credibly commit to neither intervene excessively in their [banks'] future decision-making, nor bail them out if they fail. Although important steps in this direction have been taken, the fundamental independence of these institutions from political control has not been achieved."[142]

The condition of banks is central to China's financial system health because the array of financial institutions and instruments found in the PRC is not as diversified as elsewhere. Between 2000 and 2003 China's financial system became more bank dependent. In 2000 banks were the source of 72.8 percent of funds raised in the domestic market, with treasury and corporate bonds accounting for 14.9 percent and stocks 12.3 percent. By 2003 the comparable figures were 85.2 percent, 11 percent, and 3.9 percent.[143] To give comparative perspective, about 5 percent of Chinese own stocks compared to about 49 percent of Americans.[144] As Riedel, Jin, and Gao indicate in their 2007 study, financial system reform is essential to keep high-speed growth going.[145]

Since the late 1990s the private sector's percentage of GDP has grown quite rapidly, rising to nearly half by 2002.[146] Part of this growth represents spontaneous entrepreneurial activity at the bottom rungs of the economy, but it also reflects the various forms of "corporatization" of state enterprises (including the sales of equity stakes to foreign investors). The number of state enterprises fell from 238,000 in 1998 to 150,000 in 2003, a drop only partly accounted for by the transfer of firms into at least nominally private hands.[147] Such corporatization has not yet generally produced independent, profit-maximizing firms, as we might expect in the West.

"In the process of corporatization in China, the most prominent problem was unchecked insider control."[148]

This privatization raises a host of questions: On what basis are public assets transferred to "private" investors? How solid are new ownership rights? How do local and national political authorities shape the initial transfer of the asset and the subsequent management of the resulting "privatized" firm? It is difficult even to define what *private* actually means, a challenge seen in the situation that arises when a state enterprise creates a privatized subsidiary in which it maintains the majority ownership. Moreover, how are boards of directors composed and organized internally (do they have committees?), what are the rights of minority shareholders, and how are corporate officials compensated?[149]

Chinese scholars, regulators, and businesspersons are aware of these issues, and this is why institutions like the Chinese Securities Regulatory Commission, the State Asset Management Commission, and the Research Centre of Corporate Governance of Nankai University, complete with a Web site that has foreign case studies and information about global best practices (www.cg.org.cn), have been created. Nonetheless, the persistent combination of lack of corporate and political transparency, a sketchy legal and ownership system (despite the March 2007 adoption of a property law), and the dearth of large, active institutional investors to oversee management means that the Chinese people and investors periodically will be presented with astounding cases of corporate failure, corruption, and unpredictability.

The world and Chinese citizens had a taste of this in late 2004 in a case involving the collapse of China Aviation Oil (Singapore) Corporation (CAO), which was 60 percent owned by China Aviation Oil Holdings. At the time, CAO accounted for nearly all the PRC's aircraft fuel imports. At year-end 2004 the firm was revealed to "[have] lost [US]$550 million in derivatives transactions" in five weeks, touching "off an international scramble to determine who will cover the losses."[150] The holding company sold off a significant fraction of its CAO shares before the troubles were publicly disclosed. CAO's CEO, Mr. Chen Jiulin, who left Singapore and returned to China for "personal reasons" in the wake of the scandal's disclosure, was publicly returned to the tender mercies of Singapore, where he was arrested. In mid-March 2006 Chen pleaded guilty and shortly thereafter was sentenced to a four-year prison term and fined substantially by the Singapore courts.[151]

Beyond its economic effects, corporate governance has implications for political reform and political participation. As Richard Ewing and Edward Epstein suggest, individuals and organizations that can vote for corporate leaders and shape corporate policy may eventually ask why the same principles of participation and accountability do not exist in the broader political realm.[152] This process of changing corporate governance is unfolding, but it will take time and there will be many surprises.

The foregoing discussions of political actors, arenas, and key issues make obvious the compression of developmental crises and the difficulty of keeping balance between institutional capacities and popular demands. The insufficient capacity of education, health, and social safety net institutions is related to the weakness of extractive institutions. Weak regulatory institutions are the rule rather than the exception. Further, an anemic legal structure permeates the entire system. Institutional capacities face swelling demands generated by demographic trends, information availability, rising expectations at home and abroad, very strong desires for self-improvement, and rapid urbanization. China's National Development Research Center acknowledged all this in late 2004 when it made recommendations on how to address the mounting problems: "The direction for the solution of this problem seems to be the need to clearly define the limited responsibility of the government, and stress the roles and responsibilities of people's organizations in public affairs."[153] But how to build such institutions without allowing them to become "renegade" sources of further demands worries Beijing greatly.

CHALLENGES BRIDGING THE INTERNAL AND EXTERNAL: NATIONALISM AND TAIWAN

Both nationalism and Taiwan are appropriate to mention in the context of demands on the system because they are challenges that have one foot in China's domestic politics and society and the other in external relations. Additionally, both are issues that could jeopardize China's domestic stability and the supportive external environment the PRC requires for continued development. In an ironic twist noted by Professor Peter Gries, many of the most ardent nationalists in China are members of the emerging urban middle class upon whom the regime otherwise is counting as a stabilizing force.[154]

Nationalism is a force in China that covers a range of behaviors from patriotism to assertiveness to aggressiveness. As Yongnian Zheng suggests, Chinese nationalism is built on the widely shared belief among Chinese that future humiliations at the hands of foreigners, like those of the past, can be prevented only by building "a wealthy and strong central government that could defy such victimization."[155] Chinese nationalism seeks to change China in order to more adequately protect itself from the outside. American nationalism, in contrast, often seeks to change the world to secure itself. In the words of the March 2006 *National Security Strategy of the*

United States of America, "The survival of liberty at home increasingly depends on the success of liberty abroad."[156]

If China's leaders are perceived to be lackadaisical in pursuing the nation's interests, domestic rage against the outsider can easily turn on the elite itself. As Gries put it, "The legitimacy of the current regime depends upon its ability to stay on top of popular nationalist demands."[157] Issues germane to Japan, territorial claims, and violations of Chinese sovereignty historically have been the most likely to produce hostility to foreigners, assertive external behavior, and domestic criticism of China's own leaders for weakness. Recent nationalistic episodes have included spring 2005 demonstrations and violence directed against Japanese diplomatic and business establishments as well as violence directed at the U.S. Embassy and other consular facilities in the PRC following the 1999 U.S./NATO bombing of the Chinese Embassy in Belgrade. The potential for Chinese nationalism to erupt leads most of China's neighbors and big powers at greater distance to hedge their bets when thinking about the maintenance of stability in the region. Beijing's recognition of this fact partly accounts for its "peaceful rise" and "peaceful development" campaign to reassure outsiders.

The Taiwan issue is another problem that bridges internal and external, with its origins in Chinese nationalism, domestic politics, and international security. From Beijing's perspective, Taiwan is a wild card of demand because whether cross-Strait ties become a crisis could be decided by Taipei rather than Beijing. The PRC's strategy of short- and medium-term deterrence of de jure independence and long-term integration holds out the prospect of managing, and perhaps eventually resolving, this problem. But the prospect that time may be working for Beijing leads some in Taipei to be willing to take risks soon. Taiwan President Chen Shui-bian seemed so alarmed at the drift of events throughout his terms in office (2000 through this writing in 2007) that he at times seemed willing to push for increased autonomy in the face of the explicit opposition of his primary security backer, the United States. This raises the possibility that Beijing could be drawn into conflict in circumstances not of its own choosing. Economic or military conflict in the Taiwan Strait would fundamentally change the behavior of the PRC's neighbors and the big powers. Its negative impact on U.S.-China ties would be hard to exaggerate.[158]

EXTERNAL CHALLENGES

China is vulnerable to many developments in the international system, but two broad categories are particularly noteworthy: issues arising from economic interdependence and reactions of big powers to China's rise. One senior Chinese scholar put it this way: "China's rise depends on trade, investment, and a high rate of [domestic] savings. China can control only the savings rate, not the other two factors, so this is leverage on China."[159]

The Risks of Interdependence: China's Stakes in the World Economy   Interdependence and its risks are the natural outcome of Deng Xiaoping's strategy to obtain management, technology, capital, markets, and natural resources from abroad to fuel domestic growth and social transformation. Deng bet on globalization. Weaving the PRC into the fabric of global interdependence, what Singapore's ambassador to the United States, Chan Heng Chee, referred to as the "Gulliver strategy," has been the essence of thinking among China's neighbors, particularly in Southeast Asia, and it has been the underlying rationale in America for "engagement" with China. Interdependence means reciprocal dependence and hence constrains China's economic partners as well as the PRC itself. Chinese leaders are acutely aware of their interests in a stable international system and a stable relationship with the major actors in it.

China confronts interdependence risks along many fronts, three of which I briefly focus on here: the high dependence on foreign trade for revenue and employment, foreign exchange risk, and energy dependence. Three additional critical areas of interdependence that will not be discussed here (but should be noted) are the need for a steady, high-volume flow of FDI into China (US$60.63 billion in 2004 in utilized FDI), the availability and price of key raw materials, and food. With respect to the latter, China's leaders are so concerned about food security (their agricultural products trade surplus of $4.2 billion in 2001 turned into a deficit of $4.64 billion in 2004) and the implications of large grain imports that shortly after entering office Hu Jintao commissioned studies on the subject, and in 2004 China Agricultural University opened a "China Food Security Research Centre."[160]

EMPLOYMENT AND REVENUE DEPENDENCIES   As noted above, in January 2005 Chinese Commerce Minister Bo Xilai documented the centrality of the foreign-invested and foreign trade sectors to total national tax revenue when he acknowledged that "the import and export tax revenue accounts for about 18 percent of the nation's total. The tax revenue of foreign-related enterprises makes up over 20 percent of the national total."[161] If one considers the core domestic problems and vulnerabilities discussed above, the degree of China's fiscal dependence on trade-related revenues and foreign enterprises is startling. Total urban employment was reported to be 210.1 million in 1999–2000,[162] which means that the 80 million people cited by Minister Bo as working "in the field of foreign trade" constitute a little over a third of the urban workforce; if one considers total employment in China (705.8 million), this 80 million would constitute about 11 percent of the total workforce. Whatever the percentage, employment in foreign trade is very significant.

What leaders in Beijing realize in the new millennium, leaders in Shanghai have appreciated for a long time. At one memorable January 1998 meeting in Shanghai, then Mayor Xu Kuangdi noted that there were seventeen thousand foreign-invested ventures in the city, that 35 percent of the city's exports were from foreign-invested firms, and that one-third of Shanghai's GDP was from foreign-invested firms. He noted that these firms accounted for significant employment.[163] Others in the municipal government noted that when the United States catches an economic cold, Shanghai catches pneumonia. By year-end 2004 Shanghai was announcing that 67 percent of the city's total foreign trade came from foreign-invested firms, and two years later the percentage was nearly 70 percent.[164]

The conclusion to draw from these data is not that the United States or others have unlimited leverage over the PRC but rather that Beijing, given its domestic focus, has many reasons to keep sound relations with the world's major strategic and economic actors. Likewise, China has woven itself into the fabric of the international economy in a way that gives others strong incentives for at least minimal cooperation too. China would be quickly affected by any substantial downturn in the global economy or by any sudden change in the PRC's access to the global economy, whether those changes occurred for economic or political reasons. This is one reason Beijing has pushed so hard on the EU, Latin American countries, and others to designate the PRC a "market economy," something that as of 2007 the United States and the EU have refused to do for defensible economic reasons. Were the PRC to be designated a "market economy," Beijing would be less vulnerable to "antidumping" actions by trade partners.

FOREIGN EXCHANGE RISK   As of January 2006 China possessed $818.9 billion in foreign exchange reserves (excluding gold), second only to (but not far behind) Japan's $846.9 billion. By the end of June that year, the PRC had shot past Japan, with its holdings reaching $941.1 billion. By early 2007 these reserves exceeded $US1 trillion. These holdings expose China to huge foreign exchange risk. If the U.S. dollar declined in value vis-à-vis the RMB (as it gradually did in 2006 and through this writing in 2007), the value of China's U.S. dollar denominated reserves and other assets would decline in (RMB) value correspondingly. Similar risk exists with respect to assets denominated in other currencies. In short, Beijing has very real interests in international monetary stability. These interests are so large that Beijing looks inflexible in the face of U.S. demands that its currency be revalued to help Washington adjust its trade and current account deficits, as well as help reduce the increasingly serious global trade imbalance.

ENERGY DEPENDENCE   China was 48 percent dependent on petroleum imports in 2004, and "although estimates of its [future] dependency on foreign oil differ, they all point to an alarming trend, foreseeing the dependency rate to be above . . . 60 percent in 2020, and above 70 percent in 2030."[165] Beyond availability, petroleum imports are subject to sizable international price fluctuations that can affect domestic economic growth. Nonetheless, because coal accounts for over 67.1 percent of the PRC's total energy consumption (in 2003) and is relatively plentiful in the PRC, Beijing's dependence on imports for total energy supply is still modest—about 4 percent in 2004.[166] The problem with coal is that China's most abundant energy source has highly adverse environmental consequences, at least as it is currently used.

With respect to oil imports, 83.7 percent came on foreign flagships in 2002, and about 80 to 85 percent of all PRC oil imports flow through the vulnerable Straits of Malacca.[167] More troubling for Beijing, 48.2 percent of its oil imports were from four countries: Saudi Arabia, Iran, Oman, and Yemen. Beijing's "imports are heavily focused on only a few countries which happen to sit in an area prone to instability and volatility."[168] In short, in terms of liquid energy needs, China is dependent on others for supplies that come from a highly volatile region of the world, on the ships of other countries, which need protection by the navies of others. It is hardly surprising, therefore, that the PRC is building a strategic petroleum reserve, that it contemplates building a pipeline through Burma, or that energy-rich countries in Africa, Latin America, the Middle East, Central Asia, and Southeast Asia have an allure, even if the United States wishes Chinese attentions were drawn away from places like Sudan, Iran, Cuba, Venezuela, and Burma. Indeed, China finds itself in competition with democratic India for the energy affections of the same human rights–offending states.[169] China's reluctance to alienate itself from Iran is understandable in this context, not to mention Beijing's desire for growing quantities of clean-burning Iranian and Burmese natural gas.[170] As of late 2006 China's Sinopec was negotiating a twenty-five-year-long oil and natural gas deal with Tehran worth a reported $100 billion, and PRC oil imports from Iran were 11 percent higher in the first third of 2007 than in the same period the year before.[171]

Consequently, Beijing is pursuing a multipronged strategy to overcome these vulnerabilities: make friends with every regime that has energy in the ground (whether or not the partner regime observes internationally recognized human rights, and whether or not new relationships intrude into sensitive regions); diversify suppliers; establish stable supply and pricing relationships, if possible; build a strategic petroleum reserve; increase energy efficiency; diversify delivery modes; build a much larger civilian maritime fleet; and expand the navy. This multidimensional strategy reflects the acute vulnerability that Beijing feels on the liquid energy front.

Energy is essential for economic growth, and economic growth is essential for social stability. By political algebra, energy, therefore, is essential to domestic stability. In Shanghai in mid-2005, for example, demonstrations broke out as a result of repeated power shortages that were affecting household power service—air conditioning.

Wary Big Powers and Neighbors   As Stephen Walt notes in his *The Origins of Alliances,* states balance against one another more out of consideration of threat than calculations of balance of power. Threat perception level is affected by overall power, as well as "by geographic proximity, offensive capabilities, and perceived intentions."[172] Beijing pursues the peaceful rise strategy because it knows that its internal development efforts could be adversely affected by others' concerted efforts to limit capital and technology flows and access to markets and to create an external environment that would require the diversion of resources away from domestic development to even greater military expenditure.

By virtue of its history and geographic location—fourteen land neighbors and several seaward powers with which China has had a checkered history—mutual trust is not high in its region, as discussed in the preceding chapter. In contrast, the United States has only two land neighbors with which there has been no armed conflict for a long time. Add the fact that China's military is gradually gaining the power to project its strength and is an increasingly capable nuclear power, and there are further reasons for caution. While many territorial disputes have been resolved in recent years, significant unresolved territorial issues remain, and nationalism lies only just beneath the surface in China and in neighboring countries such as Japan, Korea, and India. All this creates a situation in which the PRC is surrounded by wary neighbors and big powers at a greater distance. As Walt notes, "balancing" against such a power is common, and such behavior has less to do with ideology than with perceptions of threat.

This wariness is seen in economic behavior as well, in that investors hedge their bets. Both investing countries and the PRC's rivals for FDI keep a sharp eye on China's behavior and internal developments for signs of increased risk. Some foreign investors are ready to redeploy resources away from China, with competitors for that investment pointing out the dangers of overrelying on China. For example, a senior foreign official posted in Vietnam told me, "We have heard that the Japanese, Koreans, and Taiwanese all look at Vietnam as the hedge to [avoid] placing all their eggs in the Chinese basket. [They were] scared by March–April 2005 nationalistic outbursts [against Japan in the PRC]. Vietnamese say [there is] increased interest in Vietnam."[173]

This tendency for China's neighbors and surrounding big powers to balance against it accounts for two features of Beijing's foreign policy. The first tendency is to see big powers (variously the Soviet Union/Russia, India, Japan, and the United States) as pursuing a "containment" strategy. The second tendency is for China to suspect that its closer, smaller neighbors (e.g., Vietnam, Mongolia, and the Koreas) will align with the more distant bigger powers to hedge against it.

A principal goal of China's diplomacy is to minimize others' perception that China's rise is threatening and that international politics is zero sum. Beijing embraces globalization and comparative advantage not only because these have worked economically for China but also because the core premise of both ideas is that everyone can win from economic interdependence. The vulnerability is that the big powers may embrace John Mearsheimer's "offensive realism," which posits almost inevitable conflict between currently dominant and rising powers, rather than embracing the interdependence that liberal internationalists hope will foster cooperation among those powers and that China hopes will give it the time necessary to modernize.

THE STRUGGLE TO MAINTAIN STABILITY

The difficulty in maintaining a balance between institutional capacities and the demands described above is reflected in the reported rise in social disturbances. In late 2004 a research group of the National Development and Reform Commission in Beijing publicly released the findings of a study it had undertaken to determine the ten major risk factors confronting China's development before 2010. The report noted that "at present, rural group incidents are on the increase in terms of quantity, scale and antagonism, farmers' political appeals are growing increasingly strong."[174] In 2005 Minister of Public Security Zhou Yongkang reportedly said that in 2004 there had been seventy-four thousand "mass incidents" nationwide, up 27 percent over the preceding year.[175] One year later, the Ministry of Public Security reported that "public order disturbances" had risen yet again—to eighty-seven thousand—with mob violence up 13 percent.[176] In March 2007 Chinese figures showed that more than 65 percent of "massive incidents, or petitions and protests," were ignited by land expropriations.[177]

In discussions with PRC leaders I have been struck by how open, and obviously worried, they have been about these phenomena. In a 2002 group meeting, Premier Zhu said: "Every day such things [disturbances of workers] happen, and each day I have a report telling me where workers have taken to the streets. From January 1 to March 28 [2002], from my bulletins, altogether there have been 265 cases of protests with more than 50 workers. But 99 percent, not 100 percent, of workers who participated in making trouble have basic [unmet] needs."[178]

Beijing is trying desperately to build new institutions and strengthen old ones. We associate efforts to build a new social security system, a more effective legal system, rural cooperative medical care, and limited electoral experiments, for example, with the "reform" agenda. But there are other dimensions to the system's response to growing demands, one of which is Beijing's strategy of identifying itself with grass-roots dissatisfactions and blaming local officials. Where institutions and resources do not exist to address issues, and the population is no longer willing to suffer in quiet resignation, there is repression from both local officials and central authorities, as well as continued efforts on the part of the aggrieved to organize to advance their interests. China, therefore, is moving in all directions simultaneously—reform, meeting of demands when possible, government repression, and nascent efforts by society (enhanced by new communications) at counterorganization. Almost by default, the Chinese government has arrived at a four-pronged strategy for dealing with the imbalance of institutional capacity and internal and external demands:

1. *Grow the middle class as rapidly as possible*, hoping that it will reinforce the status quo. Rather than being seen exclusively as a Trojan horse for regime change, the middle class is seen as a moderating force endeavoring to pre-serve and gradually enlarge its gains, unwilling to gamble on a roll of the revolutionary dice.

2. *Build a societal coalition of intellectuals, the emerging middle class, and the elite itself.* In this regard, the Fifteenth Party Congress's 2002 decision to actively recruit into the Communist Party's ranks emerging business and technical classes ("The Three Represents"), the party's recruitment of nonparty victors in local elections, the dramatic increase in the pay and working conditions of intellectuals in the 1990s and thereafter, and the party elite's almost ostentatious consultation with intellectuals in the for-mulation of policy are all part of this effort. Critics of the strategy, such

as Kang Xiaoguang, assert that it creates a new class-based society with a permanent underclass.[179]

3. *Reduce popular demands for change by reducing both urban-rural and inter-regional inequalities and blaming local officials for many of the inequities that exist.* Some of this equalization is to occur through massive rural migration into new cities, while part will occur through the redistribution of resources to impoverished areas and the construction of infrastructure connecting remote locales to areas of greater economic activity. The mid-2006 completion of the railroad from Beijing to Tibet is a dramatic and expensive example of this effort.

4. *Repress demand by arresting leaders of demonstrations or movements,* while minimally placating the rank and file. Prevent the discontented of one locality from linking up with kindred spirits in another. Repress media information and communication modes supportive of organized political opposition.[180] It is notable that well into the first decade of the new millennium there is virtually no discernible organized, significant, nationwide group or organization that plausibly could constitute an alternative to the Communist Party and its over seventy million members.

While this four-pronged strategy has been effective thus far, and may remain so for a considerable time, it leaves open a number of questions, including: How long will this strategy be able to manage the mounting pressures?

Regarding China's struggle to keep institutional capacity running ahead of surging demands, one conclusion dominates all others: its leaders will be preoccupied with their domestic agenda for decades unless the outside world forces itself upon China in unwelcome ways. Yes, Chinese capabilities are growing. Yes, those capabilities have competitive, economic, security, and spillover effects. But the most fundamental point is that Chinese leaders cannot afford to ignore domestic challenges, and they are unlikely to do so unless the outside world makes itself a bigger problem than the titanic domestic agenda that has been the topic of this chapter.

Other central conclusions of this chapter are:

· It is not foreordained that China's central leaders will succeed in achieving balance between high-speed growth and social stability or between institutional capacity and demands placed on the system.

- All of the significant problems confronting the PRC are long term in character. Those observers who implicitly assume that China will quickly resolve its severe internal problems and then turn its attentions to settling old scores externally will almost certainly be proven wrong.
- It is in the outside world's interests that China be effectively governed because if Chinese do not do so, no one else can. This common interest in avoiding system breakdown ought to energize American and Western cooperation in China's development.
- A China either unable to control its external behaviors or seeking to direct attention abroad to divert attention from its domestic failures is a much bigger risk than a strong China becoming a military predator.

The preceding chapters on "might, money, and minds" are not meant to be viewed in isolation from this chapter, because mounting comprehensive strength must be viewed in relationship to the rising total volume of demands placed upon that strength. This chapter reminds us why Beijing wishes to preserve an international context that permits the domestic agenda to be addressed effectively. Further, given the Chinese propensity to believe that China can never be strong abroad until it is strong at home, there is no particular reason to expect Beijing to jeopardize a precarious domestic stability for adventures abroad, though Taiwan is the greatest wild card in this respect.

This chapter has also underscored how complex a policy problem it is for the United States to attempt to productively relate to China, and vice versa. China is a governing entity larger than any other administration on the face of the earth. It is a mix of market economy and political authoritarianism. Simultaneously, it is a mix of poverty and illiteracy (in rural areas) and pockets of excellence capable of putting people safely in space. And it is a country moving in contradictory directions simultaneously—institutional reform and liberalization, accommodation with emerging social forces, and repression. It is difficult for a pluralized country such as the United States to deal with such complexity because many American interest groups make one piece of Chinese reality the poster child for their concerns. But it is critical that America, Europe, and Japan relate to China not just as an emerging power but also as a developing nation. The combination of PRC strength and weakness requires America to be cooperative in addressing developmental issues with China while understanding that its growing strengths will affect U.S. and global interests. Above all, Americans must remember that China's growing strengths also can help solve common problems.

The hard-headed realist might ask: "Why is it in our interest to be helpful as the Chinese people address their daunting domestic agenda?" Beyond humanitarian considerations and opportunity costs, the answer is very simple—the consequences of failure in China will not remain confined within its borders. If China's leaders cannot effectively deal with the problems enumerated in this chapter, a toxic combination of popular nationalism, domestic frustration, and elite desperation to divert attention from domestic failings will spill into the international system. The environmental and refugee implications of Chinese failure are self-evident. There also is the ever-present danger that if the Chinese feel threatened, incipient Chinese nationalism will be harnessed to assertive, perhaps aggressive, purposes abroad. In terms of international trade and finance, Chinese ailments will become contagious; as we have seen, failures in China's domestic regulatory system affect health and safety abroad when the PRC suddenly is central to global supply chains. The best way to address this bundle of dangers is to support Chinese efforts to solve their enormous domestic challenges and to establish an East Asian order that has at its disposal both positive and negative incentives for regionwide cooperation.

SEVEN

· What Chinese Power Means
for America and the World

We should view our bilateral relations from a long-term, strategic perspective. We should not subject our relations to one single event. In the Tang Dynasty, Wang Wei had a two-line poem that said, "I walk where the streams rise and the clouds drift away and the water falls to the earth below" [Premier Wen points to the mural behind him and to the ceiling above with clouds]. All things are connected to one another. . . . We should seek harmony without becoming the same.

PREMIER WEN JIABAO, Great Hall of the People,
January 2005

Our main hope for disenthralling ourselves from our overemphasis on power lies more in a theoretical, or at least conceptual, effort, than in an empirical one. It lies not only in recognizing that not all human influences are necessarily coercive and exploitative, that not all transactions among persons are mechanical, impersonal, ephemeral. . . . It lies in a more realistic, a more sophisticated understanding of power, and of the often far more consequential exercise of mutual persuasion, exchange, elevation, and transformation—in short, of leadership.

JAMES MACGREGOR BURNS, 1978

I don't have confidence the U.S. will invest in herself— this year's budget is going backwards. I don't think we'll solve the visa problems. So China becomes a target of what we have failed to do. We react to China through the prism of our own missed opportunities. We say that everything is important to solve, we have no priorities, and we are not tough enough on things that matter.

SENIOR MEMBER OF U.S. HOUSE OF REPRESENTATIVES,
April 13, 2006

Bad American policy is the most significant driver of where China heads.

PROFESSOR OF STRATEGY, Singapore, June 2005

The challenge that Chinese power presents to the rest of the world is to use it productively, not to tame it.

China is not, and will not become, another Soviet Union, though what it may become will be determined by Chinese leaders who have not yet emerged, future domestic developments, and an international environment that is continually changing. As suggested by the subtitle of this book, "Might, Money, and Minds," China has evolved from Mao Zedong's reliance on coercive power (military force and the coercive use of ideology), through Deng Xiaoping's emphasis on economic or remunerative power, to current leaders' more balanced strategy that, while emphasizing economic power, is trying to increase China's "ideational power" as well as its military might. Unlike the Soviet Union, which was a military giant and economic dwarf, and Japan, which has been an economic power with stunted military development and little normative attraction beyond its borders, China explicitly aims to be a great power of comprehensive strength. It has made impressive strides. It has a great distance yet to travel. Success, whatever that means, is not assured.

China is not the Soviet Union because it is not placing the same emphasis on acquiring coercive capacity that the Kremlin did during its seventy-four-year communist history. China has also bet on globalization, a bet that has paid off thus far. Unlike the revolutionary and Cold War Soviet Union, the PRC of the past thirty years has identified economic power, the most fungible form of power, as the keystone of its strategy. "Economic growth solves all problems," one Chinese academic told me, almost as a passing thought. While this simplistic notion is untrue, economic power does have the most expressions and can be most efficiently converted into coercive and ideational power. The lesson the USSR's implosion taught Beijing is that overinvestment in coercive might undermines economic capability and political legitimacy at home and produces counter-reactions from others and that the combination of domestic weakness and external pressure can culminate in regime change. Instead, Beijing has opened its economy to give outsiders a stake in its success, steps that Japan, by contrast, has taken only recently, slowly, and rather reluctantly.

There are a range of possibilities for China's future. Outside observers and policy makers should be skeptical of simplistic assessments of China as "strong" or "weak." Each assessment holds dangers. If China is presumed to be weak, some will be tempted to coerce Beijing in ways that are unnecessary, infeasible, and reckless. If China is perceived to be strong, this could become the rationale for the United States to stimulate an unproductive arms race that will weaken its competitive position in the real races—economic and intellectual. In the first decade of the twenty-first century, many American assessments of the three faces of Chinese power are erroneous. Americans tend to overestimate China's military power (except in the Taiwan Strait). With respect to economic power, they often overemphasize China as a "seller" and underestimate it as a "buyer" and "investor." And they tend to underestimate Chinese ideational power along more than one dimension.

Several themes have been woven throughout this book. Beijing's national strategy does not rest principally upon either acquisition or utilization of coercive power, a partial exception being its strategy with respect to Taiwan. China is not a superpower of comprehensive capacity and will not be one for a long time, even if the current favorable trends continue. The multiple expressions of each face of Chinese power have their uses and liabilities, both for Beijing and for the outside world. The PRC is most accurately understood as a developing country. While it possesses large pools of excellence, it has far larger oceans of domestic poverty and weakness that will preoccupy its leaders for a considerable period. Nonetheless, China's globally competitive sectors are of such a scale, quality, and dynamism that they constitute formidable economic, intellectual, and, upon occasion, military competition for the United States and others. Nations higher on the value-added ladder must keep moving upward to preserve their advantages.

If the United States transforms an economic and intellectual competitor focused on its own internal development into an international adversary, it will have committed a strategic blunder of breathtaking and historic proportions. With much of the Muslim world antagonistic toward the United States, America's post–World War II alliance structures loosening, relations with Russia problematic, and American soft power in tatters, alienating another continent-spanning, dynamic population would be reckless. Sino-American conflict would represent a failure of leadership in both societies.

Perhaps the most fundamental point to emerge from the preceding chapters is that China's exercise of power creates counter-reactions and future constraints. In the preceding chapters we have seen an interstate version of Newton's Third Law of Motion—"For every action, there is an equal and opposite reaction." If China sends laborers to Mozambique to work on infrastructure projects or to Zambia to log, thereby using less indigenous labor, it creates resentment among locals. Indeed, there have been anti-Chinese riots in Zambia. PRC exports to Mexico create protectionist pressures from locally affected industries there. Chinese efforts to renegotiate soybean contracts using their leverage as the volume buyer anger Brazilians. If Beijing promises billions of dollars in investment to Indonesia, African nations, and Latin American economies, the failure to satisfy the expectations can itself become a problem. If China has leverage over North Korea, Americans expect it to be used to achieve nonproliferation objectives. The acquisition of power projection aimed at Taiwan creates anxieties among neighboring countries in all directions, even when they have little prospect of being a target. In short, to have power is to set in motion reactions and generate expectations over which Beijing has relatively little control. The exercise of power is a management problem—goal definition, management of implementation, management of expectations, and management of consequences.

Statesmanship involves (1) appreciating the strengths and limitations of one's own power resources and those of the other principal players in the system; (2) understanding how the other key international actors view their own goals, interests, and capabilities; and, above all, (3) having clearly defined objectives that are feasible and appropriate in light of the mix of power resources one possesses and the context in which one is operating. Without feasible goals and the application of the appropriate face of power in the appropriate context, the exercise of military, economic, or intellectual muscle can simply produce undirected, often unpredictable impacts. Power, on the other hand, is the successful use of strength to achieve prespecified goals. Just as economies have different factor endowments (land, labor, and capital), so polities have different power endowments (coercive, economic, and intellectual). The efficient use of power requires the optimal mix of power types to achieve objectives with the least expenditure of resources.

THE THREE FACES OF CHINESE POWER

Each of the three faces of power is useful in different circumstances. Each has multiple expressions. Coercive military strength usually is employed to threaten or punish, but it can sometimes be used to reassure. Coercive capability can be a reassuring part of a comprehensive diplomatic strategy. Economic power is usually an attractive face of power but can, on occasion, be used to coerce. Economic power also can have normative appeal when virtue is associated with wealth. Finally, ideational power is usually employed to positively persuade, but it can be used coercively when it leads to ostracism or directs threatening mass mobilization. Of these three forms of power, economic power is the most convertible, most flexible form of power. Ideational power may be the most desirable, the most efficient, inasmuch as it is cheaper than bribery or threat.

China is focusing upon the economic face of power. Nonetheless, Beijing also seeks to increase its national ideational strength and to develop a sufficient military deterrent to discourage assaults on vital national interests. At the same time, PRC leaders seek to avoid becoming so threatening as to encourage the formation of offsetting international coalitions and other adverse responses.

Though there is general consensus in China about this strategy, the recurrent decisions required to implement it ignite endless internal debate. What strikes the Ministry of Foreign Affairs, for example, as a satisfactory balance between economic, diplomatic, and coercive resources may seem insufficient, perhaps imprudent, to the Central Military Commission. While the Ministry of Commerce may wish to control foreign aid and use it to gain commercial advantage, the Ministry of Foreign Affairs may wish foreign assistance to serve diplomacy. Coastal cities with thriving business ties with Taiwan may be more flexible on policy toward the island than regions with less at stake economically. Local bureaus of public and state security, dedicated to taking alleged subversives out of circulation and maintaining domestic political control, may be indifferent to the foreign policy costs of their actions. Because the various social sectors and geographic regions of China experience differing impacts from globalization, they have different policy preferences. Some groups and localities push for deeper integration into the global system; others seek more insulation from it. As for the outside world, it can never be sure where the balance of PRC forces and objectives may come to rest or how lasting the current balance will be.

Because outsiders cannot be sure of a nation's intentions, and because new capabilities often create new purposes, all nations engage in hedging—maintaining sufficient (often coercive) capability to handle negative, unexpected threats to vital interests.[1] The problem is that Nation A's hedge can become Nation B's rationale for boosting its own "hedge." A process of mutual and interactive upward adjustment can evolve into a spiraling adversarial relationship. This is why dialogue, transparency, and the development of linkages at every bureaucratic and societal level between the two nations are critical. It is unclear whether Washington and Beijing will overcome or manage the mutual strategic suspicions that are built into the international system, but doing so should be a first-order priority for both.

A number of generalizations about Chinese power emerge from the preceding. First, if one subscribes to the proposition that large, pluralistic, diverse countries or organizations find it difficult to develop, articulate, and consistently implement a broad strategy, then the degree to which the PRC has done so since Deng Xiaoping in the late 1970s is impressive. Beijing has consistently emphasized economic power, kept its foreign policy consistent with economic development needs, reassured nervous neighbors as its strength has grown, and kept the flow of capital and technology from abroad coming in as it has maintained and enlarged market access for its exports. Equally impressive is that Beijing has adapted its strategy to changing circumstances, first by augmenting military resources, then by reassuring the international system that this growing strength is not to be feared. Domestically, as a middle and professional class has grown, the party gradually has recruited these new social segments to membership. And as growth has rocketed ahead along China's coasts and in its cities, the party has gradually shifted attention toward those regions and parts of the population left behind, to what tangible effect remains to be seen. In short, in China's acquisition of power one sees the rare combination of perseverance and adaptability.

Second, the difficulties of maintaining the necessary domestic support to both persevere and remain adaptable should not be underestimated: economic reform and globalization inflict pain on many domestic constituencies that demand altered policy. As one senior Chinese scholar put it, "There are lots of expectations not being met. State institutions are fragile. There are lots of restive people. . . . So whether China can go through these transitions peacefully is not clear. Historical precedents are not that encouraging."[2] Moreover, consider the possible repercussions of educating large numbers of youth at the tertiary level as employment opportunities decrease in a sharp downturn in the business cycle.

A principal threat to China's broad national strategy, therefore, is the precarious balance between institutional capacity and rising societal and international demands. The Chinese political and policy system perpetually hovers near overload. At home, an aging population, resource and environmental constraints of all sorts, rising expectations, and the demands of the rest of the world that Beijing reduce its harmful externalities are but a small part of the total burden on stressed Chinese institutions and leaders.

Third, because the enormous internal challenges China faces are all long term in character, it is difficult to envision a time when Beijing will not judge its foreign policies by reference to how they lighten or make more manageable domestic burdens. Though Beijing will assume more global responsibilities, the drain of domestic requirements will make Chinese participation in addressing long-term transnational issues less robust than others might prefer. Nations outside sometimes will judge China's contributions to transnational difficulties to be greater than its contributions to their management.

With respect to coercive strength specifically, China's capacity to defend the homeland against conventional, regime-threatening attack is considerable, and while its deterrent against strategic attack is increasing, Beijing has shown little inclination to build the kind of excessive strategic arsenal that was a staple of the super-powers of the Cold War era. The PRC's capacity to project conventional military power at great distances is quite limited, though gradually increasing, as is its ability to command and control its military in timely and intelligent ways. Beijing recognizes that it must create a positive context for its acquisition of military power or it will encourage unproductive arms races and the formation of countervailing coalitions. China is using its military as a diplomatic instrument with increasing effect by employing it in reassuring roles and interacting more with the armed forces of other societies.

Nonetheless, the United States is not being pushed out of Asia by Beijing, and Asia is not becoming Sino-centric, though China probably already is the predominant regional power. If U.S. regional influence is less potent than in the past, this reflects American policies, commitments, and preoccupations elsewhere as much as growing Chinese strength. China's neighbors increasingly must take account of PRC interests. Beijing wishes to increase its capacities to prevent actions in the region inimical to its core interests and increasingly has the ability to do so. At the same time, almost all of China's neighbors want an active, constructive, and multidimensional U.S. presence in the region.

There are worries, of course, and Chinese nationalism is among them, even though it is focused more on gaining security by strengthening and changing China than on changing the world, and more on upholding and protecting national and cultural dignity than on converting others. The desire to gain security and uphold dignity can assume threatening expressions when it veers in xenophobic directions—as it did against Americans and Japanese in 1999 and 2005, respectively. This is a danger that the PRC and its people need to guard against. Nationalism in the United States, by way of contrast, often tries to achieve U.S. security by changing the world. From this seed, in part, grows the motivation for democracy promotion globally and interventionism.

In terms of economic power, while most people associate China's strength with that of the "seller," its power as a "buyer" is what wins Beijing influence. In international financial markets, for instance, China's willingness to adjust its holdings of debt instruments denominated in dollars, yen, or euros gives Beijing some leverage over Americans, who wish to see their currency remain globally dominant and interest rates low, and Europeans, who aspire to compete with or supplant U.S. monetary dominance. China's ability to invest abroad is becoming an important diplomatic asset, and in regions such as Africa and Latin America, where other major powers have been distracted, its capacity to have an impact at modest cost is considerable.

Beijing's willingness to forego political and environmental conditionality on assistance and investment is attractive to many impoverished, autocratic regimes.

The face of Chinese power most subject to underestimation is ideational power, particularly the PRC's ability to innovate by improving production processes and creating new architectures for old components. Americans also are prone to underestimate the attraction of China's foreign policy in a world that increasingly resents the exercise of U.S. coercive strength and the use of sanctions to impoverish populations to get at their leaders. China is rapidly developing global communications and cultural diffusion capacities that will be more effective than most Americans seem to assume.

CHINA'S LEADERS LOOK AT
THEIR NATIONAL SITUATION

Overall, China's leaders would describe the nation's current situation as follows:

- There is a window of development opportunity.
- China is in a race to maintain internal stability as rising demand continually threatens to overtake institutional capacity.
- Economic growth is the pillar supporting Chinese hopes for the future and is central to regime legitimacy.
- Getting the massive Chinese population to a point of even modest physical security will take decades.
- Globalization is generally supportive of China's interests, though it has some important negative side effects.
- The international environment can be helpful, indeed very helpful, and is not now mortally hostile to Chinese aspirations.

China's leaders increasingly act as though they understand that they have an interest in maintaining a stable international system and that as time passes and China becomes stronger so too will its obligations. Chinese nationalism can be balanced by the idea of China as a responsible, equal power. The idea of China and America "as two responsible powers" is creeping into the Chinese lexicon; Beijing likes the idea, though the two countries do not define *responsibility* in identical terms. Beijing tends to view responsibility as respect for sovereignty and noninterference in the internal affairs of others ("procedural responsibility"), whereas the United

States is more interested in what I call "substantive responsibility"—good governance and respect for political rights, though in prosecuting the global war on terrorism the United States has employed means that have considerably eroded the high ground from under its position. A related point of friction is that Beijing rejects what it views as the assumption in Washington that U.S. preferred policy is necessarily the same thing as being globally responsible. Both countries can agree about being responsible powers as a general proposition but fall out over what the content of "responsibility" may specifically be. Most fundamentally, China's leaders have learned lessons from the failed policies of previous regimes (at home and abroad)—namely, that excessive military expenditure and adventures can set back economic and social development, thereby undermining regime legitimacy and fostering a countervailing international coalition.

There are, of course, diverse opinions in China on all of these issues. Not everyone learns the same lessons from history. Some younger PRC intellectuals, for example, associate globalization with a loss of Chinese cultural identity and blame globalization for pernicious domestic injustice, corruption, and inequality. They see *globalization* as a code word for American hegemony and/or "westernization." Like counterparts in the United States and elsewhere, some (perhaps many) Chinese wish to restrict foreign investment in certain strategic sectors of the economy and society. This rejection of globalization by some could transmogrify into an assertive, sometimes xenophobic nationalism.[3] But for now the center of gravity in political and intellectual discourse is a cosmopolitanism that sees China's integration into the global economy as being, on the whole, in the PRC's interests and as contributing to the fulfillment of nationalistic aspirations: making China strong, rich, respected, and equal has been a dream fundamental to the legitimacy of the Chinese Communist Party since its founding in 1921. If this trend toward cosmopolitanism and international responsibility is to be maintained, however, Chinese leaders must effectively deal with some of the destabilizing aspects of globalization and economic modernization domestically. A China floundering at home probably will be destabilizing abroad.

CHINA AS A MATURING POWER IN AN INCREASINGLY INTERDEPENDENT WORLD

China is becoming comprehensively stronger. As its power grows, the international community will expect Beijing to assume more responsibility for maintaining the global infrastructure necessary for peace and development. China's leaders have an essentially developmental view in which the strong have greater obligations than the weak; thus, as China's strength grows, so will its obligations. The point of friction with Washington, therefore, is not Beijing's denial of responsibility in the abstract but rather debate over the content of responsibility and present expectations, given China's rather limited capabilities and its enormous domestic challenges. For example, are Chinese being more or less "responsible" than Americans when they view AIDS and other epidemic diseases as a bigger threat than the weapons proliferation that Americans worry about?[4] I found the vision of the Chinese scholar Yuan Peng striking—a vision widely shared in the PRC:

> When a 15-year-old boy has grown into an 18-year-old youth, he himself
> may not be aware of the change, but in the eyes of his neighbors or the inter-
> national community, he has grown taller in comprehensive national strength,
> with a heavy voice of international clout and even sporting a beard of military
> modernization, evidently no longer a boy, but an adult. If you still regard
> yourself as a boy, troubles may be awaiting you around the corner. In essence,
> the debate over peaceful development or peaceful rise is a matter of opinion
> concerning an 18-year-old in the eyes of himself and his neighbors.
>
> Though China is rising, the journey ahead is still long and arduous. Yes, an
> 18-year-old may be considered as coming of age, yet she is still not in her thir-
> ties and forties, not yet in the prime of life. China cannot afford to boast its
> vigor and vitality and can be excused for possible rudeness. Maturity requires
> further efforts in all fields like bodybuilding and nutrition (economic and mili-
> tary development), good manners, obeying discipline and abiding by the law
> (building international image and observing international norms), conducting
> oneself in society and harmonizing social relations (striking a balance between
> a developing country and a big power in its dual status), complementing good
> neighborly relations with big power connections support for developing coun-
> tries in its multilateral diplomacy and implementing its foreign policy guide-
> lines of peace, development and cooperation. Only by so doing can China
> grow up and mature.[5]

THE POSSIBILITY OF PEACEFUL RELATIONS
WITH THE UNITED STATES

Despite the belief of some security and scholarly analysts in the United States and in China that conflict between a more capable China and an America determined to preserve its hegemony is almost inevitable (see chapter 1), the dominant Chinese perspective is more relaxed, though subject to change. The center of gravity of Chinese scholarly and strategic thinking on bilateral ties with the United States is that war with America is unlikely for four main reasons, in addition to U.S. economic interests.

The first is that the United States now, and for the foreseeable future, faces demonstrably bigger challenges to its economic and national security than China: Iraq, Afghanistan, Iran, North Korea, and its "global war on terrorism" come to mind. Moreover, whether the United States likes it or not, the world has many power centers, even though each on its own is weaker than America. In the aggregate, these potential or actual counterweights serve to limit what Washington can do. Also, the United States is squandering its own normative (ideational) power in its efforts to transform countries into democracies in regions that lack most of the preconditions to successfully accomplish this task any time soon. Finally, Washington faces pressing transnational problems that require Beijing's cooperation.

Though in pure economic and military might Washington is far and away the world's single strongest actor, strength is contextual: it must be judged in relation to the problems being confronted, the objectives being sought, and the cooperation (or opposition) one may expect in addressing them. In the dominant Chinese perspective, Washington faces many challenges that are as or more pressing than those presented by Beijing: China is not the biggest problem the United States faces, and if Beijing plays its cards wisely it will not make itself the solitary object of American antagonism. America is overstretched, its goals of hegemony are unrealistic, and its traditional allies often are in opposition. On almost every issue some other international actor can take the lead in opposing Washington, so Beijing does not need to take the point position even on issues of great importance to it. For example, while Beijing worries about the propensity of some in Washington to use force against Iran, Beijing counts on Moscow (and perhaps some in the EU) to take the lead in opposing such action, even though Beijing does not have particular faith in Russian steadfastness. Similarly, Seoul is as adamantly opposed to any use of force or coercion against Pyongyang as Beijing is, so Beijing can step away from the point position.

Strategic analysts in China believe that Washington confronts a challenging strategic landscape beyond the wars in Iraq, in Afghanistan, and against terrorism (a campaign that the U.S. Department of Defense officially dubbed "the long war" in 2006). The additional challenges are to be found in four incipient power centers: the EU, Russia, Japan, and India. With respect to the EU, the dominant Chinese view is that an increasingly integrated Europe will resist a subordinate relationship with Washington. "Europe's integration has the track and logic of its own that will eventually be at loggerheads with the global strategy of America."[6] This resistance is evident in many European states' attempts to end EU participation in the arms embargo against the PRC in early 2005; general EU reluctance to support Washington in Iraq; U.S. reluctance to see a greater German role on the UN Security Council; the desire of some Americans to limit Airbus technology transfers to the PRC and European determination to reap the economic rewards of sales; and ongoing frictions with Paris.

With respect to Russia, Beijing perceives a fundamental contradiction between Washington's desires for a Russian democracy and Moscow's engrained authoritarianism, as well as between Moscow's desire to dominate its "near abroad" and Washington's resistance to Russian dominance of the vast land that was formerly part of the USSR. Concerning Japan, Chinese suspect that Japanese nationalists will not remain satisfied for long with having their country be the American deputy in Asia, though the current degree of security cooperation between Washington and Tokyo is deeply troubling to Beijing. Then there is India, whose rise, like China's, is becoming a major economic and geopolitical event. New Delhi has never wanted to be the pawn of Washington, though Beijing has its anxieties about the current Washington–New Delhi embrace. Yuan Peng and many other Chinese conclude that "U.S.-China contradictions have not deteriorated to the extent of [being] the single centerpiece in world politics. As a matter of fact, China's rise takes place side by side with Europe's integration, Russia's revival, and India's rise almost at the same time. U.S. contradictions with China only rank among the other pairs, not to be exaggerated on purpose."[7]

The end of the Cold War is having effects far beyond the demise of the Soviet Union. Two such effects are the weakening of old alliance patterns and the reemergence of long-submerged patterns of international and intranational strife. Earlier we noted the corrosive effects of China's rise on some of America's alliances in Asia, most notably with South Korea, though many conservative analysts and politicians in Seoul suspect that Beijing actually opposes reunification and some fear that Beijing might intervene to prevent it in the event of a North Korean collapse. All this is part of an emerging world configuration in which nations increasingly seek to balance their interests between Washington and other power centers. The principal objective of China's Asian neighbors is to avoid having to choose between Washington and Beijing.

An underlying stability exists in U.S.-China relations not only because Washington faces multiple constraining power centers but also because Beijing's cooperation is required to address such problems as avian flu, North Korean nuclear efforts and illicit activities, Iran's nuclear programs, weapons proliferation, UN reform, transborder environmental challenges, and humanitarian assistance and peacekeeping. A senior Chinese government research official put it this way:

> The 9/11 attacks awaken us to the paradox that even a most powerful America has a soft underbelly. Full-blown modernization has given birth to a genetic freak—a powerful yet fragile society. . . . As mankind enters the 21st century, nontraditional issues stand out, natural disasters like earthquake, tsunami, hurricane, epidemic disease[s] like SARS, mad cow, [and] bird flu, and negative consequences of industrialization like environmental pollution [and the] greenhouse effect, to name just a few. In [the] face of them, not a single country can stand aloof. . . . The history of [the] international community shows that a weakening individualistic part or subjective aspect of the international order coupled with its correspondingly strengthening collective part or objective aspect will represent the general trend of growing democratization of international relations, a process independent of the will of anyone whosoever he may be.[8]

"In a word," Yuan Peng tells us, "in the face of the international situation for its national rise, China needs to have both a sense of crisis and strategic self-confidence."[9] For Beijing, disagreement with America is inevitable, intense conflict is avoidable, and both nations will cooperate when it is in their mutual interest to do so. Cooperation will not be easy, but it will often be essential—this is a manageable relationship.

THE DANGERS OF EXCESSIVE MILITARIZATION

Though not everyone agrees on what constitutes "excessive military expenditure" either in the PRC or in America, the consensus position in China is that the acquisition of excessive coercive power is a formula, not for state security, but for insecurity. The Chinese conclude from their long national history and the experience of empires in more recent times that an excessive emphasis on coercive power retards domestic economic development. The internal consequences of a militarized society can be excessive spending and regime decay; the external reactions may produce containment efforts by others. As one Chinese analyst put it, "The price for confronting [the] existing world order would far outweigh the illusory gains and even ruin the cause of the country's peaceful rise."[10] All this is not to deny that there are strident voices in the PRC; they exist. But these voices are not dominant, either in number or in strategic location within the policy process. An important objective of U.S. diplomacy ought to be to keep things this way.

Chinese scholars and intelligence analysts are analyzing the causes of the rise and fall of great powers historically in an attempt to understand America's current predicament. Their analysis of imperial history—whether European, Soviet, modern Japanese, or their own—has led them to conclude that overstretch is a problem. As one former senior Singaporean diplomat put it to me, "The Soviet experience showed that weapons are meaningless; they [Chinese] want a peaceful rise."[11] An influential Chinese scholar has concluded that throughout history attempts to transform influence into dominance or into control over large geographic spaces have generally led to ruin:

> Edward Gibbon said, if an empire wanted to ever last, its rulers must avoid over-expansion of their borders. Robert Gilpin also observed that if an empire over-expanded its borders, it would decline because its hegemonic costs exceeded the returns. Historically, no empire could escape from the law of "decrease of marginal effect." That is to say, over-expansion would lead to more costs with less return, and finally lead to a decline or even downfall of the empire. Some countries like the ancient Roman Empire, Napoleon-dominated France, Hitler-ruled Germany, and the Soviet Union in the 1960s–70s are of the same kind. Now the United States is suffering the same setbacks in Iraq and the Middle East as the above-mentioned empires.[12]

IMPLICATIONS OF CHINESE POWER FOR THE UNITED STATES AND THE WORLD

In his book *To Change China: Western Advisors in China 1620–1960*, Jonathan Spence described how a succession of Westerners bent on producing change in China continually ran aground on the immovable rocks of Chinese history and society. While there is this ongoing dimension to Western interaction with the PRC, today's dominant challenge is for the rest of the world to productively and peacefully adjust to a rapidly changing China, even as the outside continues to shape China's integration into the world. Change in China requires change in the outside world. China finally has attained the equality it has sought since the mid-nineteenth century, though it is the equality of the treadmill. Change in one society requires change in the others in a never-ending process of mutual adaptation and competition. As one senior member of the U.S. House of Representatives put it in a conversation in April 2006, "In the early days we engaged with [the PRC] to change China, but now we engage for other reasons [having to do with its power]."[13]

Specifically, Chinese power has five main implications internationally. First, *the outside world will feel China through negative impacts, spillovers, and externalities resulting from the PRC's institutional weaknesses and the unintended consequences of its headlong rush for economic growth.* Even though outsiders are most vigilant about areas of PRC strength, China's weaknesses require equal or greater attention. America needs to accept that China is a poor, overloaded, great power, and it needs to cooperate with China on developmental issues while treating its strengths with respect. Some members of the U.S. Congress from the West Coast were jolted when they learned at a 2006 seminar that up to one-third of the air pollution in their region comes from China.[14] A member of the U.S. Congress from the Midwest energized his audience when he said that "20 percent of the mercury in the Great Lakes is [fallout from windborne coal particulate and dust] from China."[15]

When China inflicts harm on others or proves uncooperative in its international relations, the reasons often are to be found in its own internal weaknesses. If China does not pressure North Korea on its nuclear weapons program to the degree Washington wants, it is in part because of fear of what North Korean collapse could mean for its own nearby and unstable northeast, which is rife with unemployment. If China pollutes rivers flowing through multiple downstream countries (such as the Amur or the Mekong), it is because China's own internal water, urban development, and environmental control systems are woefully inadequate. Sometimes the Chinese simply will not permit issues of regional and global interdependence to interfere with their rush for economic growth that the regime in Beijing believes is essential for its survival. A good example is the Greater Mekong system, where China is busy building dams on the upper reaches of the river without much regard for Vietnam on the lower reaches and neighbors in between (or its own biodiverse ecosystem). As one Western government official in Vietnam put it:

> The Mekong River affects the south [of Vietnam] more than the north. Massive damming will change the ecosystem of Vietnam's rice bowl. . . . In terms of the Mekong, plans were laid a decade ago. Whether [the Vietnamese were] asleep or too weak, the bottom line is—all their [Chinese] dams are being built. This will diminish the flow of fresh water. The Chinese are helping the Lao. The Mekong will be increasingly saline. . . . We have changes in the ecosystem. Why didn't the Vietnamese speak up? There is a Mekong River Commission, but it is powerless and China is not a member.[16]

Recall the distinction between *power* (the capacity to achieve purposes) and *impact* (effect on others without reference to goals): China's dynamic growth guarantees that it will generate huge unintended and often negative consequences (impacts) for the rest of the world, and these impacts will often reflect weakness more than strength.

China's middle class is growing rapidly, and its consumption preferences are similar to those associated with the resource-intensive American lifestyle—witness the ongoing Chinese love affair with the automobile that has made the PRC the fastest-growing auto market in the world as of 2006. China currently has eight autos per thousand persons, compared to the American six hundred.[17] Imagine the impact if the PRC achieves the auto penetration rate of the United States at anything like current energy technology levels. This rapid growth of a resource-intensive lifestyle among hundreds of millions of new consumers is having numerous effects. Most notable among them is environmental deterioration in China, but the effects spill over into the global system as acid rain, carbon dioxide and other global-warming gases, windborne particulates, polluted water in the global ocean commons, ozone-depleting substances, and increased demand (and prices) for resources. The single biggest issue China and the world face is simply: Is growth in an energy-intensive American-like lifestyle for such huge numbers of people sustainable for either China or the world? Then add in India and ask this question again—India's greenhouse gas emissions grew 57 percent from 1996 to 2005.[18] And yet, how do current energy-intensive and wealthy nations argue for restraint among Chinese who want air conditioning, for example?[19]

The expanding domestic demand is further amplified by China's growing roles as global processor and importer. For instance, China has quickly become a furniture exporter. To obtain the wood not available at home, the PRC imports huge quantities of (sometimes illegal) logs from rainforests in places such as Brazil and Indonesia. Similarly, as its people are eating more meat, the expanding herds of livestock require soya protein, so China has become the biggest soya importer in the world. This in turn has led to the felling of forests in Brazil's Amazon region to grow the soya to support the cattle. China then becomes part of the global deforestation problem. The point is that the domestic and global environmental spillovers of these huge new increments of demand at home and abroad, and China's growing role in global production chains, generate internal and international demands for the creation of regulatory institutions in the PRC, Beijing's constructive participation in transnational regulatory schemes, and opportunities for joint research to solve problems. China's tradition of noninterference in the internal affairs of others makes it just that much harder to address these transnational problems, as indicated when the Chinese official Wang Hujun said, "Since 2003 China has pursued a policy of sustainable development. But how Brazil protects its environment is up to them."[20] In all these spillover areas, the problems generated are everyone's problems.

For its part, the United States should adopt a cooperative stance to develop transnational institutions and mitigate spillover effects. Chinese good citizenship abroad must start with building capable domestic institutions. PRC institutional development at home and more benign international behavior and impacts are intimately related. America must cooperate on the former if it wants the latter.

Second, *China is a big power and will acquire and maintain an effective deterrent.* The PRC is on the cusp of change in its nuclear deterrence capacity with its soon-to-be deployed road-mobile, intercontinental nuclear missile system and a more usable submarine-launched missile capability. What partly drives this expansion is the increased number and accuracy of U.S. conventional weapons, which, the Chinese fear, could be employed to attack the PRC's nuclear deterrent without violating the strong taboo against the first use of nuclear weapons.[21] Some elements within the U.S. security establishment have not yet explicitly accepted what was long obvious with respect to the Soviet Union: that Moscow would spare no cost to achieve a secure second-strike nuclear capacity and that consequently the goal had to be crisis-stable mutual nuclear deterrence at the lowest possible level. China's acquisition of a survivable nuclear deterrent requires the unwelcome recognition and acceptance of U.S. strategic vulnerability. During the Cold War, nuclear strategists for the most part also believed that superpower development of offensive or defensive systems that threatened a secure second strike would be destabilizing. But today some U.S. strategists have not accepted China's right, ability, or determination to achieve a secure deterrent. China can and will do so at tolerable cost.

This means that Beijing and Washington should begin a sustained dialogue about how to achieve stable deterrence at the lowest possible level. To date, there has been little dialogue on how this might be achieved. Some would say that we do not "owe" China the opportunity to visit a devastating blow on America or its friends. But the only real question is at what level mutual deterrence will be built and how stable it will be. As one Chinese scholar on strategic nuclear issues put it in a 2006 discussion with members of Congress, "ABM is an obstacle to our second strike [capability]. China is wary about ABM and wants dialogue on this. [The United States] should respect our retaliatory [needs]; we have the capacity to do so [maintain second-strike capability,] and it is not very expensive."[22] This concern also relates to U.S. plans for space, the possible development of future weapons systems and platforms there, and Sino-American dialogue and cooperation in and about space. The United States should seek more bilateral and multilateral cooperation in this area.

In early 2007 China destroyed an aging satellite in orbit, partly to show that it was not going to supinely concede to Washington a threatening space dominance.

Third, *Taiwan's strategic position with respect to the mainland is eroding.* China is dedicated to maintaining what it would call a "deterrent" in the Taiwan Strait with respect to the island's possible declaration of de jure independence. Beijing will pay almost any price to prevent formal, permanent separation but is in no hurry for reunification. Indeed, there is no agreement among Chinese as to what the actual content of "reunification" should be. Given its own internal political and social problems, and given increasing cross-Strait interdependence that offers the prospect of eventual, peaceful, political resolution, Beijing does not desire to engage in adventurism that could upset its entire national grand strategy.

Washington has played a constructive and essential role in modulating occasionally reckless impulses on the island, as well as on the mainland, and occasionally will need to do so in the future. Washington's policies in recent decades have focused on trying to ensure sufficient Taiwan military capability to prevent either quick occupation of the island or the application of a decapitating blow that could produce Taipei's political capitulation before U.S. forces could arrive in the area, should a decision be made to send them at all.

However, the level and sophistication of PRC forces, particularly missiles, plus growing cross-Strait economic and social interdependence, raise the following issues:

- Can Taiwan be defended any longer by traditional military means? If it cannot, doesn't the island's security ultimately reside in working out a long-term interim or permanent political arrangement with the mainland?

- With China's growing power, doesn't deferral of adopting such an arrangement simply postpone decisions to an ever-more disadvantageous time for Taipei?

- If an arms spiral in the Strait accelerates, with Taiwan already acquiring its own offensive capabilities, are not all parties entering a period in which each side's escalation of military capability purchases only higher and more costly levels of insecurity for everyone?

- From an American point of view, doesn't Taipei's acquisition of strike capability against the PRC give Taipei the capacity to unilaterally drag Washington into a conflict with another nuclear power, a conflict America has ever more economic and strategic reasons to avoid?

- Over the longer run, can and should Washington provide a security back-stop to a regime that acts contrary to U.S. interests, as the Chen Shui-bian administration has done, when the costs to America of doing so continually rise? What price are Americans going to be willing to pay, for how long? The earlier-mentioned public opinion survey by the Chicago Council on Global Affairs reported that 61 percent of Americans would oppose deploying U.S. troops "if China invaded Taiwan."[23]

In light of all this, Washington ought to actively explore ways to cap arms race pressures in the Strait at the lowest possible level and encourage some form of interim or permanent political arrangement. Current U.S. law and practice inhibit doing so. Is this sensible? If Taipei's future political relationship with Beijing is inde-terminate but could become closer, what are America's interests in various possible outcomes? How can we constructively shape that outcome?

The answers to these questions are not obvious, and they certainly will depend on the evolving role China plays in the region and the world. Yet I find little reason to think that peaceful change in the cross-Strait political relationship in the direction of closer association, particularly in the context of a cooperative China, would be adverse to core American interests. Indeed, resolution of this issue would foster regional stability. If China has productive and stable relations with the United States, Japan, and its region, it is unlikely to risk everything on an adventurous roll of the dice by using force against Taiwan, as long as Taipei does not precipitate conflict.

Fourth, *the character of the U.S. alliance system is changing.* The tone and content of the U.S. post–World War II alliance system in the Asia-Pacific region are grad-ually changing for many reasons, but two are primary: China's growing power and Japan's quest (already well under way) to play a security role more befitting a dem-ocratic, economically central big power. The changes are most apparent in U.S. ties with South Korea and Thailand but are discernible even in ties with Washington's longtime friend and ally Australia. Further afield geographically, we see their effect with respect to the European Union and NATO countries and even Israel.

The hub-and-spokes system of bilateral U.S. alliances in Asia (with Japan, the Republic of Korea, Thailand, the Philippines, and Australia), for much of these alli-ances' histories, took Beijing to be either an enemy or a destabilizing factor. Though this alliance system still performs reassuring and stabilizing roles and keeps Japanese power tethered in a way that is regionally comforting, security mechanisms in South-east, East, and Northeast Asia need to be developed or strengthened to incorporate and reassure China and take advantage of Beijing's resources to solve problems.

Given their rising economic and security equities with Beijing, several American allies (notably South Korea, Thailand, and even Australia) are becoming progressively less willing to have their alliance with Washington viewed as directed against Beijing or for intervention in the Taiwan Strait. In the most likely conflict scenarios involving the United States and the PRC, it is unclear how much help America would have from regional allies. The purpose of China's regional and global diplomacy, as Sun Tzu suggested in about 400 BCE, is to "sometimes drive a wedge between a sovereign and his ministers; on other occasions separate his allies from him. Make them mutually suspicious so that they drift apart."[24] American allies, with the exception of perhaps Japan, increasingly will argue for a more restrained and modulated policy from Washington. Washington's allies have mounting economic and cultural ties with Beijing, and the costs of conflict with China will only progressively increase. South Korea, for instance, has been very reluctant to give Washington a blank check to use its territory for off-peninsula security operations without prior approval from Seoul;[25] as South Korea's ambassador to the United States put it more delicately in June 2006, "With respect to U.S. out of area [operations], we will recognize the need for strategic flexibility, and the U.S. recognizes our need not to be drawn into conflicts contrary to our will."[26] This means, I believe, that in the future if U.S. forces initially stationed in Korea are committed elsewhere in Asia, they will first have to be "laundered" through third areas (e.g., Japan).[27]

U.S. allies will be reluctant to end the bilateral treaties with Washington, still seeing them as a useful hedge against things going awry in China and elsewhere in the region and as a means of tethering growing Japanese military capability. At the same time, they will increasingly limit the degree to which they will follow Washington's lead in directions they find ill advised. U.S. allies in Asia increasingly see their problem as balancing two great powers—Washington and Beijing.

Fifth and last, *Chinese reform requires American change.* As China was emerging from its Cultural Revolution isolation and economic autarky in 1978, it was difficult to imagine it as a global, competitive force. But the combination of Chinese reform, rising labor costs elsewhere, and enormous quantities of newly available and relatively educated Chinese labor, in the context of a world economy with lower trade, transport, and financial barriers (globalization), has created a situation in which change in China requires change in America and in every other economy. Globalization is not something Americans do to others; it is a treadmill requiring continuous improvement and change among all parties involved in the global economy and intellectual life.

The United States (and other nations) face three stark choices. One is to actively seek to slow the PRC. In my view, this would be futile, since developments in China largely will be determined by the Chinese and since, under current circumstances, efforts to constrain China would not receive cooperation from other essential players. Further, the consequences of Chinese failure would be more difficult to address than the consequences of Chinese success. History suggests that a weak and resentful China has been more trouble for its region and the world than a strong one. Finally, is it ethically defensible to seek to keep weak one-fifth of the global population for fear of remote future contingencies?

A second course of action, more defensive and more narrowly economic, is to throw up barriers to Chinese goods and services. But given the multinational supply and production chains and interdependencies that have developed, these would simultaneously be barriers against much of the rest of the world and America's own multinational corporations. Such a policy would forego the huge benefits of comparative advantage. Because Chinese exports are composed of parts and subsystems from throughout the region and world, retaliation intended to hurt the PRC would inflict unwanted pain on friends globally. Further, if China's exports were artificially limited, the PRC's ability to invest and purchase from abroad would be correspondingly limited. Americans would simply buy from higher-cost suppliers.

The only feasible course of action, therefore, is the last one: to compete by upgrading the U.S. workforce, continually increasing efficiency, and providing essential public services and infrastructure more intelligently, at less cost. The U.S. government at all levels must perform essential functions more adequately than currently is being done—educate the citizenry; heal the sick and provide for the public's health in cost-effective ways; provide a social safety net for the aged and economically dislocated that is affordable, humane, and conducive to economic flexibility; and provide for national defense in ways that do not overwhelm all other priorities of spending on essential public goods. China's progress means that Americans must make progress in these basic areas or their overhead will be too high and the quality of their human resources insufficient. If Americans and others rise to this challenge, China's competition will have done them a favor.

China's challenge to the United States and others is not principally military. Washington should seek to foster an environment in which the PRC's principal emphasis remains directed inward and will not be turned outward, coercively. If Washington treats Beijing as though Beijing is placing primacy on its military, when it is not, it will push Beijing in undesirable directions and squander U.S. resources better employed to meet the actual economic and intellectual challenges that the PRC represents. A United States that is strong economically and intellectually will be secure in the face of China's progress. Realizing the competitive dynamic where it exists, and cooperating where necessary and possible, is the only sensible way forward under current and likely future conditions. I recall the wise words of an Australian corporate leader:

> We are all in a competitive world—take it or leave it. I don't want Americans to forget their values. But by the same token, I notice, I lived in the Middle East, and Arabs have their mores, ethics, as we have. Chinese have their approaches. This is the big problem for American policy, society. You need to have immense patience. On competition, I am a great admirer of America. You are economically and militarily number one. How long will it last? India will be powerful but never be a blockbuster. Will China compete with America for world leadership? As far as I can imagine, it will never be a competitor for that global leadership, and the reason is that the Americans have unique abilities— they are innovative and have the ability to make quick decisions. You have the power of politics, and you have a geographical platform from which to operate that is unique. Innovation and fast decision making you have, but not China. If you [America] focus on your strength, they [China] can focus on their strength, discipline/regimentation of manpower, and perseverance. Innovation comes naturally to Americans.[28]

Sino-American competition need not be the next example of growth, hegemonic expansion, overstretch, conflict, and decay. There are dangers, of course: one is that growing Chinese power can give rise to new, more muscular PRC purposes irrespective of current intentions, and that possibility needs to be guarded against. Another danger is that currently dominant powers, most notably Japan and the United States, will assume that a zero-sum relationship exists between China's growing strengths and their own national interests. This could lead to the creation of an external environment to which China's offensive realists would feel they had to respond, thereby setting off an upward military spiral. A third danger is that China's growing power, particularly economic expansion, will create huge, conflict-generating spillovers. The energies of China and the outside world ought to be directed toward mitigating and avoiding these spillovers. The United States should improve ties with the big powers around China (and elsewhere) not because they can be a bulwark or counterbalance to China but because such relationships have intrinsic merit and are essential to solve the global and regional challenges arising from interdependence.

For China, part of its challenge in maintaining a relatively benign security environment will be to further change the national psychology away from an aggrieved nationalism, as is dramatically evident in its relations with Japan. For the United States and Japan, this means rethinking security efforts in Asia so that China is less the object of them than a partner in them. And for all three nations, as well as the broader international community, it means developmental cooperation so that the negative spillovers from China's (and India's) modernization are as small as possible.

THE FIRST WORD IS THE LAST WORD

America and China have made a double gamble, bets that I believe are prudent. Nonetheless, significant constituencies in each nation feel anxious. Washington has bet that as China becomes more powerful it will be socialized into the norms of the international system and, because of interdependence, will become what then Deputy Secretary of State Robert Zoellick called a "responsible stakeholder" in a stable international system. Beijing has bet that despite misgivings about Chinese power, Washington will not seek to systematically frustrate the growth of PRC power and that it will, in fact, contribute mightily to it. These "bets" have been placed not only by the leadership of each country but by their middle classes and societal organizations as well, and the stakes are high.

Developments since 1978 have broadly affirmed the prudence, indeed wisdom, of these bets. The wisest course for both nations is to keep their wagers as they are. Of course, they are bets and could be lost; in this situation, if one nation's bet turns out to have been wrong, it means that the other's was as well. The job of Chinese statesmen and citizens, their counterparts in America, and those in the rest of the world is to do all within their power to increase the odds that these were the right wagers to make for a better world.

NOTES

INTRODUCTION

Epigraphs: Richard L. Armitage, "Interview with Charlie Rose on PBS," December 10, 2004, www.state.gov/s/d/rm/39973.htm (accessed December 27, 2004); Wang Jisi, "Wang Jisi Views Sino-U.S. Relations," *Zhongguo Dangzheng Ganbu Luntan* [China's Party Cadre Forum], January 5, 2005.

1. "Hu Jintao Summarizes China's World View in Political Bureau Study Session," Xinhua, February 24, 2004, Foreign Broadcast Information Service (hereafter FBIS), February 24, 2004, FBIS-CHI-2004-0224.

2. Peter Nolan and Robert F. Ash, "China's Economy on the Eve of Reform," *China Quarterly*, no. 144 (1995): 989.

3. Pang Zhongying, "China's Self-Defined Role in [the] International System," *Contemporary International Relations* 16 (April 2006): 28–40.

4. "China Seeks Investments in Ecuador, Latin America," *Guayaquil El Universo*, July 6, 2004, FBIS.

5. Wade Boese, "Missile Regime Puts Off China," *Arms Control News*, November 2004, www.armscontrol.org/act/2004_11/MTCR.asp (accessed June 22, 2006).

6. "China Backs Nepal against Maoist Insurgency," *Daily Times* (Pakistan), November 26, 2005, www.dailytimes.com.pk/default.asp?page=2005%5C11%5C26%5Cstory_26-11-2005_pg4_8 (accessed June 8, 2006).

7. Hans J. Morgenthau, *Politics among Nations*, 4th ed. (New York: Alfred A. Knopf, 1968), pp. 150–51.

8. K. S. Nathan, "Remarks," presented at the Conference on Regional Structures in

the Asia-Pacific, sponsored by the Center for International and Strategic Studies, January 18, 2005, Washington, DC.

1. THINKING ABOUT POWER

Epigraph: Interview with Foreign Ministry official, Hanoi, Vietnam, March 22, 2006, p. 3 of author's notes.

1. Max Weber, quoted in David L. Sills, ed., *International Encyclopedia of the Social Sciences,* vol. 12 (New York: Macmillan, 1968), p. 406.

2. Hans J. Morgenthau, *Politics among Nations,* 4th ed. (New York: Alfred A. Knopf, 1968), pp. 26–27.

3. John J. Mearsheimer, *The Tragedy of Great Power Politics* (New York: W. W. Norton, 2001), p. 55.

4. Joseph S. Nye Jr., "The Changing Nature of World Power," *Political Science Quarterly* 105 (Summer 1990): 177.

5. Joseph S. Nye Jr., *Soft Power: The Means to Success in World Politics* (New York: Public Affairs, 2004), pp. 32, 147.

6. Amitai Etzioni, *A Comparative Analysis of Complex Organizations* (New York: Free Press, 1975), p. 5.

7. Nye, *Soft Power.*

8. Etzioni, *Comparative Analysis,* p. 6.

9. Nye, *Soft Power,* p. x.

10. Interview with Chinese scholar, Shanghai, China, August 19, 2004, p. 3 of author's notes.

11. Charles F. Doran, "Economics, Philosophy of History, and the 'Single Dynamic' of Power Cycle Theory: Expectations, Competition, and Statecraft," *International Political Science Review* 24 (January 2003): 31.

12. Wang Zaibang, "Changes in Balance of Forces in the World in the Next Five to Ten Years Are Bound to Lead to Restructuring and Adjustment of Strategic Relations," *Liaowang* [Outlook], November 4, 2005, FBIS, NewsEdge Doc. No. 200511041477.1_6364096b478b3cf8.

13. National Security Council, *The National Security Strategy of the United States of America,* September 17, 2002, www.whitehouse.gov/nsc/nss.html.

14. Interview with senior Chinese foreign policy analyst, Beijing, China, August 16, 2004, pp. 7–8 of author's notes.

15. Interview with Chinese analyst, Narita, Japan, August 15, 2004, p. 4 of author's notes.

16. Yang Wenjing, "Probing into the Theories on the Rise of Great Powers," *Contemporary International Relations* 14, no. 6 (2004): 47.

17. Notes of remarks by John Mearsheimer made in debate ("China's Peaceful

Rise?") with Zbigniew Brzezinski, Carnegie Endowment, Washington, DC, September 20, 2004, and subsequent conversation with him.

18. Mearsheimer, *Tragedy of Great Power Politics*, pp. 53–56.

19. Notes of remarks by John Mearsheimer.

20. Interview with senior Chinese scholar, Beijing, China, August 16, 2004, p. 4 of author's notes.

21. Yang, "Probing into the Theories," pp. 47–48.

22. Alastair Iain Johnston, *Cultural Realism: Strategic Culture and Grand Strategy in Chinese History* (Princeton: Princeton University Press, 1995).

23. Peng Guangqian and Yao Youzhi, *The Science of Military Strategy* (Beijing: Military Science Publishing House, 2005), p. 3.

24. Wang Li, *Zhong mei guanxi yanbian de quzhe licheng* [The Zigzag Process in the Evolution of U.S.-China Relations] (Beijing: Shijie Zhizhi Chubanshe, 1998), p. 278; see also Wang Yusheng, "Hiding One's Capacities and Time *[sic]* Is Weapon to Cope with Strong Enemy," *People's Daily*, August 13, 2001, http://english.people.com.cn/english/200108/10/eng20010810_77024.html (accessed June 7, 2006).

25. Alastair Iain Johnston, "China's Militarized Interstate Dispute Behavior, 1949–1992: A First Cut at the Data," *China Quarterly*, no. 153 (March 1998): 28–29.

26. Andrew Scobell, *China's Use of Military Force: Beyond the Great Wall and the Long March* (Cambridge: Cambridge University Press, 2003), p. 5.

27. For a superb account of Chinese strategic thinking from Sun Tzu to today, see John Wilson Lewis and Xue Litai, *Imagined Enemies: China Prepares for Uncertain War* (Stanford: Stanford University Press, 2006), especially ch. 1.

28. Sun Tzu, *The Art of War*, trans. Samuel B. Griffith (London: Oxford University Press, 1971), p. 63. A somewhat different translation is found in Ralph D. Sawyer, trans., *One Hundred Unorthodox Strategies: Battle and Tactics of Chinese Warfare* (Boulder, CO: Westview Press, 1996), p. 1.

29. On *Seven Military Classics*, see Johnston, *Cultural Realism*, p. 46.

30. Lo Kuan-chung, *Romance of the Three Kingdoms*, trans. C. H. Brewitt-Taylor, vol. 1 (Hong Kong: Kelly and Walsh, 1959), p. 74.

31. Ibid., p. 82.

32. Notes of conversation with Chinese policy analyst and scholar, Shanghai, China, August 19, 2004, pp. 1–2.

33. Michael D. Swaine and Ashley J. Tellis, *Interpreting China's Grand Strategy: Past, Present, and Future* (Santa Monica, CA: RAND, 2000), p. 65.

34. Notes of Preventive Defense Project meeting with Zheng Bijian, New York City, November 11, 2003.

35. Quoted in William C. Kirby, "Traditions of Centrality, Authority, and Management in Modern China's Foreign Relations," in *Chinese Foreign Policy: Theory and*

Practice, ed. Thomas W. Robinson and David Shambaugh (Oxford: Oxford University Press, 1997), p. 16.

36. Interview with senior Chinese official, April 1993, quoted in David M. Lampton, *Same Bed, Different Dreams: Managing U.S.-China Relations, 1989–2000* (Berkeley: University of California Press, 2001), p. 40.

37. Jiang Zemin, "Full Text of Jiang Zemin's 'Report' at 16th Party Congress," Section 9, "On the International Situation and Our External Work," Sixteenth National Congress of the Communist Party of China, Beijing, China, November 8, 2002, http://english.people.com.cn/200211/18/eng20021118_106985.shtml (accessed August 19, 2006).

38. Michael Pillsbury, *China Debates the Future Security Environment* (Washington, DC: National Defense University Press, 2000), p. 204. For a fuller discussion of comprehensive national power, see pp. 203–58.

39. Huang Shuofeng, *New Theory on Comprehensive National Strength: Comprehensive National Strength of China* (Beijing: China Social Sciences Press, 1999), cited in Hu Angang and Men Honghua, "The Rise of Modern China (1980–2000): Comprehensive National Power and Grand Strategy," 2002, http://irchina.org/en/xueren/china/pdf/mhh3.pdf (accessed July 20, 2007), p. 2; see also Huang Shuofeng, *Zonghe guoli lun* [On Comprehensive National Power] (Beijing: Zhongguo Shehui Kexue Chubanshe, 1992), p. 7, cited in Pillsbury, *China Debates*, p. 204.

40. Hu and Men, "Rise of Modern China," p. 2.

41. Michael Porter, *The Competitive Advantage of Nations* (New York: Free Press, 1990), cited in Hu and Men, "Rise of Modern China," p. 3.

42. R. J. Barro and Jong-wha Lee, "International Data on Educational Attainment: Updates and Implication," National Bureau of Economic Research Working Paper No. W7911, 2000, cited in Hu and Men, "Rise of Modern China," p. 5.

43. The Correlates of War Project has for decades been collecting such data and ranking nations according to their relative power because the concept of "relative" power is key to "power cycle theory," as explained above, and therefore to theories of war causation. See, for example, Melvin Small and J. David Singer, *Resort to Arms: International and Civil Wars, 1816–1980* (Beverly Hills, CA: Sage Publications, 1982).

44. Memorandum of conversation with senior Chinese scholar, Shanghai, China, August 17, 2004, pp. 3–4.

45. Their original article, published in 2002, covered only up to the year 2000. In an updated table provided by Professor Hu Angang to me in March 2007, the data in table 1 cover up until the year 2003.

46. Hu and Men, "Rise of Modern China," p. 17.

47. Ibid., p. 17.

48. Li Zhoncheng, quoted in Pillsbury, *China Debates*, p. 250.

49. Wu Xinbo, "To Be an Enlightened Superpower," *Washington Quarterly* 24 (Summer 2001): 71.

50. Chicago Council on Global Affairs, *The United States and the Rise of China and India: Results of a 2006 Multination Survey of Public Opinion* (Chicago: Chicago Council, 2006), p. 33, www.thechicagocouncil.org.

51. International Monetary Fund, World Economic Outlook Database, April 2006, www.imf.org/external/pubs/ft/weo/2006/01/data/index.htm. This quadrupling factor is derived from data for 2003–7.

52. One Chinese economics-oriented think tank opined in 2003: "[The] Japanese economy has grown slowly, restructuring has been stagnant, conservative forces have risen and the ruling group has been unstable. It is difficult for Japan to play an important political role in the future international arena." Research Group, "On China's International Strategy," *SIIS Journal* (Shanghai) 10 (November 2003): 46.

53. "Experts Predict: China's 10 Major Risk Factors before 2010," *People's Daily*, September 1, 2004, http://english.peopledaily.com.cn/200409/01/eng20040901_155578 .html (accessed June 7, 2006).

54. Interview with senior Chinese foreign policy analyst, Beijing, China, August 16, 2004, p. 4 of author's notes.

55. Hu and Men, "Rise of Modern China," pp. 24, 25.

56. Notes of roundtable meeting at think tank, Shanghai, January 14, 2005, p. 2.

57. Interview with senior Chinese scholar, Beijing, China, August 16, 2004, p. 7 of author's notes.

58. Hu and Men, "Rise of Modern China," p. 23.

59. Interview with Chinese analyst, Narita, Japan, August 15, 2004, p. 1 of author's notes.

60. Swaine and Tellis, *Interpreting China's Grand Strategy*, pp. 97–98.

61. Jiang Zemin, "Full Text of Jiang Zemin's 'Report' at 16th Party Congress," Section 9, "On the International Situation and Our External Work," Sixteenth National Congress of the Communist Party of China, Beijing, China, November 8, 2002, http://english.people.com.cn/200211/18/eng20021118_106985.shtml (accessed August 19, 2006).

62. Interview with Chinese scholar, Shanghai, China, August 19, 2004, pp. 3–4 of author's notes.

63. Jia Qingguo, "Learning to Live with the Hegemon: Evolution of China's Policy toward the U.S. since the End of the Cold War," *Journal of Contemporary China* 14, no. 44 (2005): 395–407.

64. Notes of conversation with Chinese policy analyst and scholar, Shanghai, China, August 19, 2004, pp. 2–3.

65. Ibid., pp. 4–5.

66. Interview with senior Chinese foreign policy analyst, Beijing, China, August 16, 2004, p. 6 of author's notes.

67. Interview with senior Chinese scholar, Beijing, China, August 16, 2004, pp. 1–2 of author's notes.

68. Interview with Chinese analyst, Narita, Japan, August 15, 2004, p. 2 of author's notes.

69. Interview with senior Chinese scholar, Beijing, China, August 16, 2004, p. 5 of author's notes.

70. David Shambaugh, *Modernizing China's Military: Progress, Problems, and Prospects* (Berkeley: University of California Press, 2002), pp. 188–89; see also "China's Defense Budget," www.globalsecurity.org/military/world/china/budget.htm (accessed June 15, 2006).

71. Notes of Preventive Defense Project meeting with Zheng Bijian, New York City, November 11, 2003.

72. Robert L. Suettinger, "The Rise and Descent of 'Peaceful Rise,'" *China Leadership Monitor,* no. 12 (Fall 2004), http://chinaleadershipmonitor.com, p. 8.

73. Hu Jintao, "China's Development Is an Opportunity for Asia," speech to Boao Forum on Asia, April 24, 2003, http://english.people.com.cn/200404/24/eng20040424 _141419.shtml.

74. Interview with senior Chinese scholar, Beijing, China, August 16, 2004, pp. 1–2 of author's notes.

75. Zheng Bijian, "Heping jueqi di zhongguo shi weihu shijie heping di jianding liliang" [Peacefully rising China is a firm defender of world peace], speech given at the International Conference on East Asia Cooperation and Sino-U.S. Relations, Diaoyutai Hotel, Beijing, China, November 3, 2005.

76. Notes of International Conference on East Asia Cooperation and Sino-U.S. Relations, Diaoyutai Hotel, Beijing, November 3–4, 2005, notes on day 2, pp. 5–6.

77. *U.S.-China Relations 2006,* Report of the Eighth Congressional Conference of the Aspen Institute (Washington, DC: Aspen Institute, 2006), p. 4.

78. Ronald L. Tammen, "The Impact of Asia on World Politics: China and India Options for the United States," *International Studies Review,* no. 8 (2006): 564.

2. MIGHT

Epigraphs: Notes of William Perry Delegation meeting with senior Chinese military leader, Beijing, China, January 28, 2005, p. 2; interview with senior Singaporean flag officer, Singapore, June 13, 2005, pp. 1–2 of author's notes.

1. Amitai Etzioni, *A Comparative Analysis of Complex Organizations* (New York: Free Press, 1975), p. 5.

2. Ibid.

3. "Suggestions to Promote Sino-Japanese Relations," *Contemporary International Relations* 14 (June 2004): 22, remarks by Tsinghua University's Yan Xuetong.

4. Notes of meeting with Liu Huaqing, Beijing, China, May 26, 1994.

5. State Council Information Office, People's Republic of China, *White Paper on National Defense, 2004* (Beijing: State Council, December 27, 2004), p. 6, http://news.xinhuanet.com/english/2004-12/27/content_2384679.htm (accessed December 27, 2004).

6. Deng Xiaoping, "The Task of Consolidating the Army," July 14, 1975, in *Selected Works of Deng Xiaoping* (Beijing: Foreign Languages Press, 1984), p. 27.

7. James Mulvenon, *Soldiers of Fortune: The Rise and Fall of the Chinese Military-Business Complex, 1978–1998* (Armonk, NY: M. E. Sharpe, 2001).

8. GlobalSecurity.org, "China's Defense Budget," www.globalsecurity.org/military/world/china/budget.htm (accessed June 15, 2006). The official defense budget rose from $3.9 billion in 1991 to $29.9 billion in 2005. The percentage increase in military spending per year also ranged from a 9.6 percent increase in 2002 to a 28.8 percent jump in 1993.

9. State Council Information Office, People's Republic of China, *China's National Defense in 2006*, December 2006, www.china.org.cn/english/features/book/194421.htm (accessed August 10, 2007), p. 6.

10. John Wilson Lewis and Xue Litai, *Imagined Enemies: China Prepares for Uncertain War* (Stanford: Stanford University Press, 2006), especially ch. 8.

11. Alan D. Romberg and Michael McDevitt, "Executive Summary," in *China and Missile Defense: Managing U.S.-PRC Strategic Relations*, ed. Alan D. Romberg and Michael McDevitt (Washington, DC: Henry L. Stimson Center, 2003), pp. 1–5. See also U.S. Department of Defense, "FY04 Report to Congress on PRC Military Power," in *Annual Report to Congress: Military Power of the People's Republic of China, 2004* (Washington, DC: U.S. Department of Defense, 2004), pp. 5, 13.

12. Su Ruozhou, "A Great Military Reform—Roundup of Strategic Changes in Our Army Building," *Jiefangjun Bao* [Liberation Army Daily], December 18, 1998, 1–2, Foreign Broadcast Information Service (hereafter FBIS), FBIS-CHI-99-018; Alexander C. Huang, "The Chinese Navy's Offshore Active Defense Strategy: Conceptualization and Implications," *Naval War College Review* 47 (Summer 1994): 15.

13. Wang Yiwei, "Maliujiaka wang zhongdong shiyoulu zhongguo haiwai shiyou mingxuan yixian" [Malacca and Middle East oil routes: China's overseas oil lifeline], *Zhonghua Gongshang Shibao* [China Business Times], July 28, 2003, http://finance.sina.com.cn/g/20030728/0723383862.shtml (accessed June 16, 2006).

14. John Calabrese, "The Risks and Rewards of China's Deepening Ties with the Middle East," *Jamestown Foundation China Brief*, May 24, 2005, http://jamestown.org/publications_details.php?volume_id=408&issue_id=3344&article_id=2369790 (accessed June 16, 2006).

15. U.S. Department of Defense, "FY04 Report to Congress," p. 19; see also "Beijing 'Has E-Blockade Strategy,'" Associated Press, November 17, 2004, http://taiwan security.org/AP/2004/AP-171104.htm (accessed June 17, 2006).

16. James C. Mulvenon et al., *Chinese Responses to U.S. Military Transformation and Implications for the Department of Defense* (Santa Monica, CA: RAND, 2006).

17. James Mulvenon, "The PLA Army's Struggle for Identity," in *The People's Liberation Army and China in Transition,* ed. Stephen Flanagan and Michael Marti (Washington, DC: National Defense University Press, 2003), p. 109, www.ndu.edu/inss/China/PLA_Conf_Oct01/Jmulvenon.htm (accessed December 13, 2004).

18. State Council Information Office, *China's National Defense in 2006,* p. 8; also U.S. Department of Defense, "FY04 Report to Congress," p. 17; Office of the Secretary of Defense, *Annual Report to Congress: Military Power of the People's Republic of China, 2006* (Washington, DC: U.S. Department of Defense, 2006), pp. 19–21, www.defense link.mil/pubs (accessed August 25, 2006); see also Stockholm International Peace Research Institute, "The SIPRI Military Expenditure Data Base," http://first.sipri.org/non_first/milex.php (accessed July 19, 2007); and Xu Guangyu, "What's Behind Increase in the Military Budget," *China Daily,* March 15, 2007, p. 9.

19. Dr. John Hill, "China's PLA Reform Success," *Jane's Intelligence Review* 15 (December 2003).

20. Dennis J. Blasko et al., *Defense-Related Spending in China: A Preliminary Analysis and Comparison with American Equivalents* (Washington, DC: United States–China Policy Foundation, May 2007).

21. "Communique of the Sixth Plenum of the 16th Central Committee," Xinhua, October 11, 2006, www.news.xinhuanet.com/english/2006-10/11/content_5191071 .htm (accessed July 10, 2007).

22. State Council Information Office, *White Paper on National Defense, 2004.*

23. Interview with senior Chinese military officer, Washington, DC, October 11, 2004, p. 2 of author's notes. I closely paraphrase the interviewee here.

24. Mulvenon, "PLA Army's Struggle," p. 115. See also Dennis Blasko, "PLA Force Structure: A 20-Year Retrospective," in *Seeking Truth from Facts,* ed. James C. Mulvenon and Andrew N. D. Yang (Santa Monica, CA: RAND, 2001), CF-160-CAPP.

25. "Hu Jintao Promotes CMC Members Zhang Dingfa, Jing Zhiyuan as Generals," Xinhua, September 25, 2004, FBIS-CHI-2004-0930.

26. Interview with senior Chinese military officer, Washington, DC, November 22, 2004, p. 2 of author's notes.

27. Mulvenon et al., *Chinese Responses,* pp. xii–xvi.

28. U.S. Department of Defense, "FY04 Report to Congress," p. 21.

29. Susan M. Puska, "Rough but Ready Force Projection: An Assessment of Recent PLA Training," in *China's Growing Military Power,* ed. Andrew Scobell and Larry M.

Wortzel (Carlisle, PA: Strategic Studies Institute, Army War College, September 2002), p. 230.

30. David Shambaugh, *Modernizing China's Military: Progress, Problems, and Prospects* (Berkeley: University of California Press, 2002), p. 99.

31. U.S. Department of Defense, "FY04 Report to Congress," p. 44.

32. Chicago Council on Global Affairs, *The United States and the Rise of China and India: Results of a 2006 Multination Survey of Public Opinion* (Chicago: Chicago Council, 2006), p. 64, www.thechicagocouncil.org.

33. Xiong Guangkai, "The Global Counter-terrorism Campaign: Its Current Situation and Future Prospects," *International Strategic Studies* 68 (April 2003): 2.

34. Meeting notes of roundtable at think tank, Shanghai, China, January 14, 2005, p. 3; see also Wu Nanlan, "PRC Government Increasingly Considers Safety of Nationals Abroad," *Zhongguo Wang* [China Net], September 28, 2004, FBIS *Daily Report*, September 28, 2004.

35. Jeffrey Gettleman, "Rebels Storm a Chinese-Run Oil Field in Ethiopia, Killing 70," *New York Times*, April 25, 2007, p. A6.

36. SCO originally was named the Shanghai Five and consisted of China, Russia, Kazakhstan, Tajikistan, and Kyrgyzstan. The group changed names and introduced a new constitution when it broadened its membership to include Uzbekistan. The Shanghai Five was created on April 26, 1996.

37. Hong Jianjun, "NATO's New Strategy in C. Asia and Its Impacts," *Contemporary International Relations* 16 (February 2006): 10.

38. Edward Cody, "Six-Nation Bloc Plans Anti-terror Maneuvers," *Washington Post*, April 27, 2006, p. A20.

39. Interview with a senior scholar in Shanghai, China, August 17, 2004, p. 1 of author's notes.

40. Discussion with senior PLA officers, Beijing, China, January 11, 2005, p. 1 of author's notes.

41. "Total Mileage of China's Freeway Ranks 2nd in World," *People's Daily*, October 29, 2004, http://english.peoplesdaily.com.cn/200410/29/3ng20041029_162122 .html (accessed July 20, 2007).

42. "China's Road Construction Uses 6 Billion USD Foreign Investment," Xinhua, October 27, 2004, FBIS-CHI-2004-1027.

43. M. Taylor Fravel, "Regime Insecurity and International Cooperation: Explaining China's Compromises in Territorial Disputes," *International Security* 30, no. 2 (2005): 46–83.

44. John Hill, "China Upgrades Border Security," *Jane's Intelligence Review*, October 1, 2004.

45. "China, Mongolia Finalize 4,677-km Border," Kyodo, November 30, 2005,

www.chinadaily.com.cn/english/doc/2005-11/30/content_499235_2.htm (accessed June 19, 2006).

46. "Indian Security Official to Meet Vice FM Dai Bingguo on Border Dispute," Agence France Presse, November 16, 2004, FBIS-NEC-2004-1116; "Shift in China's Foreign Policy under Hu," Indo-Asian News Service, October 21, 2004, Lexis-Nexis.

47. Interview with senior Chinese military officer, Washington, DC, October 11, 2004, p. 3 of author's notes.

48. Alexander L. George, David K. Hall, and William R. Simons, *The Limits of Coercive Diplomacy* (Boston: Little, Brown, 1971), pp. 18–19.

49. Shen Dingli, "Nuclear Deterrence in the 21st Century," *China Security* 1 (Autumn 2005): 10–14, www.wsichina.org (accessed August 25, 2006); see also Sun Xiangli, "Analysis of China's Nuclear Strategy," *Zhongguo Guoguan Zai Xian* [China's International Relations Online], www.irchina.org/en/news/view.asp?id=401 (accessed August 30, 2006); Evan Medeiros, "China's Second Artillery and Concepts of Escalation," paper presented at "Escalation Control in the Taiwan Strait," CAPS-RAND-CEIP International Conference on PLA Affairs, Taipei, October 21–22, 2004, pp. 9–11.

50. Peng Guangqian and Yao Youzhi, *The Science of Military Strategy* (Beijing: Military Science Publishing House, 2005), p. 213.

51. John D. Negroponte, Director of National Intelligence, "Annual Threat Assessment," delivered to U.S. Senate Select Committee on Intelligence, January 11, 2007, p. 10, www.intelligence.senate.gov (accessed January 24, 2007).

52. Office of the Secretary of Defense, *Annual Report to Congress: Military Power of the People's Republic of China, 2005* (Washington, DC: U.S. Department of Defense, 2005), p. 36.

53. Office of the Secretary of Defense, *Annual Report to Congress: Military Power of the People's Republic of China, 2006*, pp. 38, 50.

54. Medeiros, "China's Second Artillery," pp. 8, 13–15.

55. Mao Tse-tung [Mao Zedong], "On the Ten Major Relationships" (April 1956), in *The Selected Works of Mao Tse-tung* (Beijing: Foreign Languages Press, 1977), p. 288.

56. John W. Lewis and Xue Litai, *China Builds the Bomb* (Stanford: Stanford University Press, 1988), p. 2 and ch. 3.

57. Center for Defense Information, "The World's Nuclear Arsenals," February 2003, www.cdi.org/issues/nukef&f/database/nukearsenals.cfm#china (accessed June 19, 2007); see also Jeffrey Lewis, "Nuclear Numerology Chinese Style," letter to the editor, *Arms Control Today*, www.armscontrol.org/act/2005_03/LetterstotheEditor.asp (accessed August 30, 2006).

58. "U.S. Experts Cut by Half Size Estimate of China Nuclear Arsenal," Agence France Presse, May 3, 2006, Lexis-Nexis; Ministry of Foreign Affairs of the People's Republic of China, "Fact Sheet: China: Nuclear Disarmament and Reduction of [sic],"

April 27, 2004, www.fmprc.gov.cn/eng/wjb/zzjg/jks/cjjk/2622/t93539.htm (accessed June 25, 2006).

59. Peng Guangqian and Yao Youzhi, *Science of Military Strategy*, pp. 217–25; see also Sun Xiangli, "Analysis of China's Nuclear Strategy"; Medeiros, "China's Second Artillery," pp. 9–10.

60. John W. Lewis and Xue Litai, *China Builds the Bomb* (Stanford: Stanford University Press, 1988), p. 211.

61. William Burr and Jeffrey T. Richelson, "The United States and the Chinese Nuclear Program 1960–1964," *National Security Archive*, January 21, 2001, www2.gwu .edu/~nsarchiv/NSAEBB/NSAEBB38/ (accessed June 20, 2006).

62. Medeiros, "China's Second Artillery," p. 10.

63. Romberg and McDevitt, "Executive Summary," p. 3; Paul H. B. Godwin, "Potential Chinese Responses to U.S. Ballistic Missile Defense," in Romberg and McDevitt, *China and Missile Defense*, p. 66.

64. Mark A. Stokes, "Chinese Ballistic Missile Forces in the Age of Global Missile Defense: Challenges and Responses," in Scobell and Wortzel, *China's Growing Military Power*, p. 110.

65. Bruce G. Blair and Chen Yali, "The Fallacy of Nuclear Primacy," *China Security* 2 (Autumn 2006): 68–72, www.wsichina.org.

66. Romberg and McDevitt, "Executive Summary," pp. 2–3; David M. Finkelstein, "National Missile Defense and China's Current Security Perceptions," in Romberg and McDevitt, *China and Missile Defense*, pp. 40–42.

67. Godwin, "Potential Chinese Responses," p. 62.

68. Office of the Secretary of Defense, *Annual Report to Congress: Military Power of the People's Republic of China, 2006*, p. 27.

69. Shen Dingli, "Nuclear Deterrence"; see also Pan Zhenqiang, "China Insistence on No-First-Use of Nuclear Weapons," *Zhongguo Guoguan Zai Xian* [China's International Relations Online], www.irchina.org/en/news/view.asp?id=403 (accessed August 30, 2006), originally published in *China Security* (Autumn 2005).

70. Discussion with senior PLA officers, Beijing, China, January 11, 2005, pp. 2–3 of author's notes.

71. State Council Information Office, People's Republic of China, *China's National Defense, 2004* (Beijing: State Council, December 27, 2004), www.fas.org/nuke/guide/china/doctrine/natdef2004.html (accessed June 26, 2006).

72. U.S. Department of Defense, "FY04 Report to Congress," p. 37.

73. Ibid., p. 7.

74. Ibid., p. 39.

75. Ibid., p. 40.

76. Ibid., pp. 39–40.

77. Evan S. Medeiros et al., *A New Direction for China's Defense Industry* (Santa Monica: RAND, 2005).

78. Interview with senior Chinese military officer, Washington, DC, October 11, 2004, p. 3 of author's notes.

79. State Council Information Office, People's Republic of China, *China's Space Activities in 2006*, http://china.org.cn/english/2006/Oct/183588.htm (accessed October 17, 2006).

80. State Council Information Office, People's Republic of China, *White Paper: China's Space Activities*, November 22, 2000, www.cdi.org/PDFs/ChinaSpace.pdf (accessed June 27, 2006), p. 8.

81. State Council Information Office, *White Paper on National Defense 2004*, p. 78.

82. Office of the Secretary of Defense, *Annual Report to Congress: Military Power of the People's Republic of China, 2006*, p. 34.

83. David L. Chandler, "Confident China Joins Space Elite," *New Scientist*, October 25, 2003, Lexis-Nexis; Joan Johnson-Freese, "China's Manned Space Program," *Naval War College Review* 56 (Summer 2003): 63; see also "China Plans Moonwalk, Space Station by 2020," *Los Angeles Times*, December 3, 2005, p. A14.

84. "China 1st Lunar Orbiter Costs as Much as 2 km of Subway," Xinhua, July 21, 2006.

85. Chang Xianqi and Sui Junqin, "Active Exploration and Peaceful Use of Outer Space," *China Security*, no. 2 (2006): 21–22. This issue of *China Security* is entirely devoted to the PRC's space efforts.

86. Ibid., pp. 16–23, esp. p. 19.

87. David L. Chandler, "Why Do the Chinese Want to Conquer Space?" *New Scientist*, October 25, 2003, Lexis-Nexis.

88. State Council Information Office, People's Republic of China, "China's Space Activities: A White Paper," November 22, 2000, www.spaceref.com/China/China.white.paper.nov.22.2000.html (accessed July 7, 2007). See also Desmond Ball, "China Pursues Space-Based Intelligence Gathering Capabilities," *Jane's Intelligence Review* 15 (December 1, 2003): 36–39; Office of the Secretary of Defense, *Annual Report to Congress: Military Power of the People's Republic of China 2006*, pp. 31–35.

89. Johnson-Freese, "China's Manned Space Program," p. 53.

90. Edward Cody, "China Builds and Launches a Satellite for Nigeria," *Washington Post*, May 14, 2007, p. A11.

91. "China Joins Galileo Program for Civil Purposes, FM Spokeswoman," Xinhua, October 26, 2004, FBIS-CHI-2004-1026.

92. David Lague, "GPS Substitute for China?" *International Herald Tribune*, April 19, 2005, www.iht.com/articles/2005/04/18/news/galileo.php (accessed June 30, 2006); also notes on lecture by Dean Cheng at Johns Hopkins-SAIS, Washington, DC,

February 21, 2007, p. 4; and Jim Yardley, "China's New Frontier in Diplomacy: Space," *International Herald Tribune*, May 24, 2007, pp. 1, 4.

93. Andrew Bounds, "Work on European Version of GPS Stalls," *Financial Times*, March 15, 2007, p. 1.

94. Jeff Foust, "China, Competition, and Cooperation," *Space Review*, April 10, 2006, www.thespacereview.com/article/599/1 (accessed August 30, 2006).

95. Warren E. Leary, "NASA Chief, on First China Trip, Says Joint Spaceflight Is Unlikely," *New York Times*, September 28, 2006, p. A9.

96. For estimate of "Chinese space expenditures," see Johnson-Freese, "China's Manned Space Program," p. 69, n. 5. The figure for Chinese expenditures on its space program is really quite soft. According to another Western report, "Analysts estimate that it [China] has spent $2.2 billion so far on its space programme [as of 2003]." See Chandler, "Why Do the Chinese?"

97. "Zhongguo fazhan zairen hangtian gongcheng 13 nian huafei budao 200 yi yuan" [China's manned space projects spend less than 20 billion RMB in 13 years], Xinhua, November 29, 2005, http://news.xinhuanet.com/fortune/2005-11/29/content_3854006.htm (accessed June 30, 2006). For more on the space budget, see Stacey Solomone, "China's Space Program: The Great Leap Upward," *Journal of Contemporary China* 15 (May 2006): 315, 324.

98. Foust, "China, Competition, and Cooperation."

99. Notes of remarks by Admiral Dennis Blair, National Press Club, Washington, DC, December 17, 2004.

100. Evan S. Medeiros et al., *A New Direction for China's Defense Industry* (Santa Monica: RAND, 2005), p. xxiv.

101. Herb Keinon, "Ally in the Making," *Jerusalem Post*, February 4, 2005, FBIS, NewsEdge Doc. No. 200502041477.1_d747071f2c7c8f79.

102. "Interest in Russian Fighters at Show in China, Export Plans Seen; Officials Cited," Izvestia, November 16, 2004, p. 7, FBIS-CHI-2004-1117.

103. Ministry of Foreign Affairs, "Strengthening Cooperation for Mutual Benefit and a Win-Win Result," November 29, 2004, www.fmprc.gov.cn/eng/wjb/zzjg/gjs/gjsxw/t172730.htm (accessed August 24, 2006).

104. "Philippines, China Agree on Annual Security Talks," Agence France Presse, FBIS-EAS-2004-1117.

105. Interview with senior Chinese scholar, Helsinki, Finland, May 11, 2004, p. 1 of author's notes.

106. Pew Global Attitudes Project, "China's Neighbors Worry about Its Growing Military Strength," September 21, 2006, www.pewglobal.org.

107. "Suggestions to Promote Sino-Japanese Relations," *Contemporary International Relations* 14 (June 6, 2004), remarks by Tsinghua's Yan Xuetong, p. 26.

108. Kenneth W. Allen and Eric A. McVadon, *China's Foreign Military Relations* (Washington, DC: Henry L. Stimson Center, 1999); see also Stefan Staehle, "China's Participation in the United Nations Peacekeeping Regime" (MA thesis, George Washington University, 2006).

109. "Kazakhstan, China Discuss Bilateral Military Cooperation," Interfax-Kazakhstan, November 23, 2004, FBIS-SOV-2004-1123.

110. "Foreign Military Officers Conclude Training Courses in China," Xinhua, September 30, 2004, FBIS-CHI-2004-0930.

111. Robert Karniol, "China to Host Seminar on Humanitarian Law," *Jane's Defence Weekly*, June 2, 2004, http://jdw.janes.com (accessed May 27, 2004).

112. Staehle, "China's Participation," p. 73.

113. Ibid.

114. State Council Information Office, *White Paper on National Defense, 2004*, Appendix VI.

115. Allen and McVadon, *China's Foreign Military Relations*, p. 27.

116. Staehle, "China's Participation," p. 84.

117. United Nations, "Contributors to United Nations Peacekeeping Operations: Monthly Summary of Contributions, as of July 2006," www.un.org/Depts/dpko/dpko/contributors/index.htm (accessed August 25, 2006).

118. Embassy of the People's Republic of China, "China Sends Riot Police to Haiti for Peace Mission," *China Review*, no. 16 (October 2004), www.china-embassy.org/eng/xw/t165833.htm (accessed June 27, 2006).

119. State Council Information Office, *White Paper on National Defense, 2004*, p. 32.

120. Hu Xiao and Tonny Chan, "PLA Troops Active in Tsunami Relief Work," *China Daily*, January 5, 2005, p. 1.

121. Memorandum of conversation with ministerial-level official of State Council, Beijing, China, January 12, 2005, p. 2.

122. Kenneth I. Juster, "Remarks," Conference on Asian Security and Hong Kong's Role in the War on Global Terrorism, Center for Strategic and International Studies, Washington, DC, April 28, 2003, www.bis.doc.gov/news/2003/HongKongJuster Speech4_28.htm (accessed June 30, 2006).

123. This entire section draws heavily on David M. Lampton and Richard Daniel Ewing, *The U.S.-China Relationship Facing International Security Crises* (Washington, DC: Nixon Center, 2003), pp. 8–9.

124. "Container Security Proposal Cooperation between Customs of China, US Launched," Xinhua, April 27, 2005, FBIS, NewsEdge Doc. No. 200504271477.1_893a002fda64d7a7.

125. Ministry of Foreign Affairs, "Strengthening Cooperation."

126. "Russian-Chinese Declaration Supports Russian Involvement in Asia-Pacific Region," ITAR-TASS, October 14, 2004, FBIS-SOV-2004-1014.

127. "First Security Policy Conference of ASEAN Regional Forum Will Be Held in Beijing," Xinhua, October 26, 2004, FBIS-CHI-2004-1026.

128. Bates Gill, "China's Evolving Regional Security Strategy," in *Power Shift: China and Asia's New Dynamics,* ed. David Shambaugh (Berkeley: University of California Press, 2005), pp. 247–65.

129. State Council Information Office, *China's National Defense, 2004,* p. 107.

130. Office of the Secretary of Defense, *Annual Report to Congress: Military Power of the People's Republic of China, 2006,* p. 28.

131. Shen Dingli, "Nuclear Deterrence," 12.

132. Notes of remarks to congressional staff by Caterpillar Corporation representative William C. Lane, U.S. Senate, Mansfield Room, S-207, Washington, DC, May 31, 2006, p. 1.

133. "Mainland Pushes Forward Direct Links with Taiwan," *Financial Times,* January 24, 2006, Lexis-Nexis; Bureau of East Asian and Pacific Affairs of the United States Department of State, "Background Note: Taiwan," April 2006, www.state.gov/r/pa/ei/bgn/35855.htm (accessed July 3, 2006); "Taiwan Premier Reveals 71% of Country's FDI Is in China," *Asia Pulse,* May 5, 2006, Lexis-Nexis.

134. Andrew Scobell, "China and North Korea: From Comrades-in-Arms to Allies at Arms Length," unpublished manuscript, March 2004, pp. 23–24.

135. Anna Fifield and Stephanie Kirchgaessner, "China Bank Freezes N Korean Accounts," *Financial Times,* July 26, 2006, p. 1.

136. Jeremy Paltiel, "How China Got North Korea Back to the Table," *Globe and Mail,* November 1, 2006, p. A25.

137. Greg Torode, "N Korean Ship Cleared to Leave," *South China Morning Post,* January 4, 2007, p. A2.

138. David Murphy, "Softening at the Edges," *Far Eastern Economic Review,* November 4, 2004, p. 36, www.feer.com/articles/2004/0411_04/p032china.html (accessed July 3, 2006).

139. "Chinese People Enjoy Better Life after 3 Years in WTO," *People's Daily,* December 29, 2004, http://english.people.com.cn/200412/29/eng20041229_169034.html (accessed June 30, 2006).

140. Chen-yuan Tung, "China's Economic Leverage and Taiwan's Security Concerns with Respect to Cross-Strait Economic Relations" (PhD diss., Johns Hopkins University, May 2002), p. 478.

141. Confucius, *The Analects of Confucius,* ed. Arthur Waley (New York: Vintage Books, 1989), book 13, verse 3.

142. Nicholas R. Lardy and Daniel H. Rosen, *Prospects for a Taiwan Free Trade Agreement* (Washington, DC: Institute for International Economics, 2004), p. 45.

143. Notes of remarks by Daniel Rosen at Institute for International Economics book release, Washington, DC, December 10, 2004, p. 2.

144. United Nations Conference on Trade and Development, *World Investment Report* 2005, www.unctad.org/wir or www.unctad.org/fdistatistics; for 2000–2003 statistics, see American Chamber of Commerce in Taipei, *2004 Taiwan White Paper* (Taipei: American Chamber of Commerce, May 2004), pp. 7–8.

145. Interview with senior official, June 2005, p. 1 of author's notes.

146. Editorial, "It's Taiwan's Right to Change," *Taipei Times*, December 9, 2004, p. 8, www.taipeitimes.com/News/editorials/archives/2004/12/09/2003214375 (accessed July 3, 2006).

147. Interview with Minister James Huang, Taipei, Taiwan, June 5, 2007, p. 3 of author's notes.

148. "Chinese Ambassador to Vanuatu Says Hit by Fist-Waving Prime Minister?" *China Post*, December 6, 2004, www.chinapost.com.tw/i_latestdetail.asp?id=24761 (accessed December 13, 2004); see also "Australia Towing China's Line: Taiwan," Australian Associated Press, November 28, 2004, http://taiwansecurity.org/News/2004/AAP-281104.htm (accessed July 3, 2006).

149. Joy Su, "Are Vanuatu Ties for Real? Who Knows?" *Taipei Times*, November 14, 2004, FBIS-CHI-2004-1115.

150. Joy Su, "Opponent to Diplomatic Ties Moved," *Taipei Times*, November 17, 2004, FBIS-CHI-2004-1117.

151. Joe McDonald, "China-Taiwan Rivalry Helps Poor Countries," Associated Press, November 18, 2004, Lexis-Nexis.

152. Virginia Marsh, "Australia Reaffirms Interventionist Stance on South Pacific," *Financial Times*, December 13, 2004, http://news.ft.com/cms/s/8244809e-4cac-11d9-835a-00000e2511c8.html (accessed July 3, 2006).

153. Melody Chen, "Vanuatu's Prime Minister Gets the Boot," *Taipei Times*, December 12, 2004, p. 6, www.taipeitimes.com/News/taiwan/archives/2004/12/12/2003214749 (accessed July 3, 2006).

154. Craig Skehan, "Chinese Hail Diplomatic Win in Vanuatu," *Sydney Morning Herald*, December 14, 2004, www.smh.com.au/news/World/Chinese-hail-diplomatic-win-in-Vanuatu/2004/12/13/1102787017702.html.

155. Wu Yi, "Speech on Taiwan-Related Proposal," Fifty-sixth World Health Assembly, May 19, 2003, www.china-un.ch/eng/zmjg/jgthsm/t85542.htm (accessed July 3, 2006).

156. Dr. Wu-Lien Wei, "Taiwan in the World Health Organization: A Prescription for Good Health," *Asia Pacific Network*, May 17, 2004, www.roc-taiwan.org/la/press/20040519/2004051901.html (accessed July 3, 2006).

157. U.S. Department of State, "Taiwan—Severe Acute Respiratory Syndrome and the World Health Organization," April 9, 2003, www.state.gov/r/pa/prs/ps/2003/19472.htm.

158. Memorandum of conversation with senior Australian official, Washington, DC, September 30, 2004, p. 2.

159. Notes of conversation with senior Foreign Ministry official, Beijing, China, August 7, 2006, p. 1.

160. "Zambian Leader Apologizes to Chinese Gov't," Xinhua, September 1, 2006, www.chinadaily.com.cn/china/2006-09/01/content_678884.htm (accessed September 1, 2006).

161. Stephen M. Walt, *The Origins of Alliances* (Ithaca: Cornell University Press, 1987), p. 284.

3. MONEY

Epigraphs: "GM Launches Aggressive Expansion in China," Xinhua, June 23, 2004, http://news.xinhuanet.com/english/2004-06/23/content_1542772.htm (accessed July 5, 2006); Edmund L. Andrews, "Snow Urges Consumerism on China Trip," *New York Times*, October 14, 2005, pp. C1, C5.

1. Angus Maddison, *The World Economy: A Millennial Perspective* (Paris: Organisation for Economic Co-operation and Development, 2001), Appendix B, p. 263.

2. International Monetary Fund, *World Economic Outlook Database, April 2007*, www.imf.org/external/pubs/ft/weo/2007/01/data/weorept.aspx?sy=1990&ey=2008&scsm=1&ssd=1&sort=country&ds=.&br=1&c=924&s=PPPSH&grp=0&a=&pr.x=50&pr.y=10#download (accessed July 20, 2007); for similar figures, see Maddison, *World Economy*, Appendix B, Table B-20, p. 263, http://www.imf.org/external/pubs/ft/weo/2007/01/data/weoselgr.aspx.

3. Alan Heston, Robert Summers, and Bettina Aten, Penn World Table, Version 6.1, Center for International Comparisons at the University of Pennsylvania, October 2002, http://pwt.econ.upenn.edu/php_site/pwt61_form.php (accessed July 5, 2006).

4. Notes of meeting with Premier Wen Jiabao, New York City, December 7, 2003, p. 1.

5. James Kynge, Chris Giles, and James Harding, "China Tells US to Put Its House in Order," *Financial Times*, November 23, 2004, p. 1.

6. Notes of remarks by senior Chinese scholar, Washington, DC, February 2, 2005, p. 1.

7. Lester R. Brown, "China Replacing the United States as World's Leading Consumer," Earth Policy Institute, Washington, DC, February 16, 2005, www.earth-policy.org/Updates/Update45.htm (accessed July 11, 2007).

8. L. Alan Winters and Shahid Yusuf, eds., *Dancing with Giants: China, India, and the Global Economy* (Washington, DC: World Bank and Institute of Policy Studies, 2007), p. 6, table 1.1.

9. Nicholas R. Lardy, *China: Toward a Consumption-Driven Growth Path*, Policy

Briefs in International Economics (Washington, DC: Institute for International Economics, October 2006).

10. Pieter Bottelier, China Seminar, American Enterprise Institute, January 10, 2005, p. 4; see also Economist Intelligence Unit, "China Economy: The Frugal Giant," EIU Viewswire, September 23, 2005, www.viewswire.com/index.asp?layout=display_print &doc_id=589440844 (accessed October 5, 2005); and Pieter Bottelier, "Is China Investing and Saving Too Much While Consuming Too Little?" unpublished manuscript, January 6, 2006, pp. 1 and 5.

11. For 2003 rate, see International Monetary Fund, *People's Republic of China: 2004 Article IV Consultation* (Washington, DC: International Monetary Fund, 2004), p. 30. For 2005 rate, see International Monetary Fund, *People's Republic of China: 2006 Article IV Consultation* (Washington, DC: International Monetary Fund, 2006), p. 5.

12. Lawrence H. Summers, "The U.S. Current Account Deficit and the Global Economy," Per Jacobsson Lecture, Per Jacobsson Foundation, Washington, DC, October 3, 2004, www.perjacobsson.org/2004/100304.pdf (accessed July 5, 2006), p. 6.

13. "New 5-Year Plan to See Revolutionary Changes," Xinhua, October 11, 2005, http://news.xinhuanet.com/english/2005-10/11/content_3606173.htm (accessed August 2, 2006).

14. Global Fund to Fight AIDS, Tuberculosis, and Malaria, "Stopping Tuberculosis in China," www.theglobalfund.org/en/in_action/china/tb1/ (accessed August 28, 2006). See also Global Fund to Fight AIDS, Tuberculosis, and Malaria, "China Signs New Global Fund HIV and TB Grants Worth US$52 Million," www.theglobalfund .org/en/media_center/press/pr_050602.asp (accessed August 28, 2006).

15. Ministry of Education of the People's Republic of China, "2002 nian gelei jiaoyu fazhan jiben tongji" [Various key educational development statistics in 2002], www.moe .edu.cn/edoas/website18/info7901.htm (accessed August 2, 2006). For U.S. figures, see National Center for Education Statistics, *Digest of Education Statistics, 2002* (Washington, DC: U.S. Department of Education, 2003), tables 252–54. For data on science and engineering students in the United States, see President's Council of Advisors on Science and Technology, *Assessing the U.S. R&D Investment* (Washington, DC: Office of Science and Technology Policy, 2002), www.ostp.gov/PCAST/FINAL%20R&D %20REPORT%20WITH%20LETTERS.pdf.

16. Diana Farrell and Andrew J. Grant, "China's Looming Talent Shortage," *McKinsey Quarterly*, no. 4 (2005), www.mckinseyquarterly.com/article_page.aspx?ar =1685&L2=18&L3=31 (accessed July 12, 2006).

17. EIU Riskwire, "China Finance: Japanese and South Korean Investment Migrates South," February 11, 2005, http://riskwire.eiu.com/index.asp?layout=display_print &doc_id=308021630 (accessed February 15, 2005).

18. Liu Li, "Top Firms Join Fight against AIDS, TB in Guangdong," *China Daily*, September 12, 2006, p. 1.

19. World Bank, *2005 World Development Indicators* (Washington, DC: World Bank, 2005), pp. 120–22; and *2004 World Development Indicators* (Washington, DC: World Bank, 2004), pp. 108–9.

20. World Bank, *2005 World Development Indicators*, pp. 120–21; and *2004 World Development Indicators*, p. 108.

21. "Middle Class Society a Long Way Off," *China Daily*, February 18, 2005, http://en.ce.cn/National/Government/200502/18/t20050218_3102951.shtml (accessed July 7, 2006).

22. Xin Zhigang, "Dissecting China's 'Middle Class,'" *China Daily*, October 27, 2004, www.chinadaily.com.cn/english/doc/2004-10/27/content_386060.htm; "China's Middle Class Ushered in at 60,000 Yuan," Xinhua, January 20, 2005, www.chinadaily.com.cn/english/doc/2005-01/20/content_410777.htm (accessed July 8, 2006).

23. "Zhongguo de zhongchan jieceng zai nali?" [Where is China's middle class?], *Caijing Zongheng* [Tom Finance News], http://finance.tom.com/1327/2005120-149458.html (accessed August 2, 2006); Xin Zhigang, "Dissecting China's 'Middle Class,'"; "Middle Class Society"; "China's Middle Class."

24. "Diaocha: Yueru wuqian zhongchan jieceng zhan jiuye renkou jin 12% ping" [Survey: Monthly income 5000 yuan—middle class composes 12% of working population], Xinhua, September 5, 2005, http://news.xinhuanet.com/fortune/2005-09/05/content_3445657.htm (accessed August 2, 2006).

25. "China Has 80 Million Middle Class Members," *China Daily*, June 19, 2007, www.chinadaily.com.cn/bizchina/2007-06/19-content_897583.htm (accessed July 20, 2007).

26. Hong Liang and Ning Ma, "China's Property Market: Fallacies of an Imminent Bubble Burst," *Goldman Sachs Economic Flash*, December 10, 2004, www.gs.com/hkchina/insight/research/pdf/China_Property_Market_Fallacies_of_Bubble_Burst_12-10-04.pdf, pp. 3–4.

27. "Diaocha xinxian chulu 30wan dajuan jie 'zhongchan jieceng,' de shenmi miansha" [Newly completed survey of 300,000 lifts the mysterious shroud surrounding "the middle class"], *Caijing Zongheng* [Tom Finance News], January 21, 2005, http://finance.news.tom.com/1001/1002/2005121-149955.html (accessed August 2, 2006).

28. Ernst and Young, "China: The New Lap of Luxury," September 2005, www.ey.com; see also "China on a Spree in Luxury Market," *International Herald Tribune*, March 25–26, 2006, p. 17, originally published in the *Boston Globe*.

29. Mark Landler, "Short History, Long View," *New York Times*, March 3, 2007, p. B1.

30. Stephen Fitzgerald, *China and the Overseas Chinese: A Study of Peking's Changing Policy, 1949–1970* (Cambridge: Cambridge University Press, 1972).

31. "Overseas Chinese Entrepreneurs Shift Investment Focuses," *People's Daily*, February 13, 2004, http://english1.people.com.cn/200402/13/print20040213_134728.html (accessed August 2, 2006).

32. Chan Heng Chee, "ASEAN's Relations with China: An Evolving Relationship," address delivered at Johns Hopkins-SAIS, Washington, DC, April 25, 2005, p. 4.

33. "Overseas Chinese Firms Awarded for Contributions to China's Economy," *People's Daily,* September 29, 2003, http://english.people.com.cn/200309/29/eng 20030929_125204.shtml (accessed August 2, 2006).

34. U.S.-China Business Council, "Foreign Investment in China," March 14, 2005, table 2, www.uschina.org/statistics/2005foreigninvestment.html (accessed August 2, 2006).

35. Zhan Lisheng, "Fujian to Soak Up More Investment," *China Business Weekly,* September 14, 2004, www.chinadaily.com.cn/english/doc/2004-09/14/content_374380 .htm (accessed August 2, 2006).

36. David Zweig, Chen Changgui, and Stanley Rosen, "Globalization and Transnational Human Capital: Overseas and Returnee Scholars to China," *China Quarterly,* no. 179 (September 2004): 735–57.

37. AnnaLee Saxenian, "Secret of Success: Immigrant Networks Keep Silicon Valley on Top," Public Policy Institute of California, May 2002, www.ailf.org/ipc/policy _reports_2002_secret.asp (accessed August 2, 2006).

38. National Science Foundation, "Human Resource Contributions to U.S. Science and Engineering from China," Division of Science Resources Studies Issue Brief, January 12, 2001, www.nsf.gov/statistics/issuebrf/nsf01311/sib01311.htm (accessed August 2, 2006).

39. Hong Liu, "New Migrants and the Revival of Overseas Chinese Nationalism," *Journal of Contemporary China* 14, no. 43 (May 2005): 308, citing *Yazhou Zhoukan* [Asia Weekly], January 20, 2002.

40. AnnaLee Saxenian, *Local and Global Networks of Immigrant Professionals in Silicon Valley* (San Francisco: Public Policy Institute of California, 2002), vii, www .ppic.org/content/pubs/report/R_502ASR.pdf (accessed August 11, 2007).

41. Congressional Research Service, "China's Economic Conditions," CRS Issue Brief for Congress, January 12, 2006, www.fas.org/sgp/crs/row/IB98014.pdf (accessed August 2, 2006); see also John Henley, Colin Kirkpatrick, and Georgina Wilde, "Foreign Direct Investment (FDI) in China: Recent Trends and Current Policy Issues," 1998, table 4, pp. 12–13, http://unpan1.un.org/intradoc/groups/public/documents/ APCITY/UNPAN014359.pdf (accessed August 2, 2006).

42. Zuliu Hu and Mohsin S. Khan, *Why Is China Growing So Fast?* Economic Issues Paper No. 8 (Washington, DC: International Monetary Fund, April 1997), p. 4.

43. Yasheng Huang, "Institutional Environment and Private Sector Development in China," in *China's Economy: Retrospect and Prospect,* ed. Loren Brandt, Thomas G. Rawski, and Gang Lin (Washington, DC: Asia Program of Woodrow Wilson International Center for Scholars, July 2005), p. 26. In Zhejiang Province in 2004, 91 percent

of all enterprises were privately owned. See "On the Capitalist Road," *Economist Intelligence Unit*, March 19, 2004, www.viewswire.com (accessed March 20, 2004).

44. "Private Business Mushrooming in East China Province," Xinhua, September 23, 2004, FBIS-CHI-2004-0923.

45. Richard McGregor, "China Economy: Private Sector 'in Control of China Economy,'" *Financial Times*, September 14, 2005, www.viewswire.com (accessed October 5, 2005); "China Economy: A Model of Reform," *Economist*, September 16, 2005, www.viewswire.com (accessed October 5, 2005).

46. Lee Branstetter and Nicholas Lardy, "China's Embrace of Globalization," in Brandt, Rawski, and Gang Lin, *China's Economy*, p. 6; see also "PRC Administrative Licensing Law, Revised Foreign Trade Law to Take Effect 1 July," Xinhua, June 30, 2004, FBIS-CHI-2004-0630.

47. Nicholas R. Lardy, "Trade Liberalization and Its Role in Chinese Economic Growth," paper prepared for an International Monetary Fund and National Council of Applied Economic Research Conference, "A Tale of Two Giants: India's and China's Experience with Reform and Growth," New Delhi, November 14–16, 2003.

48. "New 5-Year Plan."

49. David Dollar, Anqing Shi, Shuilin Wang, and Lixin Colin Xu, "Improving City Competitiveness through the Investment Climate: Ranking 23 Chinese Cities," unpublished manuscript, World Bank, December 2003.

50. Hu and Khan, *Why Is China Growing So Fast?* p. 8.

51. Keith Bradsher, "China Economy Rising at Pace to Rival U.S.," *New York Times*, June 28, 2005, pp. A1, C6.

52. Kimberly McGinnis, "Searching for Autopia," *Insight*, magazine of the Shanghai Branch of the American Chamber of Commerce, April 2006, p. 21.

53. Gary Clyde Hufbauer and Yee Wong, "China Bashing 2004," International Economics Policy Briefs, Institute for International Economics, no. PB04-5 (September 2004), p. 27.

54. Branstetter and Lardy, "China's Embrace of Globalization," p. 11.

55. Art Pine, "China Steals the Spotlight on the Global Stage," *Independent Online Ltd. Business Report*, July 7, 2004, www.businessreport.co.za/general/print_article.php ?fArticleId=2140425&fSectionId=553&fSetId=304 (accessed August 2, 2006).

56. Hufbauer and Wong, "China Bashing 2004," p. 27.

57. Louis Uchitelle, "When the Chinese Consumer Is King," *New York Times*, December 14, 2003, p. 5.

58. "Han dui zhongguo jingji yilaidu zheng 3.6bei 400wan renkou zhongguo shenghuo" [South Korea's economic dependence on China increases 3.6 fold, 4 million people depend on China for living], *Renmin Ribao* [People's Daily], January 28, 2005, http://world.people.com.cn/GB/1029/3152061.html (accessed August 2, 2006).

59. UN Commodity Trade Statistics Database, http://unstats.un.org/unsd/comtrade/.

60. Chan Heng Chee, "ASEAN's Relations with China," p. 7.

61. Kristi Heim, "As Competition Heats Up, Jobs Fly into China," *Seattle Times,* June 20, 2005, http://seattletimes.nwsource.com/html/businesstechnology/2002319842_boeingchina07.html (accessed August 2, 2006); see also "Airbus to Look at Building Jets in China," *New York Times,* December 5, 2005, p. A5. For deal in Tianjin, see "Airbus Inks Tianjin Plant Deal," *China Daily* (Business), June 29, 2007, p. 13.

62. "Putin Aide Says Issues of Russian Oil Supplies to China Resolved," RIA, April 6, 2005, FBIS, Doc. No. 200504061477.1_187f0034ececfd8e.

63. Pieter Bottelier, Chart, "China Is Driving Global Commodity Demand for Key Commodities," unpublished charts and tables provided to me by Professor Bottelier.

64. See Kerry Dumbaugh and Mark P. Sullivan, "China's Growing Interest in Latin America" (Washington, DC: Congressional Research Service, 2005), RS22110 (April 20, 2005), p. 2; "China Industry: Will China Be Allowed to Find Trade Markets in Latin America?" *Economist Intelligence Unit,* February 15, 2005, www.viewswire.com (accessed February 15, 2005).

65. Interview with strategic analyst, Canberra, Australia, June 24, 2005, p. 1 of author's notes. In fact, Australia possesses less than this percentage of global uranium reserves.

66. Interview with senior official, Canberra, Australia, June 23, 2005, p. 3 of author's notes.

67. "Colombian President Welcomes PRC Investment in Oil," Xinhua, April 7, 2005, FBIS, Doc. No. 200504071477.1_54620001fafadd7f3.

68. "Oil Primary Russian Export to China, Cooperation on Joint Projects to Continue," ITAR-TASS, April 6, 2005, FBIS, Doc. No. 200504061477.1_b57c00b24396bbb.

69. Howard W. French, "China in Africa: All Trade, with No Political Baggage," *New York Times,* August 8, 2004, p. 4.

70. Hu Shuli, "CNOOC, Unocal and the 'Go-Out Strategy,'" *Caijing* [Finance], no. 139 (June 25, 2005), http://caijing.hexun.com/english/detail.aspx?issue=139&id=1251372 (accessed August 2, 2006).

71. George Chellah and Kwenda Paipi, "Zambians Will Rise if Polls Are Rigged Says Sata," *Post* (Lusaka), August 22, 2006, http://allafrica.com/stories/printable/200608220747.html (accessed September 2, 2006).

72. Igor Verba, "Timber as a Mirror of Neighborly Relations," *Moscow Nezavisimaya Gazeta,* November 1, 2004, FBIS-CHI-2004-1103.

73. Patricia Campos Mello and Jo Baumer, "Losses Resulting from Rejected Shipments Already Amount to $250 Million," *O Estado de Sao Paulo,* June 1, 2004, FBIS-LAT-2004-0601. For the Chinese side of the story, see "China, Brazil Reach Understanding in Soybean Trade Dispute," Xinhua, June 22, 2004, FBIS-CHI-2004-0622.

74. Notes of conversation with former Brazilian minister, Portugal, May 18, 2006, p. 1.

75. Notes of remarks by former European foreign minister, Portugal, May 20, 2006, p. 4 (quoted with permission of the minister given the conference rules).

76. Zhang Dingmin, "Country Not Cutting US Dollar Holdings," *China Daily*, December 11–12, 2004, p. 1.

77. "Bank Official Attaches Importance to Holding Euro Assets," Xinhua, March 7, 2005, FBIS, Doc. No. 200503071477.1_2917001d9d924b34.

78. United Nations Industrial Development Organization, *Industrial Development Report 2005: Capability Building for Catching-Up* (Vienna: United Nations Industrial Development Organization, 2005), p. 131.

79. Ibid., pp. 131, 157, and 160.

80. U.S.-China Business Council, "China's Trade Performance," http://uschina .org/statistics/economy.html, April 2006, and "PRC Economic Statistics through 2005," http://uschina.org/statistics/economy.html (both accessed August 3, 2006).

81. "FIEs Accounted for More Than 50% of China's Exports in 2005," *China Knowledge*, June 9, 2006, www.chinaknowledge.com/news/news-detail.aspx?ID=3333 (accessed June 15, 2006). For the 2003 figure, see Pieter Bottelier, chart, "Share of Foreign Invested Companies in China's Exports, 1985–2003," sources Chinese Ministry of Commerce and IMF, unpublished charts and tables provided to me by Professor Bottelier.

82. "China Technology: I Spy Spies," *Economist Intelligence Unit*, February 5, 2005, www.viewswire.com (accessed February 5, 2005).

83. "Foreign-Funded Firms Contribute to Nearly 90 Pct of High-Tech Exports via Shanghai Port," Xinhua, January 24, 2005, FBIS, NewsEdge Doc. No. 200501241477.1 _567100174eb9a1db.

84. Michael S. Chase, Kevin L. Pollpeter, and James C. Mulvenon, *Shanghaied? The Economic and Political Implications of the Flow of Information Technology and Investment across the Taiwan Strait* (Santa Monica, CA: RAND, 2004), p. xiii.

85. Lawrence J. Lau, "China's Economy and Implications for U.S. Policy," in *U.S.-China Relations*, Report of the Fourth Congressional Conference of the Aspen Institute, ed. Dick Clark (Washington, DC: Aspen Institute, 2002), p. 23.

86. Andy Xie, "Don't Fear U.S. Backlash," *Morgan Stanley Equity Research Newsletter*, January 12, 2005, p. 2. Pieter Bottelier, "China Import Surcharges Bill Will Damage US," *Financial Times* (London), February 8, 2005, p. 12, Lexis-Nexis, gives an estimated range of four to six million "jobs in the US related to the domestic distribution and sale of imports from China."

87. For a thorough study of FDI and its successes and problems, see Yasheng Huang, *Selling China: Foreign Direct Investment during the Reform Era* (New York: Cambridge University Press, 2003).

88. "China's Champions: The Struggle of the Champions," *Economist*, January 6, 2005, www.economist.com/display_story.cfm?story_id=3535818 (accessed August 3, 2006).

89. "China's Defence, Economy at Risk from Machine Tool Technology Imports: Official," Xinhua, April 21, 2007, http://news.xinhuanet.com/english/2007-04/21/content_6007730.htm (accessed August 11, 2007).

90. Chinese Academy of Engineering, "Getting the Market to Play a Guiding Role and Cultivating Innovation Capacity," *CAE Newsletter*, March 2006, www.cae.cn/english/publications/content.jsp?id=1060 (accessed September 8, 2006).

91. See Jiang Wei, "EU Seeking Shoe Protectionism," *China Daily* (Business), June 9, 2005, p. 9, http://app.ccpit.org/servlet/org.servlet.fronthomepage.org.en.OrgOrg/NewsViewEnG?org_id=56&id=27964 (accessed July 12, 2007).

92. "Twenty Now Held over Attacks on Chinese Businesses in Spain," *El Pais*, September 30, 2004, FBIS-WEU-2004-0930.

93. Jia Heping, "Textile Producers Rush to Foreign Lands," *China Business Weekly*, November 22–28, 2004, p. 8.

94. Daniel Rosen, personal communication, August 2, 2005.

95. Celia W. Dugger, "U.N. Report Cites U.S. and Japan as the 'Least Generous Donors,'" *New York Times*, September 8, 2005, p. A6.

96. Conversation with Mexican scholars, Washington, DC, cited in David M. Lampton, testimony, *Hearing on the "Role of China in Latin America," Senate Foreign Relations Subcommittee on Western Hemisphere, Peace Corps and Narcotics Affairs*, September 20, 2005, p. 6.

97. Interview with Australian strategic policy analyst, Canberra, Australia, June 24, 2005, p. 2 of author's notes.

98. John Weiss, "People's Republic of China and Its Neighbors: Partners or Competitors for Trade and Investment?" ADB [Asian Development Bank] Institute Discussion Paper no. 13 (August 2004), p. 7, www.adbi.org/discussion-paper/2004/08/24/547.prc.and.neighbors/ (accessed July 11, 2007).

99. "South Korean Steelmakers Wary of Rising Chinese Steel Imports," *Yonhap*, January 4, 2005, FBIS-CHI-2005-0104.

100. Ministry of Commerce, People's Republic of China, "Main Mandate of the Ministry of Commerce," http://english.mofcom.gov.cn/mission/mission/html (accessed July 25, 2005).

101. Friedrich Wu, "The Globalization of Corporate China," *NBR Analysis* 16 (December 2005): 6.

102. "Philippines, China Sign Loan, Investment Agreements," Agence France Presse, April 27, 2005, FBIS, Doc. No. 200504271477.1_004e0031d2f626c.

103. "China Briefing," *Far Eastern Economic Review*, November 20, 2003, www.feer.com/articles/2003/0311_20/po28china.html (accessed July 27, 2006).

104. Notes of remarks by East African businessperson, Portugal, May 18 and 20, 2006, pp. 1, 4.

105. "Singapore Can Help Chinese Companies Internationalize: Minister," Xinhua, October 12, 2004, FBIS-CHI-2004-1012.

106. "Cheery News from the DPRK: Wenzhou Merchants Seize Groundfloor Business Opportunity," *CND*, www.cnd.org, August 2, 2004.

107. Asia Pacific Foundation of Canada and China Council for the Promotion of International Trade, *China Goes Global-II: A Survey of Chinese Companies' Outward Direct Investment Intentions* (December 2006), p. 13, www.asiapacific.ca.

108. Jiang Wei and Hu Meidong, "Council Set Up to Promote Investment," *China Daily*, July 26, 2006, p. 9, www.chinadaily.com.cn/bizchina/2006-07/26/content _649478.htm (accessed July 11, 2007). Another Chinese source provides the figure of $57.2 billion of cumulative Chinese FDI through the end of 2005, http://news.xinhua net.com/fortune/2006-09/04/content_5046631.htm (accessed September 4, 2006).

109. "Ministry: Chinese Firms' Overseas Investments up 27 Percent in 2004 Year-on-Year," February 7, 2005, Xinhua, FBIS, Doc. No. 200502071477.1_8c36 00157f8b1246; also Owen Brown, "China's Direct Investment Abroad Rises 27%," *Wall Street Journal*, February 8, 2005, p. A16.

110. Economist Intelligence Unit, "Rising Overseas Investment by Chinese Companies Will Help Keep Despots around the World in Business Longer," Viewswire, November 21, 2006, www.viewswire.com (accessed November 26, 2006).

111. Wu, "Globalization of Corporate China," p. 7.

112. Eunsuk Hong and Laixiang Sun, "Dynamics of Internationalization and Outward Investment: Chinese Corporations' Strategies," *China Quarterly*, no. 187 (September 2006): 615.

113. "China Pours More Money Overseas," *China Daily*, October 22, 2004, http:// news.xinhuanet.com/english/2004-10/22/content_2124563.htm (accessed August 3, 2006).

114. "China's Hu Boosts Kenyan Business," *BBC News*, http://news.bbc.co.uk/ 2/hi/africa/4953588.stm (accessed August 4, 2006).

115. Nick Bunkley, "Revival in Oklahoma," *New York Times*, July 12, 2006, pp. C1– C2; see also Bloomberg.com, "Chinese Company to Build MGs in Oklahoma," *Business Ticker*, July 13, 2006.

116. Li Xin, "Lobbying the United States," *Caijing* [Finance], no. 165 (August 7, 2006).

117. Greater London Authority Economics, *Enter the Dragon: An Analysis of Chinese FDI into London* (London: Greater London Authority, December 2004), pp. 10 and 12, figures 8 and 10.

118. "Celebration in London Marking Closer Business Links with China," Xinhua, February 8, 2005, FBIS, Doc. No. 200502081477.1_91fc004793101a3e.

119. Boris Savelyev, "Russia, China Agree to Step Up Investment Cooperation," Moscow ITAR-TASS, June 9, 2004, FBIS-SOV-2004-0609; see also "Russian Minister Says China 'Main Strategic Partner,'" ITAR-TASS, June 9, 2004, FBIS-SOV-2004-0609.

120. "National Social Security Fund to Invest Overseas," *Economist Intelligence Unit,* April 27, 2004, www.viewswire.com (accessed May 2, 2004).

121. "China Allows Investing Abroad," *Honolulu Advertiser,* April 14, 2006, p. A8; Zhang Ran, "Private Foreign Currency to Be Invested Abroad," *China Daily,* July 25, 2006, p. 9.

122. David Wessel, "Rubin Presses China on Size of Its Reserves," *Wall Street Journal,* September 29, 1997, p. 6.

123. Notes of conversation with senior Australian officials, Canberra, Australia, June 22, 2005, p. 5.

124. Notes of business roundtable meeting, Jakarta, Indonesia, June 17, 2005, p. 5.

125. "Roundup on Press Reaction to Chinese President Hu Jintao's Visit [to] Brazil," *FBIS Report,* November 16, 2004, FBIS-EAS-2004-1116.

126. "Editorial: China's Disquieting Bid for Noranda," *Toronto Star,* October 5, 2004, p. A18.

127. Bruce D. Larkin, *China and Africa, 1949–1970: The Foreign Policy of the People's Republic of China* (Berkeley: University of California Press, 1971), p. 93.

128. World Bank, *World Development Indicators 2005,* p. 350.

129. World Bank, World Development Indicators database, http://devdata.world bank.org/dataonline/SMResult.asp (accessed June 15, 2006).

130. "Meiguoren yanzhong de zhongguo jiuzai xingxiang: Haixiaozhong shengqi de zhongguo xing" [Americans' image of China's disaster aid: In the tsunami China's star rises], *Huashengdun Guancha* [Washington Observer], January 19, 2005, http://news. xinhuanet.com/overseas/2005-01/19/content_2479503.htm (accessed August 3, 2006).

131. Memorandum of conversation with ministerial-level official of the State Council, Beijing, China, January 12, 2005, pp. 1–2.

132. Jim Fisher-Thompson, "China No Threat to United States in Africa, U.S. Official Says," press release, July 29, 2005, www.usembassy-china.org.cn/press/ release/2005/072905chi.html (accessed September 2, 2005); see also Vivienne Walt, "China's African Safari," *Fortune,* February 20, 2006, p. 41.

133. Lei Min, "China Will Gradually Expand the Scope of Its Aid to Africa," Xinhua, December 19, 2006, FBIS, Doc. No. 200612191477.1_f6aa004b6f7487f7.

134. Jonathan Watts, "China Shifts from Receiving to Giving Foreign Aid as Economic Boom Continues," *Guardian,* December 15, 2004, http://guardian.co.uk/ china/story/0,7369,1373830,00.html (accessed July 19, 2005).

135. Peter Van Ness, *Revolution and Chinese Foreign Policy: Peking's Support for Wars of National Liberation* (Berkeley: University of California Press, 1971), p. 250.

136. French, "China in Africa," p. 4.

137. Ibid.

138. Lindsay Hilsum, "China's Big Investment," transcript of a *NewsHour with Jim Lehrer* report, July 5, 2005, www.pbs.org/newshour/bb/asia/july-deco5/china_7-05 .html (accessed August 3, 2006).

139. Walt, "China's African Safari," p. 41.

140. David Murphy, "Softening at the Edges," *Far Eastern Economic Review*, November 4, 2004, p. 36.

141. For speech in Chinese, see "Wen Jiabao zai dibaci zhongguo—dongmeng ling-daoren huiyishang de jianghua" [Wen Jiabao speech at the Eighth Leadership Summit of ASEAN], Xinhua, November 29, 2004, http://news.xinhuanet.com/world/2004-11/ 29/content_2274734.htm (accessed July 26, 2006). For English-language version, see "Main Points of Wen's Speech at ASEAN+3 Summit," Xinhua, November 29, 2004, Vientiane, Laos, http://news.xinhuanet.com/english/2004-11/29/content_2274344 .htm (accessed August 3, 2006).

142. "East Asia Summit: In the Shadow of Sharp Divisions," *People's Daily*, December 7, 2005, http://english.people.com.cn/200512/07/print20051207_226350.html (accessed December 7, 2005).

143. Notes of remarks by senior Chinese diplomat, Washington, DC, February 2, 2005, p. 4.

144. Notes of roundtable with Singapore analysts, Singapore, June 13, 2005, pp. 2–3.

145. "China Plans to Increase Energy, Telecommunications Cooperation within SCO," Interfax, September 14, 2004, FBIS-SOV-2004-0914.

146. Wang Feng, "US Emissary Urges Floating RMB," *Caijing*, June 20, 2004, http://caijing.hexun.com/english/detail.aspx?issue=161&id=1357728 (accessed August 3, 2006).

147. Memorandum of conversation with senior Australian official, Canberra, Australia, June 22, 2005.

148. "It's Stupid to Be Afraid: Spiegel Interview with Singapore's Lee Kuan Yew," *Der Spiegel*, August 8, 2005, http://service.spiegel.de/cache/international/spiegel/ 0,1518,369128,00.html (accessed July 25, 2006).

4. MINDS

Epigraphs: Notes of meeting with NPC Chairman Li Peng, New York City, August 30, 2000, p. 3; notes of meeting with senior Australian official, June 22, 2005, p. 5; "On the Record: Jack Ma," *San Francisco Chronicle*, May 7, 2006, pp. F1, F3; Wang Chong, "China Takes the Opportunity to Dispel 'China Threat' at Pacific Asia Regional Meeting of the Trilateral Commission in Beijing," *Zhongguo Qingnian Bao* [China Youth Daily], November 30, 2005, FBIS, NewsEdge Doc. No. 200511301477.1_bad0015782e9744e.

1. Wang Chueh, "Central Leadership Attach Importance to 'Soft Power,'" *Wen Wei*

Po, October 6, 2004, FBIS-CHI-2004-1006; see also Pang Zhongying, "Connotation of the Soft Power of China," *Liaowang* [Outlook], November 27, 2005, FBIS, NewsEdge Doc. No. 200511271477.1_9b5e00efe23f9414.

2. Joseph S. Nye Jr., *Soft Power: The Means to Success in World Politics* (New York: Public Affairs, 2004).

3. Notes of meeting with senior Chinese foreign affairs official, Beijing, China, November 4, 2005, p. 3.

4. Notes of remarks by important Chinese foreign policy official, Beijing, China, November 3, 2005, p. 1.

5. Lee Kuan Yew, *From Third World to First: The Singapore Story, 1965–2000* (New York: HarperCollins, 2000), p. 624.

6. Interview with economist in Singapore, June 14, 2005, pp. 2–3 of author's notes.

7. Notes of remarks at conference, Beijing, China, September 27, 2005, p. 1.

8. Zhiyue Bo, "The Provinces," in *China's Leadership in the 21st Century: The Rise of the Fourth Generation,* ed. David M. Finkelstein and Maryanne Kivlehan (Armonk, NY: M. E. Sharpe, 2003), pp. 66–117.

9. Cheng Li, "New Provincial Chiefs: Hu's Groundwork for the 17th Party Congress," *China Leadership Monitor,* no. 13 (Winter 2005): 3, www.chinaleadership monitor.org.

10. Ibid., pp. 4–5.

11. Ibid., pp. 3–6.

12. James Mulvenon, "The King Is Dead! Long Live the King! The CMC Leadership Transition from Jiang to Hu," *China Leadership Monitor,* no. 13 (Winter 2005): 6, www.chinaleadershipmonitor.org.

13. David Shambaugh, *Modernizing China's Military: Progress, Problems, and Prospects* (Berkeley: University of California Press, 2002), p. 13.

14. Bruce J. Dickson, *Red Capitalists in China: The Party, Private Entrepreneurs, and Prospects for Political Change* (Cambridge: Cambridge University Press, 2003); Margaret M. Pearson, *China's New Business Elite: The Political Consequences of Economic Reform* (Berkeley: University of California Press, 1997); Kang Xiaoguang, "An Analysis of Political Stability in Mainland China in the Next Three to Five Years," *Strategy and Management,* June 1, 2002, pp. 1–15.

15. Cheng Li, "The Rise of China's Yuppie Corps: Top CEOs to Watch," *China Leadership Monitor,* no. 14 (Spring 2005): 2, http://chinaleadershipmonitor.org.

16. Ibid., p. 17.

17. Jae Cheol Kim, "From the Fringe to the Center: The Political Emergence of Private Entrepreneurs in China," *Issues and Studies* 41 (September 2005): 119.

18. Richard McGregor, "China Goes beyond the Party for Key Post," *Financial Times,* June 29, 2007, www.ft.com/cms/s/1b1c3e40-2623-11dc-8e18-000b5df10621 .html (accessed July 11, 2007).

19. Cheng Li, "Rise of China's Yuppie Corps."

20. Ibid., p. 6, and pp. 9–12 for other data in this paragraph.

21. Zhang Lu and Vincent Lam, "Dairy Firm Looks Abroad for New Head," *China Daily*, September 28, 2005, Business Section, p. 9.

22. Notes of meeting with Professor Zhao Shuming, School of Business, Nanjing University, Johns Hopkins-SAIS, Washington, DC, March 13, 2006, p. 1.

23. "Training for Chinese Software Personnel," *Hindu*, January 27, 2005, FBIS, NewsEdge Doc. No. 200501271477.1_a3530028d65flcb7.

24. Mansour Javidan and Nandani Lynton, "The Changing Face of the Chinese Executive," *Harvard Business Review* 83 (December 2005): 28, 30.

25. World Bank, *World Development Indicators 2005* (Washington, DC: World Bank, 2005), p. 88.

26. National Science Foundation, *Science and Engineering Indicators 2006* (Arlington, VA: National Science Foundation), ch. 2, "Higher Education in Science and Engineering," pp. 2–34, www.nsf.gov/statistics/seind06/.

27. Nye, *Soft Power*, p. 46.

28. Institute of International Education, "Open Doors 2005: Report on International Educational Exchange. Leading Places of Origin," http://opendoors.iienetwork .org/?p=69691 (accessed November 8, 2005).

29. Organisation for Economic Co-operation and Development [OECD], *OECD Science, Technology and Industry Outlook 2006* (Paris: OECD, 2006), pp. 36–37.

30. "Human Resources in S&T in Non-OECD Economies," *OECD Science, Technology and Industry Scoreboard 2005* (Paris: OECD, 2005), p. 65.

31. "Over 700,000 Chinese Receive Overseas Education," Xinhua, http://news .xinhuanet.com/english/2004-05/22/content_1484369.htm (accessed July 19, 2006).

32. UNESCO Institute for Statistics, "Foreign Students by Country of Origin," http://stats.uis.unesco.org/TableViewer/tableView.aspx (accessed November 8, 2005).

33. OECD, *OECD Science, Technology and Industry Outlook 2006*, p. 117.

34. Notes of remarks by Joseph Nye, Center for Strategic and International Studies, Washington, DC, November 15, 2005, p 4.

35. Interview with senior NGO officer, Jakarta, Indonesia, June 18, 2005, p. 3 of author's notes.

36. Interview with former senior Australian government official, Canberra, Australia, June 23, 2005, pp. 1–2 of author's notes. For the official quotation, see "We Won't Punish Defector, Says China," *The Age*, June 6, 2005, www.theage.com.au/news/ National/We-wont-punish-defector-says-China/2005/06/06/1117910235775.html. The official quotation of Ambassador Fu is as follows: "It has become a very interesting point and a joke. If I can't attend a dinner with one of my colleagues in the diplomatic corps, if I say, 'I am busy, I'm sorry, I can't come,' they say, 'Oh, it's okay, you are busy with your spy network.'"

37. Neil King Jr., "Charm Offensive: To Win Friends, China Takes Its Message on a U.S. Road Trip," *Wall Street Journal*, November 18, 2005, p. A1.

38. Xiaohong Liu, *Chinese Ambassadors* (Seattle: University of Washington Press, 2001), pp. 203–4.

39. Phillip C. Saunders, *China's Global Activism: Strategy, Drivers, and Tools* (Washington, DC: Institute for National Strategic Studies, National Defense University, 2006), pp. 19–20.

40. "China Receives 52 Heads of State, Government in 2004: FM," Xinhua, March 6, 2005, FBIS, NewsEdge Doc. No. 200503061477.1_1a4e001b4cc6e7b.

41. "VIP Appearances," *China Vitae*, 2005, www.chinavitae.com/vipappearances/index.php (accessed October 5, 2005).

42. "China Politics: Here's Hu," *Economist*, November 3, 2005, www.economist.com/research/articlesBySubject/displayStory.cfm?story_id=5116702&subjectid=1530567.

43. Notes of conversation with senior American NGO officer, Jakarta, Indonesia, June 17, 2005, p. 3.

44. Jia Qingguo, "Peaceful Development: China's Policy of Reassurance," *Australian Journal of International Affairs* 59 (December 2005): 492–507.

45. Zhang Lihong, "President Hu Outlines Tasks for Building Innovation-Oriented Country," Xinhua, January 9, 2006, http://english.gov.cn/2006-01/09/content_151696.htm (accessed February 20, 2006); see also "China Focus: China Aims to Be One of Science Powers in World," Xinhua, February 9, 2006, FBIS, NewsEdge Doc. No. 200602091477.1_2ea2006c258fc706.

46. OECD, *OECD Science, Technology and Industry Outlook 2006*, pp. 43–44.

47. Ernst points out that "the US 'innovation score' has more than doubled from 41 (in 1985) to almost 101 (in 2002), a rate far better than for any other country. In 2002, all 15 leading companies with the best record on patent citations were based in the US, with nine of them in the electronics industry." Dieter Ernst, "Late Innovation Strategies in Asian Electronics Industries: A Conceptual Framework and Illustrative Evidence," East-West Center Working Papers, no. 66 (March 2004): 4, www.eastwestcenter.org/fileadmin/stored/pdfs/econwp066.pdf (accessed July 20, 2007). See also Jon Sigurdson et al., *Technological Superpower China* (Northampton, MA: Edward Elgar, 2005).

48. Notes of meeting with former senior CIA official, Washington, DC, June 27, 2005, p. 1; see also Dan Steinbock, "New Innovation Challenges: The Rise of China and India," *National Interest*, no. 87 (January/February 2007): 67–73.

49. "It's Stupid to Be Afraid: Spiegel Interview with Singapore's Lee Kuan Yew," *Der Spiegel*, August 8, 2005, http://service.spiegel.de/cache/international/spiegel/0,1518,369128,00.html (accessed July 19, 2006).

50. Ernst, "Late Innovation Strategies," p. 1.

51. Dieter Ernst and Barry Naughton, "Building Capabilities within Global Networks: China's Upgrading and Innovation in the IT Sector," draft paper presented at the East-West Center Conference "China's Capitalist Transition," August 11–13, 2004, pp. 1–2.

52. Geoff Dyer, "China Overtakes Japan in R&D," *Australian*, December 5, 2006, www.theaustralian.news.com.au/printpage/0,5942,20872169,00.html (accessed January 31, 2007).

53. Sonia Kolesnikov-Jessop, "Open Sesame: Alibaba.com Founder Unlocks China," *International Herald Tribune*, January 6–7, 2007, p. 12.

54. "On the Record: Jack Ma," p. F3.

55. "Chinese Manufacturers Beat U.S. Rivals," *Far Eastern Economic Review*, October 28, 2004, p. 28; also Jonathan Bell, "China's New Mantra: Innovate Not Imitate," *Far Eastern Economic Review* 170 (March 2007): 37–40.

56. Jim Pinto, "Global Manufacturing: The China Challenge," www.automation.com/sitepages/pid1779.php (accessed May 8, 2007).

57. Kathleen Walsh, *Foreign High-Tech R&D in China: Risks, Rewards, and Implications for U.S.-China Relations* (Washington, DC: Henry L. Stimson Center, 2003), p. 67.

58. U.S. Patent and Trademark Office, "Number of Utility Patent Applications Filed in the United States, by Country of Origin, Calendar Years 1965 to Present," www.uspto.gov/go/oeip/taf/appl_yr.htm (accessed July 24, 2007); OECD, *OECD Science, Technology and Industry Outlook 2006*, p. 45.

59. UNESCO, *UNESCO Science Report 2005* (Paris: UNESCO, 2005), p. 9.

60. Ibid., table "World Shares of Scientific Publications, 1991 and 2001 (in %)," p. 9.

61. "University Head Says China's Academic Ethics at Rock Bottom," *People's Daily*, July 15, 2006, http://english.people.com.cn/200607/15/eng20060715_283320.html (accessed July 19, 2006).

62. Andrew Pollack, "Cancer Therapy Dropped in U.S. Is Revived in China," *New York Times*, February 25, 2005, p. C4.

63. Francisco Moris, "U.S.-China R&D Linkages: Direct Investment and Industrial Alliances in the 1990s," InfoBrief NSF04-306 (Arlington, VA: National Science Foundation, February 2004), pp. 1–3, table 1; see also Larry Weber, testimony, U.S.-China Economic and Security Review Commission, *Hearing on China's High Technology Development*, April 21–22, 2005, www.uscc.gov/hearings/2005hearings/written_testimonies/05_21_22wrts/weber_larry_wrts.php (accessed July 20, 2007).

64. OECD, *OECD Science, Technology and Industry Outlook 2006*, p. 45.

65. "Commerce Minister Bo Xilai on Foreign Trade, Economy," *Renmin Ribao*, January 1, 2005, FBIS-CHI-2005-0103.

66. "Foreign Investors Select China as Research and Development Base," Xinhua, February 9, 2006, FBIS, NewsEdge Doc. No. 200602091477.1_a42b002be3b3a389.

67. U.S.-China Business Council, "Foreign Investment in China," p. 4, www.uschina.org/statistics/2005foreigninvestment.html (accessed July 15, 2005).

68. James Brooke, "South Korea Becoming a Big Asian Investor," *New York Times*, October 20, 2005, pp. C1, C4.

69. Walsh, *Foreign High-Tech R&D*, pp. 23–24.

70. Jiang Wei, "Outward Direct Investment to Increase," *China Daily*, September 27, 2005, p. 10.

71. "China Industry: SMTG Expands Overseas," *Economist Intelligence Unit*, November 24, 2004, www.viewswire.com (accessed November 28, 2004).

72. Dennis Normile, "Is China the Next R&D Superpower?" *Electronic Business*, July 1, 2005, www.reed-electronics.com/eb-mag/article/CA610433 (accessed July 20, 2006).

73. Eunsuk Hong and Laixiang Sun, "Dynamics of Internationalization and Outward Investment: Chinese Corporations' Strategies," *China Quarterly*, no. 187 (September 2006): 611.

74. Friedrich Wu, "The Globalization of Corporate China," *NBR Analysis* 16 (December 2005): 13.

75. Walsh, *Foreign High-Tech R&D*, p. xiv.

76. Ibid., pp. 63–64.

77. Martin Schaaper, "An Emerging Knowledge-Based Economy in China: Indicators from OECD Databases," Science, Technology and Industry Working Paper 2004/4 (OECD, March 22, 2004), p. 47.

78. Moris, "U.S.-China R&D Linkages," p. 2.

79. Gary Clyde Hufbauer and Yee Wong, "China Bashing 2004," *International Economics Policy Briefs* (Washington, DC: Institute for International Economics, September 2004), p. 25.

80. OECD, *OECD Science, Technology and Industry Outlook 2006*, p. 42. For a different view, see Zhao Gang, "Zhongguo keji shili zhen you nenma qiang?" [Is China's S&T really that strong?], *Huanqiu Shibao* [Global Times], December 12, 2006.

81. Simona Frank, "R&D Expenditure in the European Union," *Statistics in Focus: Science and Technology*, February 2005, p. 1.

82. Ibid., p. 3; see also OECD, *OECD Science, Technology and Industry Outlook 2006*, p. 43.

83. Cao Cong, "China Planning to Become a Technological Superpower," *EAI Background Brief*, no. 24 (May 26, 2005), East Asian Institute, National University of Singapore, p. ii.

84. "Hefei to Become PRC's Silicon Valley," Xinhua, March 3, 2005, FBIS, NewsEdge Doc. No. 200503031477.1_d4600051903062e4.

85. Notes of remarks by Hendrik Meijer, CEO Meijer Inc, Beijing, China, September 28, 2005, p. 7.

86. "Technological Gap between ROK-China Stands at 2.1 Years," *Tong-a Ilbo*, September 30, 2004, FBIS-EAS-2004-0930.

87. Howard W. French, "A Lifetime in Recovery from the Cultural Revolution," *New York Times*, October 22, 2005, p. A4.

88. Interview with senior corporate leader, Canberra, Australia, June 24, 2005, p. 2 of author's notes.

89. Martin Wolf, *Why Globalization Works* (New Haven: Yale University Press, 2004), p. 262.

90. Notes of meeting with Chinese official, Washington, DC, April 15, 2005, pp. 1–2.

91. Interview with former senior Singaporean diplomat, Singapore, June 13, 2005, p. 4 of author's notes.

92. Joshua Cooper Ramo, *The Beijing Consensus* (London: Foreign Policy Centre, 2004).

93. Interview with social science scholars, southern Vietnam, March 24, 2006, pp. 2–4 of author's notes.

94. "Middle Eastern Governments Would Do Well to Follow China's Example" (editorial), *Daily Star* (Lebanon), February 12, 2005.

95. Bradley Klein, "Democracy Optional: China and the Developing World's Challenge to the Washington Consensus," *UCLA Pacific Basin Law Journal* 22 (Fall 2004): 89–149.

96. Qian Qichen, "US Strategy Seriously Flawed," *China Daily*, November 1, 2004.

97. Lee Chung-min, "Domestic Politics and the Changing Contours of the ROK-US Alliance: The End of the Status Quo," in *The Future of America's Alliances in Northeast Asia*, ed. Michael H. Armacost and Daniel I. Okomoto (Stanford: Asia-Pacific Research Center, Stanford University, 2004), p. 212.

98. Zheng Bijian, "China's 'Peaceful Rise' to Great-Power Status," *Foreign Affairs* 84 (September/October 2005): 20–21.

99. Interview with senior NGO officer in Jakarta, Indonesia, June 18, 2005, p. 2 of author's notes.

100. Ian Seckington, "Nationalism, Ideology and China's 'Fourth Generation' Leadership," *Journal of Contemporary China* 14 (February 2005): 23–33.

101. For more on these incidents and Chinese nationalism in general, see Peter Hays Gries, *China's New Nationalism: Pride, Politics, and Diplomacy* (Berkeley: University of California Press, 2004).

102. "World Briefing," *New York Times*, September 14, 2005, p. A12.

103. "PowerNet and China Communist Youth League Develop 'Anti-Japan War Online' Game," Interfax-China, August 23, 2005, www.interfax.cn/showfeature .asp?aid=4907&slug=INTERNET-ONLINE%20GAME-JAPAN-POWERNET.

104. John J. Mearsheimer, "Realism Is Right," *National Interest*, no. 81 (Fall 2005): 10.

105. "Dujia diaocha: Zhongguoren renhe kan zhong mei guanxi?" [Exclusive inves-

tigation: How do Chinese view China-U.S. relations?], *Huanqiu Shibao* [Global Times], March 2, 2005, www.sohu.com. See also "Wu da chengshi minyi diaocha 56.7% renwei mei zai ezhi zhongguo" [Public opinion survey in five big cities shows 56.7 percent believe the United States is containing China], *Huanqiu Shibao*, March 2, 2005, www .ynet.com/view.jsp?oid=4774610&pageno=1.

106. Conference notes of remarks by professor at China Youth College for Politics, Beijing, China, September 27, 2005, p. 4; see also Chen Shengluo, "Zhongguo daxuesheng dui meiguoren guanzhu de shi da wenti de taidu yu kanfa diaocha yanjiu" [Survey research on the attitudes and views of Chinese university students on ten big issues with respect to Americans], unpublished manuscript, September 2005, Beijing.

107. Allen S. Whiting, "Chinese Nationalism and Foreign Policy after Deng," *China Quarterly*, no. 142 (June 1995): 295–96. See also Chen Zhimin, "Nationalism, Internationalism and Chinese Foreign Policy," *Journal of Contemporary China* 14 (February 2005): 35–53.

108. Alastair Iain Johnston, "Chinese Middle Class Attitudes towards International Affairs: Nascent Liberalism?" *China Quarterly*, no. 179 (September 2004): 603. Also suggestive of more "liberal" attitudes as economic development proceeds is a study on political culture by Yanlei Wang, Nicholas Rees, and Bernadette Andreosso-O'Callahan, "China's Political Development, Leadership Transition and Local Elections," *Journal of Contemporary China* 13 (May 2004): 203–22.

109. Stephen M. Walt, *Taming American Power: The Global Response to U.S. Primacy* (New York: W. W. Norton, 2005); see also Stephen M. Walt, "Taming American Power," *Foreign Affairs* 84 (September/October 2005): 105–20.

110. Pew Global Attitudes Project, "U.S. Image Up Slightly, but Still Negative," June 23, 2005, http://pewglobal.org/reports/display.php?ReportID=247 (accessed August 29, 2005).

111. BBC World Service, "World View of US Role Goes from Bad to Worse," 2007, www.globescan.com/news_archives/bbcusop/ (accessed January 24, 2007).

112. Pew Research Center, "Global Unease with Major World Powers," June 27, 2007, http://pewglobal.org/reports/pdf/256.pdf (accessed June 27, 2007).

113. Chicago Council on Global Affairs, *The United States and the Rise of China and India: Results of a 2006 Multination Survey of Public Opinion* (Chicago: Chicago Council, 2006), p. 39.

114. Pew Global Attitudes Project, "U.S. Image Up Slightly."

115. Pew Research Center, "Global Unease," p. 7.

116. Wolf Blitzer Reports, "Cheney on Osama and Gitmo," CNN, June 24, 2005, www.cnn.com/2005/US/06/24/cheney/ (accessed October 19, 2005).

117. Ipsos-Reid, "A Public Opinion Survey of Canadians and Americans about China," June 2005, report prepared for the Canada Institute of the Woodrow Wilson

International Center for Scholars and the Toronto-based Canada Institute on North American Issues, p. 1.

118. "U.S. Image Slides as World Mess Deepens," July 24, 2006, http://feeds.big newsnetwork.com/?sid=29afaab22e34843b (accessed July 24, 2006).

119. Pew Global Attitudes Project, "U.S. Image Up Slightly."

120. Ipsos-Reid, "Public Opinion Survey," p. iv.

121. Pew Global Attitudes Project, "U.S. Image Up Slightly."

122. Ibid.

123. Ipsos-Reid, "Public Opinion Survey," p. iv.

124. "China's Influence Seen Positive," *BBC News*, March 5, 2005, http://news .bbc.co.uk/2/hi/asia-pacific/4318551.stm (accessed July 20, 2006).

125. Ibid.

126. Steven Kull, "It's Lonely at the Top," *Foreign Policy*, no. 149 (July/August 2005): 36.

127. Philip P. Pan, "China's Improving Image Challenges U.S. in Asia," *Washington Post*, November 15, 2003, pp. A1, A15.

128. Pew Research Center, "Global Unease," pp. 39–44.

129. Committee of 100 and Zogby International, "China's Hill to Climb," *Foreign Policy*, no. 150 (September/October 2005): 23, based on Zogby International polling for the Committee of 100.

130. David M. Lampton, *Same Bed, Different Dreams: Managing U.S.-China Relations, 1989–2000* (Berkeley: University of California Press, 2001), p. 385; Gallup Poll, "China," http://poll.gallup.com/content/default.aspx?ci=1627 (accessed September 21, 2005).

131. Committee of 100 and Zogby International, "China's Hill to Climb," p. 23; also Committee of 100 Zogby International Survey, *American Attitudes toward China* (New York: Committee of 100, April 6, 2005), www.committee100.org/publications/survey/ phase2/English_pressrelease.pdf (accessed July 20, 2007), table 9.

132. Pew Research Center for the People and the Press and the Council on Foreign Relations, *America's Place in the World 2005* (Washington, DC: Council on Foreign Relations, November 17, 2005), p. 19. CNN/USA Today/Gallup poll data show the same pattern in late 2005; see PollingReport.com, "China," www.pollingreport.com/ china.htm (accessed February 8, 2006).

133. Interview with former senior Australian government official, Canberra, Australia, June 23, 2005, p. 2 of author's notes.

134. Cato Institute, "Executive Summary," in *Economic Freedom of the World: 2005 Annual Report* (Washington, DC: Cato Institute, 2005), p. 3. "The index published in *Economic Freedom of the World* measures the degree to which the policies and institutions of countries are supportive of economic freedom in five areas: (1) size of government; (2) legal structure and protection of property rights; (3) access to sound money; (4) international exchange; and (5) regulation."

135. Ibid., pp. 3–4.

136. Yanzhong Huang, Bates Gill, and Sheng Ding, "The Dragon's Underbelly? An Assessment of China's Soft Power," draft, August 2005, p. 21.

137. Interview with former senior Singaporean diplomat, Singapore, June 13, 2005, p. 3 of author's notes.

138. Yuan Yuan, "Use the Facts to Defuse the 'China Threat Theory,'" *Liaowang* [Outlook], October 6, 2005, FBIS, NewsEdge Doc. No. 200510061477.1_d06406f5 20284be6.

139. "2004 nian Taiwan xuesheng dao dalu qiuxue renshu chuang lishi xin gao" [The number of Taiwan students coming to the mainland for study reaches historic high in 2004], Xinhua, http://news.xinhuanet.com/newscenter/2005-08/24/content_3397508 .htm (accessed August 24, 2005).

140. Notes of William Perry Delegation meeting with Premier Wen Jiabao, Beijing, China, January 28, 2005, p. 2.

141. "Dalu yu jinnian qiuji kaixue kaishi shishi taisheng tongdeng shoufei zhengce" [This fall semester the mainland begins implementing policy of equal tuition for Taiwan students], Xinhua, August 28, 2005, http://news.xinhuanet.com/newscenter/2005-08/ 24/content_3397481.htm (accessed August 24, 2005).

142. Josephine Ma, "HK Students in Great Leap Northward," *South China Morning Post*, January 4, 2007, p. A4.

143. Consulate General of the PRC in New York, "More Foreign Students Coming to China," www.nyconsulate.prchina.org/eng/xw/t80128.htm (accessed August 24, 2005), quoting Ministry of Education figures; see also Ministry of Education of the People's Republic of China, "International Students in China," www.moe.edu.cn/ english/international_2.htm (accessed September 23, 2005).

144. "China Sees Record High Number of Overseas Students in 2004," *People's Daily*, May 21, 2005, http://english.people.com.cn/200505/21/eng20050521_186164 .html (accessed November 8, 2005).

145. "China Expects Influx of Foreign Students," *China Daily*, September 29, 2004, www2.chinadaily.com.cn/english/doc/2004-09/29/content_378812.htm (accessed August 24, 2005); see also Consulate General of the PRC, "More Foreign Students."

146. Yan Zhen, "Foreign Students Tested," *Shanghai Daily*, June 6, 2005, p. 2.

147. Jane Perlez, "China's Reach: Chinese Move to Eclipse U.S. Appeal in South Asia," *New York Times*, November 18, 2004, www.nytimes.com/2004/11/18/ international/asia/18asia.html?ex=1101770465&ei=1&en=4a2e759312185edb.

148. David Murphy, "Softening at the Edges," *Far Eastern Economic Review*, November 4, 2004, p. 34.

149. Perlez, "China's Reach," pp. A1, A10.

150. Interview with Chinese professor from Shanghai, Washington, DC, July 21, 2005, p. 1 of author's notes.

151. Consulate General of the PRC, "More Foreign Students Coming to China," citing Ministry of Education of the PRC.

152. Interview with social science scholar, Ho Chi Minh City, Vietnam, March 24, 2006, p. 3 of author's notes.

153. Interview with U.S. government official, Hanoi, Vietnam, March 21, 2006, p. 2 of author's notes.

154. Hu Jintao, "Constantly Increasing Common Ground," October 24, 2003, www.australianpolitics.com/news/2003/10/03-10-24b.shtml (accessed August 24, 2005).

155. Interview with senior Australian official, Canberra, Australia, June 23, 2005, p. 3 of author's notes.

156. Perlez, "China's Reach."

157. Donald M. Bishop, "Chinese Students at American Colleges and Universities," remarks at the American Center for Educational Exchange, January 26, 2005, www.iienetwork.org/?p=56814 (accessed July 20, 2006); see also Institute of International Education, "Open Doors 2004: Report on International Educational Exchange. Leading Places of Origin," http://opendoors.iienetwork.org?p=49933 (accessed September 23, 2005).

158. IIE Network for Members, April 6, 2005, http://222.iienetwork.org/?ct=member&m_v=lusub&m_rid=1885.

159. David Shambaugh, "China and Europe: The Emerging Axis," *Current History* 103 (September 2004): 245.

160. Jiaoyubu [Ministry of Education], "2003 niandu ge lei liuxue renyuan qingkuang tongji jieguo gongbu" [Statistical results announced on the situation for all types of students abroad in 2003], www.moe.edu.cn/news_2004_02/15/htm.

161. "China, Egypt Sign Agreement on Establishing Chinese University," Xinhua, April 25, 2005, FBIS, NewsEdge Doc. No. 200504251477.1_b54500232e3f960d.

162. "First Foreign University Office in China Established," Xinhua, April 27, 2005, FBIS, NewsEdge Doc. No. 200504271477.1_57420013e7c12cf8.

163. China National Office for Teaching Chinese as a Foreign Language, "Introduction to the 'Confucius Institute' Project," http://english.hanban.edu.cn/market/HanBanE/412360.htm (accessed July 20, 2006).

164. Geoffrey York, "Beijing Uses Confucius to Lead Charm Offensive," *Globe and Mail*, September 9, 2005, p. A1.

165. "China Launches First Confucius Institute in Pakistan," Xinhua, April 10, 2007, NewsEdge Doc. No. 200704101477.1_bfac0026185fb79e.

166. China National Office, "Introduction to the 'Confucius Institute' Project."

167. Ibid.

168. Gretchen Ruethling, "Classes in Chinese Grow as the Language Rides a Wave of Popularity," *New York Times*, October 15, 2005, www.nytimes.com/2005/10/15/national/15chinese.html?incamp=article_popular (accessed October 16, 2005).

169. "Chinese Language Turning out Globally Popular," *People's Daily*, December 24, 2003, http://english.people.com.cn/200312/24/eng20031224_131133.shtml (accessed July 20, 2006).

170. "Chinese Tourists 'Flood' Abroad, Spending $48 Billion," Bloomberg.com, October 26, 2004, http://quote.bloomberg.com/apps/news?pid=nifea&&sid=aPHwi NY7mA10# (accessed October 17, 2004).

171. James C. McKinley Jr., "Mexico Builds Trade Ties with China," *New York Times*, September 13, 2005, p. A3.

172. Notes of meeting with senior foreign ministry official, Washington, DC, August 31, 2005, p. 9.

173. "China's Tourism Speeds Up after WTO Entry," *People's Daily*, November 25, 2004, http://english.people.com.cn/200411/25/eng20041125_165134.html. This is also based on my own research on possible destinations for Chinese tour groups, spanning various Web sites and articles, February 6, 2005.

174. "Roundup: China Pacific Island Countries Explore Ways to Enhance Ties in Tourism and Transportation," Xinhua, April 5, 2006, FBIS, NewsEdge Doc. No. 200604051477.1_94bd00623d288a60.

175. John Leicester, "China's Travel Revolution Ripples across the Globe," Associated Press, October 23, 2004, Lexis-Nexis.

176. Ibid.

177. Adam Jones, "Fury at French Tactics to Woo the Chinese," *Financial Times*, January 6, 2007, p. 3.

178. Notes of meeting at East Asia Institute, National University of Singapore, Singapore, June 14, 2005, p. 2.

179. Agence France-Presse, "Mainland to Win Gold in Tourism," *South China Morning Post*, July 3, 2007; see also Amy Yee, "Great Wall Overtakes Florence for Tourists," *Financial Times*, May 22, 2005, p. 1.

180. "Tourism Becomes Main Non-trade Channel to Bring Foreign Currency Income," Xinhua, September 10, 2004, FBIS-CHI-2004-0910.

181. "Let China's 'Soft Strength' Be Real Strength," *Renmin Ribao*, October 11, 2005, FBIS, NewsEdge Doc. No. 200510111477.1_5b9200ad68aadof2.

182. State Council Information Office, *Space Policy: China's Space Activities* (White Paper), November 2000, www.fas.org/spp/guide/china/wp112200.html (accessed July 20, 2006).

183. "China Launches Satellite TV Service in Asian Region," Xinhua, February 1, 2005, FBIS, NewsEdge Doc. No. 200502011477.1_7eba0016e42fb033.

184. Jane Perlez, "Chinese Move to Eclipse U.S. Appeal in Southeast Asia," *New York Times*, November 18, 2004, pp. A1, A10.

185. Hong Liu, "New Migrants and the Revival of Overseas Chinese Nationalism," *Journal of Contemporary China* 14 (May 2005): 315.

186. David Hancock, "Power Projectors," *Foreign Policy,* no. 149 (July/August 2005): 30–31.

187. "Hollywood's China Venture," *Far Eastern Economic Review,* October 28, 2004.

188. "International Box Office Surges: China Is the World's Fastest Growing Theatrical Market," *Screen Digest,* February 1, 2005.

189. "China to Amend Policies, Laws to Encourage Publishing Industry to Go Abroad," Xinhua, November 21, 2004, FBIS-CHI-2004-1121.

190. Xin Dingding, "Press Wholesale Market Opens to Overseas," *China Daily,* August 19, 2004, p. 1.

191. Interview with non-Chinese businessperson, Beijing, China, September 30, 2005, author's notes.

192. S. Jayasankaran, "Chasing the World's Chinese Readers," *Far Eastern Economic Review,* August 7, 2003, p. 37.

193. Internet Coaching Library, "Internet Users by Language," *Internet World Stats,* www.internetworldstats.com/stats7.htm (accessed July 20, 2006). In China itself there were 103 million netizens as of June 2005.

194. "Xinhua News Products Enter Japan's Cellphone On-Line Service Market," Xinhua, April 5, 2005, FBIS, NewsEdge Doc. No. 200504051477.1_870b001e5d60b302.

195. "Chinese Ask for Help in Sparking 'Chinese Wind' in Korea," *Chosun Ilbo,* November 17, 2004, FBIS-CHI-2004-1116.

196. Ambassador Chan Heng Chee, "ASEAN Relations with China: An Evolving Relationship," lecture delivered at Johns Hopkins-SAIS, Washington, DC, April 25, 2005.

5. CHINA AND ITS NEIGHBORS

Epigraphs: Notes of conversation with Vietnamese scholar, Ho Chi Minh City, Vietnam, March 24, 2006, p. 3; notes of luncheon conversation with senior Australian official, Canberra, Australia, June 22, 2005, p. 3; notes of conversation with Singapore official, Washington, DC, March 14, 2005, p. 1; notes of conversation with Vietnamese NGO official, Hanoi, Vietnam, March 21, 2006, p. 1.

1. Chen Xiangyang, "Draw Up New 'Greater Periphery' Strategy as Soon as Possible," *Liaowang* [Outlook], no. 6 (July 17, 2006): 64.

2. David Shambaugh, *Power Shift: China and Asia's New Dynamics* (Berkeley: University of California Press, 2005).

3. King C. Chen, *Vietnam and China, 1938–1954* (Princeton: Princeton University Press, 1969), p. 7.

4. Wu Hongying, "How Real Is the So-Called China Threat to U.S. Backyard?" *Contemporary International Relations* 15 (December 2005): 1–13.

5. Cheng-Chwee Kuik, a PhD candidate at John Hopkins-SAIS, is writing a dissertation on small states' hedging strategies dealing with the responses of Indonesia, Sin-

gapore, Thailand, and Malaysia to China's rise. I owe him a debt of intellectual gratitude for his thinking on this subject.

6. Notes of meeting involving senior academic of Indian extraction, Portugal, May 19, 2006, p. 2.

7. Interview with senior Australian defense official, Canberra, Australia, June 23, 2005, p. 2 of author's notes.

8. Lu Ning, *The Dynamics of Foreign-Policy Decisionmaking in China* (Boulder, CO: Westview Press, 1997), p. 111.

9. "Declaration of Heads of Member States of Shanghai Cooperation Organization," *Astana*, July 5, 2005, www.sectsco.org/htm/00500.html.

10. Ann Scott Tyson, "Russia and China Bullying Central Asia, U.S. Says," *Washington Post*, July 15, 2005, p. A19.

11. Interview with Vietnamese social science researcher, Hanoi, Vietnam, March 20, 2006, p. 2 of author's notes.

12. Embassy of the Philippines, Beijing, "Philippines-China Relations: List of Philippines-China Bilateral Agreements, 1975–2005," 2005, www.philembassy-china .org/relations/agreements.html (accessed May 26, 2006).

13. "Philippines: Military Relations with China Do Not Conflict with Any Third Country," Xinhua, March 3, 2005, FBIS, NewsEdge Doc. No. 200503031477.1 _4d8d0025793b09b0.

14. Interview with Vietnamese scholars of China, Hanoi, Vietnam, March 21, 2006, p. 2 of author's notes.

15. Interview with member of National Assembly, Hanoi, Vietnam, March 21, 2006, p. 2 of author's notes.

16. "Chinese Official Vows to Seek Cooperation in South China Sea Exploitation," Xinhua, April 22, 2005, FBIS, NewsEdge Doc. No. 200504221477.1_98a2002b80881ecc.

17. Donald E. Weatherbee, "Cooperation and Conflict in the Mekong River Basin," *Studies in Conflict and Terrorism* 20 (1997): 176.

18. White House, "Memorandum of Conversation" (Summary of the President's First Meeting with PRC Vice Premier Deng Xiaoping), January 29, 1979, 10:40 a.m.– 12:30 p.m., Document No. CK3100155962, Declassified Document Reference System, http//galenet.galegroup.com, p. 8.

19. Jimmy Carter, handwritten notes on White House stationery, January 30, 1979, National Security Council Doc. No. NCC-98-215, National Archives release date July 2, 1999.

20. Anna Fifield and Stephanie Kirchgaessner, "China Bank Freezes N Korean Accounts," *Financial Times*, July 26, 2006, p. 1.

21. Ambassador Chan Heng Chee, "ASEAN Relations with China: An Evolving Relationship," lecture delivered at Johns Hopkins-SAIS, Washington, DC, April 25, 2005, p. 7.

22. "Vietnam Buys Electricity from China for the First Time," Xinhua, FBIS-CHI-2004-0408; see also "China Sells Electricity to Vietnam Despite 'Acute' Power Shortage at Home," Agence France Presse, February 8, 2005, FBIS, NewsEdge Doc. No. 200502081477.1_a3cf003b2cfa6e2c.

23. "North Korea," *Harper's Magazine*, www.harpers.org/NorthKorea.html (accessed May 25, 2006). Regarding the January 2006 trip, Kim is reported to have been accompanied by President Hu Jintao on at least part of his nine-day tour. Antoaneta Bezlova, "China Chooses Its Own Pace," Inter Press Service and *Asia Times*, July 14, 2006; see also "Backgrounder: Kim Jong-il's three visits to China," *China Daily*, April 21, 2004, www.chinadaily.com.cn/english/doc/2004-04/21/content_325196.htm (accessed May 30, 2006).

24. Wonhyuk Lim, "Kim Jong Il's Southern Tour: Beijing Consensus with a North Korean Twist?" Brookings Institution, February 13, 2006, www.brookings.edu/printme .wbs?page=/pagedefs/6a78odd4d558ff3f7fff27780a1415cb.xml (accessed May 30, 2006).

25. Interview with social scientists, Ho Chi Minh City, Vietnam, March 24, 2006, pp. 1–2 of author's notes.

26. Interview with senior Australian defense official, Canberra, Australia, June 23, 2005, p. 1 of author's notes.

27. Notes of conversation with senior Australian officials, Canberra, Australia, June 22, 2005, p. 4.

28. Interview with senior Australian defense official, Canberra, Australia, June 23, 2005, p. 2 of author's notes.

29. Interview with former senior defense official, Canberra, Australia, June 23, 2005, p. 2 of author's notes.

30. "Australia and Japan Forge Ever Closer Ties," *International Herald Tribune*, March 14, 2007, pp. 1, 8.

31. Notes of luncheon conversation with senior Australian official, Canberra, Australia, June 22, 2005, p. 1.

32. Interview with former senior defense official, Canberra, Australia, June 23, 2005, p. 3 of author's notes; also notes of conversation with former and current Australian officials, Canberra, Australia, June 22, 2005, p. 1.

33. U.S. Department of Defense, "Quadrennial Defense Review Report," September 30, 2001, p. 4, www.defenselink.mil/pubs/qdr2001.pdf (accessed August 15, 2006).

34. Condoleezza Rice, "Promoting the National Interest," *Foreign Affairs* 79 (January/February 2000): 57.

35. "Excerpt from 'Good Morning America' on Interview with President Bush on Protecting Taiwan," Charles Gibson, interviewer, http://web.lexis-nexis.com (accessed July 25, 2006). For a complete review of developments in this period, see David M. Lampton and Richard Daniel Ewing, *U.S.-China Relations in a Post-September 11th World* (Washington, DC: Nixon Center, 2002).

36. Peter Allport, "Australians Expected to Join Defense of Taiwan: U.S. Official," *Agence France Presse*, August 17, 2001, Lexis-Nexis.

37. Interview with senior Australian corporate leader, Canberra, Australia, June 24, 2005, p. 4 of author's notes.

38. Interview with senior Australian defense official, Canberra, Australia, June 23, 2005, p. 3 of author's notes.

39. Raymond Bonner and Donald Greenlees, "Australians View U.S. as a Threat to Peace," *International Herald Tribune,* March 29, 2005, p. 8.

40. Notes of conversation with senior Australian officials, Canberra, Australia, June 22, 2005, p. 6. Whether the message "got through to Taipei" is highly debatable.

41. Interview with former senior defense official, Canberra, Australia, June 23, 2005, p. 3 of author's notes.

42. Interview with senior Australian corporate leader, Canberra, Australia, June 24, 2005, p. 3 of author's notes.

43. Notes of conversation with senior Australian officials, Canberra, Australia, June 22, 2005, p. 5.

44. Bloomberg.com, "Australia's Current Account Gap Narrows to A$14 Bln (Update2)," www.Bloomberg.com/apps/news?pid=71000001&refer=australia&sid =aUDu78rtUZRg (accessed June 6, 2006).

45. Alexander Downer, MP, Minister of Foreign Affairs, Australia, "Doorstop Interview Trilateral Strategic Dialogue, Sydney," March 18, 2006, www.foreign minister.gov.au/transcripts/2006/060318_ds-3lat.html (accessed June 7, 2006); see also Rich Bowden, "Concerns Expressed over Australia's Uranium Deal with China," Worldpress.org, April 26, 2006, www.worldpress.org/print_article.cfm?article_id =2447&dont=yes (accessed June 7, 2006).

46. Uranium Information Center, "Australia's Uranium," 2005, www.uic.com.au/ ozuran.htm (accessed August 15, 2006); also interview with Australian strategic policy analyst, Canberra, Australia, June 24, 2005, p. 1 of author's notes; Jane Perlez, "China's Role Emerges as Major Issue for Southeast Asia," *New York Times,* March 14, 2006, p. A3.

47. Ambassador Fu Ying, "Premier Wen Jiabao's Visit and China-Australia Relations," speech at the China-Australia Media Industry Leaders' Meeting, April 14, 2006, http://au.china-embassy.org/eng/sgjs/sghd/t247388.htm (accessed June 6, 2006); see also "China, Australia Ink Uranium Trade Deal," www.chinadaily.com.cn/china/ 2006-04/03/content_558239.htm (accessed July 17, 2007).

48. Patrick Goodenough, "Allies Downplay Differences over China," CNS NEWS.com, March 20, 2006, www.cnsnews.com/ViewForeignBureaus.asp?Page=%5 CforeignBureaus%5Carchive%5C200603%5CFOR20060320d.html (accessed August 15, 2006).

49. Downer, "Doorstop Interview."

50. Perlez, "China's Role," p. A3.

51. Lee Kuan Yew, *From Third World to First: The Singapore Story: 1965–2000* (New York: HarperCollins, 2000), ch. 4.

52. Ibid., p. 57.

53. Ibid., p. 58.

54. Ibid., pp. 497–98.

55. Discussion with analysts, Singapore, June 13, 2005, p. 2 of author's notes.

56. Ibid., p. 4.

57. Ibid., pp. 4–5.

58. Ibid., p. 5.

59. Interview with economist, Singapore, June 14, 2005, p. 2 of author's notes.

60. Discussion with analysts, Singapore, June 13, 2005, p. 11 of author's notes.

61. Ibid., p. 9.

62. Ibid., p. 10.

63. Interview with professor of strategy, Singapore, June 14, 2005, p. 3 of author's notes.

64. Chan Heng Chee, "ASEAN'S Relations with China," p. 7.

65. Edward Cody, "Asian Leaders Establish New Group," *Washington Post*, December 15, 2005, p. A25.

66. "East Asia Summit: In the Shadow of Sharp Divisions," *People's Daily Online*, December 7, 2005, http://english.people.com.cn/200512/07/eng20051207_226350.html (accessed August 15, 2006).

67. Chan Heng Chee, "ASEAN'S Relations with China," p. 12.

68. Among works essential to supplement what can be said here are George McTurnan Kahin, *Nationalism and Revolution in Indonesia* (Ithaca: Cornell University Press, 1970); *Indonesia: The Great Transition*, ed. John Bresnan (Lanham, MD: Rowman and Littlefield, 2005); *Religion and Religiosity in the Philippines and Indonesia: Essays on State, Society, and Public Creeds*, ed. Theodore Friend (Washington, DC: Johns Hopkins-SAIS, 2006); *Indonesia beyond Suharto: Polity, Economy, Society, Transition*, ed. Donald K. Emerson (Armonk, NY: East Gate Books, 1999); Qian Qichen, *Qian Qichen: Ten Episodes in China's Diplomacy* (New York: HarperCollins, 2005), ch. 4.

69. Kahin, *Nationalism and Revolution*, particularly p. 475; see also Arnold C. Brackman, *The Communist Collapse in Indonesia* (New York: W. W. Norton, 1969).

70. Tim Johnston, "Chinese Diaspora: Indonesia," *BBC News*, March 3, 2005, http://news.bbc.co.uk/2/hi/asia-pacific/4312805.stm (accessed August 15, 2006).

71. Michael Richardson, "Singapore and Malaysia Watch with Alarm: Indonesia's Neighbors Fear Wave of Refugees," *International Herald Tribune*, February 11, 1998, Lexis-Nexis. It also should be noted that there is debate over how many Indonesians are, in fact, of Chinese ancestry. See Johnston, "Chinese Diaspora."

72. Chan Heng Chee, "ASEAN'S Relations with China," p. 3; Nyan Chanda, *Brother Enemy: The War after the War* (New York: Collier Books, 1986), pp. 240–44, explains how this suspicion led to a massive exodus of Chinese from Vietnam in the late 1970s.

73. Human Rights Watch, "Indonesia and Timor," in *World Report 1999*, www .hrw.org/worldreport99/asia/indonesia.html (accessed June 13, 2006).

74. Interview with U.S. development NGO leader, Jakarta, Indonesia, June 17, 2005, p. 1 of author's notes.

75. Interview with senior Indonesian strategic analyst, Jakarta, Indonesia, June 18, 2005, p. 4 of author's notes.

76. Mark J. Valencia, *China and the South China Sea Disputes*, Adelphi Paper No. 298 (Oxford: Oxford University Press, October 1995), p. 65.

77. I am indebted to former ambassador to Indonesia J. Stapleton Roy for this observation, June 12, 2006.

78. Interview with senior Indonesian strategic analyst, Jakarta, Indonesia, June 18, 2005, pp. 2–3 of author's notes.

79. Ibid., p. 5.

80. Ibid., p. 6.

81. "Hu Jintao Holds Talks with Indonesian President Susilo," Xinhua, April 26, 2005, FBIS, NewsEdge Doc. No. 200504261477.1_7f89018fc6b3e305.

82. Notes of remarks by U.S. NGO leader at congressional breakfast, Washington, DC, March 10, 2005, p. 1.

83. BPS Statistics Indonesia, "Value and Growth of Foreign Trade with Main Partner Countries, Indonesia, 2004–2005," www.bps.go.id/sector/ftrade/exim/table2 .shtml (accessed June 14, 2006).

84. Interview with senior Indonesian strategic analyst, Jakarta, Indonesia, June 18, 2005, p. 6 of author's notes.

85. Ibid., p. 8.

86. Central Intelligence Agency, "Rank Order—Military Expenditures—Dollar," in *The World Factbook*, www.cia.gov/cia/publications/factbook/rankorder/2067 rank.html (accessed June 14, 2006).

87. Interview with U.S. development NGO leader, Jakarta, Indonesia, June 17, 2005, p. 2 of author's notes.

88. Ibid., p. 3.

89. Interview with senior Indonesian strategic analyst, Jakarta, Indonesia, June 18, 2005, p. 4 of author's notes; interview with Dr. Gumilar Rusliwa Somantri, University of Indonesia, Jakarta, Indonesia, June 20, 2005, p. 1 of author's notes.

90. Interview with senior Indonesian strategic analyst, Jakarta, Indonesia, June 18, 2005, p. 5 of author's notes.

91. The following works provide essential supplementation to what can be provided in the text: Chen Jian, *Mao's China and the Cold War* (Chapel Hill: University of North

Carolina Press, 2001), ch. 5; Qiang Zhai, *China and the Vietnam Wars, 1950–1975* (Chapel Hill: University of North Carolina Press, 2000); Brantly Womack, *China and Vietnam: The Politics of Asymmetry* (Cambridge: Cambridge University Press, 2006); Chanda, *Brother Enemy*, esp. pp. 235–47.

92. Interview with official, Ho Chi Minh City, Vietnam, March 23, 2006, p. 2 of author's notes.

93. Interview with Vietnam Chamber of Commerce and Industry, Hanoi, Vietnam, March 20, 2006, p. 3 of author's notes.

94. Ibid., p. 2.

95. Interview with Vietnamese NGO official, Hanoi, Vietnam, March 21, 2006, p. 3 of author's notes; Jane Perlez, "U.S. Competes with China for Vietnam's Allegiance," *New York Times*, June 19, 2006, p. A3.

96. Interview with Vietnam Chamber of Commerce and Industry, Hanoi, Vietnam, March 20, 2006, p. 3 of author's notes.

97. "Roundup: China-Vietnam Friendly Ties on Fast-Growing Pace," Xinhua, November 12, 2006, FBIS, Doc. No. 200611121477.1_030c00b44cb164a7.

98. Interview with Vietnamese NGO official, Hanoi, Vietnam, March 21, 2006, p. 3 of author's notes.

99. Memorandum of conversation with a senior U.S. official in Vietnam, Hanoi, Vietnam, March 21, 2006, p. 1.

100. "Vietnam Dismisses China's Fury over Spratlys Oil Bid," Agence France Presse, October 21, 2004, FBIS-EAS-2004-1021.

101. Memorandum of conversation with Foreign Ministry official, Hanoi, Vietnam, March 22, 2006, p. 2.

102. Memorandum of conversation at social science institution in Ho Chi Minh City, Vietnam, March 24, 2006, p. 3.

103. Interview with Vietnamese NGO official, Hanoi, Vietnam, March 21, 2006, pp. 2–3 of author's notes.

104. Interview with senior foreign government official in Vietnam, Ho Chi Minh City, Vietnam, March 23, 2006, p. 2 of author's notes.

105. Dr. Frank Frost, "Vietnam's Membership of ASEAN: Issues and Implications," Parliamentary Research Service, Current Issue Brief No. 3, 1995–96, August 31, 1995, p. i.

106. Weatherbee, "Cooperation and Conflict," p. 180. For more on Chinese regional infrastructure construction, see "China Expands Its Southern Sphere of Influence," *Jane's Intelligence Review*, June 1, 2005, www.janes.com (accessed October 23, 2005). See also John W. Garver, "Development of China's Overland Transportation Links with Central, South-West and South Asia," *China Quarterly*, no. 185 (March 2006): 1–22.

107. Interview with member of National Assembly, Hanoi, Vietnam, March 21, 2006, p. 4 of author's notes.

108. Michael R. Gordon, "Rumsfeld, Visiting Vietnam, Seals Accord to Deepen Military Cooperation," *New York Times,* June 6, 2006, p. A8.

109. Raymond Burghardt, "U.S.-Vietnam: Discreet Friendship under China's Shadow," *YaleGlobal,* November 22, 2005, pp. 1–3, http://yaleglobal.yale.edu/display .article?id=6546 (accessed August 15, 2006).

110. "VN, China Party Delegations Meet," *Viet Nam News,* March 21, 2006, p. 3.

111. "China's Insincerity Feeds Anti-Chinese Sentiment Ryu Jin," *Korea Times,* January 28, 2005, FBIS, NewsEdge Doc. No. 200501281477.1d732006638407aa7.

112. Conference notes, Seoul, Korea, November 11–12, 2004, p. 2.

113. "Rumsfeld Challenges Chinese Military Buildup, Slams North Korea," Associated Press, June 4, 2005, Lexis-Nexis.

114. People's Daily Online, "Interview with Chinese Ambassador to Japan, Wang Yi," *Huanqiu Shibao,* December 13, 2006, NewsEdge Doc. No. 200612131477.1 _cfaa05fd681a07ac.

115. "Japan Divided on Neighbourly Ties," *People's Daily,* January 9, 2006, http:// english.peopledaily.com.cn/200601/09/eng20060109_233895.html (accessed June 28, 2006); see also Norimitsu Onishi, "Koizumi Blames China and South Korea for Rift," *New York Times,* January 5, 2006, p. A6.

116. Keizo Nabeshima, "Japan, China Wasting Time," *Japan Times,* April 18, 2005, Lexis-Nexis; see also "Record-Low 38% of Japanese Feel Good about China," Kyodo News Service, December 18, 2004, Lexis-Nexis.

117. "Sankei Poll Shows 51 Percent See China as Threat," *Sankei Shimbun,* September 14, 2004, FBIS-CHI-2004-0914.

118. Paul Lin, "China Cannot Ignore the Japanese," *Taipei Times,* January 12, 2005, www.taipeitimes.com/News/editorials/archives/2005/01/12/2003219084 (accessed June 28, 2006). See also "Poll: China-Japan Ties Need Mending," *China Daily,* August 24, 2005, www.chinadaily.com.cn/english/doc/2005-08/24/content_471671.htm (accessed August 15, 2006); Onishi, "Koizumi Blames China," p. A6.

119. Masaru Tamamoto, "How Japan Imagines China and Sees Itself," *JIAA Commentary,* no. 3 (May 31, 2006), www2.jiia.or.jp/en_commentary/200605/31-Masaru Tamamoto.html (accessed June 28, 2006).

120. "Publics of Asian Powers Hold Negative Views of One Another," http://pew global.org/reports/display.php?ReportID=255 (accessed October 6, 2006).

121. Norimitsu Onishi and Howard French, "Ill Will Rising between China and Japanese," *New York Times,* August 3, 2005, p. A6.

122. Li Xiaogang, "US-Japan Alliance Faces Fresh Set of Challenges," *China Daily,* September 26, 2005, p. 4.

123. "Japanese Lawmakers Recommend Cutting ODA to China," Agence France Presse, November 10, 2004, FBIS-EAS-2004-1110.

124. Peter Hays Gries, "China's 'New Thinking' on Japan," *China Quarterly*, no. 184 (December 2005): 831–50.

125. Daiki Shibuichi, "The Yasukuni Shrine Dispute and the Politics of Identity in Japan," *Asian Survey* 45, no. 2 (2005): 197–215. To get a chilling impression of the shrine, go to www.yasukuni.or.jp. There are reports that the shrine Web site was attacked from China by up to nine hundred thousand messages a minute. "Barrage of Hostile E-Mail from China Shuts Down Japanese War Shrine Site," *RTHK Radio 3*, January 6, 2005, FBIS-CHI-2005-0106.

126. Norimitsu Onishi, "Koizumi Further Deepens Debate over Shrine," *New York Times*, August 15, 2006, p. A6.

127. People's Daily Online, "Interview with Chinese Ambassador."

128. "Ozawa Warns about China, Says Japan Could Easily Go Nuclear," Kyodo News Service, April 6, 2002, Lexis-Nexis.

129. David Turner, "US and Japan in Missile Defence Accord," *Financial Times* (London), June 24–June 25, 2006, p. 2.

130. "World Briefing: Asia: 24 New Launching Pads for Okinawa," *New York Times*, July 14, 2006, Lexis-Nexis.

131. Joseph Kahn, "If 22 Million Chinese Prevail at UN, Japan Won't," *New York Times*, April 1, 2005, Lexis-Nexis.

132. "FM Spokesman: UN Is Not a 'Board of Directors,'" *China Daily*, September 22, 2004, www.chinadaily.com.cn/english/doc/2004-09/22/content_376639.htm (accessed August 15, 2006).

133. David Pilling, "Koizumi Trip to Elvis Home Will Seal US Alliance," *Financial Times* (London), June 26, 2006, p. 5.

134. Japanese External Trade Organization, "Japanese Exports/Imports 2005 Calendar Year," table 1, www.jetro.go.jp/en/stats/statistics (accessed July 14, 2006).

135. U.S.-China Business Council, "U.S.-China Trade Statistics and China's World Trade Statistics," tables 7 and 9, www.uschina.org/statistics/tradetable.html (accessed June 29, 2006).

136. David Ibison, "China/Japan Economy: Japanese Investment into China Hits Record High," *Economist Intelligence Unit*, April 3, 2006, www.viewswire.com (accessed April 5, 2006).

137. Eamonn Fingleton, "East Asian Alliance," *Prospect*, May 2004, Lexis-Nexis.

138. "US-Japan Statement on Taiwan Opposed," *China Daily*, February 20, 2005, www.chinadaily.com.cn/english/doc/2005-02/20/content_417717.htm (accessed June 26, 2006).

139. "Beijing Protests U.S.-Japan 'Crisis Plan,'" *Standard* (HK), January 5, 2007, pp. A1, A7.

140. Shi Yinhong, "The Taiwan Issue and 'Common Strategic Objectives' of the

United States and Japan," *Wen Wei Po*, April 26, 2005, NewsEdge Doc. No. 2005 04261477.1_b66e0244e3366fd9.

141. To supplement what can be said here, see Sherman W. Garnett, ed., *Rapprochement or Rivalry? Russia-China Relations in a Changing Asia* (Washington, DC: Carnegie Endowment for International Peace, 2000); Judith Thornton and Charles E. Ziegler, eds., *Russia's Far East: A Region at Risk* (Seattle: National Bureau of Asian Research, 2002), pp. 319–47, 375–95.

142. Xing Guangcheng, "Mutual Trust, Mutual Benefit, and Reciprocity: Deepening Sino-Russian Relations," *Renmin Ribao*, April 20, 2004, FBIS-CHI-2004-0420.

143. "China, Russia Sign Joint Statement, Pledge Closer Ties," Xinhua, March 21, 2006, FBIS, NewsEdge Doc. No. 200603211477.1_8035009bd6864c45. It is difficult to say the issue is thoroughly settled when in 2006 the two sides said it was "completely settled" and then went on to say that "preparations for boundary settlement are proceeding" and that "the remaining two sections will be completed before the end of 2007." See "Sino-Russian Joint Statement Says Border Issues Completely Resolved," Xinhua, March 21, 2006, NewsEdge Doc. No. 200603211477.1_9a00002b668c5b52.

144. "SCO-CSTO Anti-terror Exercises Key to Security in Central Asia," *Agentstvo Novostey*, November 7, 2006, FBIS, Doc. No. 200611071477.1_7d11002875b1239f.

145. "Russian Official Says India, China to Remain Top Arms Buyers," *Agentstvo Voyennykh Novostey*, February 9, 2005, FBIS, NewsEdge Doc. No. 200502091477.1 _1066001f4613d2f4; Richard F. Grimmett, *Conventional Arms Transfers to Developing Nations, 1998–2005* (Washington, DC: Congressional Research Service, October 23, 2006), p. 10.

146. "Russian, Chinese Defense Ministers Discuss UN's Role in World," ITAR-TASS, April 21, 2004, FBIS-SOV-0422.

147. US-China Business Council, "China's Trade Performance," April 2006, www .uschina.org/info/chops/2006/foreign-trade.html (accessed June 27, 2006).

148. "Russia Wants to Cooperate, Not Compete with China," Interfax, March 20, 2006, FBIS, NewsEdge Doc. No. 200603201477.1_f4bb0058582e08d4.

149. Mikhail Vorobyev, "Great Wall of Oil; Russia Is Becoming Raw Materials Tributary of China," *Vremya Novostey*, November 8, 2006, FBIS, Doc. No. 20061108 1477.1_280f020fbldec80b.

150. Sergey Gennadyevich Luzyanin, "Five against One: The Priorities of Russia and China within the Shanghai Cooperation Organization Do Not Coincide," *Moscow Nezavismaya Gazeta*, September 28, 2004, FBIS-CHI-2004-0928.

151. "Putin Says Russia Should Consider China's Interests in Building Far East Pipelines," ITAR-TASS, October 13, 2004, FBIS-SOV-2004-1013.

152. "Lukoil's '05 China Exports in Doubt," Reuters, December 24, 2005, p. 7, www .themoscowtimes.com/stories/2004/12/24/046.html (accessed July 17, 2006).

153. Andrew Jack and David Pilling, "Russian Strategists Content to Play China off

against Japan over Siberian Oil Pipeline Route," *Financial Times* (London), May 13, 2004, p. 6.

154. "Putin Says"; see also "China to Encourage Companies to Invest in Russia," Interfax, November 2, 2004, FBIS-SOV-2004-1102.

155. "Russian Defense Minister to Discuss Military and Technical Cooperation in China," RIA *Novsti*, December 9, 2004, http://en.rian.ru/onlinenews/20041209/39775308.html (accessed August 15, 2006).

156. Paradorn Rangsimaporn, "Russia's Debate on Military-Technological Cooperation with China: From Yeltsin to Putin," *Asian Survey* 46, no. 3 (2006): 495.

157. Mikhail Kukushkin, "China Does Not Want Ready Aircraft," *Moscow Vremya Novostey*, November 5, 2004, FBIS-CHI-2004-1105. For more on Sino-Russian aircraft cooperation, see "Russia's Sukhoy Exports State-of-the-Art Aircraft to China," ITAR-TASS, March 21, 2006, FBIS, NewsEdge Doc. No. 2006032111477.1_46030015bce33faf.

158. "Chinese Prime Minister Voices Support for Russia's Accession to WTO," Interfax, September 21, 2004, FBIS-SOV-2004-0921.

159. "China Politics: Another Crisis Mishandled," *Economist Intelligence Unit*, December 2, 2005, www.viewswire.com (accessed December 7, 2005).

160. For more on China-India relations, see Neville Maxwell, *India's China War* (New York: Anchor Books, 1972); Waheguru Pal Singh Sidhu and Jing-dong Yuan, *China and India: Cooperation or Conflict?* (Boulder, CO: Lynne Rienner, 2003); Francine R. Frankel and Harry Harding, eds., *The India-China Relationship* (New York: Columbia University Press, 2004); Rollie Lal, *Understanding China and India: Security Implications for the United States and the World* (Westport, CT: Praeger Security International, 2006).

161. Francine R. Frankel, introduction to Frankel and Harding, *India-China Relationship*, p. 14.

162. "Sino-Indian Trade Crosses $10 Bn," NDTVProfit.com, December 17, 2004, www.ndtv.com/money/showbusinessstory.asp?id=22854&firmsrch=1&txtsrch=%22sino%2indian+trade-crosses%22 (accessed August 15, 2006); "Interview with Chinese Ambassador to India," Xinhua, April 1, 2005, FBIS, NewsEdge Doc. No. 20050401 1477.1_5e4300dad9cod72e.

163. Frankel, introduction to Frankel and Harding, *India-China Relationship*, p. 4.

164. Geoffrey Kemp, "The East Moves West," *National Interest*, no. 84 (Summer 2006): 75–78.

165. "Foreign Ministry Spokesman Kong Quan on Political Guiding Principles for Settling Sino-Indian Boundary Issue," Xinhua, April 13, 2005, FBIS, NewsEdge Doc. No. 200504131477.1_4f7900696fb75le4.

166. Liu Szu-lu, "No Need to Rush Settlement of Sino-Indian Border Dispute," *Wen Wei Po*, November 25, 2006, NewsEdge Doc. No. 200611251477.1_ddedo6odob 5ab741.

167. Mark W. Frazier, "Quiet Competition and the Future of Sino-Indian Relations," in Frankel and Harding, *India-China Relationship*, pp. 294–318.

168. "The United Nations," September 16, 1946, in *Selected Works of Jawaharlal Nehru*, 2nd ser., vol. 1, ed. S. Gopal (New Delhi: Jawaharlal Nehru Memorial Fund, 1984), p. 439, cited in Frankel, introduction to Frankel and Harding, *India-China Relationship*, p. 26.

169. Harry Harding, "The Evolution of the Strategic Triangle: China, India, and the United States," in Frankel and Harding, *India-China Relationship*, p. 323.

170. Pranab Mukherjee, Defense Minister, "Concluding Address at the 7th Asian Security Conference," January 29, 2005, www.idsa.in/speeches_at_idsa/7ASC Concluding.htm (accessed August 18, 2006); see also "More Areas of Agreement Than Differences with China," *Hindu*, January 30, 2005, FBIS, NewsEdge Doc. No. 200501301477.1_4b2a00a111fbcasd0.

6. A PRECARIOUS BALANCE

Epigraphs: Interview with senior Australian defense official, Canberra, Australia, June 23, 2005, p. 3 of author's notes; Cheng Li, "New Provincial Chiefs: Hu's Groundwork for the 17th Party Congress," *China Leadership Monitor*, no. 13 (Winter 2005): 11, http://chinaleadershipmonitor.org (accessed July 17, 2006); memorandum of conversation with senior Chinese scholar, Shanghai, China, August 17, 2004, pp. 5–6.

1. Notes of meeting with senior former intelligence official, Washington, DC, June 27, 2005, p. 1.

2. Quoted in William C. Kirby, "Traditions of Centrality, Authority, and Management in Modern China's Foreign Relations," in *Chinese Foreign Policy: Theory and Practice*, ed. Thomas W. Robinson and David Shambaugh (New York: Oxford University Press, 1997), p. 20.

3. Samuel P. Huntington, *Political Order in Changing Societies* (New Haven: Yale University Press, 1968); Gabriel A. Almond and G. Bingham Powell Jr., *Comparative Politics: A Developmental Approach* (Boston: Little, Brown, 1966); Dankwart A. Rustow, *A World of Nations* (Washington, DC: Brookings Institution, 1967).

4. Almond and Powell, *Comparative Politics*, p. 314. Rustow identifies three categories that are conceptually similar to those of Almond and Powell.

5. Henry S. Rowen, "The Short March: China's Road to Democracy," *National Interest*, no. 45 (Fall 1996): 61, 68–69.

6. Feng Jianhua, "Coping with Disaster," *Beijing Review* 49 (February 16, 2006), www.bjreview.com.cn/06-07-e/china-3.htm (accessed July 25, 2006).

7. Zeng Qinghong, "A Programmatic Document for Strengthening the Party's Ability to Govern: Study and Implement the Spirit of the Fourth Plenum of the 16th Party Committee, Strengthen the Party's Ability to Govern," *Renmin Ribao*, October

8, 2004, FBIS, http://english.peopledaily.com.cn; "CPC Central Committee Key Plenum Opens to Address 'Disharmonious' Issues," *People's Daily Online*, October 8, 2006, http://english.people.com.cn/200610/08/eng20061008_309909.html (accessed February 2, 2007).

8. Huntington, *Political Order*, p. 79.

9. Ian Bremmer, *The J Curve: A New Way to Understand Why Nations Rise and Fall* (New York: Simon and Schuster, 2006).

10. Francis Fukuyama, *State-Building: Governance and World Order in the Twenty-first Century* (Ithaca: Cornell University Press, 2004).

11. Evan S. Medeiros, *Chasing the Dragon: Assessing China's System of Export Controls for WMD-Related Goods and Technologies* (Santa Monica, CA: RAND, 2005).

12. United Nations Development Programme [UNDP] in China, "China by the Numbers," unpublished document released in conjunction with *China's Human Development Report 2005*, December 16, 2005, p. 3.

13. "CPC Self-Regulation," *China Daily*, August 8, 2006, p. 4.

14. Hu Angang, "Jiegou binge de chuanzaoxing cuihui" [The creative destruction of structural change], May 24, 2002, www.dajun.com.cn/huangang.html (accessed October 20, 2005); also Sun Zifa, "Hu Angang Comes Up with 'One China, Four Worlds,' Theory," Zhongguo Xinwen She, February 21, 2001, FBIS.

15. Jinglian Wu, *Understanding and Interpreting Chinese Economic Reform* (Singapore: Thomson South-Western, 2005), p. 276.

16. National Bureau of Statistics of China, *China Statistical Yearbook 2004* (Beijing: China Statistics Press, 2004); also Wang Shaoguang and Hu Angang, *The Political Economy of Uneven Development: The Case of China* (Armonk, NY: M. E. Sharpe, 1999), p. 186. The figures in these two sources are close but not identical.

17. Jinglian Wu, *Understanding and Interpreting*, p. 268.

18. Barry Naughton, "China's Political System and China's Future Growth," in *China's Economy: Retrospect and Prospect*, ed. Loren Brandt et al. (Washington, DC: Woodrow Wilson International Center for Scholars, July 2005), p. 64.

19. Wang Shaoguang and Hu Angang, *Political Economy*, p. 186.

20. Jinglian Wu, *Understanding and Interpreting*, p. 269.

21. National Bureau of Statistics of China, *Chinese Statistical Yearbook 2004*, tables 8–16.

22. Naughton, "China's Political System," p. 64.

23. Jing Jin, "Fiscal Federalism or Tax Farming: Political Economy of Fiscal Decentralization in China" (PhD diss., Johns Hopkins University, 2003), p. 171.

24. World Bank, *China 2020* (Washington, DC: World Bank, 1997), p. 25.

25. "Commerce Minister Bo Xilai Gives Exclusive Interview to Renmin Ribao on China's Foreign Trade and Economy," *Renmin Ribao*, January 1, 2005, FBIS, NewsEdge Doc. No. 200501051477.1_d91500fe5f258e06.

26. Kenneth G. Lieberthal and David M. Lampton, eds., *Bureaucracy, Politics, and Decision Making in Post-Mao China* (Berkeley: University of California Press, 1992), chs. 1 and 2; see also David M. Lampton, "Chinese Politics: The Bargaining Treadmill," *Issues and Studies* 23 (March 1987): 11–41.

27. David M. Lampton, ed., *Policy Implementation in Post-Mao China* (Berkeley: University of California Press, 1987), ch. 1.

28. Kong Bo, "Institutional Insecurity," *China Security* 2 (Summer 2006): 72. www.wsichina.org.

29. Zeng Qinghong, "Programmatic Document."

30. Wang Feng, "Can China Afford to Continue Its One-Child Policy?" *Asia-Pacific Issues* (Honolulu) [East-West Center], no. 77 (March 2005): 3.

31. Ibid., p. 6; for 2005 data, see Howard W. French, "China: One-Child Policy Spurred Gender Gap," *New York Times*, January 24, 2007, p. A6.

32. "Sex-Ratio Imbalance 'a Danger,'" *China Daily*, January 23, 2007, p. 1.

33. Peter Wonacott, "India's Skewed Sex Ratio Puts GE Sales in Spotlight," *Wall Street Journal*, April 18, 2007, pp. A1, A14.

34. Wang Feng, "Can China Afford to Continue?" p. 4.

35. Ibid., pp. 4–5.

36. Around the Nation, "100m Only-Children Born under One-Child Policy," *South China Morning Post*, January 12, 2007, p. A9.

37. Richard Jackson and Neil Howe, *The Graying of the Middle Kingdom: The Demographics and Economics of Retirement Policy in China* (Washington, DC: Center for Strategic and International Studies, April 2004), p. 3.

38. China Development Research Foundation [CDRF], "Abstract," in *China Human Development Report 2005* (New York: UNDP, 2005), www.undp.org.cn/downloads/nhdr2005/05abstract.pdf (accessed July 25, 2006).

39. Jared Diamond, *Collapse: How Societies Choose to Fail or Succeed* (New York: Penguin, 2005), p. 360.

40. CDRF, *China Human Development Report 2005*, p. 63.

41. Jackson and Howe, *Graying of the Middle Kingdom*, p. 6.

42. Wang Xiangwei, "Backlash from Rebounding Conservatives Challenges Pace of Reforms," *South China Morning Post*, February 13, 2006, Lexis-Nexis.

43. Memorandum of meeting with Premier Wen Jiabao, Zhongnanhai, Beijing, April 1, 2005, pp. 4–5.

44. "China Revises 2004 GDP Up 16.8 Pct, Service Sector behind Rise," *AFX International Focus*, December 20, 2005, Lexis-Nexis.

45. The Gini coefficient is a measure of inequality in which 0 represents absolute equality and 1.0 represents absolute inequality, a situation in which all individuals, except one, have zero. For 1999 figure, see "Income Disparity in China," *MC*, August 10, 2001,

www.macrochina.com.cn/english/focus/20010810002002.shtml (accessed March 16, 2005). For 2004 figure, see CDRF, *Human Development Report 2005*, p. 55; also "How to Interpret Gini Coefficient in China," *China Economic Net* (Zhongguo Jingji Wang), September 16, 2005, http://en.ce.cn/Insight/200509/13/t20050913_4669147.shtml (accessed September 16, 2005). The CDRF reported the Gini coefficient level at .447 in its *Human Development Report 2005*, p. 55. (Note that in this source the above number was displayed as 44.7, presumably multiplied by 100.)

46. CDRF, *China Human Development Report 2005*, p. 2; see also Loren Brandt and Thomas G. Rawski, "Introduction," in Brandt et al., *China's Economy*, p. 4.

47. Geoff Dyer, "Gap between Rich and Poor in China Widens," *Financial Times*, December 27, 2006, p. 3.

48. UNDP in China, "China by the Numbers," p. 1.

49. CDRF, *China Human Development Report 2005*, p. 80.

50. Ibid.

51. Ibid., pp. 167–68.

52. Ibid., p. 25.

53. Ibid., pp. 42, 65, 87.

54. "Work Injury Insurance Covers 13.4 Percent of Migrant Workers in China," Xinhua, April 25, 2007, FBIS, NewsEdge Doc. No. 200704251477.1_d7d200254d8bcft2.

55. On urban poverty, see Athar Hussain, *Urban Poverty in China: Measurement, Patterns and Policies* (Geneva: International Labour Office, 2002). On rural poverty, see Azizur Rahman Khan and Carl Riskin, "China's Household Income and Its Distribution, 1995 and 2002," *China Quarterly*, no. 182 (June 2005), esp. pp. 382–83. On the conversion of agricultural land to other uses, see UNDP in China, "China by the Numbers," p. 3; Daniel Griffiths, "China Faces Growing Land Disputes," *BBC News*, August 2, 2005, http://news.bbc.co.uk/2/hi/asia-pacific/4728025.stm (accessed July 25, 2006).

56. World Bank, *World Development Indicators 2005* (Washington, DC: World Bank, 2005), p. 120.

57. UNDP in China, "China by the Numbers," p. 2.

58. Charles Wolf Jr. et al., *Fault Lines in China's Economic Terrain* (Santa Monica, CA: RAND, 2003), p.43. Data from "Malaria, 1982–1997," *Weekly Epidemiological Review* 74, no. 32 (1999): 265–70.

59. CDRF, *China Human Development Report 2005*, p. 55.

60. UNDP in China, "China by the Numbers," p. 2.

61. CDRF, *China Human Development Report 2005*, p. 66. The press release accompanying this report put the complex figures somewhat differently, saying: "Only 15% of rural residents had medical insurance in 2004, whereas half of urban population benefited from full insurance." See UNDP in China, "China on the Watch for Fight-

ing Social Inequality, New UNDP Report Says," press release, December 16, 2005, http://content.undp.org/go/newsroom/december-2005/china-hdr161205.en?g11n .enc=ISO-8859-1 (accessed July 25, 2006).

62. Pan Zhenqiang, "China's Security Agenda in 2004," *Foreign Affairs Journal*, no. 71 (March 2004): 13.

63. National Intelligence Council, *The Next Wave of HIV/AIDS: Nigeria, Ethiopia, Russia, India, and China* (Washington, DC: National Intelligence Council, September 2002), ICA 2002-04 D, p. 16.

64. Ibid., p. 14.

65. "Weishengbu: Quanguo leiji baogao aizibing duganran zhe 12 wan yu lie" [The Ministry of Public Health reports that nationwide (new) HIV cases top 120,000], Xinhua, October 14, 2005, http://news.xinhuanet.com/politics/2005-10/14/content _3617391.htm.

66. Ministry of Health, PRC, Joint United Nations Programme on HIV/AIDS World Health Organization, "2005 Update on the HIV/AIDS Epidemic and Response in China," January 24, 2006; see also "AIDS in China: New Legislation, Old Doubts," *Lancet* 367 (March 11, 2006): 803–4.

67. U.S. Centers for Disease Control, "China Reports 42 Percent Rise in HIV Cases," *The Body*, www/thebody.com/cdc/news_updates_archive/2005/oct14_05/ china_hiv.html (accessed January 10, 2006).

68. Bates Gill, *Assessing HIV/AIDS Initiatives in China: Persistent Challenges and Promising Ways Forward* (Washington, DC: Center for Strategic and International Studies, June 2006), p. v.

69. "China Reports 126,808 HIV Infection Cases," Xinhua, October 14, 2005, http://news.xinhuanet.com/english/2005-10/14/content_3617075.htm (accessed July 25, 2006).

70. "Experts Predict: China's 10 Major Risk Factors before 2010," *People's Daily*, September 1, 2004, http://english.peopledaily.com.cn/200409/01/eng20040901_155578 .html (accessed September 2, 2004).

71. "Chinese Law Mandates Help for AIDS Patients," *Washington Post*, February 13, 2006, p. A18.

72. "Beijing Reports 53.2 Percent Rise in Reported HIV Carriers," Xinhua, August 26, 2005, FBIS, NewsEdge Doc. No. 200508261477.1_a44e003d0c670537.

73. Pan Zhenqiang, "China's Security Agenda," pp. 13–14.

74. Edward Cody, "After WHO Request, China Reports Two More Bird Flu Deaths," *Washington Post*, January 12, 2006, p. A13.

75. "Di qijie zhongguo jingjixue luntan ji 2006 nian zhongguo shehui jingji xingshi fenxi yu yuce guoji yantaohui" [The Seventh China Economic Forum and International Forum on 2006 China's Social and Economic Situation Analysis and Forecast], conference program book, p. 112.

76. CDRF, *China Human Development Report 2005*, p. 87.

77. "China to Close All Small Coal Mines by 2007," Xinhua, April 4, 2006, FBIS, NewsEdge Doc. No. 200604041477.1_57ba002bc868d5f6.

78. Feng Jianhua, "Coping with Disaster," *Beijing Review* 49 (February 16, 2006), www.bjreview.com.cn/06-07-e/china-3.htm (accessed July 25, 2006).

79. UNDP in China, "China by the Numbers," p. 3; also CDRF, *China Human Development Report 2005*, p. 87.

80. World Bank, *China 2020*, p. 71.

81. Richard McGregor, "Beijing Clouds the Pollution Picture," *Financial Times*, July 2, 2007, www.ft.com/cms/s/69333ff8-28bb-11dc-af78-000b5df10621.html (accessed July 19, 2007).

82. Elizabeth C. Economy, *The River Runs Black* (Ithaca: Cornell University Press, 2004), p. 88.

83. Wu Yungzhao, "Duihua Zhu Zhixin" [Dialogue with Zhu Zhixin], *Zhiye Yanjiu* [Corporation Research], May 2006, www.chycf.com/Article/ArticleShow.asp?ArticleID=365 (accessed July 12, 2006).

84. Shehui Kexue Wenxian Chubanshe [Social Sciences Documentation Publishing House], *Shehui Lanpishu 2002* [Blue Book of Chinese Society 2002] (Beijing: Shehui Kexue Wenxian Chubanshe, 2002), pp. 158–59.

85. World Bank, *World Development Indicators, 2005* (Washington, DC: World Bank, 2005), p. 100 (table 2.14).

86. CDRF, *China Human Development Report 2005*, box 2.2, p. 63.

87. CDRF, "Abstract," in CDRF, *China Human Development Report 2005*.

88. "Where Are the Patients?" *Economist*, August 19, 2004, www.economist.com/World/asia/displaystory.cfm?story_id=3104453; CDRF, *China Human Development Report 2005*, box 2.2, p. 63, has similar figures.

89. World Bank, *World Development Indicators 2005*, p. 100.

90. "China to Allocate More Money to Agriculture in 2006," Xinhua, February 5, 2006, FBIS, NewsEdge Doc. No. 200602051477.1_ecda002c9b8ce37b.

91. Jinglian Wu, *Understanding and Interpreting*, p. 283.

92. "China to Improve Medical Care for Farmers," Xinhua, February 21, 2006, FBIS, NewsEdge Doc. No. 200602211477.1_3bf300202d93268c.

93. World Bank, *World Development Indicators 2005*, pp. 104–5.

94. CDRF, *China Human Development Report 2005*, p. 8.

95. Maureen Fan, "Illiteracy Jumps in China, Despite 50-Year Campaign to Eradicate It," *Washington Post*, April 27, 2007, p. A19; also UNDP in China, "China by the Numbers," p. 2.

96. "Experts Say Education Input Vital," *China Daily*, July 8, 2005, p. 2, www.chinadaily.com.cn/english/doc/2005-07/08/content_458173.htm (accessed July 25, 2006). See also CDRF, *China Human Development Report 2005*, pp. 50–51.

97. Yan Zhen, "Spending Gap a Worry," *Shanghai Daily,* August 12–13, 2006, p. A4.

98. Xin Zhigang, "Dissecting China's 'Middle Class,'" *China Daily,* October 27, 2004, www.chinadaily.com.cn/english/doc/2004-10/27/content_386060.htm.

99. "China's Middle-Income Class in the Making," Xinhua, March 26, 2004, http://news.xinhuanet.com/english/2004-03/26/content_2028599.htm (accessed July 26, 2006).

100. Pew Global Attitudes Project, "Prosperity Brings Satisfaction—and Hope," November 16, 2005, www.pewglobal.org.

101. Anthony Saich, "Political Change in China," in *U.S.-China Relations,* Report of the Seventh Congressional Conference of the Aspen Institute (Washington, DC: Aspen Institute, 2005), p. 27.

102. "One-Third of China's Private Businessmen Are CPC Members," Xinhua, February 10, 2005, FBIS, NewsEdge Doc. No. 200502101477.1_240d00140bfc85.

103. Margaret M. Pearson, *China's New Business Elite* (Berkeley: University of California Press, 1999), p, 164.

104. Kang Xiaoguang, "An Analysis of Political Stability in Mainland China in the Next Three to Five Years," *Beijing Zhanlue yu Guanli* [Strategy and Management], June 1, 2002, pp. 1–15, FBIS.

105. "Party Now Has 70.8 Million Members," *China Daily,* July 1–2, 2006, p. 1.

106. Jae Cheol Kim, "From the Fringe to the Center: The Political Emergence of Private Entrepreneurs in China," *Issues and Studies* 41 (September 2005): 113–43.

107. Gao Yongqiang and Tian Zhilong, "How Firms Influence the Government Policy Decision-Making in China," *Singapore Management Review* 28, no. 1 (2006): 77–78; see also Yongqiang Gao and Zhilong Tian, "A Comparative Study on Corporate Political Action in China," *Journal of American Academy of Business* 8 (March 2006): 67–72.

108. "Students Clash with Police in Degree Protest," Associated Press Newswires, October 26, 2006, www.hkhkhk.com/engpro/messages/2180.html (accessed February 9, 2007).

109. Alastair Iain Johnston, "Chinese Middle Class Attitudes towards International Affairs: Nascent Liberalization?" *China Quarterly,* no. 179 (September 2004): 603–28.

110. Vivien Cui, "Authorities to Scrap Sponsor Rule for NGOs," *South China Morning Post,* October 19, 2004, Lexis-Nexis.

111. World Bank, "China: Change from the Grassroots Up," http://go.worldbank.org/4YEZPXIL20 (accessed July 17, 2007).

112. "Chinese Environmental NGOs Called On to Play a Bigger Role," Xinhua, October 29, 2006, FBIS, Doc. No. 200610291477.1_cdb1005728dde4f2.

113. Jing Xiaolei, "A Green Alliance," www.bjreview.com.cn/06-03-e/china-2.htm (accessed February 9, 2006).

114. Notes of conversation between Premier Zhu Rongji and members of U.S. Congress, Zhongnanhai, Beijing, China, April 5, 2002, pp. 2–3.

115. Notes of talk by Fan Gang, Xi'an, China, March 29, 2005, pp. 2–3.

116. For official Chinese figures, see "Zhonghua renmin gongheguo laodong he shehui baozhangbu" [Ministry of Labor and Social Security], www.molss.gov.cn (accessed February 1, 2006); see also "Hu, Wen and SOE Reform," *Economist Intelligence Unit,* February 17, 2004, www.viewswire.com (accessed February 20, 2004).

117. "China Faces Six Challenges in the 21st Century, Expert," *Renmin Ribao,* September 7, 2005, FBIS, NewsEdge Doc. No. 200509071477.1_70a6007a78a71377.

118. *Business Daily,* "Farmers Protest over Alleged Lead Poisoning," September 2, 2005, http://infoweb.newsbank.com/iw-search/we/InfoWeb/?_action=print&p _docid=10C665D (accessed July 12, 2006).

119. Shai Oster and Jane Spencer, "A Poison Spreads amid China's Boom," *Wall Street Journal,* September 30–October 1, 2006, p. 1.

120. "China Reassesses Plant Plans," *Wall Street Journal* (Asia), June 8–10, 2007, p. 9.

121. David M. Lampton, "Water Politics and Economic Change in China," in *The Four Modernizations,* vol. 1 of *China's Economy Looks toward the Year 2000* (Washington, DC: U.S. Government Printing Office, 1986), pp. 387–88.

122. "Shortage of Water Twice as Costly as Flooding," Xinhua, February 18, 2006, FBIS, NewsEdge Doc. No. 200602181477.1fa010022916dad02.

123. Howard W. French, "Riots in Shanghai Suburb as Pollution Protest Heats Up," *New York Times,* July 19, 2005, p. 3.

124. Feng Jianhua, "Coping with Disaster"; see also Jim Yardley, "China Chemical Spills Spur Plan to Guard Water Supply," *New York Times,* January 12, 2006, p. A12; Edward Cody, "A Stand against China's Pollution Tide," *Washington Post,* January 12, 2006, p. A12.

125. Kimberly McGinnis, "Thirsting for Solutions," *Insight* (Journal of the American Chamber of Commerce in Shanghai), March 2006, p. 21.

126. Economy, *River Runs Black,* ch. 7.

127. Ibid., pp. 130–31.

128. Xiaobo Lu, *Cadres and Corruption* (Stanford: Stanford University Press, 2000), p. 160; for further background, see pp. 154–257.

129. Minxin Pei, *China's Trapped Transition: The Limits of Developmental Autocracy* (Cambridge, MA: Harvard University Press, 2006), p. 136.

130. Hu Angang, *Zhongguo: Tiaozhan fubai* [China: Fighting against Corruption] (Hangzhou, China: Zhejiang People's Publishing House, 2001), p. 61; see also Hu Angang, "Fu bai: Zhongguo zui da de shehui wuran" [Corruption: The largest social pollution in China], undated manuscript (circa 2000).

131. Minxin Pei, "Will China Become Another Indonesia?" *Foreign Policy*, no. 116 (Fall 1999): 96–100, and *China's Trapped Transition*.

132. Cited in Jinglian Wu, *Understanding and Interpreting*, p. 394.

133. Ibid., p. 395.

134. Minxin Pei, *China's Trapped Transition*, pp. 133–34, 152.

135. Peter S. Goodman, "China Reveals $1.1B Bank Fraud: Corruption Threatens Foreign Investment," Washington Post Foreign Service, June 27, 2006, www.washington post.com.

136. Jinglian Wu, *Understanding and Interpreting*, p. 231.

137. Ibid., pp. 341–42.

138. Naughton, "China's Political System," p. 65.

139. Ibid., p. 64.

140. Remarks by Chinese economist, March 29, 2005, pp. 2–3.

141. Wolf et al., *Fault Lines*, p. xviii.

142. Naughton, "China's Political System," p. 63.

143. Ibid., p. 63, table 1, from People's Bank of China, *2002 China Monetary Policy Report* (Beijing: People's Bank of China, 2003), 13.

144. Richard Daniel Ewing, "Chinese Corporate Governance and Prospects for Reform," *Journal of Contemporary China* 14 (May 2005): 327.

145. James Riedel, Jing Jin, and Jian Gao, *How China Grows: Investment, Finance, and Reform* (Princeton: Princeton University Press, 2007).

146. "Guanzhu minguan ziben di shehui zeren" [Heed the responsibilities of private capital], Xinhua, April 8, 2004, http://news.xinhuanet.com/fortune/2004-04/08/content_1408238.htm.

147. Naughton, "China's Political System," p. 65; BBC Monitoring, "China Economy: 60,000 SOEs Privatized in Past Decade," Viewswire, November 7, 2005, www .viewswire.com.

148. Jinglian Wu, *Understanding and Interpreting*, pp. 160–61.

149. Ewing, "Chinese Corporate Governance," p. 318.

150. Keith Bradsher and Wayne Arnold, "Trading Losses at Chinese Firm Coming to Light," *New York Times*, December 2, 2004, pp. C1, C5.

151. "Chen Claims He Did Not 'Start Fire That Consumed Company,'" *Straits Times*, March 16, 2006, p. 1; also "Chen of CAO Received a 4-Year Prison Term," *International Herald Tribune*, March 22, 2006, p. 13.

152. Ewing, "Chinese Corporate Governance," p. 332; Edward J. Epstein, *Who Owns the Corporation?* (New York: Priority Press, 1986), pp. 5–6, cited in Ewing, "Chinese Corporate Governance," p. 332.

153. "Experts Predict."

154. "China Politics: Pride and Prejudice," *Economist Intelligence Unit*, March 24, 2006, from *Economist*, www.viewswire.com (accessed March 30, 2006).

155. Yongnian Zheng, *Discovering Chinese Nationalism in China: Modernization, Identity, and International Relations* (Cambridge: Cambridge University Press, 1999), p. 17.

156. National Security Council, *The National Security Strategy of the United States of America*, March 16, 2006, p. 3, www.whitehouse.gov/nsc/nss/2006/.

157. Peter Hays Gries, *China's New Nationalism: Pride, Politics, and Diplomacy* (Berkeley: University of California Press, 2004), p. 136.

158. Richard C. Bush and Michael E. O'Hanlon, *A War Like No Other: The Truth about China's Challenge to America* (Hoboken, NJ: John Wiley, 2007).

159. Memorandum of conversation with senior Chinese scholar in Shanghai, China, August 19, 2004, p. 4.

160. "China's Agricultural Trade Deficit against U.S. Jumps 1.5 Times in Four Years," Xinhua, FBIS, February 19, 2006, NewsEdge Doc. No. 200602191477.1_88f1004f3c78c6bc; James Kynge, "China Fears Food Crisis as Imports hit $14 Bn," *Financial Times*, August 22, 2004; "China's Grain Supply Deficit Remains," *China Daily*, July 19, 2004, http://english.people.com.cn/200407/19/eng20040719_150073.html (accessed July 25, 2006).

161. "Commerce Minister Bo Xilai."

162. *Zhongguo Tongji Nianjian 2000* [China Statistical Yearbook 2000] (Beijing: China Statistical Press, 2000), pp. 118–19, cited in Wolf et al., *Fault Lines*, table 2.1, p. 13. There is uncertainty about exactly what Bo's figure of eighty million is composed of and whether some rural employment is also included. If one considers total employment in China, then the eighty million cited by Bo would constitute a little over 11 percent of total employment nationally.

163. Notes of conversation with Mayor Xu Kuangdi, Shanghai, China, January 14, 1998, p. 33.

164. "Foreign-Funded Companies in Shanghai Set Trade Record," Xinhua, January 2, 2005, FBIS-CHI-2005-0102; "Foreign Companies Contribute Nearly 70 Pct. of Shanghai's Foreign Trade," Xinhua, October 24, 2006, FBIS, Doc. No. 200610241477.1_9719001afe15ba7e.

165. Bo Kong, *An Anatomy of China's Energy Insecurity and Its Strategies* (Richland, WA: Pacific Northwest National Laboratory, December 2005), p. 11.

166. Ibid., pp. 1, 7.

167. Ibid., pp. 15–16.

168. Ibid., p. 13.

169. David Fullbrook, "Resource-Hungry China to Devour More of Burma's Gas and Oil Industry," *Irrawaddy*, February 1, 2006.

170. Dingli Shen, "Iran's Nuclear Ambitions Test China's Wisdom," *Washington Quarterly* 29 (Spring 2006): 55–66.

171. "Iran Invites China's Sinopec to Sign $100 Billion Oil, Gas Deals," Fars News

Agency, November 26, 2006, FBIS, Doc. No. 200611261477.1_bc8a007bb9e2b671. On imports, see "China May Store Iranian Crude Oil," *Wall Street Journal* (Asia), June 12, 2007, p. 4.

172. Stephen M. Walt, *The Origins of Alliances* (Ithaca: Cornell University Press, 1987), p. 5.

173. Interview with senior foreign government official, Ho Chi Minh City, Vietnam, March 23, 2006, p. 2 of author's notes.

174. "Experts Predict."

175. "Xinhua: China Sacks Officials after Pollution Riots," Reuters (Shanghai), December 31, 2005, http://go.reuters.com/newsArticle.jhtml?type=worldNews& storyID=10725625&src=rss/worldNews (accessed January 16, 2006).

176. "China Reports Rise in Public Order Disturbances," Reuters, January 19, 2006, www.alertnet.org/thenews/newsdesk/PEK137255.htm (accessed January 20, 2006).

177. "Property Law May Serve as Umbrella to Farmers' Land," Xinhua, March 8, 2007, NewsEdge Doc. No. 200703081477.1_6ecb00584c5eale2.

178. Notes of conversation between Premier Zhu Rongji and members of U.S. Congress, Zhongnanhai, Beijing, China, April 5, 2002, p. 3.

179. Kang Xiaoguang, "Analysis of Political Stability," pp. 1–15.

180. Michael Chase and James Mulvenon, *You've Got Dissent: Chinese Dissident Use of the Internet and Beijing's Counter-Strategies* (Santa Monica, CA: RAND, 2002).

7. WHAT CHINESE POWER MEANS FOR AMERICA AND THE WORLD

Epigraphs: Notes of William Perry Delegation meeting with Premier Wen Jiabao, Beijing, China, January 28, 2005, p. 1; James MacGregor Burns, *Leadership* (New York: Harper and Row, 1978), p. 11; David M. Lampton, "Rapporteur's Summary," in *U.S.-China Relations 2006*, Report of the Eighth Congressional Conference of the Aspen Institute (Washington, DC: Aspen Institute, 2006), p. 7; interview with professor of strategy, Singapore, June 14, 2005, p. 2 of author's notes.

1. David M. Lampton, "Paradigm Lost: The Demise of 'Weak' China," *National Interest*, no. 81 (Fall 2005): 73–80; see also Evan S. Medeiros, "Strategic Hedging and the Future of Asia-Pacific Stability," *Washington Quarterly* 29, no. 1 (2005): 145–67.

2. Meeting notes of Aspen Institute Congressional Conference, Honolulu, Hawaii, April 12, 2006, p. 9.

3. For more on China's "New Left" and the globalization debate in China, see Joseph Fewsmith, *China since Tiananmen: The Politics of Transition* (Cambridge: Cambridge University Press, 2001), pp. 17, 125–28; Suisheng Zhao, *Nation-State by Construction: Dynamics of Modern Chinese Nationalism* (Stanford: Stanford University Press, 2004), pp. 152–55.

4. Chicago Council on Global Affairs, *The United States and the Rise of China and India: Results of a 2006 Multination Survey of Public Opinion* (Chicago: Chicago Council, 2006), pp. 64, 69. See also Liu Zhijun, "On Bird Flu and Beyond: A Human Security Perspective," *Global Asia* 1 (September 2006): 81–89.

5. Yuan Peng, "China's Rise and External Circumstances," *Contemporary International Relations* 15 (October 2005): 11.

6. Ibid., p. 12; see also "China's Diplomacy in the Important Period of Strategic Opportunity," *Renmin Ribao,* January 19, 2006, FBIS, NewsEdge Doc. No. 200601191477.1_c8f313705c52a616.

7. Yuan Peng, "China's Rise," p. 13.

8. Cui Liru, "Thoughts on the Evolving World Order," *Contemporary International Relations* 15 (October 2005): 4–5.

9. Yuan Peng, "China's Rise," p. 13.

10. Fu Mengzi, "Rising China vs. Peaceful Transformations in International Order," *Contemporary International Relations* 15 (October 2005): 8.

11. Interview with former senior Singaporean diplomat, Singapore, June 13, 2005, p. 2 of author's notes.

12. Tian Wenlin, "U.S. Strategic Predicament in Iraq," *Contemporary International Relations* 15 (October 2005): 27–28.

13. Meeting notes of Aspen Institute Congressional Conference, Honolulu, Hawaii, April 12, 2006, p. 11.

14. Hal Harvey, "China Energy Issues," in *U.S.-China Relations,* ed. Dick Clark (Washington, DC: Aspen Institute, 2006), p. 15.

15. Meeting notes of Aspen Institute Congressional Conference, Honolulu, Hawaii, April 10, 2006, p. 9.

16. Interview with senior foreign government official, Ho Chi Minh City, Vietnam, March 23, 2006, pp. 2–3 of author's notes.

17. Kimberly McGinnis, "Searching for Autopia," *Insight* (Shanghai, American Chamber of Commerce, April 2006), p. 20.

18. Celia W. Dugger, "India and China Drive Up Emissions Rates," *New York Times,* May 10, 2006, p. A7.

19. Keith Bradsher, "The Price of Keeping Cool in Asia," *New York Times,* February 23, 2007, pp. C1, C6.

20. Jonathan Watts, "The New China: A Hunger Eating Up the World," *Guardian,* November 10, 2005, Lexis-Nexis.

21. Bruce G. Blair and Chen Yali, "The Fallacy of Nuclear Primacy," *China Security* 2 (Autumn 2006): 68–72.

22. Meeting notes of Aspen Institute Congressional Conference, Honolulu, Hawaii, April 11, 2006, p. 7.

23. Chicago Council on Global Affairs, *United States,* p. 22.

24. Sun Tzu, *The Art of War,* ed. Samuel B. Griffith (London: Oxford University Press, 1971), p. 69.

25. Choe Sang-Hun, "Shift GIs in Korea to Taiwan? Never, China Envoy Says," *International Herald Tribune,* March 23, 2006, p. 3.

26. Notes of remarks by South Korean Ambassador Lee at the Nixon Center, Washington, DC, June 13, 2006, p. 1.

27. Interview with U.S. government officials, January 19, 2007, p. 4 of author's notes.

28. Interview with senior Australian corporate leader, Canberra, Australia, June 24, 2005, pp. 2–3 of author's notes.

INDEX

Page references in *italics* refer to illustrations.

Burma. *See* Myanmar

Burns, James MacGregor, 252

Bush, George W., *28;* diplomacy of, 128; election of, 142

Bush administration (George W. Bush): ABM policy of, 41; China policy of, 177, 183; China scholars on, 27; Iraq war of, 18, 51; nuclear policy of, 53; on relative power, 12–13; Taiwan policy of, 177–78, 315n35

Bush doctrine, 52, 142

Calabrese, John, 41

Cambodia: textile industry of, 100; Vietnamese domination of, 171, 192

Canada: Asia Pacific Foundation, 102; Excel Funds Management Inc., 84; Koizumi's visit to, 198; trade relations with China, 150

Capital, Chinese: efficiency of utilization, 24; formation of, 80–81; human, 24; social, 3, 139

Capital, foreign, in China, 20, 68, 79

Carter administration: and Deng Xiaoping, 171; relations with PRC, 69

Castro, Fidel, *107*

Caterpillar Corporation, sales to China, 67

Cato Institute, *Economic Freedom of the World*, 151

CEOs, Chinese, 123. *See also* Entrepreneurs, Chinese

Cervantes Institute (Spain), 156

Chad, state institutions of, 209

"The Chain Plan" (strategy), 17

Chains, multinational, in China, 89

Challenges, Chinese, 217–51; demographic, 217–19; developmental, 208–11; in equity, 219–29; external, 242–51; internal, 217–41, 249, 253–55; in nationalism, 241–42; to security, 273–74; Taiwan, 241–42

Chan Heng Chee, 85, 162, 184, 243

Changi Naval Base (Singapore), 184

Chase, Michael S., 297n84, 334n180

Chen Jiulin, 240

Chen Shui-bian, President, 70, 73, 242; Bush administration's support for, 178

Chen Tang-sun, 73

Chen Zhimin, 147

Cheng Biding, 136

Cheng Dawei, 4

Chicago: Chinese language classes in, 158; Council on Global Affairs, 270

Child mortality, Chinese, 83, 219

China: academic misconduct in, 133; American students in, 154; big powers' constraints on, 272; brain drain from, 86; during Cold War, 120; commercial legal system of, 87; communication with outside world, 153; conservatism of, 207; consumer desire in, 84; defense industries, 55, 60; demands of international system on, 209, 210; democratization in, 210; demography of, 208, 217–19; developmental challenges facing, 208–11; "division" problems of, 19; drug use in, 223; effect of globalization on, 256, 259; energy dependence in, 245–46; external threats to, 40–42, 47–48, 54–55; fertility in, 217; "first," 214, 226; fiscal federalism in, 215; foreign companies operating in, 98; foreign direct investment (FDI) in, 79, 89, 103, 199, 243–44, 246–47, 272, 297n87; foreign investors in, 68, 79, 84; foreign students in, 153–56; "fourth," 214, 226; in global economy, 241, 242–46; in global infrastructure, 260; as global processor, 267; in global production chains, 111, 267, 272; global responsibility of, 4; HIV/AIDs in, 82, 223–25, 261; homeland defense of, 46–48, 54, 76, 183; household size in, 219; hydropower of, 172; industrial output of, 97; influence on Korean

China *(continued)*
    peninsula, 5, 67; influence in Mongolia, 67, 110; influence in Nepal, 5; influence in North Korea, 67, 109–10, 255; influence in South China Sea, 171; information availability in, 98, 213; infrastructure of, 47; institutional deficiencies in, 212–17, 224, 240–41, 266; institutional rigidity of, 80; internal threats to, 46, 47; in international power cycles, 36; in international system, 2, 26, 27, 32, 109, 259, 265; international views on, 148–52; investment in Australia, 179; and Iraq War, 18; Japanese FDI in, 199; Japanese invasion of, 164; "Korean Wave" in, 162; life expectancy in, 83; links to Silicon Valley, 86; local governments of, 103; malaria in, 222; Mongol occupation of, 164; multinational corporations in, 89, 98, 106; "multiplication" problems of, 19; National Defense University, 62; National Development Research Center, 224, 241; and NATO, 4; natural resource needs of, 91–92; New Left of, 334n3; Richard Nixon's trip to, 3; non-Han peoples of, 210; nonstate firms of, 87, 98–99; in Nuclear Suppliers Group, 5; in opinion polls, 149–51; overseas population of, 80, 85–86, 124–25, 153–56, 160, 178; peaceful rise of, 14, 32–34, 66, 125, 143–44, 152, 242, 265; periphery defense of, 34; port trade, 65; reform era of, 86, 138, 212; remittances from abroad, 85; resentment of, 93; reunification with Taiwan, 50, 69, 168, 269; road mileage in, 47; role in globalization, 2, 4, 35, 116, 120, 260–61; role in transnational problems, 267–68; rural-urban migration in, 212; SARS in, 74; "second," 226; sex ratio in, 218, 219; share of global power, 21–24; technology

imports of, 60; tourism in, 158–59, 162, 190, 312n173; trade partners of, 48, 71, 90, 91–93, 95, 150; trade surplus with United States, 90; tsunami relief (2004), 5, 64, 107–8; U.S. investment in, 134; unemployment in, 222; urban employment in, 243; use of force, 15, 16; Vietnamese emulation of, 141; Warring States Period, 16; water crisis in, 235–36; wealthiest counties of, 207; in World Trade Organization, 30, 68, 100, 120, 126. *See also* Economy, Chinese; Foreign relations, Chinese; People's Republic of China (PRC); Republic of China (ROC); Sino-American relations
China: 2020, 227
China Agricultural University, Food Security Research Centre, 243
China Aviation Oil (Singapore) Corporation, 240
China Council for International Investment Promotion, 103
China Council for the Promotion of International Trade, 102
China Democracy Party, 232
China Film Group, 161
China Food Security Research Centre, 243
China Institute of Contemporary International Relations, 23
China National Offshore Oil Company (CNOOC), 93; and Philippine National Oil Company, 170, 171; and Unocal, 105, 106
China Radio International, 160
China Scholarship Council, 154
China State Council, Research Office, 83
China Youth College for Politics (Beijing), 147
China's Space Activities: in 2000, 58; *in 2006*, 56
Chinese: exodus from Vietnam, 318n72;

in Indonesia, 184–86, 188–89, 317n71; Muslims, 18. *See also* Overseas Chinese

Chinese Academy of Engineering, 98

Chinese Academy of Sciences, 136

Chinese Academy of Social Sciences (CASS), 116; on income, 221; Institute of Sociology, 83

Chinese language, foreigners' study of, 154, 156, 157, 158

Citizenship, in Chinese culture, 139

Civil War, U.S. (1861–65), 209

Clinton, Bill, 192

CO_2 emissions, Chinese, 7

Coal mining, health hazards of, 225, *226*, 227

Coercive power, 10; alienation under, 11; isolation in, 38; of money, 78; among nations, 256; negative impacts of, 75–76; self-limiting, 38; tools of, 37

Coercive power, Chinese, 6, 114; among big powers, 205; in diplomacy, 49, 255; economic, 38, 66–68, 95, 101, 110, 112; effect on economic development, 264; growth in, 37, 38; homeland defense in, 257; ideational aspects of, 255; insecurity following, 264; isolation in, 68–75; under Mao, 38, 253; military components of, 38, 39–45, 204, 255; in national strategy, 254; nonmilitary instruments of, 65; against North Korea, 172; overinvestment in, 253; projection of, 54–60; in relations with big powers, 204; in relations with neighbors, 164, 174; strategic coherence of, 76; against Taiwan, 38, 40

Cohen, William, 193

Cold War: China during, 120; end of, 263; nuclear strategy of, 268; Sino-American relations during, 165

Colombia, relations with China, 92

Comfort women, Asian, 197, 198

Communications technology, Chinese: competitiveness of, 135; in ideational power, 162; infrastructure for, 159–63

Communist Party, Chinese (CCP): ability to govern, 217; alternatives to, 249; authority of, 212; cadre training in, 124; domestic priorities of, 43; elites in, 174; entrepreneurs in, 123, 248; Hu Jintao in, 200; and international order, 34; leadership of, 119; legitimacy of, 260; middle class and, 230; Organization Department, 230; Politburo of, 122; role in economy, 30; students in, 230; Youth League, 121, 145

Communist Party, Indonesian, 186

Communist Party, Vietnamese, Chinese influence in, 174

Comprehensive national power (CNP): American, 22, 23; Chinese studies of, 20–21; Chinese understanding of, 21; national indexes of, 22–23; strategic resources in, 21

Comprehensive national power, Chinese, 20–25, 168; grand strategy for, 25–36; maturity in, 261; weakness in, 34

Confucianism, role in Chinese development, 139–40

Confucius: *Analects,* 69; on excellence, 22; on power, 8, 15

Confucius Institute Project, 157

Conservatism, Chinese, 207

"Consider Danger in Times of Peace" (film), 116

Consumer desires, Chinese, 84

Container Security Initiative (United States), 65

Corporate governance, Chinese, as issue driver, 238–41

Correlates of War Project, 278n43

Corruption, Chinese, 208, 331n130; cost of, 236; in GDP, 237; as issue driver, 234, 236–38; in PLA, 39; popular rage against, 238; official position selling,

Economy, U.S.: freedom in, 151; government expenditures in, 214–15; ties to China, 1

Education, Chinese: distribution of, 220; in engineering, 82; equality in, 228–29; expenditures for, 25; higher, 3; of leaders, 121, 124–25; in Middle East, 156; nongovernmental schools in, 232; in poor areas, 221; problems with, 154; in reform era, 228; role in economy, 80, 81–83; in Shanghai, 229; tertiary, 121, 124–25, 155, 257; university enrollment in, 229; of workforce, 114, 271

Education, U.S., 7; Advanced Placement Chinese Language and Culture Course, 158; deficiencies in, 134

Education Forum for Asia, 154

Electronic information industry, Chinese, 98

Elites, Chinese: business, 230–31; in Communist Party, 174; and democratization, 211; fragmentation of, 214; national strategy of, 1; political, 121, 213; technocratic, 120; view of middle class, 229–30

Energy, Chinese: coal, 245; demand for, 208; demonstrations concerning, 246; dependence on, 245–46; from natural gas, 245; sources of, 24. *See also* Oil supply, Chinese

Engineering schools, Chinese, 82

Engineers, Chinese, in U.S., 86

Enterprises, Chinese: foreign-owned, 97; international competition by, 117; state-owned, 98, 208, 233, 234, 239

Entrepreneurs, Chinese, 122–23; in CCP, 123, 248; failures of, 240; in GDP, 239

Environment, Chinese: activism in, 235; deterioration of, 87, 227, 234, 266, 267; economic expansion and, 80; as

issue driver, 234–36; NGOs and, 232–33; reform of, 4; violence concerning, 234–35. *See also* Pollution, Chinese

Epstein, Edward, 240

Equality: in Chinese education, 228–29; in Chinese health care, 222–28; in Chinese society, 219–29; during Cultural Revolution, 222; in income, 221–22; urban-rural, 249

Equity, 249; in Chinese society, 219–29; during Cultural Revolution, 222

Ernst, Dieter, 130, 304n47

Etzioni, Amitai: *A Comparative Analysis of Complex Organizations*, 10; on power, 8, 118

European Union (EU), 263; arms embargo against PRC, 202; relations with China, 262–63

Ewing, Richard, 240

Excel Funds Management Inc. (Canada), 84

Exports, Chinese: cultural, 161; in gross domestic product, 97; labor services, 216; market access for, 257; regulation of, 114; safety of, 101, 152, 205–6, 212, 251; shoes, 99; textiles, 99–100; to Vietnam, 190

Fan Gang, 233

Fertility, Chinese, 217

Fewsmith, Joseph, 334n3

Films, Chinese-language, 160–61

Financial system, Chinese, 238–41; banks in, 239. *See also* Economy, Chinese

Fitzgerald, Stephen, 85

Five-Year Plan (China, 2006–10), 24, 222

Food security, Chinese, 243

Force, Chinese use of, 15, 16, 19, 34. *See also* Coercive power, Chinese

Foreign Affairs University (China), 153

Gries, Peter, 197, 241; on regime legitimacy, 242
Griffin, Michael, 58, 59
Gross domestic product (GDP), Chinese, 23; agricultural, 87; per capita, 207, 210–11, 229; in coastal areas, 41; defense spending in, 24; under Deng Xiaoping, 120; effect of air pollution on, 227; effect of corruption on, 237; exports in, 97; growth in, 79; imports in, 88; income in, 221, 222; nonperforming loans in, 238–39; private sector in, 239; revenue as percentage of, 214–15; of Shanghai, 244; *versus* U.S. GDP, 78; urban-rural disparities in, 221, 222. *See also* Economy, Chinese
Gross domestic product, global, China's share of, 78
Gross domestic product, U.S., *versus* Chinese GDP, 78
Gross national product (GNP), Chinese: per capita, 33, 207, 220; increases in, 29
Guangdong Province, middle class of, 83
Guangzhou, international airport of, 88
Guizhou, GDP per capita of, 207
Gulf War, First, military technology of, 39

Haier Group (China), foreign design centers of, 135
Haiti, Chinese riot police in, 64
Hancock, David, 160
Hanoi, Ho Hoan Kiem Lake, 166
Hard power, Chinese, 29
Harding, Harry, 204
Harris-Financial Times, poll on China, 149
He Guangwei, 159
He Sibing, 58
Health care, Chinese, 24–25; cost of, 219; distribution of, 220; equality in, 222–28; expenditures on, 227; government spending on, 228; for HIV/AIDs, 223–25; insurance for, 222, 327n61;

local subsidies in, 228; for migrant workers, 232; privatization of, 227; rural, 228, 327n61; rural-urban disparities in, 222–23; for workforce, 225, 227
Hezbollah, war with Israel, 64
HIV/AIDS: in China, 82, 261; health care for, 223–25
HIV/AIDS: China's Titanic Peril, 223
Ho Hoan Kiem Lake (Hanoi), 166
Hong, Eunsuk, 103
Hong Kong: economic freedom in, 151; students in China, 154
Household size, Chinese, 219
Howard, John, *92*
Howe, Neil, 218
Hu Angang, 24, 214, 278n45; *China: Fighting against Corruption*, 236; on CNP, 21
Hu Heli, 237
Hu Jintao, *107;* in CCP, 200; domestic programs of, 60; on food security, 243; in Indonesia, 128; on innovation, 128–29; and Kim Jong Il, 315n23; leadership of, 120–21; meeting with Shinzo Abe, 197; on national strategy, 1; oil agreements of, 103, 109; on peaceful rise, 33; PLA policy of, 39; power strategies of, 10; priorities of, 32, 121; satellite programs of, 58; travels of, 127–28; visits in Latin America, 6, 91, 92; visit to Philippines, 101; visit to U.S., 94
Hu Shuli, 93
Huang, James, 72
Huang Shuofeng, 21
Huang Yanzhong, 152
Huawei Technologies (China), 203
Hufbauer, Gary Clyde, 295n53, 306n79
Human capital, Chinese, 138
Human Development Report (UNDP), 227
Humanitarian assistance, Chinese, 107–10; following tsunami of 2004, 5, 64, 107–8; food donations, 108

Mao Zedong *(continued)*
coercive power of, 38, 253; "four olds" of, 118; guerrilla warfare under, 47; military power of, 11; military writings of, 17; on nuclear weapons, 51; strategies of, 10, 26, 30; transition from, 120; workforce under, 3

McDevitt, Michael, 281n11, 285nn63,66

McDonald's, in China, 89

McKinsey & Company, 82

McNamara, Robert, 39; and Deng Xiaoping, 120

McVadon, Eric A., 63

Mearsheimer, John: on nationalism, 145; on offensive realism, 247; on power, 9, 11, 13–14; visit to China, 14

Medeiros, Evan, 49

Media, Chinese: diplomats' use of, 128; nationalism of, 147; repression of, 249

Meishan Township, pollution in, 234

Mekong River, dams on, 171, 266

Mekong River Commission, 266

Men Honghua, 21, 24, 278n45

Meng Hongwei, 64

Mengniu Dairy (Group) Co., 123

Mexico, textile exports of, 100

Middle class, Chinese, 80, 83–85; and CCP, 230; consumption by, 267; economic growth and, 210; elites' view of, 229–30; growth of, 248; income of, 83, 84; Internet use of, 213; liberalism of, 148, 308n108; nationalism of, 231, 241; in national strategy, 114; political participation by, 84, 229–31; in Singapore, 230; size of, 83–84; stability of, 229–30

Middle East, Chinese university in, 156

Might. *See* Coercive power

Migration: internal, 233; rural-urban, 212

Military, Chinese: aircraft of, 55; budget of, 42–43, 115, 281n8; command and control in, 45; delegation to Kazakhstan, 62; education for, 43–44; evolving doctrine of, 55; expenditures of, 260; GPS systems of, 57; improvements to, 75; informationized, 40, 42; in Iron Fist—2004, 62; joint operations, 44–45, 61–62, 63, 200; in Lebanon, 64; modernization of, 37, 39–45, 47, 48, 53, 54; organizational change in, 44; power-projection capacity of, 59–60; restructuring of, 43–44; size of, 43; spending for, 29, 32; supply lines of, 55–56; in tsunami relief, 5, 64; under UN, 55, 61. *See also* People's Liberation Army (PLA)

Military, U.S.: in Asia, 182; cooperation in Vietnam, 193–94; in Indonesia, 188; PRC challenge to, 150, 152

Military power: escalation of, 49; in international relations, 13; uses of, 45

Military power, Chinese, 11; coercive, 255; conventional, 257; deterrence in, 49–54; diplomatic use of, 257; effect on neighboring states, 168–69; excessive, 264–65; external, 54–55; homeland defense in, 46–48, 54, 76; Mao on, 17; overinvestment in, 254; public opinion on, 61; reassurance through, 61–66; in regime legitimacy, 260; in relations with big powers, 204; and space program, 57–58; uses of, 45–66

Ming Dynasty, Vietnamese defeat of, 166

Ming Pao (newspaper), circulation of, 161

Mischief Reef, tensions over, 61

Missile Technology Control Regime (MTCR), China and, 5

Missiles: North Korean, 196; U.S., 52, 54, 268

Missiles, Chinese, 49, 54; modernization of, 53; in Taiwan policy, 269

Modernization, Chinese, 59; consensus on, 31; of defense industries, 60; developmental challenges in, 209; fragility in, 264; ideational power in,

tions of, 15–19; negative impacts of,
7, 117, 266–69; in relations with big
powers, 204; responsible, 259–60;
smart, 76; Sun Tzu on, 16–17; three
faces of, 254, 255–59; traditional
thinking on, 15–19; typologies of,
11, 34, 162. *See also* Coercive power,
Chinese; Economic power, Chinese;
Ideational power, Chinese; Military
power, Chinese; Soft power, Chinese
Power cycles, international, 11–15, 36
Power projection, Chinese, 95; coercive,
54–60; diplomatic consequences of,
60; of force, 76; by military, 59–60;
in space program, 56; aimed at Taiwan, 255
Power projection, Japanese, 198
PowerNet Technology (China), 145
Privatization: of health care, 227; of
public assets, 240. *See also* Entre-
preneurs, Chinese
Production chains, global, China in, 111,
267, 272
Property owners, associations of, 232
Property rights, Chinese: definition of,
238; intellectual, 135
Public assets, Chinese, privatization of,
240. *See also* Economy, Chinese
Purchasing Power Parity (PPP), 23
Putin, Vladimir, 201

Qian Qichen, 60, 142
Qing Dynasty, 144; use of force in, 15
"Quadrennial Defense Review Report,"
U.S. Department of Defense, 315n33
Quenos (ethylene producer), 179

Radio, Chinese, 160
Rainforest, Brazilian, exports to China,
267, 268
Ramo, Joshua Cooper, *The Beijing Con-
sensus*, 141
Rangsimaporn, Paradorn, 202

Rawski, Thomas G., 294n43
Realism, offensive, 13, 35, 247
Relocations, forced, 234
Remunerative power, 10, 37–38; coercion in, 38
Republic of China (ROC): isolation of,
70–71; name of, 69–70; use of isolation, 69. *See also* Taiwan
Research, Chinese, 128–37; domestic
expenditures in, 129; expenditures in,
136; facilities abroad, 129; funding of,
136–37; globalization of, 134–35; mis-
conduct in, 133; published papers, 132
Research, foreign-funded: Chinese par-
ticipation in, 135; factors influencing,
134–35; intellectual property in, 135
Research, Western, facilities in China,
130, 134
Research Centre of Corporate Gover-
nance (Nankai University), 240
Rice, Condoleezza, 177; in Indonesia,
188; and Vu Khoan, 194
Riedel, James C., 239
Riot police, Chinese, 64
RMB, Chinese. *See* Currency, Chinese
The Romance of the Three Kingdoms, 17, 49
Rosen, Daniel, 71, 100
Rowen, Henry, 210, 211, 229
Roy, J. Stapleton, 318n77
Rubin, Robert, 105
Rumsfeld, Donald: Hanoi visit of, 190,
193–94; on national security, 196
Russia: authoritarianism in, 263; border
disputes with China, 201, 322n143;
China policy of, 200–202; Chinese
investment in, 201; core interests of,
195; defense industrial base of, 201–2;
far east of, 202; relations with China,
168, 200–202, 262–63; revival of, 263;
in SCO, 200; technology exports of, 60

Saich, Anthony, 230
Sarbanes, Paul, 237–38

sources in, 199; cooperation in, 199; economic, 90, 199; strategies in, 175; trade in, 198–99; in twenty-first century, 196; U.S. role in, 168; weakness in, 182

Sino-North Korean relations, 167, 168; economic, 172, 173

Sinopec: negotiations with Iran, 245; Russian oil assets of, 104

Sino-Russian relations, 47, 60, 200–202, 262–63; border issues in, 48, 201, 322n143; cooperation in, 202; corruption in, 168; economic, 200; joint military operations in, 200; military-technological cooperation in, 201–2; "Strategic Partnership" in, 200; territorial issues in, 200, 201

Sino-Singapore relations, 180–84; economic, 183

Sino-Vietnamese relations, 164, 165–66, 168, 170–71, 189–94; anxiety in, 189; diversification in, 193; economic, 172–73, 194; FDI in, 190; multilateralism in, 192–93; trade, 190; Vietnam acquiescence in, 191

Six-Party Talks, 65, *173*

Smokers, Chinese, 82

Snow, John W., 78

Social capital, Chinese, 3, 139

Social security, Chinese, 104, 218

Socialist Republic of Vietnam (SRV). *See* Vietnam

Society, Chinese: conflicts of 1989 in, 214; Confucian, 140; consensus in, 25; distribution of essentials in, 219–29; disturbances in, 231, 247–48; pluralization of, 210; stability of, 32, 249

Sociopolitical change, and institutional capacity, 211

Soft power, 10; Chinese view of, 182; U.S., 7, 254

Soft power, Chinese, 27, 118, 162, 182; Jiang Zemin's strategy of, 11; nega-

tive, 117; through development assistance, 107; in Vietnam, 191

Software, Chinese, 123

Solomon Islands: anti-Chinese feeling in, 75; crisis in, 55

Songhua River, toxic spill in, 202, 235

South Africa, trade with China, 71

South China Sea: Chinese influence in, 171; energy resources of, 170, 190

South Korea: in ASEAN + 3, 111; patent applications of, 132; relations with China, 195; relations with U.S., 263, 271; research in, 136; steel exports of, 100; students in China, 154

Southeast Asia: Chinese of, 162; trade partners of, 172

Soviet Union: control of resources, 116; demise of, 253, 263; nuclear capability of, 52, 268; relations with China, 47

Space: non-weaponization of, 57; Sino-American relations concerning, 58–59, 66

Space program, Chinese, 5, 54, 56–59, 159–60, 250; goals of, 56–57; ideational power in, 59; investment in, 59; lunar orbiter, 56, 57; PLA in, 58; power projection in, 56; reassurance in, 66

Speltz, Paul, 114

Spence, Jonathan, *To Change China*, 265

Spratly Islands: Chinese influence in, 171; oil exploration in, 191

Stability, Chinese, 2, 207; in domestic economy, 208–9, 211; maintenance of, 247–51; and openness, 211; societal, 32, 249; sociopolitical, 214

Staehle, Stefan, 288n108

State Leading Small Group on Medium and Long-Term Planning for the Development of Science and Technology, 128

State-owned enterprises (SOEs), Chinese, 98, 208, 233, 234; in Australia, 178; loans to, 239

Steel industry, Chinese, 100
Stokes, Mark, 52
Straits of Malacca, oil supply through, 245
Strategy. *See* National strategy, Chinese
Strength, industrial-age measures of, 23
Students, Chinese: abroad, 124–25, 153–56; in CCP, 230; disturbances by, 231; engineering, 292n15; return rate of, 124–25; in U.S., 124–25, 292n15; in Vietnam, 191
Students, foreign, 153–56; American, 154; careers of, 155; in graduate programs, 155; Indonesian, 189; South Korean, 154; study of Chinese language, 154; Vietnamese, 155
Students, Taiwanese, 153–54; in China, 310n139
Su Ge, 127
Subianto, Prabowo, 185
Submission, production of, 16
Suharto, New Order of, 185
Summers, Larry, 81
Sun, Laixiang, 103
Sun Tzu, *The Art of War*, 8, 16, 277n28; on diplomacy, 271; on ideational power, 118; strategic thinking of, 277n27; on use of power, 16–17
Sun Xiangli, 49
Sun Yat-sen, 207
Supply chains, global, 272; centrality for PRC, 251; safety of, 101, 152, 205–6, 212, 251
Swaine, Michael, 19
Switzerland, economic freedom in, 151

Taipei, Chinese. *See* Taiwan
Taipei Economic and Cultural Representative Office (TECRO) in the United States, 70
Taiwan: ABM capability for, 41; and ASEAN + 3, 71; Bush administration and, 177–78; as challenge to China,

241–42; Chinese power projection at, 255; in Chinese space program, 59; citizens' identity in, 71; coercive power against, 38, 40, 68; cultural contact with China, 68; democracy for, 72, 74; as destination for FDI, 71; deterrent forces against, 49; domestic investment in, 72; electronics industry, 68; entrepreneurs of, 67; exports to China, 67; independence for, 32, 33, 41, 55, 56; investment in Vietnam, 190; isolation of, 68–75; under Kuomintang, 71; legislative elections of, 70, 73; military deterrence against, 68; Mirage jets of, 67; missiles aimed at, 53, 54; name of, 69–70; offensive capabilities of, 269; and "one-China principle," 49, 178; passport of, 70; policy challenges of, 6; PRC policy on, 41, 242; regime legitimacy of, 70; relations with Australia, 74, 177–78; relations with U.S., 72, 242; reunification with China, 50, 69, 168, 269; security of, 269; in Sino-American relations, 146, 165, 269–70; U.S. policy on, 40–41; in U.S.-Japan relations, 199; UN membership for, 70; in WHO, 73–74; in WTO, 70
Tamamoto, Masaru, 196
Tammen, Ronald, 11, 36
Tang Jiaxuan, *173*
Tanzam Railroad, 106
Technology, Chinese, proprietary, 99
Telecommunications, Chinese, *213*
Television, Chinese, 160
Tellis, Ashley, 19
Terrorism: in China, 46; Chinese opposition to, 28; of East Turkestan, 46; U.S. war on, 142, 262
Thailand: Chinese students in, 155, 156; cultural centers of, 157; relations with China, 170
The Three Represents, 141, 248

Tiananmen demonstrations (1989), 40,
120; against corruption, 238; openness
following, 86; reform following, 151
Tibet: illiteracy in, 229; trade with
Nepal, 48
Tibetan Autonomous Region (TAR),
PRC sovereignty over, 203
Tokyo University, exchange with Chinese universities, 156
Tonga, crisis in, 55
Tourism, Chinese: destinations for, 159,
312n173; spread of culture through,
158–59, 162; in Vietnam, 190
Tourists, Asian, in China, 158
Trade, Chinese: barriers to, 87; with
Japan, 198–99; with neighboring
states, 48; port, 65; revenue from,
216, 243–44; with Sikkim, 48; with
South Africa, 71; surplus in, 79; with
Nepal, 48; with U.S., 100; with Vietnam, 190. *See also* Exports, Chinese;
Imports, Chinese
Trade, global, imbalances in, 245
Treaty of Amity and Cooperation
(1976), 113
Trilateral Strategic Dialogue, 180
Trung, Hai Ba, 166
Tsunami relief (2004): Chinese, 5, 64,
107–8; from U.S., 108
Tuberculosis, in China, 82–83
Tung Chen-yuan, 68
Two-plus-two talks (2005), 169
Tz'u-hsi, Empress, 144

Unemployment, Chinese, 222
United Nations: Chinese membership
in, 69; Chinese military under, 55, 61;
Development Program (UNDP), 218,
219, 222, 225, 227, 229; in reconstruction of Iraq, 143; Taiwan in, 70; Truce
Supervision Organization, 63; vote on
Iraq, 18–19; World Food Program
(WFP), 108

United Nations Security Council: China
in, 64; Japan in, 198; permanent seats
on, 13; Resolution 1441, 18
United States: aircraft industry, 90;
allies of, 76–77, 254, 262, 270, 271;
anti-terror campaign, 142, 262; among
big powers, 195; bilateral alliances in
Asia, 270, 271; China strategy of, 264;
Chinese air pollution in, 266; Chinese
ambassadors to, 125–26; Chinese investment in, 103–4; Chinese language
speakers in, 160; Chinese students in,
124–25; coercive power in Asia, 205;
Container Security Initiative (CSI),
65; containment strategy of, 14; cultural hegemony of, 159; debt to China,
105; defense budget of, 43; developmental challenges following, 209; economic freedom in, 151; effect of Chinese economic power on, 112–13;
homeland defense of, 46; human resources of, 272; ideational power of,
262; ideological assertiveness of, 142,
143; implications of Chinese power
for, 265–74; Indonesian concerns
over, 183; industrial output of, 96–97;
influence in Asia, 181, 182, 183, 202,
206, 258; innovation in, 110, 304n47;
investment in China, 134; militarization of, 264; missile defense of, 52, 54,
268; National Missile Defense plan,
52; national security of, 35, 195–96;
National System of Interstate and
Defense Highways, 47–48; negative
attitudes concerning, 148–49; negative influence of, 149; net national
product of, 81; Pacific Rim influence,
176; patent applications in, 132; per
capita resources of, 210; post-9/11
foreign policy of, 142; presence in
Asia, 181; promotion of democracy,
109, 141, 142, 181, 183, 258; promotion
of human rights, 183; as regional

Weiss, John, 100

Wen Jiabao, *92*, 162; at ASEAN + 3, 61; on bilateral relations, 252; on Chinese currency, 79; diplomatic missions of, 127, 128; on inequality, 220; on national security, 65; on peaceful rise, 33; on regional cooperation, 111; on Taiwanese students, 153; trip to France, 90; visit to Pacific Islands, 75

White Paper on National Defense (2004), 39, 43, 66

Whiting, Allen S., 147

Wolf, Charles, Jr., 239

Wolf, Martin, 138

Workforce, Chinese: age of, 218–19; cost of, 82, 131; education of, 114, 271; health of, 81, 83, 225, 227; under Mao Zedong, 3; migrant workers in, 222, 232; political participation in, 233–34; rural, 333n162; skills of, 82; in SOEs, 234; urban, 243; worker-to-dependent ratio in, 218–19

World Bank: on Chinese economy, 120; *Dancing with Giants*, 80; Vietnam and, 192

World Health Organization (WHO): Assembly, 74; on Chinese AIDS, 223, 225; Taiwanese participation in, 73–74

World Tourism Organization, 158

World Trade Organization (WTO): China in, 30, 68, 94, 100, 120, 126; Doha Round negotiations, 94; Taiwan in, 70; Vietnam in, 192

Wu, Friedrich, 103

Wu, Jinglian, 215, 228; on corruption, 237; on corporate governance, 238

Wu Xinbo, 279n49

Wu Yi, 75; visit to U.S., 94

Xenophobia, Chinese, 184, 258, 260

Xie, Andy, 98

Xinhua News Agency, 161

Xiong Guangkai, General, 46

Xu Tian, 137

Xue Litai, 51

Yahoo! China, 84

Yasukuni Shrine (Japan), 197, 321n125

Yuan Peng, 261, 263, 264

Yunnan Province, water flows, 171

Zeng Guofan, 208

Zeng Qinghong, 217

Zhao Pengfei, 225

Zheng Bijian: on exports, 117; on globalization, 143–44; on peaceful rise, 33, 34

Zheng, Yongnian, 241

Zhou Ruijin, 220

Zhou Tianyong, 220

Zhou Wenzhong, 109; ambassadorship of, 125, 127; career of, 127

Zhou Yongkang, 247

Zhu Qingshi, 133

Zhu Rongji, 233, 237–38; on domestic disturbances, 248

Zhu Zhixin, 227

Zoellick, Robert, 35, 126, 274

ZTE Corporation (China), 135

Text:	10.25/14 Fournier
Display:	Fournier
Compositor:	BookMatters, Berkeley
Indexer:	Roberta Engleman
Illustrator:	Bill Nelson
Printer and binder:	Thomson-Shore, Inc.